Original Creator:
Yuto Tsukuda
Artist:
Shun Saeki
Contributor:
Yuki Morisaki

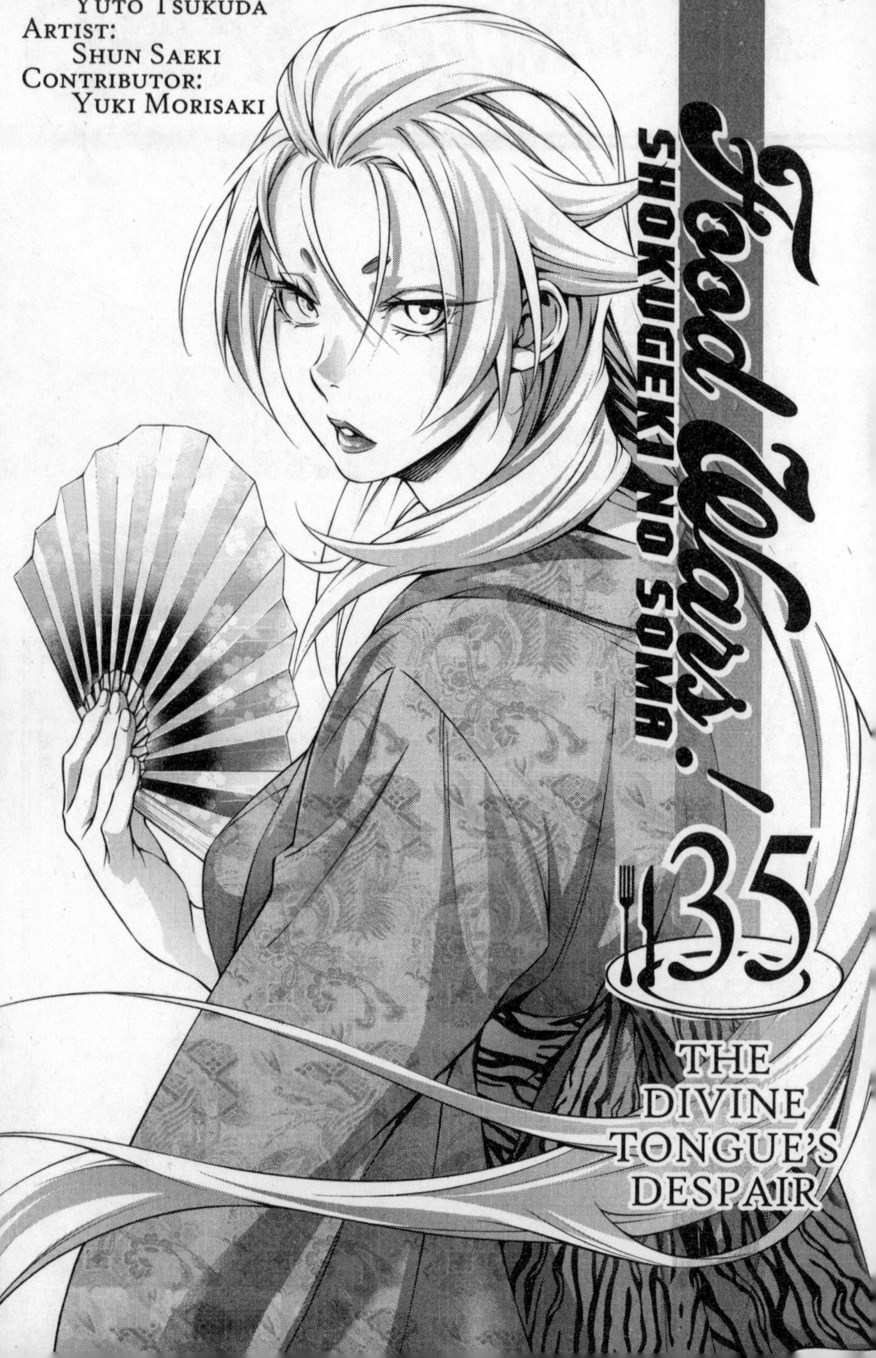
Food Wars!
Shokugeki no Soma
35
The Divine Tongue's Despair

CHARACTERS

SOMA YUKIHIRA Second Year High School

The current first seat on Totsuki's Council of Ten. Unbound by traditional notions and with a natural inquisitiveness and passion for cooking, his fresh take on cuisine leads him to create dishes no one has ever thought of before. Resides in Polaris Dormitory.

Shokugeki no
SOMA

ERINA NAKIRI Second Year High School

The current dean of Totsuki Institute and granddaughter of former dean Senzaemon Nakiri. Her sense of taste is so refined it's known as "the Divine Tongue." Though normally strict and proper, she has a girly side and loves shojo manga.

STORY

Soma grew up helping to cook at his family's restaurant, Yukihira. But one day his father enrolls him in Japan's premier culinary school, Totsuki Institute. Having met other students as skilled as he is and with similar goals, Soma has grown a little as a chef.

The tournament segment of the Blue is underway! Soma squares off with Asahi Saiba's underling, a skilled noir named Sarge, and uses all of his family-restaurant know-how to come out on top. Meanwhile, Eishi Tsukasa clashes with Asahi himself and loses. Asahi's freakish talent, crossed knives, is just too powerful. Not only can he absorb the signature skill of a chef by acquiring their primary cooking tool, he can then cross that tool with another to create new, astounding cooking skills!

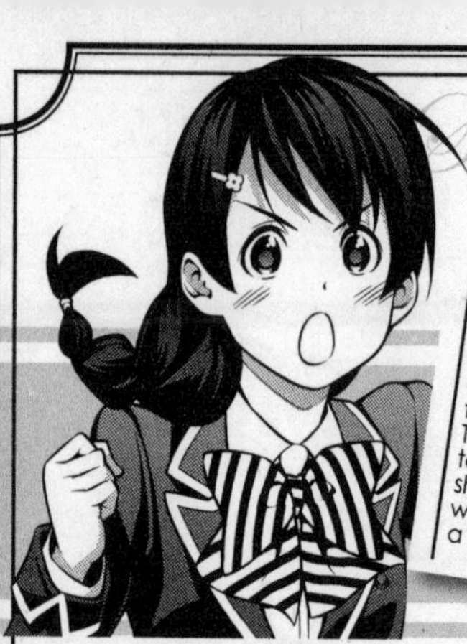

Shokugeki no SOMA

MEGUMI TADOKORO Second Year High School

Coming to the big city from the countryside, she now holds the tenth seat on Totsuki's Council of Ten. Using the privileges granted to her as a council member, she has traveled the globe learning world cultures and cuisines. Currently a Polaris dormitory resident.

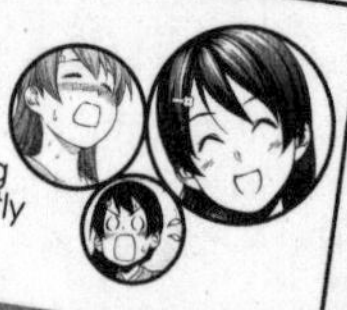

TAKUMI ALDINI Second Year High School

The current seventh seat on Totsuki's Council of Ten. He left his family's trattoria in Italy to attend Japan's Totsuki Institute. Isami is his younger twin brother.

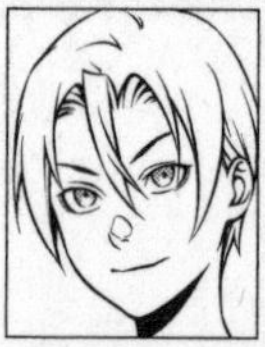

EISHI TSUKASA

A Totsuki Institute graduate and former first seat, he has a powerful talent for bringing out the best qualities of ingredients.

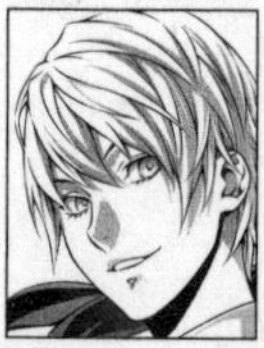

JOICHIRO YUKIHIRA

Totsuki alumnus and Soma's father, he was once the second seat on the Council of Ten. Now he's a globe-trotting chef who's famous to those in the know in the culinary world.

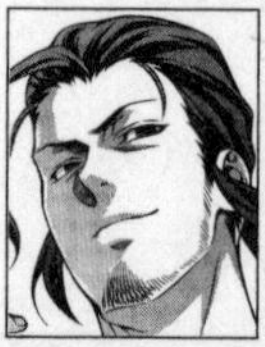

UNE

A first-rank adjudicator with the WGO, the organization that publishes *The Book*, a periodical that rates all gourmet restaurants in the world.

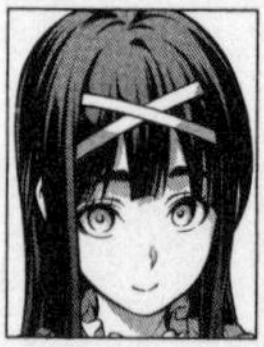

BOOK MASTER

The highest-ranking booker and top authority in the WGO who coordinates the Blue.

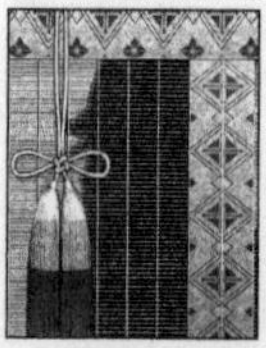

ASAHI SAIBA

Thanks to information squeezed out of some reluctant cuisiniers noir, it's believed he's involved with the recent shokugeki incidents around Japan. Supposedly an excellent chef.

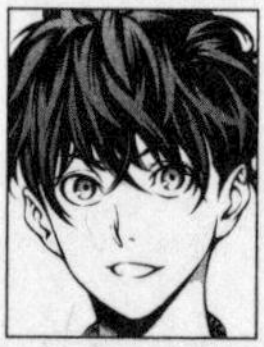

Food Wars! Shokugeki no Soma

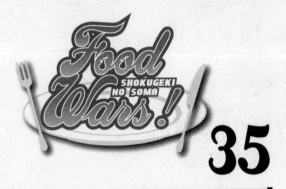

35

Table of Contents

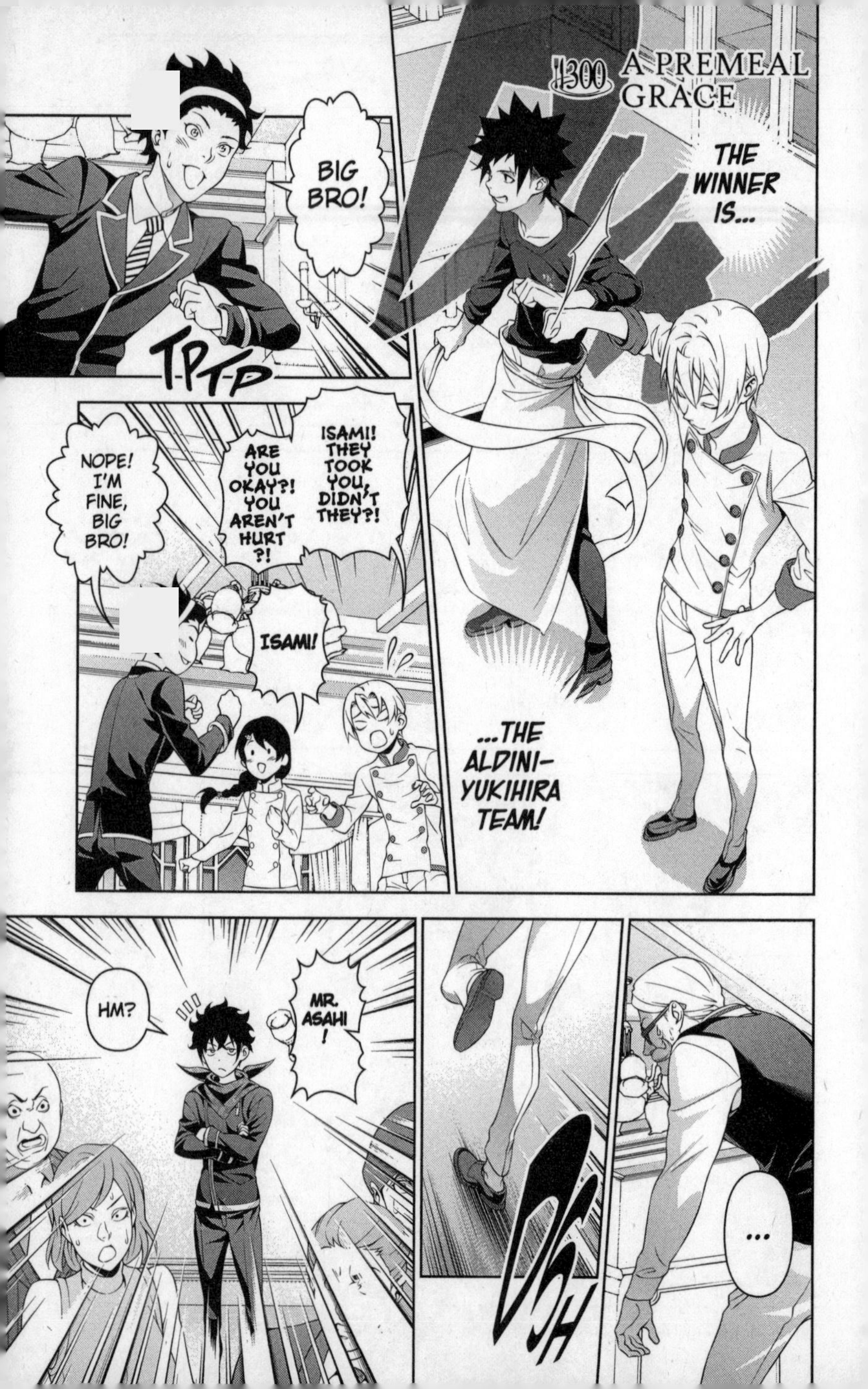
300 A PREMEAL GRACE
THE WINNER IS...
...THE ALDINI-YUKIHIRA TEAM!
BIG BRO!
T-P T-P
ISAMI! THEY TOOK YOU, DIDN'T THEY?!
ARE YOU OKAY?! YOU AREN'T HURT?!
NOPE! I'M FINE, BIG BRO!
ISAMI!
...
VSH
MR. ASAHI!
HM?

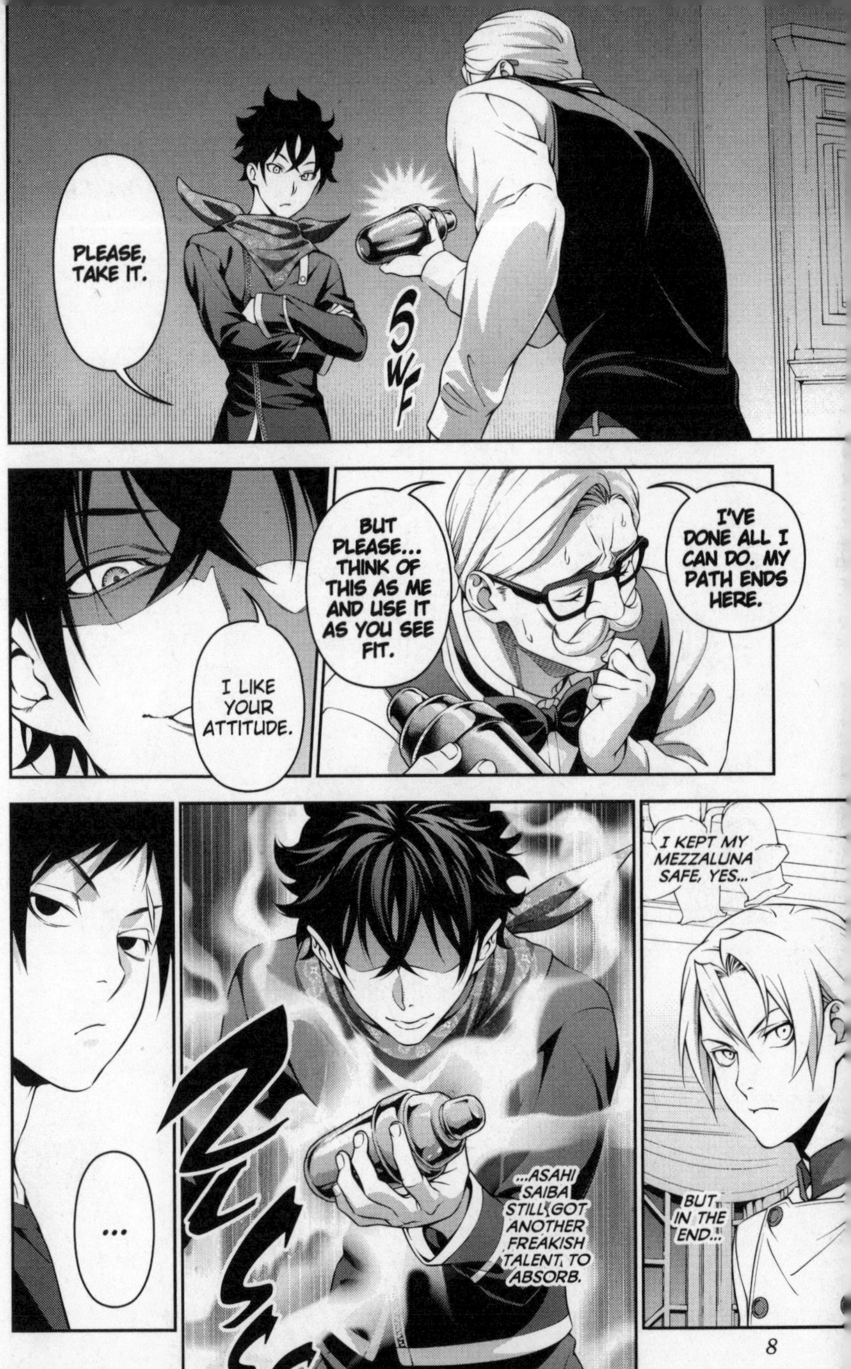
PLEASE, TAKE IT.
SWF
I'VE DONE ALL I CAN DO. MY PATH ENDS HERE.
BUT PLEASE... THINK OF THIS AS ME AND USE IT AS YOU SEE FIT.
I LIKE YOUR ATTITUDE.
I KEPT MY MEZZALUNA SAFE, YES...
BUT IN THE END...
...ASAHI SAIBA STILL GOT ANOTHER FREAKISH TALENT TO ABSORB.
...

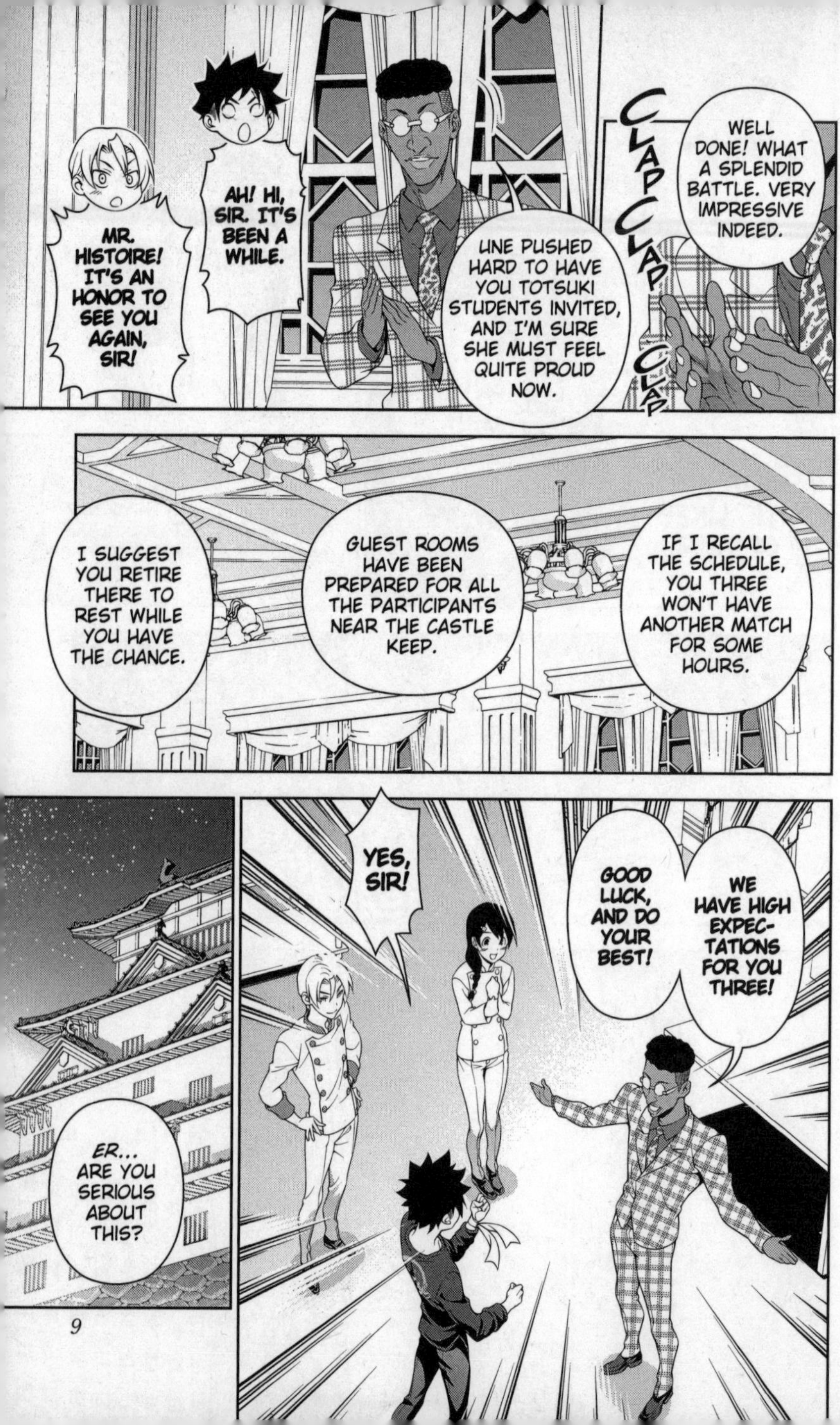
CLAP CLAP CLAP
WELL DONE! WHAT A SPLENDID BATTLE. VERY IMPRESSIVE INDEED.
UNE PUSHED HARD TO HAVE YOU TOTSUKI STUDENTS INVITED, AND I'M SURE SHE MUST FEEL QUITE PROUD NOW.
AH! HI, SIR. IT'S BEEN A WHILE.
MR. HISTOIRE! IT'S AN HONOR TO SEE YOU AGAIN, SIR!
IF I RECALL THE SCHEDULE, YOU THREE WON'T HAVE ANOTHER MATCH FOR SOME HOURS.
GUEST ROOMS HAVE BEEN PREPARED FOR ALL THE PARTICIPANTS NEAR THE CASTLE KEEP.
I SUGGEST YOU RETIRE THERE TO REST WHILE YOU HAVE THE CHANCE.
WE HAVE HIGH EXPEC-TATIONS FOR YOU THREE!
GOOD LUCK, AND DO YOUR BEST!
YES, SIR!
ER... ARE YOU SERIOUS ABOUT THIS?

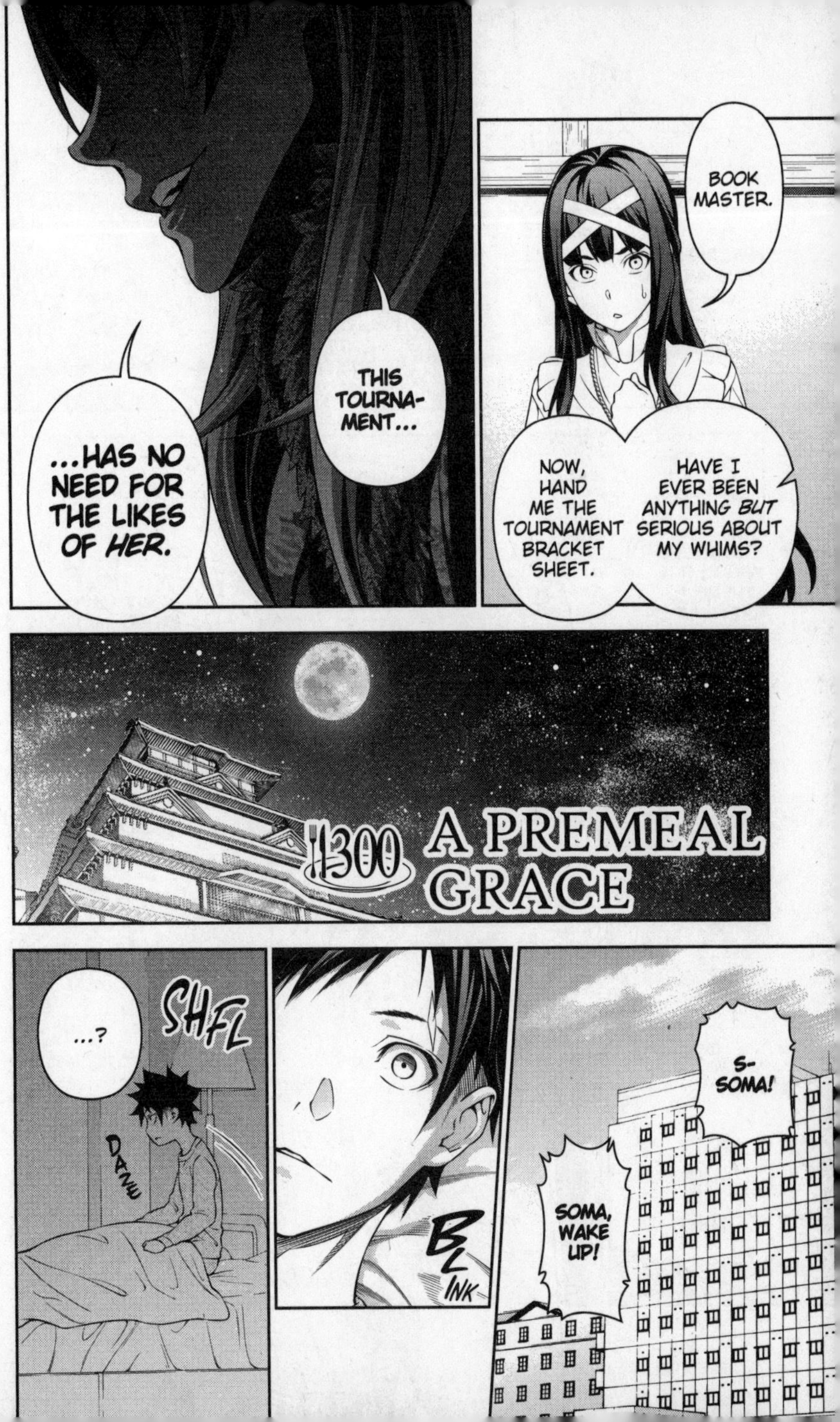
BOOK MASTER.
HAVE I EVER BEEN ANYTHING BUT SERIOUS ABOUT MY WHIMS?
NOW, HAND ME THE TOURNAMENT BRACKET SHEET.
THIS TOURNAMENT...
...HAS NO NEED FOR THE LIKES OF HER.
300 A PREMEAL GRACE
S-SOMA!
SOMA, WAKE UP!
BLINK
SHFL
...?
DAZE

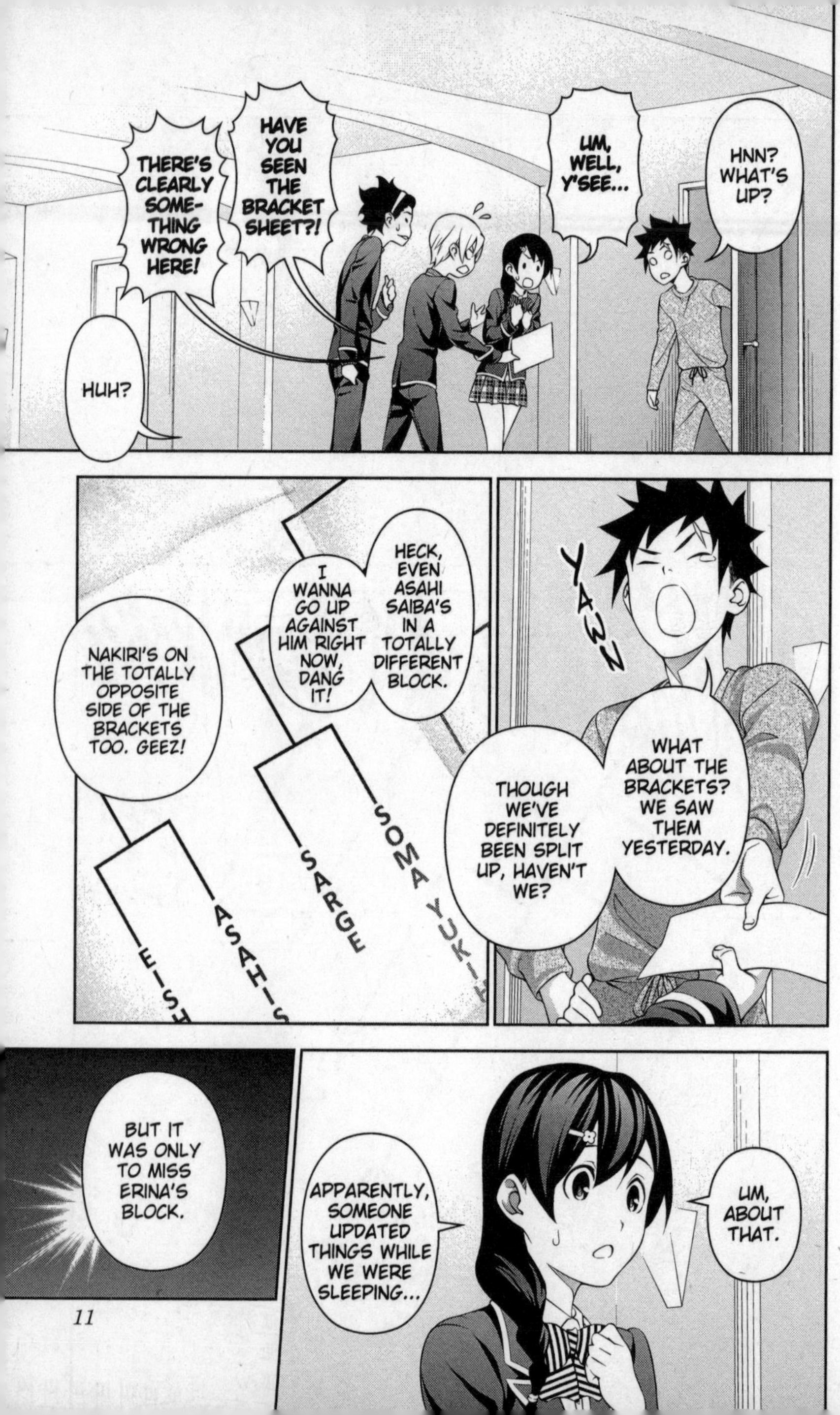
HNN? WHAT'S UP?
UM, WELL, Y'SEE...
HAVE YOU SEEN THE BRACKET SHEET?!
THERE'S CLEARLY SOME-THING WRONG HERE!
HUH?
YAWN
WHAT ABOUT THE BRACKETS? WE SAW THEM YESTERDAY.
THOUGH WE'VE DEFINITELY BEEN SPLIT UP, HAVEN'T WE?
HECK, EVEN ASAHI SAIBA'S IN A TOTALLY DIFFERENT BLOCK.
I WANNA GO UP AGAINST HIM RIGHT NOW, DANG IT!
NAKIRI'S ON THE TOTALLY OPPOSITE SIDE OF THE BRACKETS TOO. GEEZ!
SOMA YUKI
SARGE
ASAHI S
UM, ABOUT THAT.
APPARENTLY, SOMEONE UPDATED THINGS WHILE WE WERE SLEEPING...
BUT IT WAS ONLY TO MISS ERINA'S BLOCK.

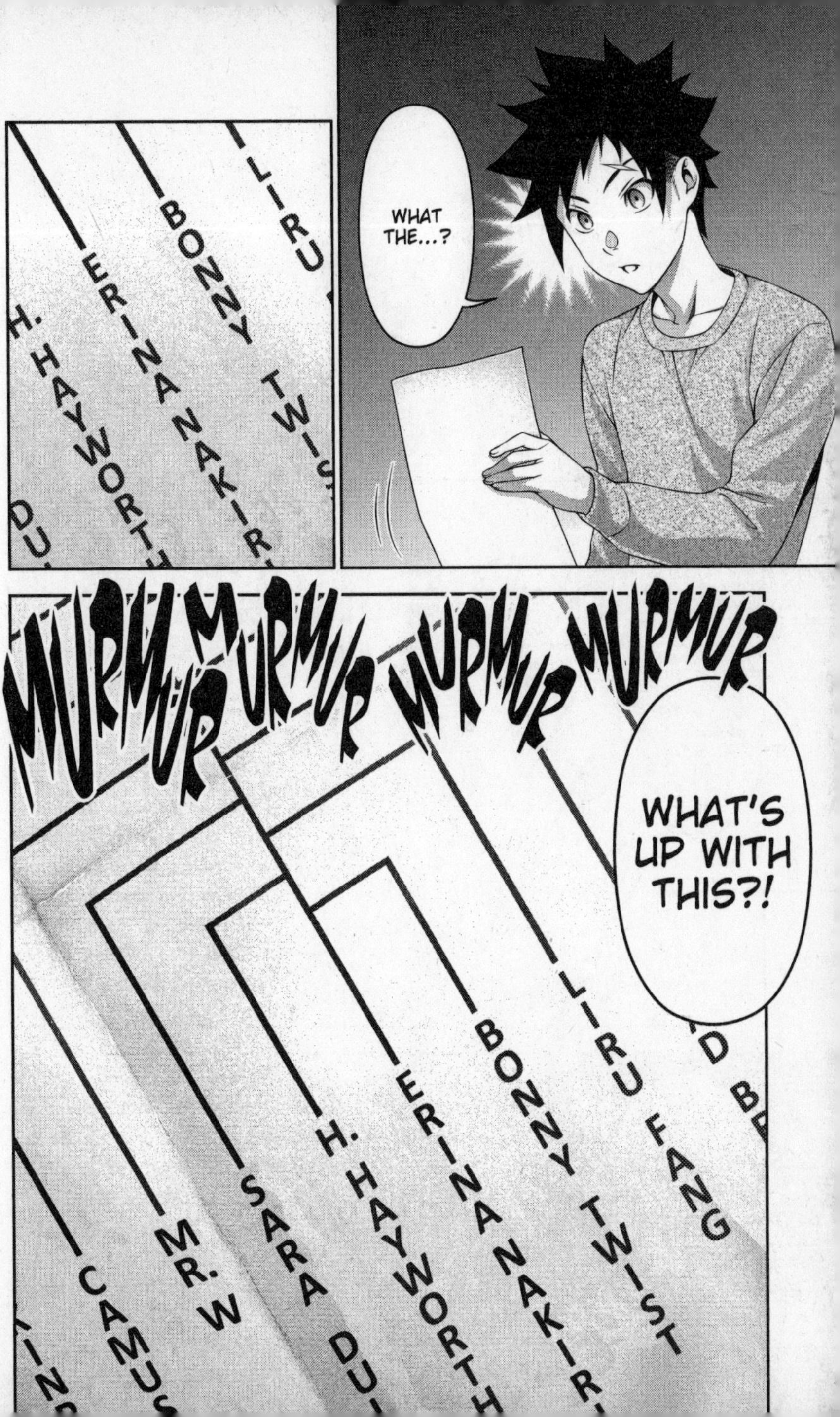
WHAT THE...?
LIRU
BONNY
H. HAYWORTH
MURMUR MURMUR MURMUR MURMUR
WHAT'S UP WITH THIS?!
LIRU FANG
BONNY TWIST
H. HAYWORTH
MR. W

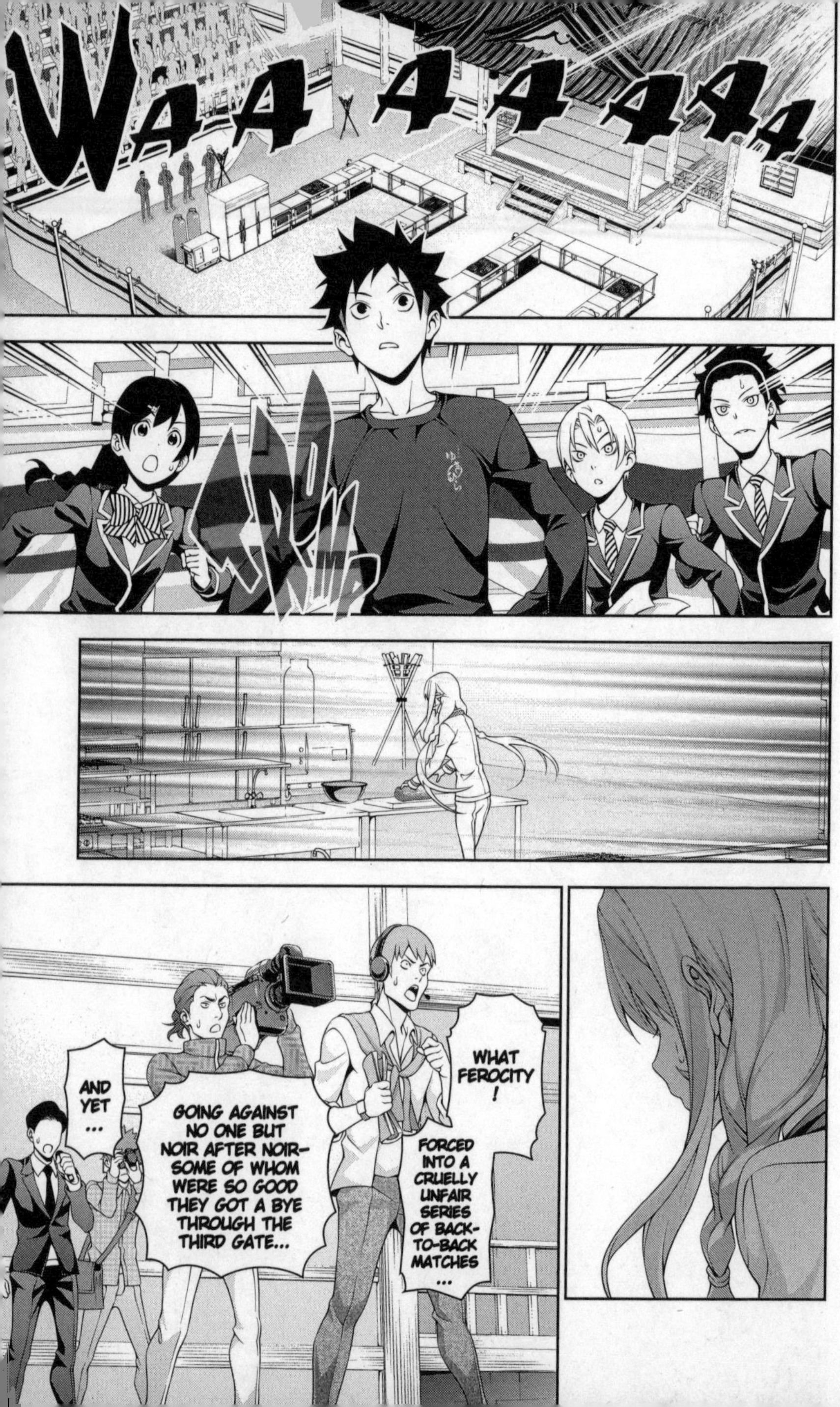
WAAAAAAA
WHAT FEROCITY!
FORCED INTO A CRUELLY UNFAIR SERIES OF BACK-TO-BACK MATCHES...
GOING AGAINST NO ONE BUT NOIR AFTER NOIR— SOME OF WHOM WERE SO GOOD THEY GOT A BYE THROUGH THE THIRD GATE...
AND YET...

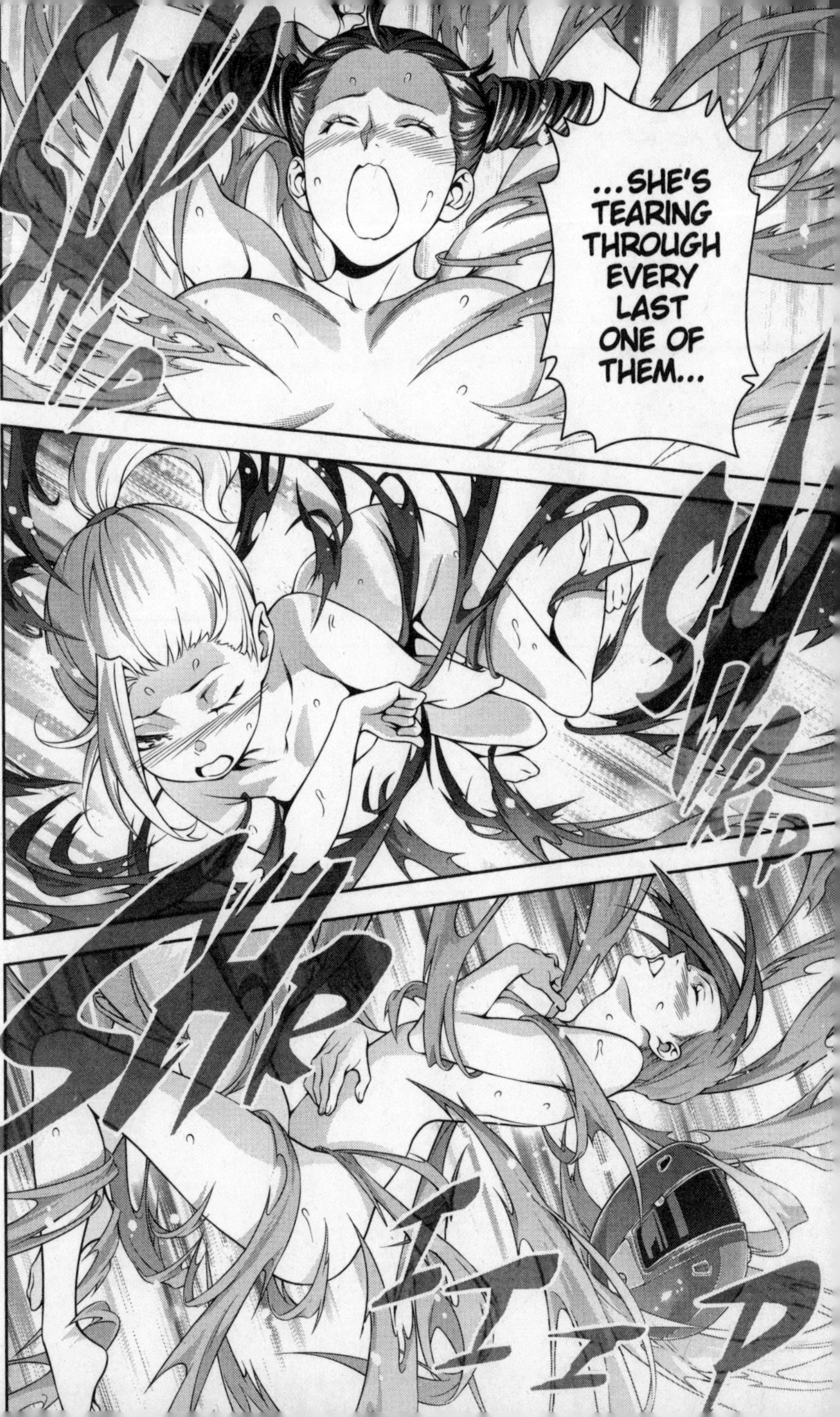
...SHE'S TEARING THROUGH EVERY LAST ONE OF THEM...

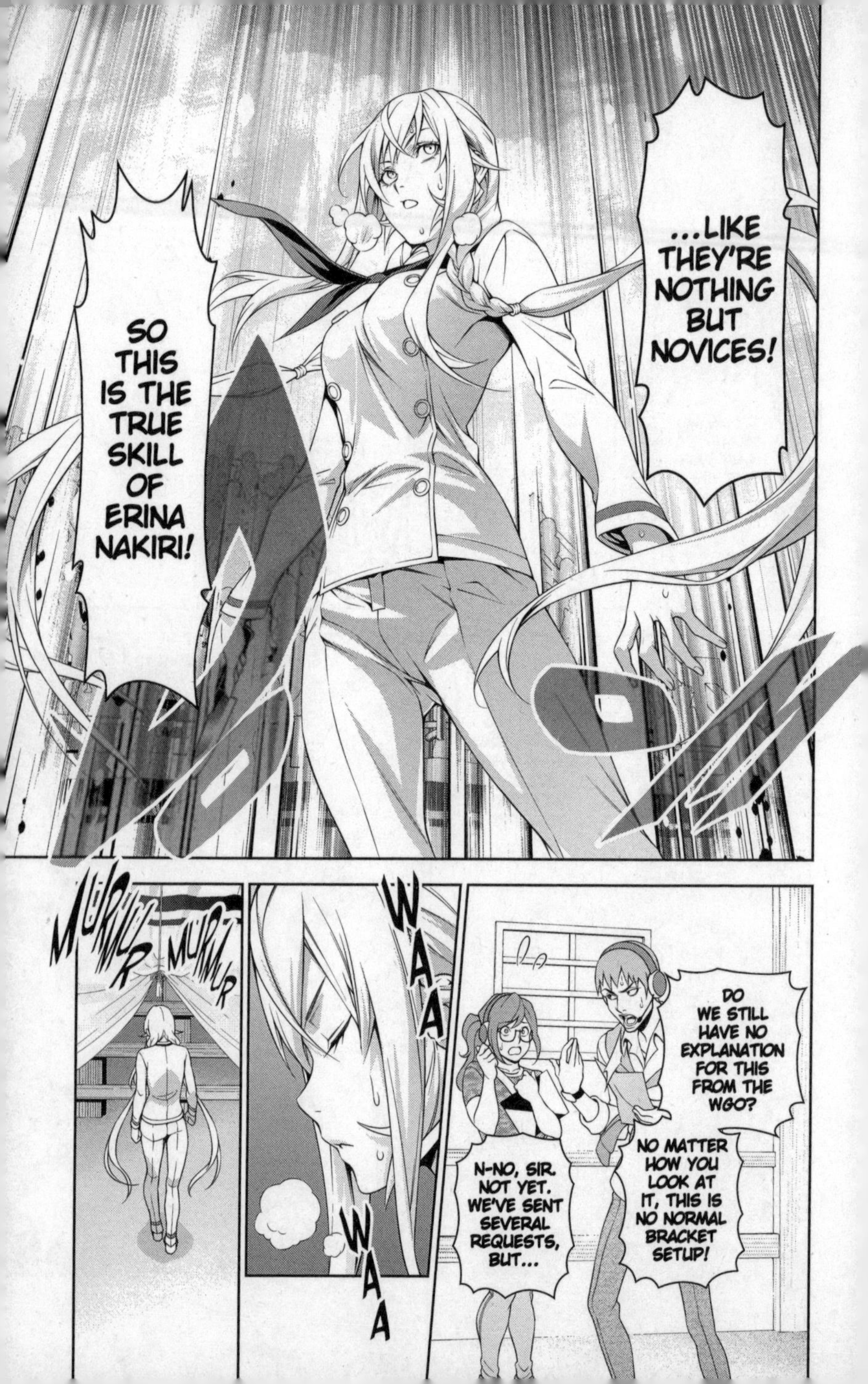
...LIKE THEY'RE NOTHING BUT NOVICES!
SO THIS IS THE TRUE SKILL OF ERINA NAKIRI!
DO WE STILL HAVE NO EXPLANATION FOR THIS FROM THE WGO?
N-NO, SIR. NOT YET. WE'VE SENT SEVERAL REQUESTS, BUT...
NO MATTER HOW YOU LOOK AT IT, THIS IS NO NORMAL BRACKET SETUP!
WAA
WAA
MURMUR
MURMUR

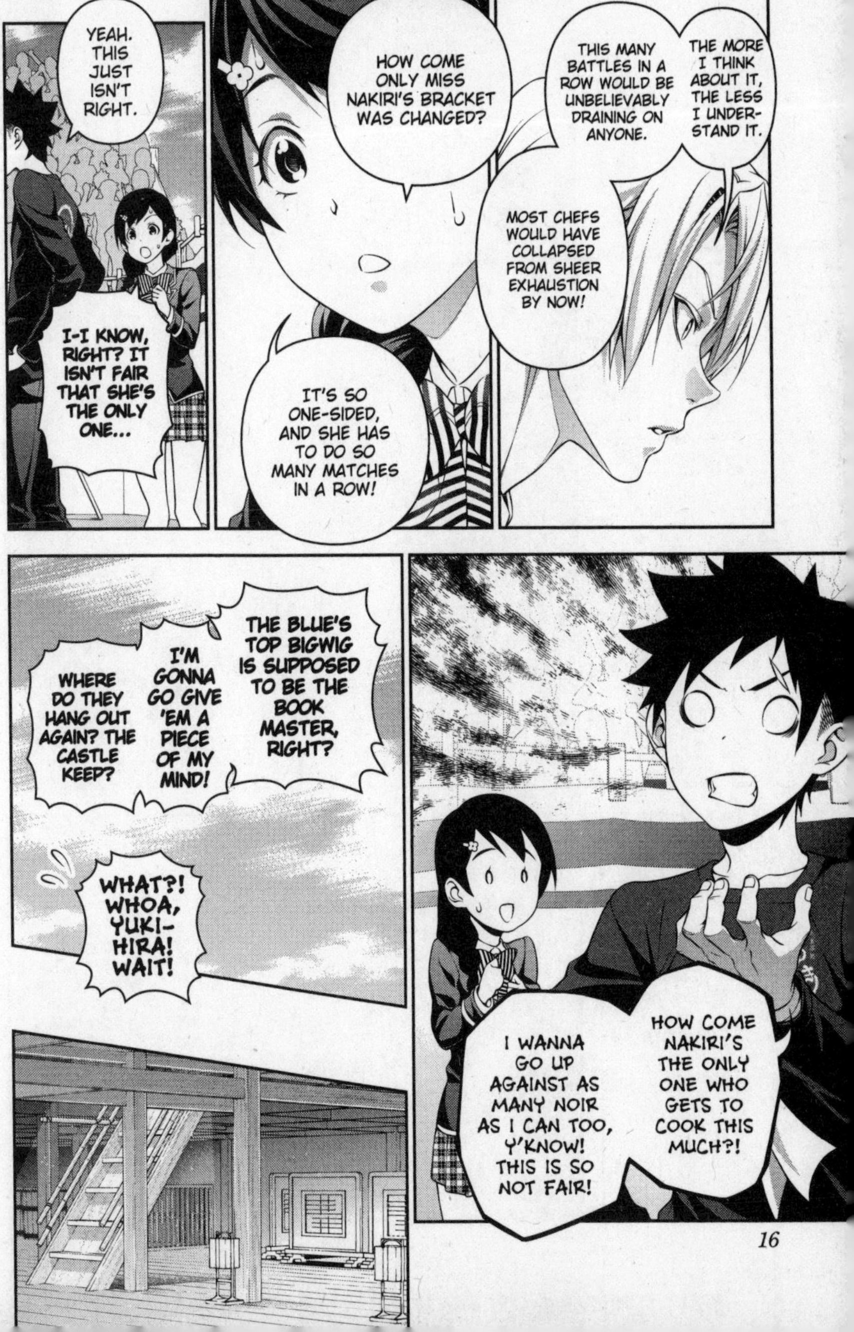
THE MORE I THINK ABOUT IT, THE LESS I UNDER-STAND IT.
THIS MANY BATTLES IN A ROW WOULD BE UNBELIEVABLY DRAINING ON ANYONE.
MOST CHEFS WOULD HAVE COLLAPSED FROM SHEER EXHAUSTION BY NOW!
HOW COME ONLY MISS NAKIRI'S BRACKET WAS CHANGED?
IT'S SO ONE-SIDED, AND SHE HAS TO DO SO MANY MATCHES IN A ROW!
YEAH. THIS JUST ISN'T RIGHT.
I-I KNOW, RIGHT? IT ISN'T FAIR THAT SHE'S THE ONLY ONE...
HOW COME NAKIRI'S THE ONLY ONE WHO GETS TO COOK THIS MUCH?!
I WANNA GO UP AGAINST AS MANY NOIR AS I CAN TOO, Y'KNOW! THIS IS SO NOT FAIR!
THE BLUE'S TOP BIGWIG IS SUPPOSED TO BE THE BOOK MASTER, RIGHT?
I'M GONNA GO GIVE 'EM A PIECE OF MY MIND!
WHERE DO THEY HANG OUT AGAIN? THE CASTLE KEEP?
WHAT?! WHOA, YUKI-HIRA! WAIT!

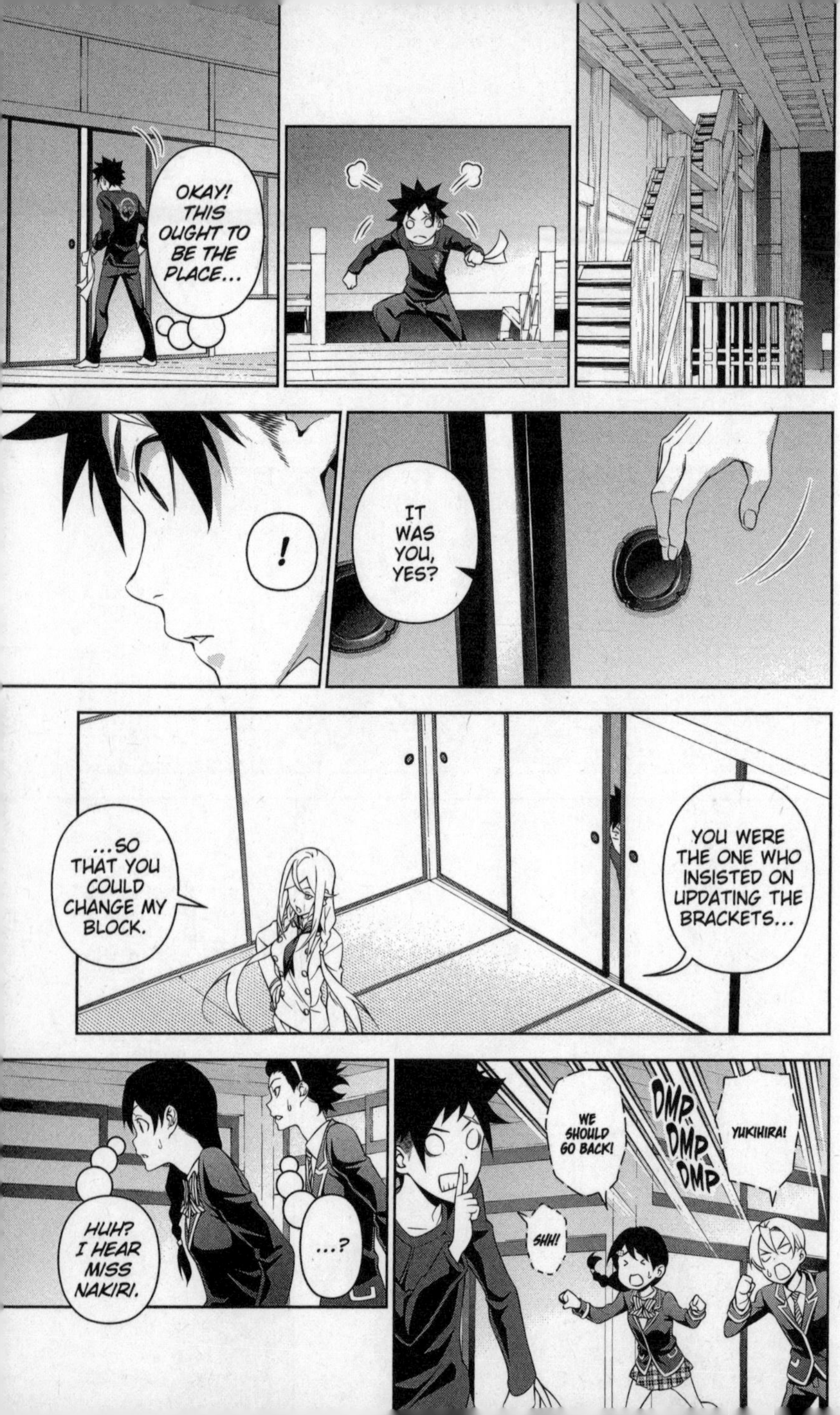
OKAY! THIS OUGHT TO BE THE PLACE...
IT WAS YOU, YES?
!
YOU WERE THE ONE WHO INSISTED ON UPDATING THE BRACKETS...
...SO THAT YOU COULD CHANGE MY BLOCK.
YUKIHIRA!
DMP DMP DMP
WE SHOULD GO BACK!
SHH!
...?
HUH? I HEAR MISS NAKIRI.

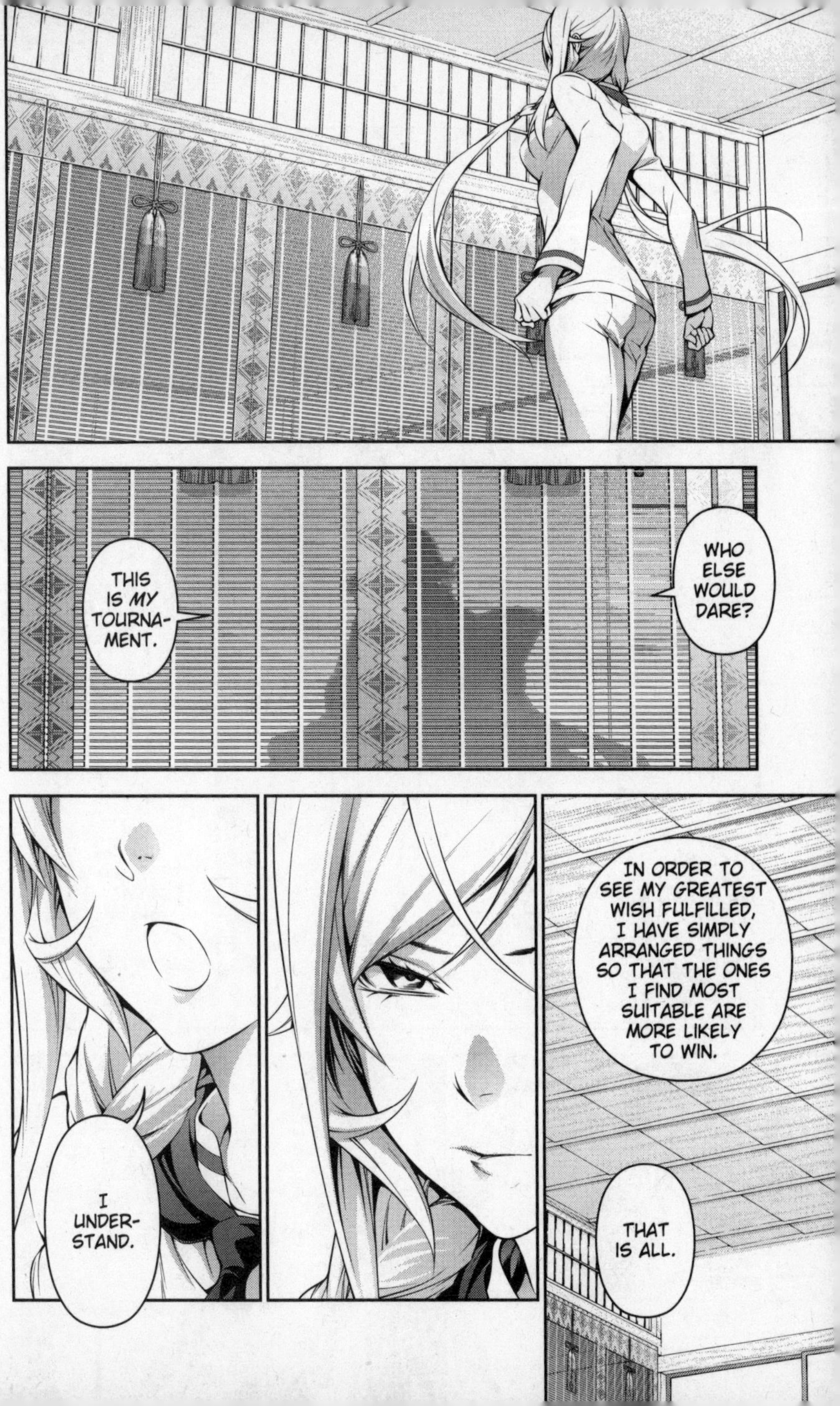
WHO ELSE WOULD DARE?
THIS IS *MY* TOURNAMENT.
IN ORDER TO SEE MY GREATEST WISH FULFILLED, I HAVE SIMPLY ARRANGED THINGS SO THAT THE ONES I FIND MOST SUITABLE ARE MORE LIKELY TO WIN.
THAT IS ALL.
I UNDERSTAND.

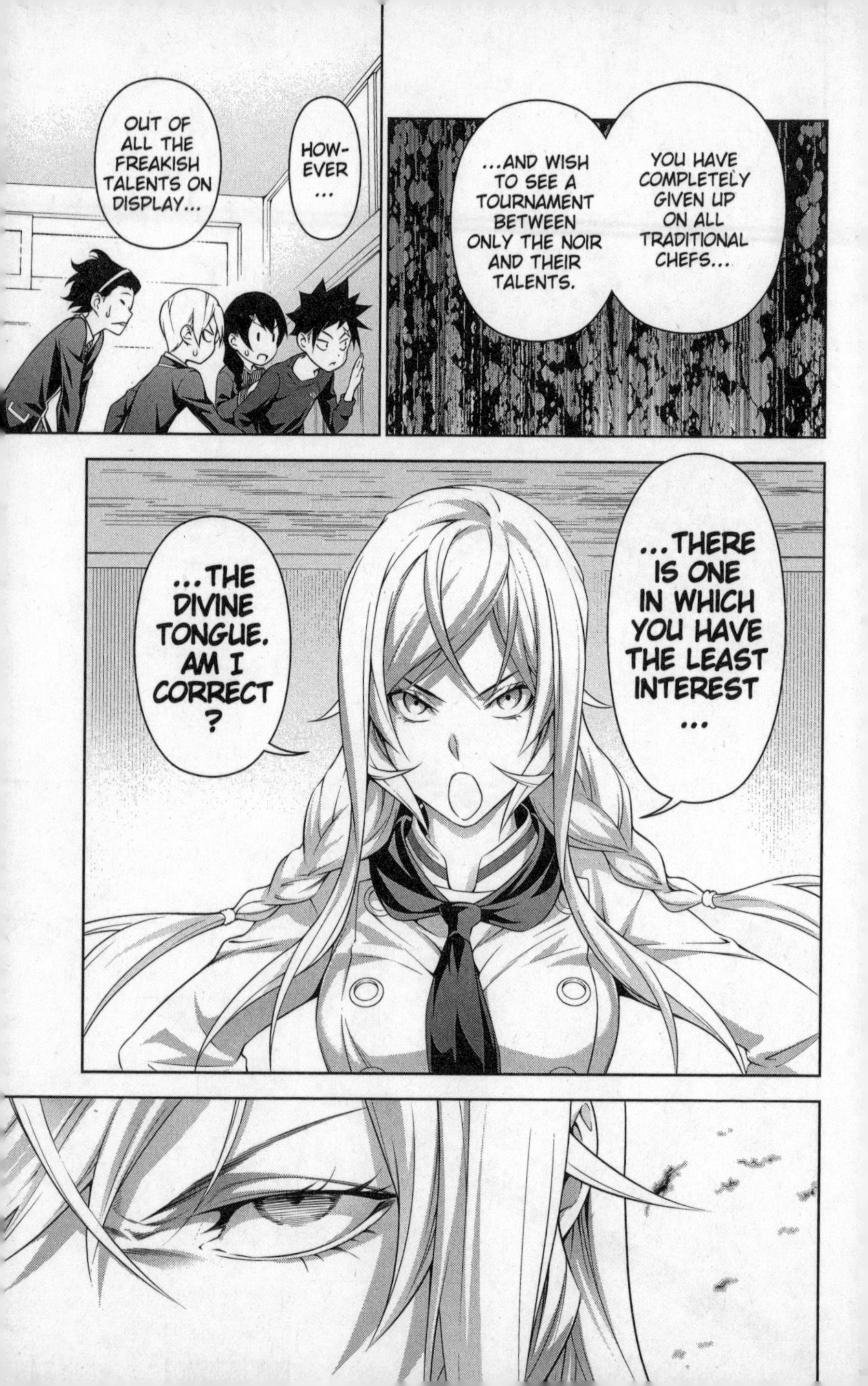
YOU HAVE COMPLETELY GIVEN UP ON ALL TRADITIONAL CHEFS...
...AND WISH TO SEE A TOURNAMENT BETWEEN ONLY THE NOIR AND THEIR TALENTS.
HOW-EVER...
OUT OF ALL THE FREAKISH TALENTS ON DISPLAY...
...THERE IS ONE IN WHICH YOU HAVE THE LEAST INTEREST...
...THE DIVINE TONGUE. AM I CORRECT?

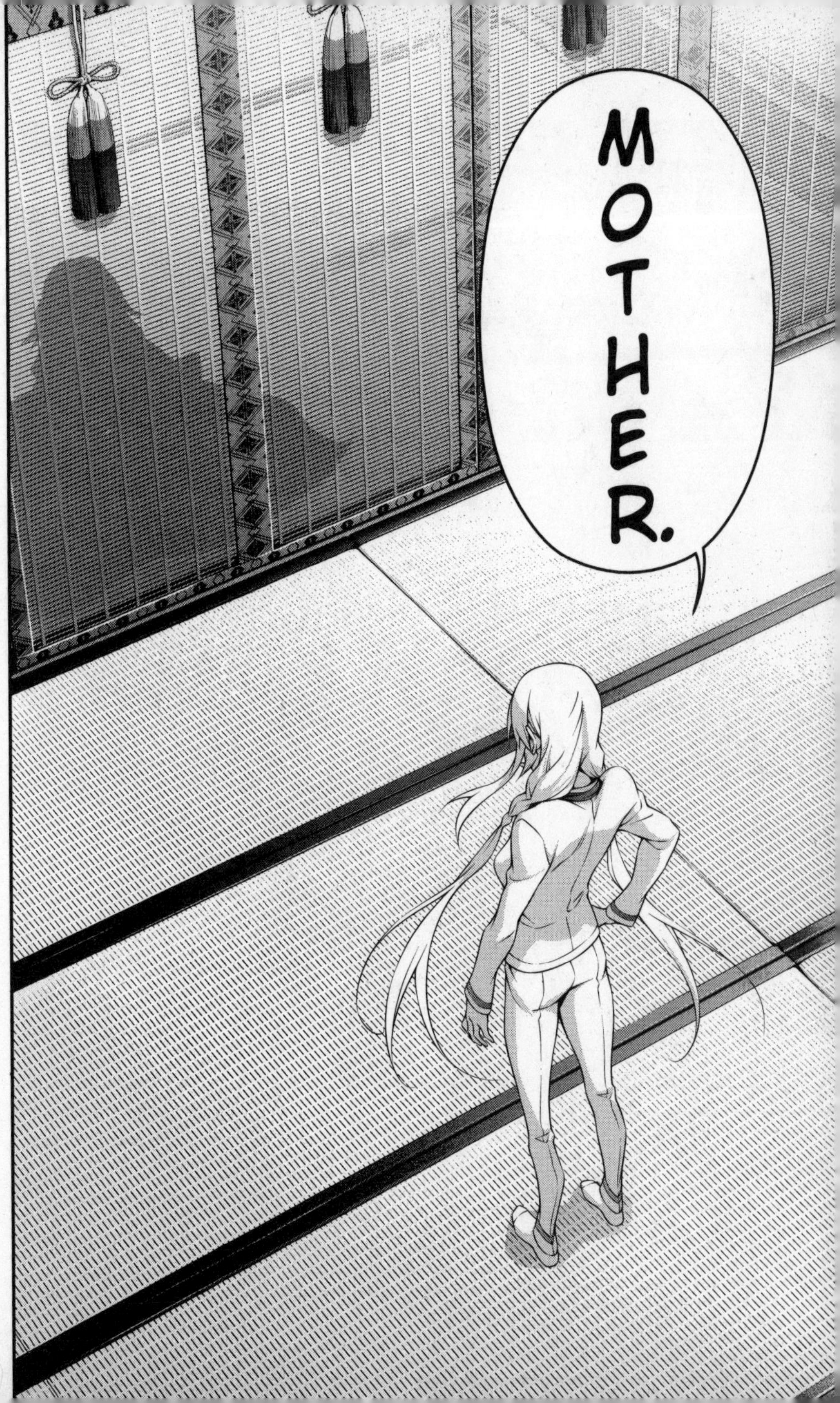
MOTHER.

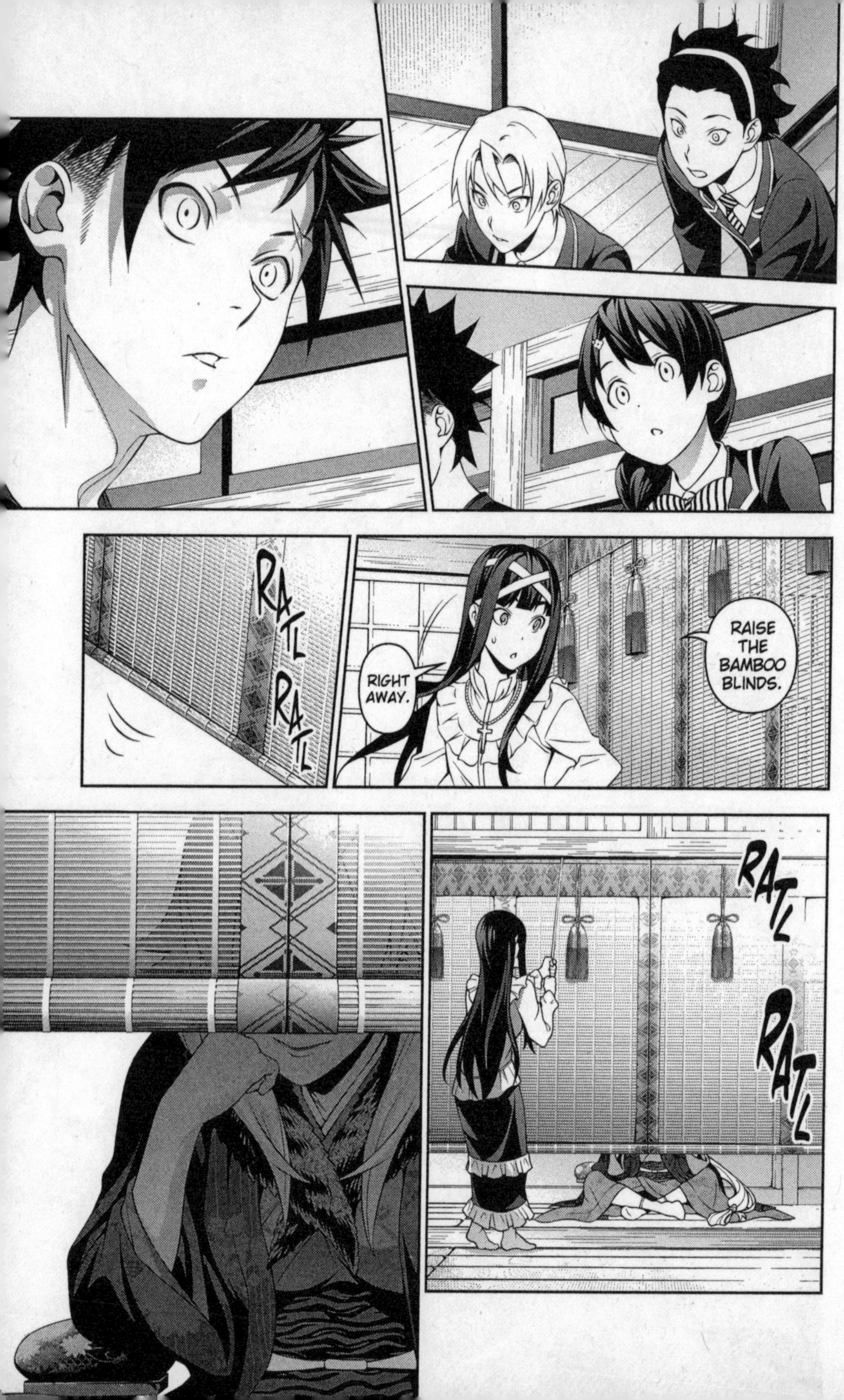
RAISE THE BAMBOO BLINDS.
RIGHT AWAY.
RATL RATL
RATL RATL

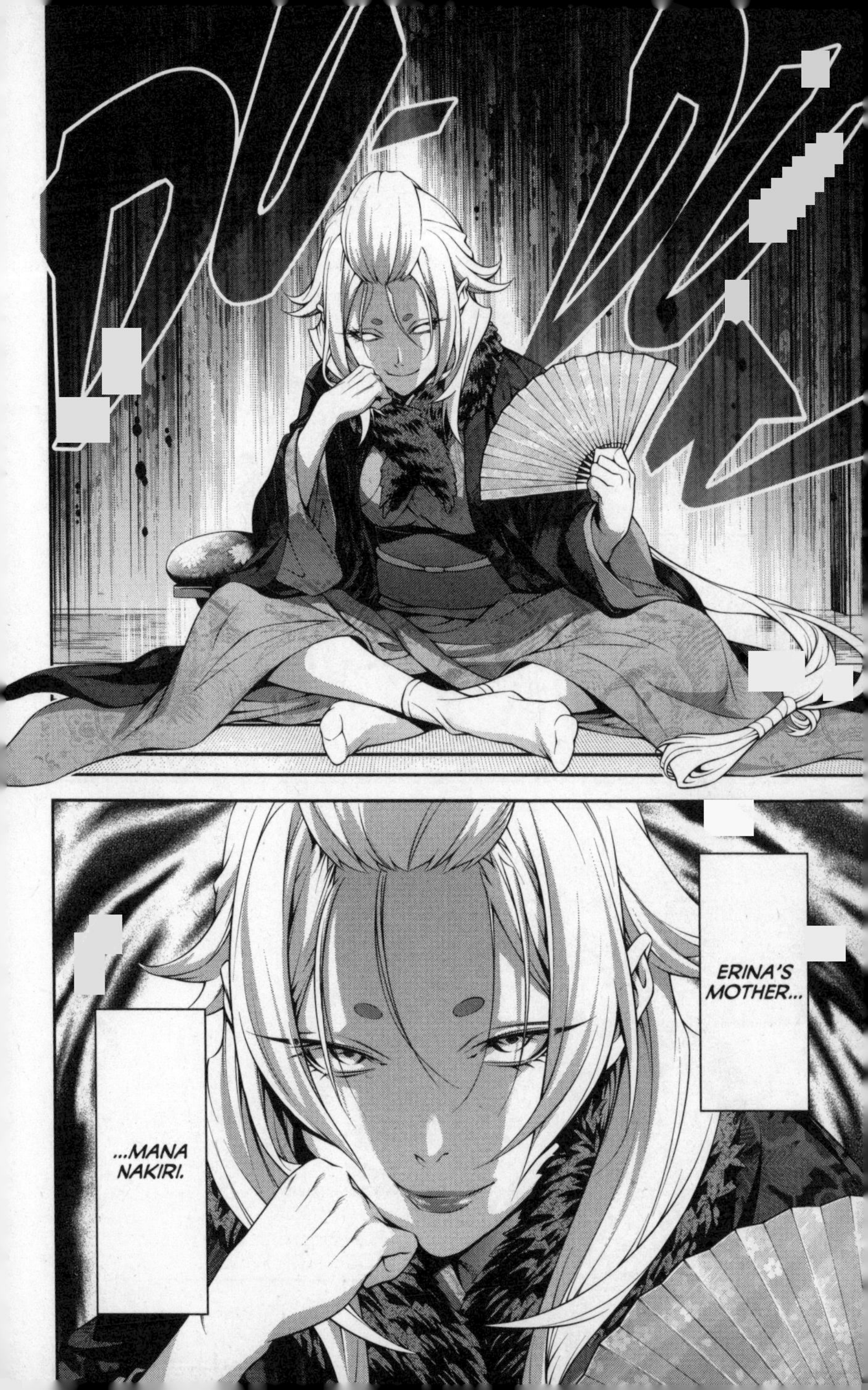
ERINA'S MOTHER...
...MANA NAKIRI.

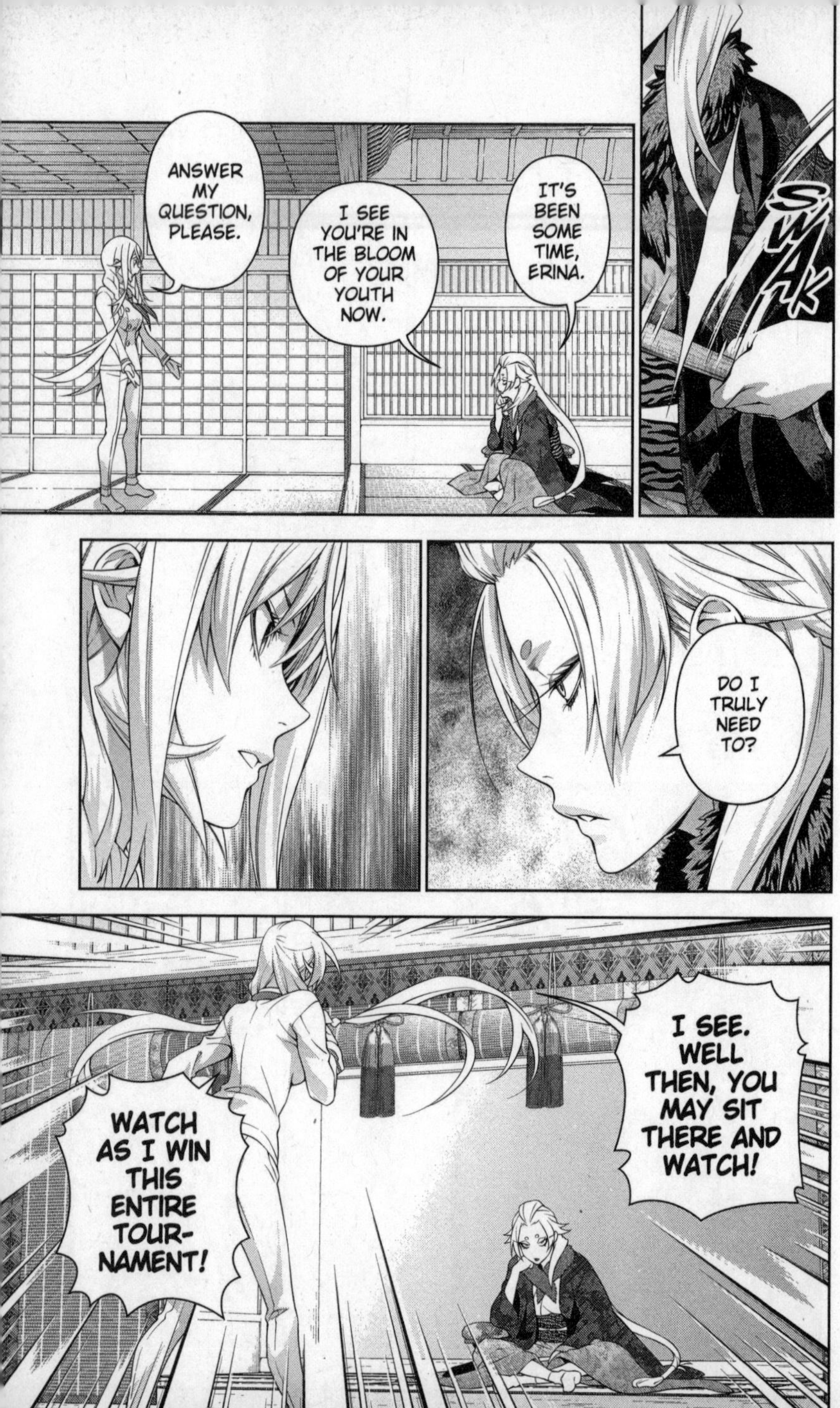
SWAK
IT'S BEEN SOME TIME, ERINA.
I SEE YOU'RE IN THE BLOOM OF YOUR YOUTH NOW.
ANSWER MY QUESTION, PLEASE.
DO I TRULY NEED TO?
I SEE. WELL THEN, YOU MAY SIT THERE AND WATCH!
WATCH AS I WIN THIS ENTIRE TOUR-NAMENT!

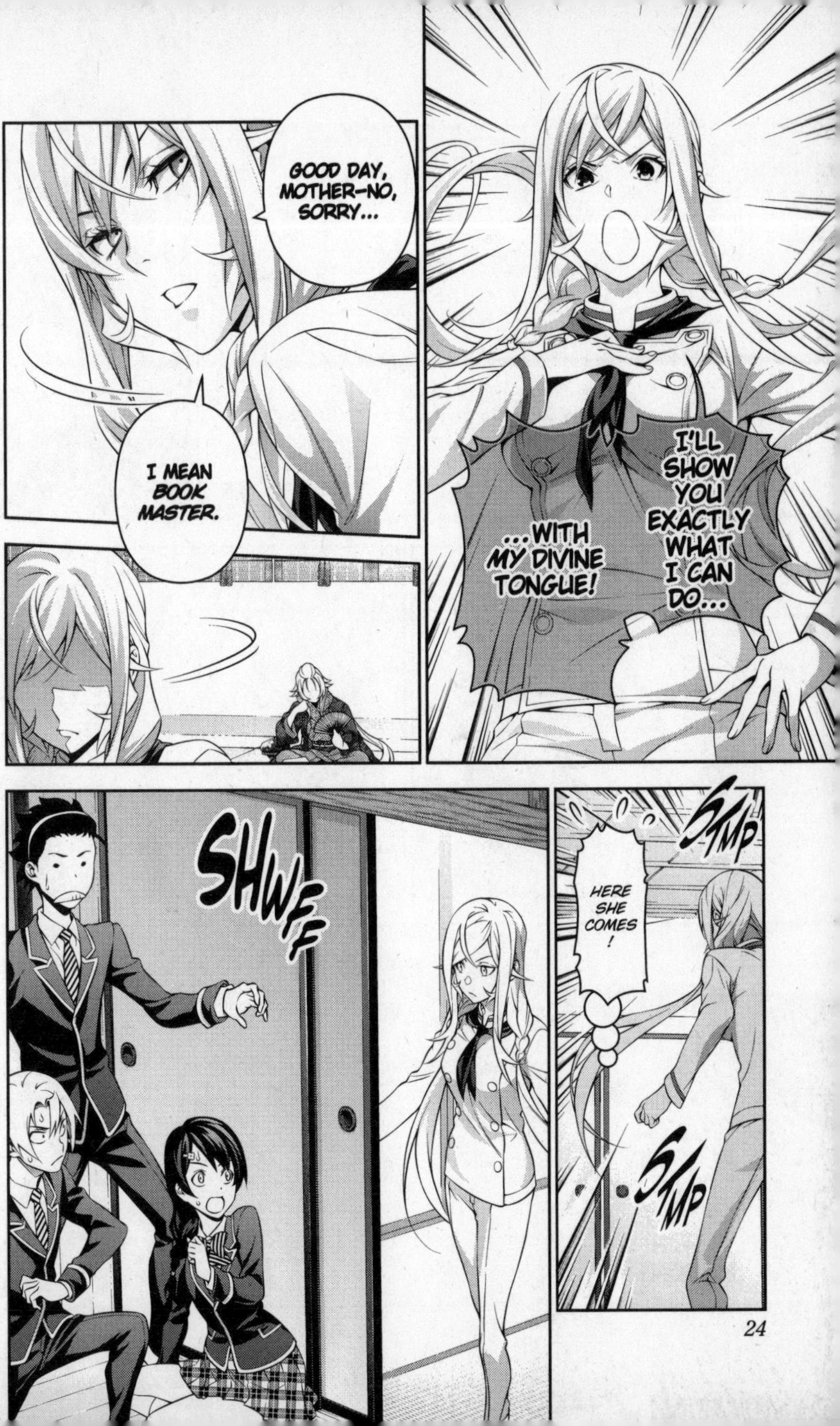
I'LL SHOW YOU EXACTLY WHAT I CAN DO...
...WITH MY DIVINE TONGUE!
GOOD DAY, MOTHER—NO, SORRY...
I MEAN BOOK MASTER.
STMP
HERE SHE COMES!
STMP
SHWFF

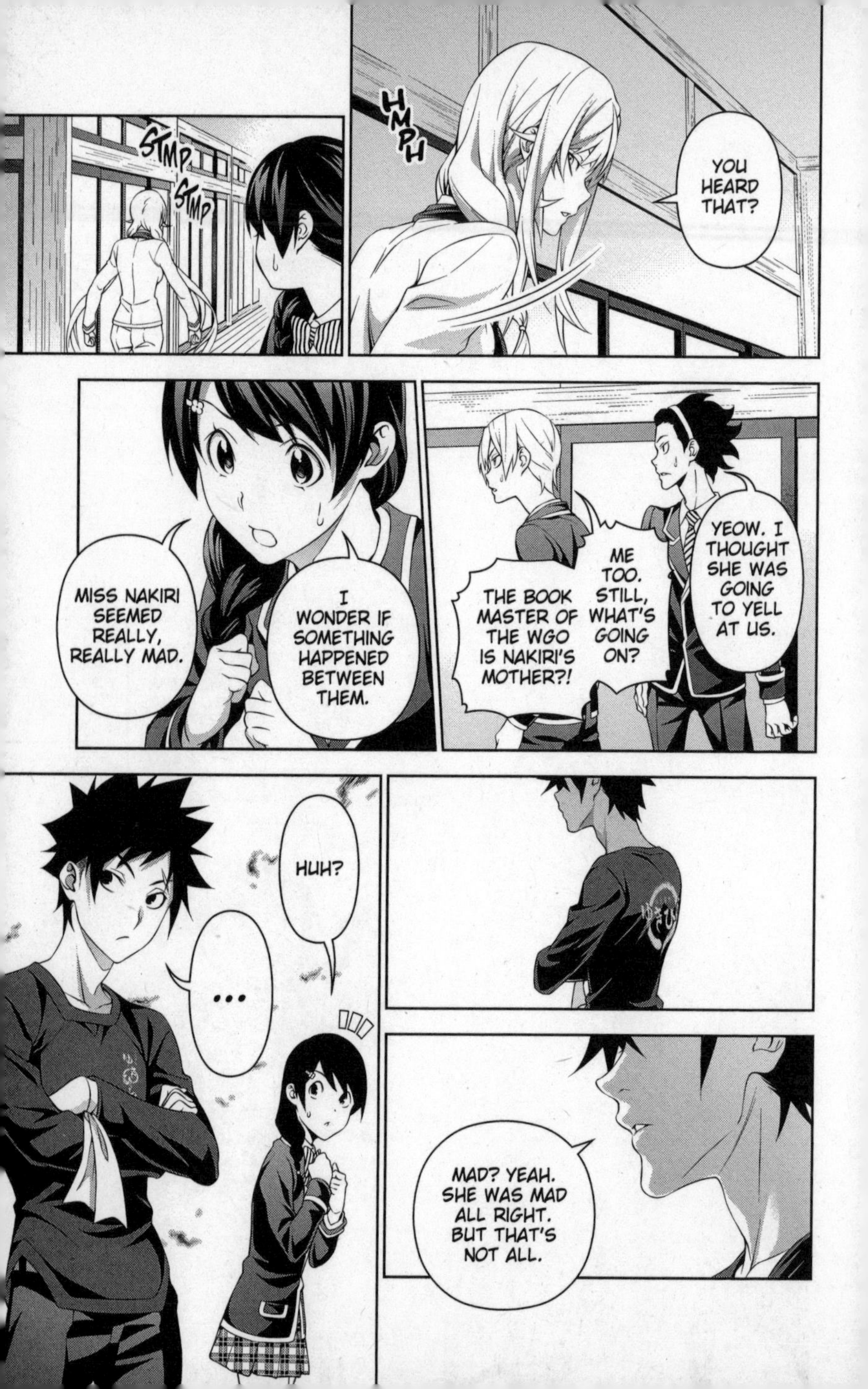
HMPH
YOU HEARD THAT?
STMP
STMP
YEOW. I THOUGHT SHE WAS GOING TO YELL AT US.
ME TOO. STILL, WHAT'S GOING ON?
THE BOOK MASTER OF THE WGO IS NAKIRI'S MOTHER?!
I WONDER IF SOMETHING HAPPENED BETWEEN THEM.
MISS NAKIRI SEEMED REALLY, REALLY MAD.
MAD? YEAH. SHE WAS MAD ALL RIGHT. BUT THAT'S NOT ALL.
HUH?
...

THERE'S JUST SOMETHING ABOUT THIS SHOT OF TADOKORO THAT I LIKE.

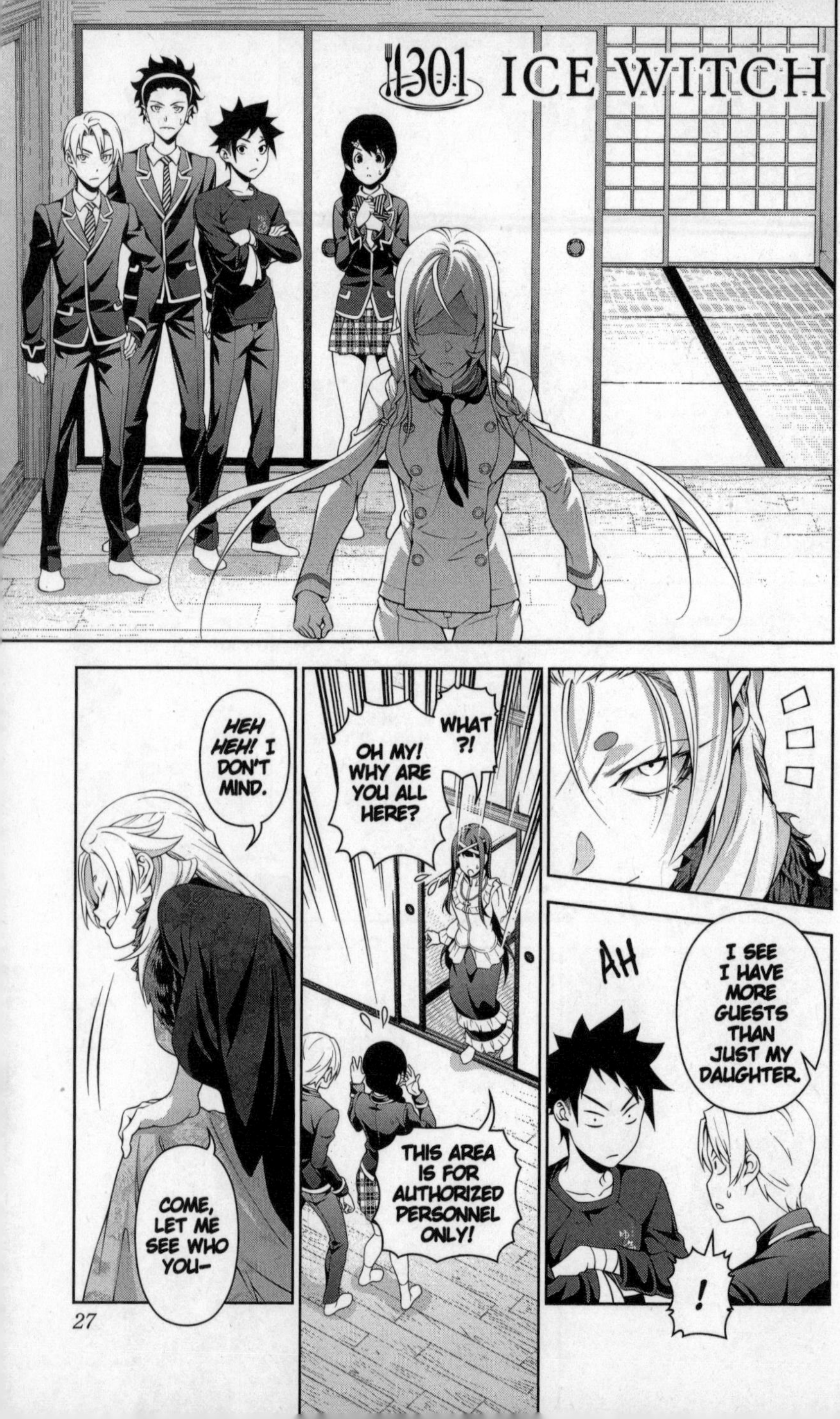
301 ICE WITCH
AH
I SEE I HAVE MORE GUESTS THAN JUST MY DAUGHTER.
!
WHAT?!
OH MY! WHY ARE YOU ALL HERE?
THIS AREA IS FOR AUTHORIZED PERSONNEL ONLY!
HEH HEH! I DON'T MIND.
COME, LET ME SEE WHO YOU-

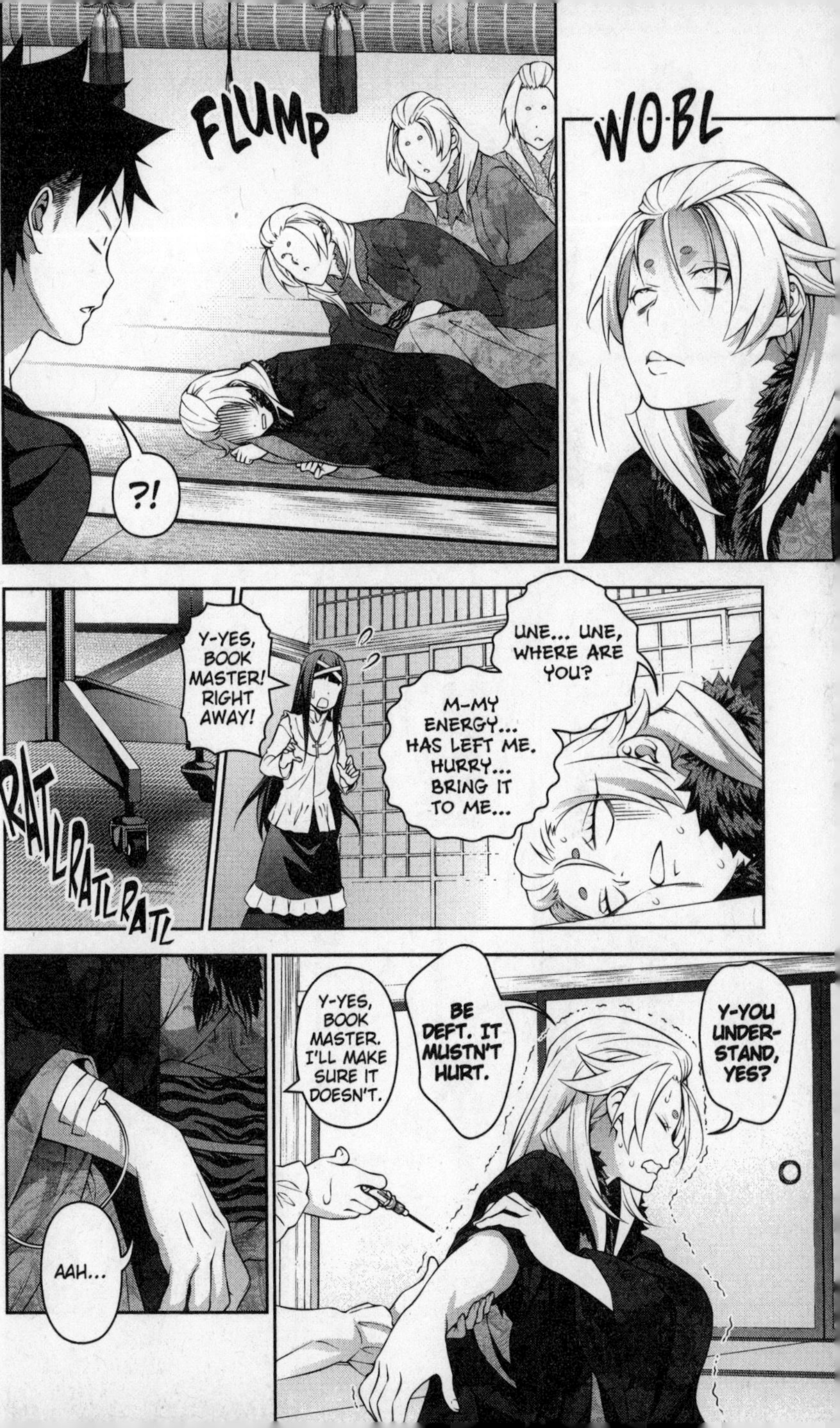
WOBL
FLUMP
?!
UNE... UNE, WHERE ARE YOU?
M-MY ENERGY... HAS LEFT ME. HURRY... BRING IT TO ME...
Y-YES, BOOK MASTER! RIGHT AWAY!
RATL RATL RATL RATL
Y-YOU UNDER-STAND, YES?
BE DEFT. IT MUSTN'T HURT.
Y-YES, BOOK MASTER. I'LL MAKE SURE IT DOESN'T.
AAH...

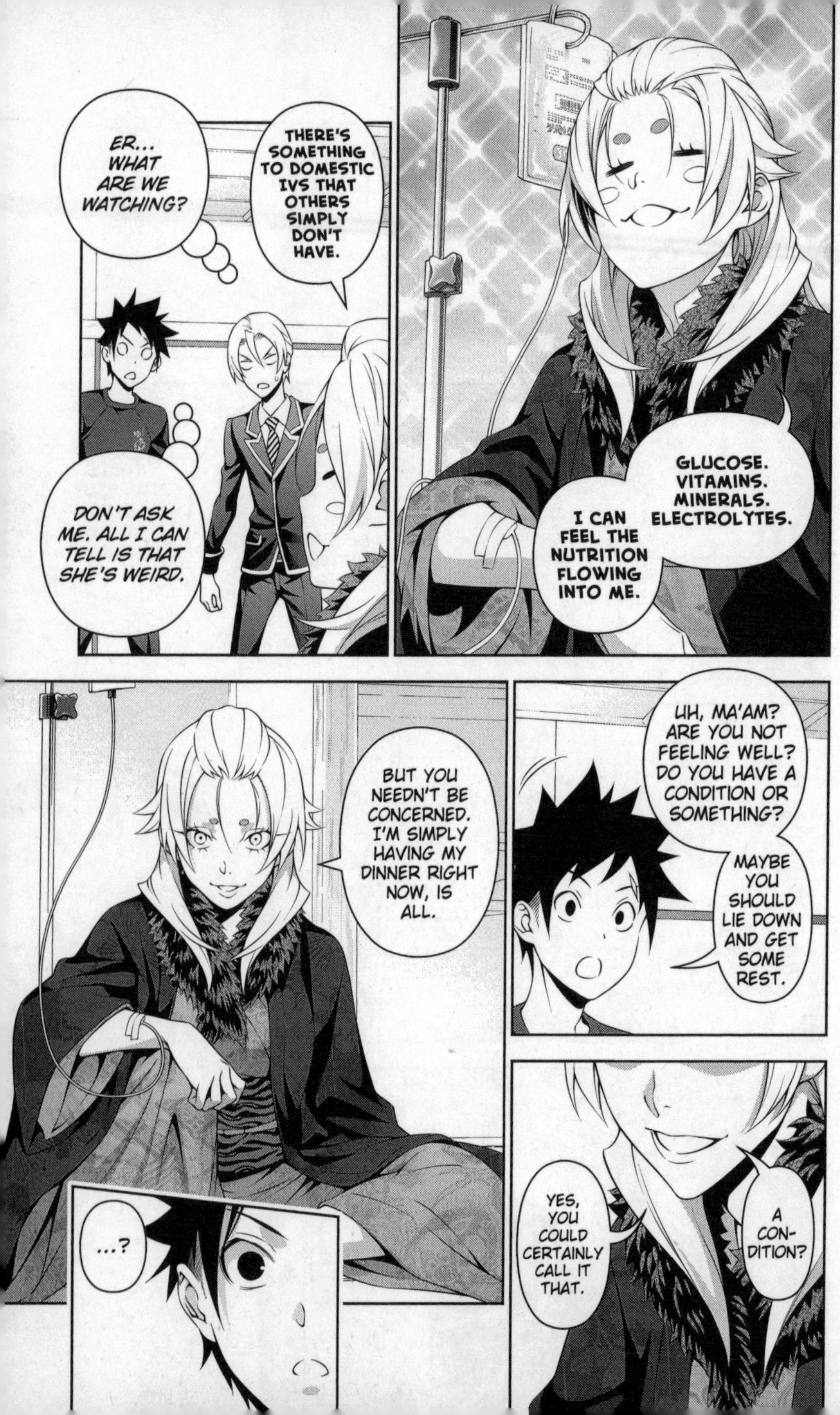
GLUCOSE. VITAMINS. MINERALS. ELECTROLYTES.
I CAN FEEL THE NUTRITION FLOWING INTO ME.
THERE'S SOMETHING TO DOMESTIC IVS THAT OTHERS SIMPLY DON'T HAVE.
ER... WHAT ARE WE WATCHING?
DON'T ASK ME. ALL I CAN TELL IS THAT SHE'S WEIRD.
UH, MA'AM? ARE YOU NOT FEELING WELL? DO YOU HAVE A CONDITION OR SOMETHING?
MAYBE YOU SHOULD LIE DOWN AND GET SOME REST.
A CON-DITION?
YES, YOU COULD CERTAINLY CALL IT THAT.
BUT YOU NEEDN'T BE CONCERNED. I'M SIMPLY HAVING MY DINNER RIGHT NOW, IS ALL.
...?

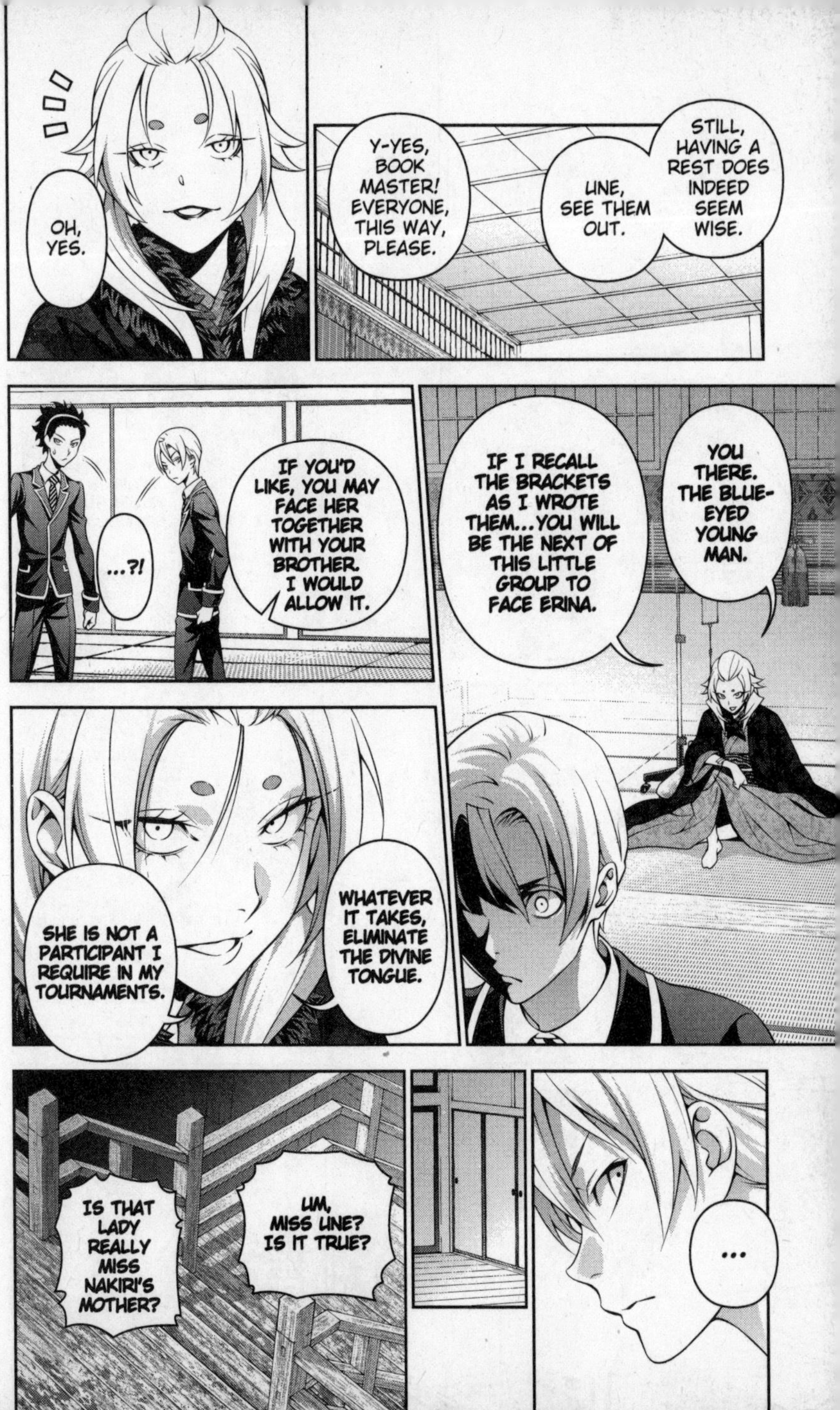
STILL, HAVING A REST DOES INDEED SEEM WISE.
LINE, SEE THEM OUT.
Y-YES, BOOK MASTER! EVERYONE, THIS WAY, PLEASE.
OH, YES.
YOU THERE. THE BLUE-EYED YOUNG MAN.
IF I RECALL THE BRACKETS AS I WROTE THEM...YOU WILL BE THE NEXT OF THIS LITTLE GROUP TO FACE ERINA.
IF YOU'D LIKE, YOU MAY FACE HER TOGETHER WITH YOUR BROTHER. I WOULD ALLOW IT.
...?!
WHATEVER IT TAKES, ELIMINATE THE DIVINE TONGUE.
SHE IS NOT A PARTICIPANT I REQUIRE IN MY TOURNAMENTS.
...
UM, MISS LINE? IS IT TRUE?
IS THAT LADY REALLY MISS NAKIRI'S MOTHER?

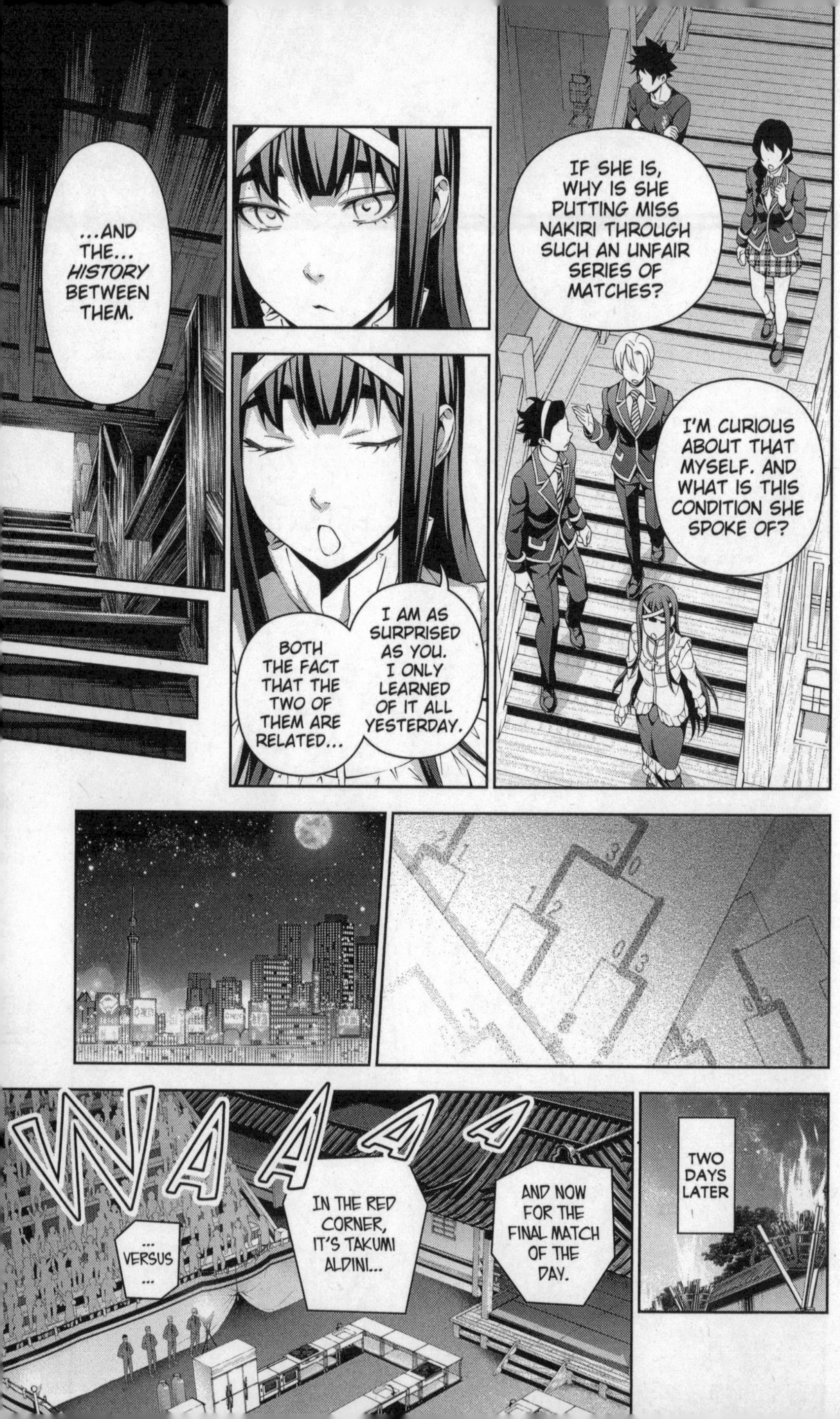
IF SHE IS, WHY IS SHE PUTTING MISS NAKIRI THROUGH SUCH AN UNFAIR SERIES OF MATCHES?
I'M CURIOUS ABOUT THAT MYSELF. AND WHAT IS THIS CONDITION SHE SPOKE OF?
I AM AS SURPRISED AS YOU. I ONLY LEARNED OF IT ALL YESTERDAY.
BOTH THE FACT THAT THE TWO OF THEM ARE RELATED...
...AND THE... *HISTORY* BETWEEN THEM.
TWO DAYS LATER
WAAAA
AND NOW FOR THE FINAL MATCH OF THE DAY.
IN THE RED CORNER, IT'S TAKUMI ALDINI...
...VERSUS...

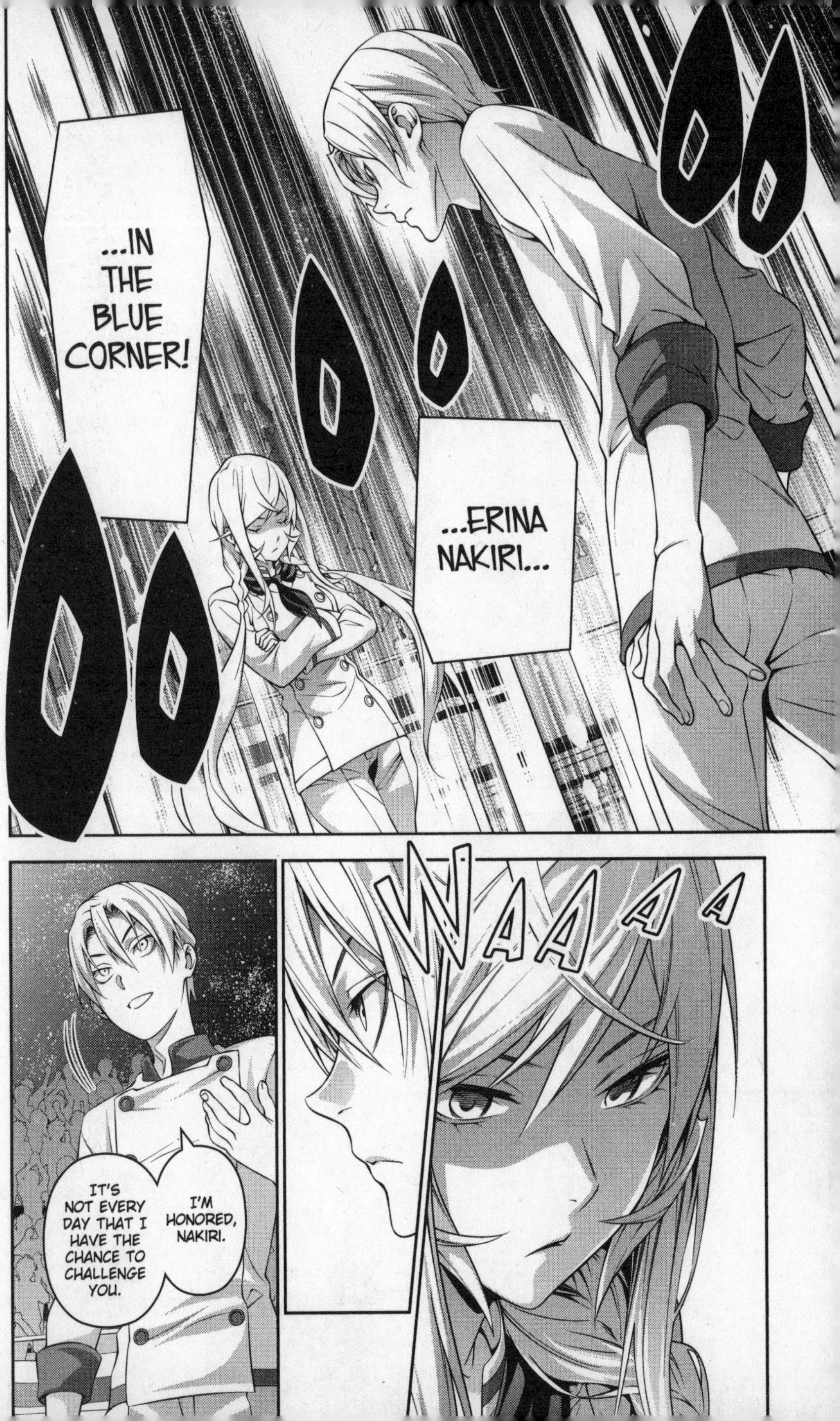
...IN THE BLUE CORNER!
...ERINA NAKIRI...
WAAAAA
I'M HONORED, NAKIRI.
IT'S NOT EVERY DAY THAT I HAVE THE CHANCE TO CHALLENGE YOU.

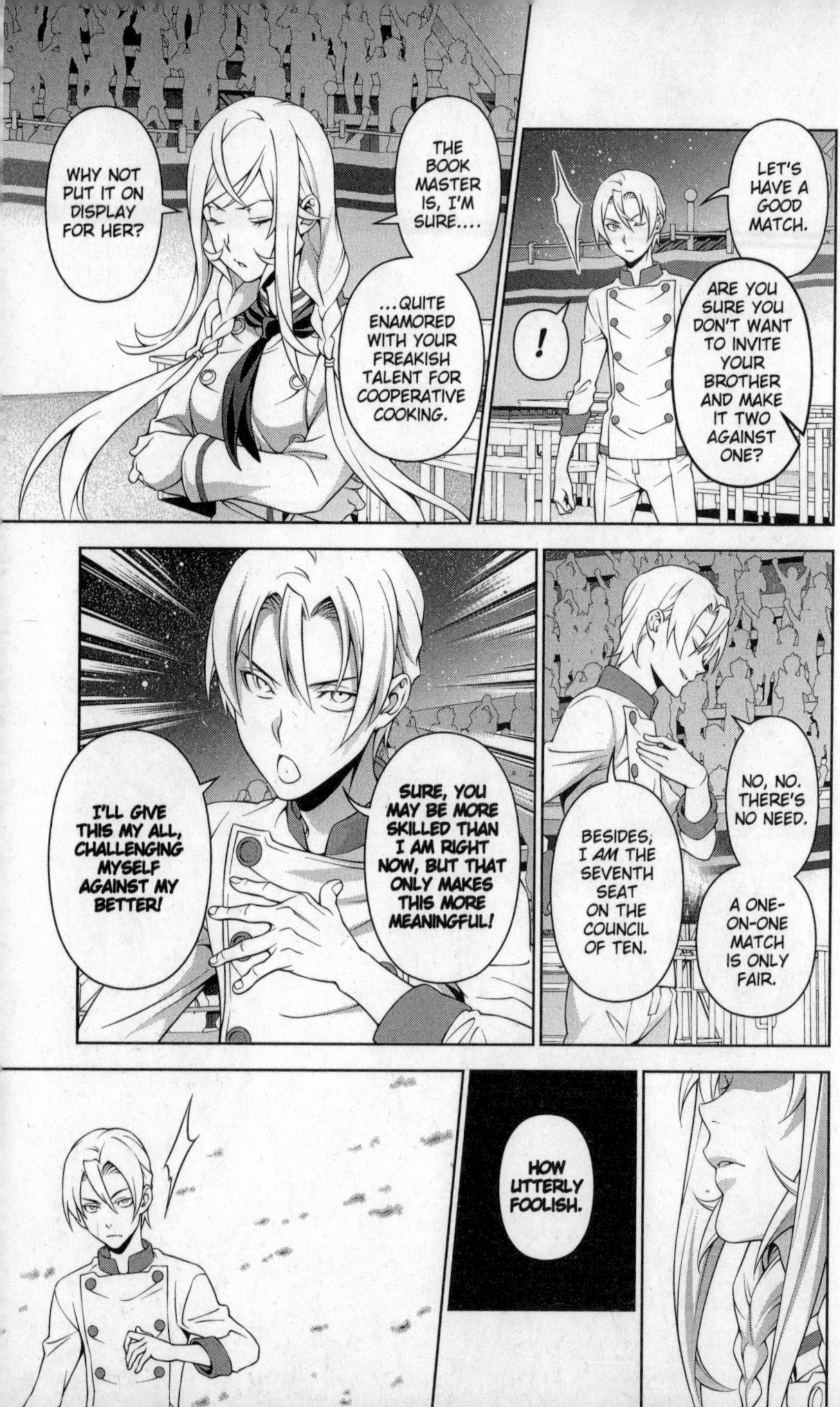
LET'S HAVE A GOOD MATCH.
ARE YOU SURE YOU DON'T WANT TO INVITE YOUR BROTHER AND MAKE IT TWO AGAINST ONE?
!
THE BOOK MASTER IS, I'M SURE....
...QUITE ENAMORED WITH YOUR FREAKISH TALENT FOR COOPERATIVE COOKING.
WHY NOT PUT IT ON DISPLAY FOR HER?
NO, NO. THERE'S NO NEED.
A ONE-ON-ONE MATCH IS ONLY FAIR.
BESIDES; I *AM* THE SEVENTH SEAT ON THE COUNCIL OF TEN.
SURE, YOU MAY BE MORE SKILLED THAN I AM RIGHT NOW, BUT THAT ONLY MAKES THIS MORE MEANINGFUL!
I'LL GIVE THIS MY ALL, CHALLENGING MYSELF AGAINST MY BETTER!
HOW UTTERLY FOOLISH.

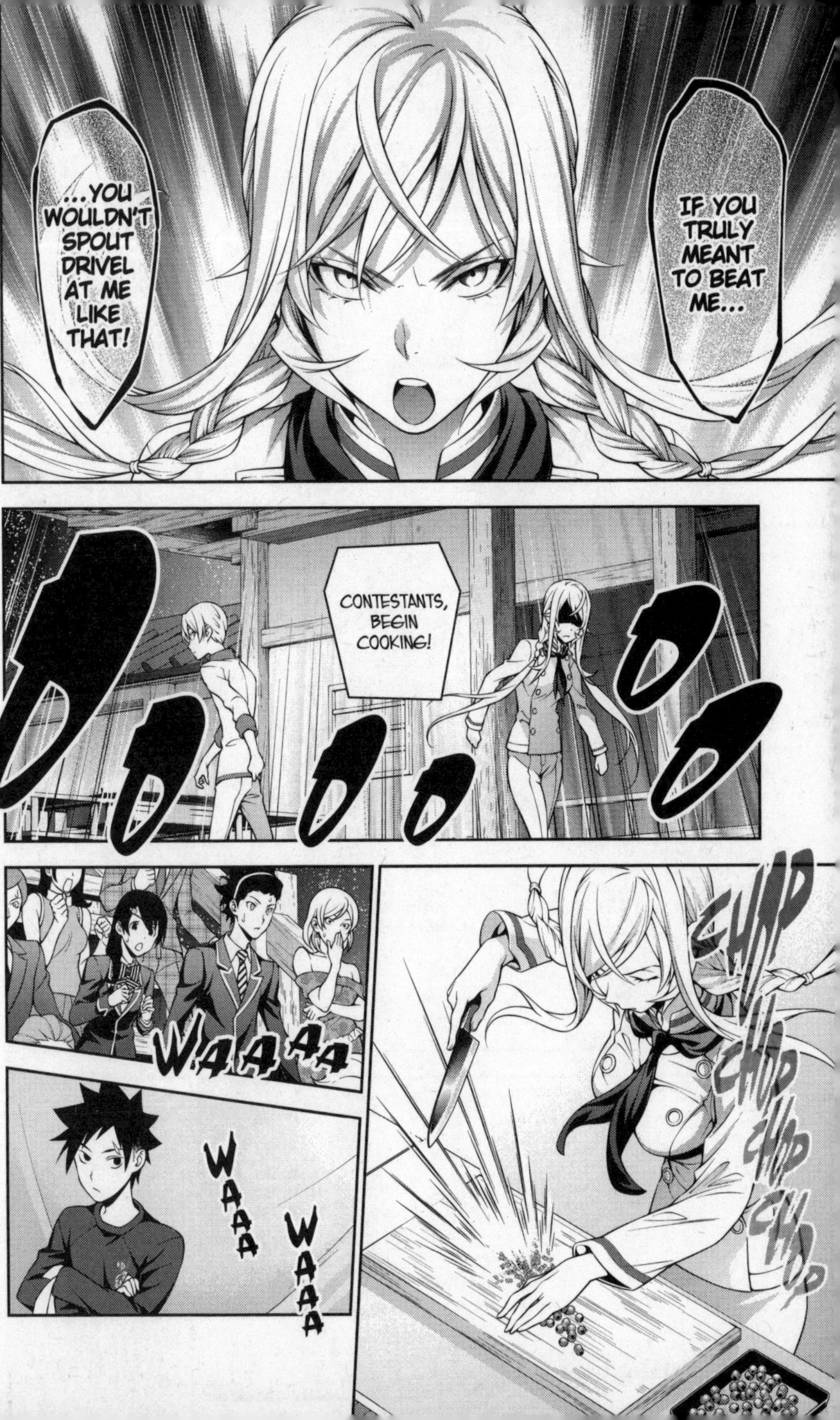
IF YOU TRULY MEANT TO BEAT ME...
...YOU WOULDN'T SPOUT DRIVEL AT ME LIKE THAT!
CONTESTANTS, BEGIN COOKING!
CHOP CHOP CHOP CHOP
WAAAAA
WAAA
WAAA

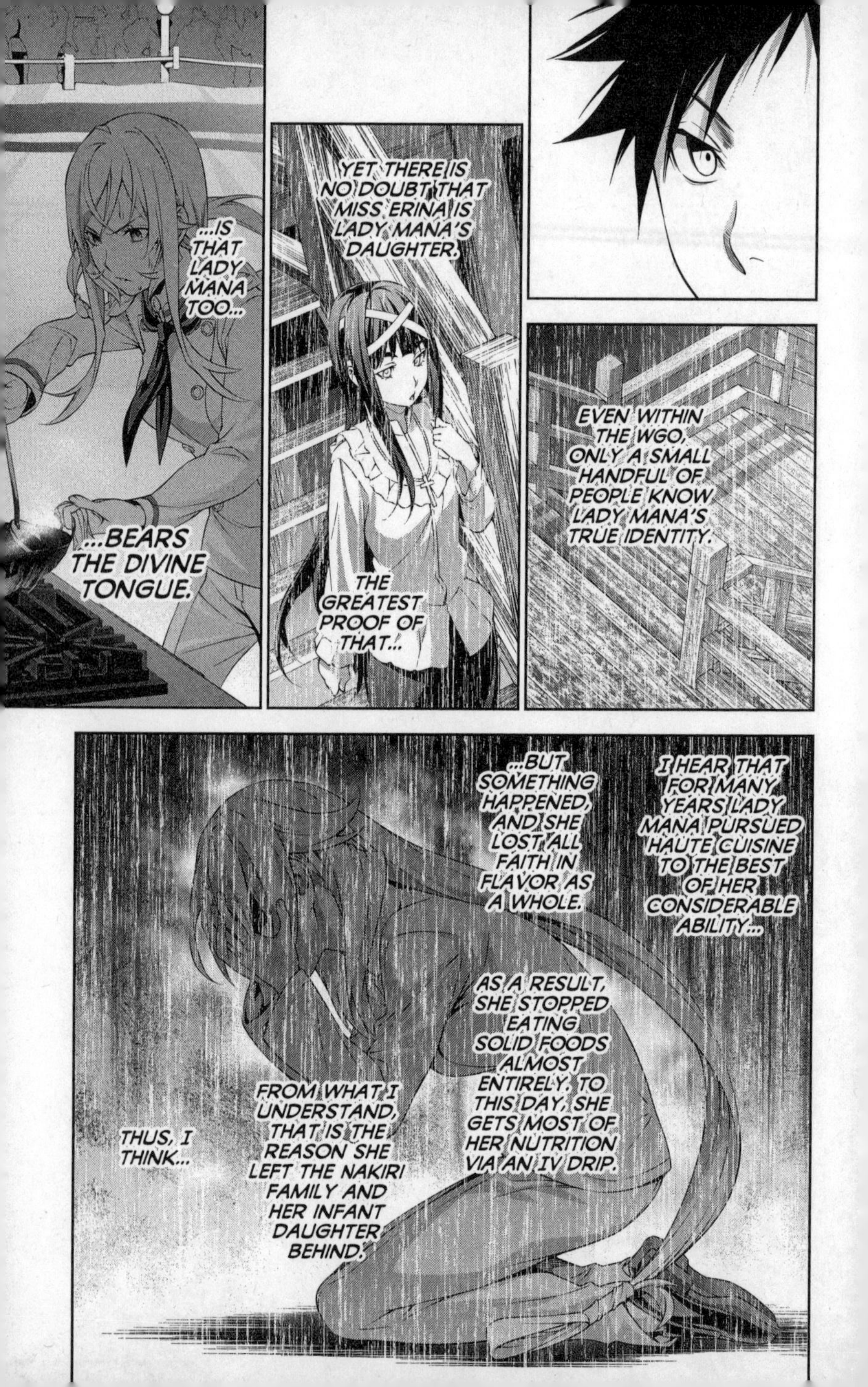
EVEN WITHIN THE WGO, ONLY A SMALL HANDFUL OF PEOPLE KNOW LADY MANA'S TRUE IDENTITY.
YET THERE IS NO DOUBT THAT MISS ERINA IS LADY MANA'S DAUGHTER.
THE GREATEST PROOF OF THAT...
...IS THAT LADY MANA TOO...
...BEARS THE DIVINE TONGUE.
I HEAR THAT FOR MANY YEARS LADY MANA PURSUED HAUTE CUISINE TO THE BEST OF HER CONSIDERABLE ABILITY...
...BUT SOMETHING HAPPENED, AND SHE LOST ALL FAITH IN FLAVOR AS A WHOLE.
AS A RESULT, SHE STOPPED EATING SOLID FOODS ALMOST ENTIRELY. TO THIS DAY, SHE GETS MOST OF HER NUTRITION VIA AN IV DRIP.
FROM WHAT I UNDERSTAND, THAT IS THE REASON SHE LEFT THE NAKIRI FAMILY AND HER INFANT DAUGHTER BEHIND.
THUS, I THINK...

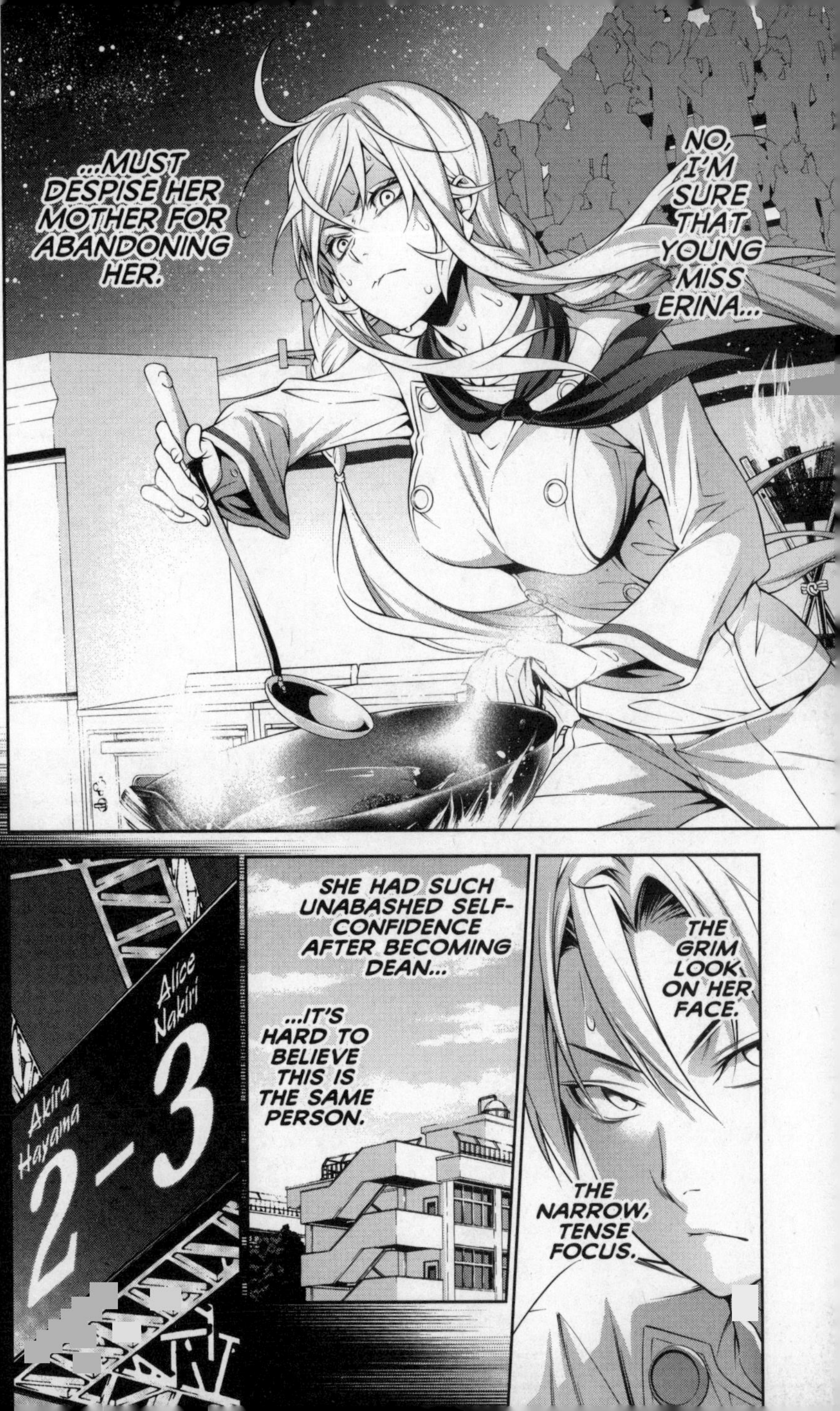
NO, I'M SURE THAT YOUNG MISS ERINA...
...MUST DESPISE HER MOTHER FOR ABANDONING HER.
THE GRIM LOOK ON HER FACE.
THE NARROW, TENSE FOCUS.
SHE HAD SUCH UNABASHED SELF-CONFIDENCE AFTER BECOMING DEAN...
...IT'S HARD TO BELIEVE THIS IS THE SAME PERSON.
Alice Nakiri
Akira Hayama
2-3

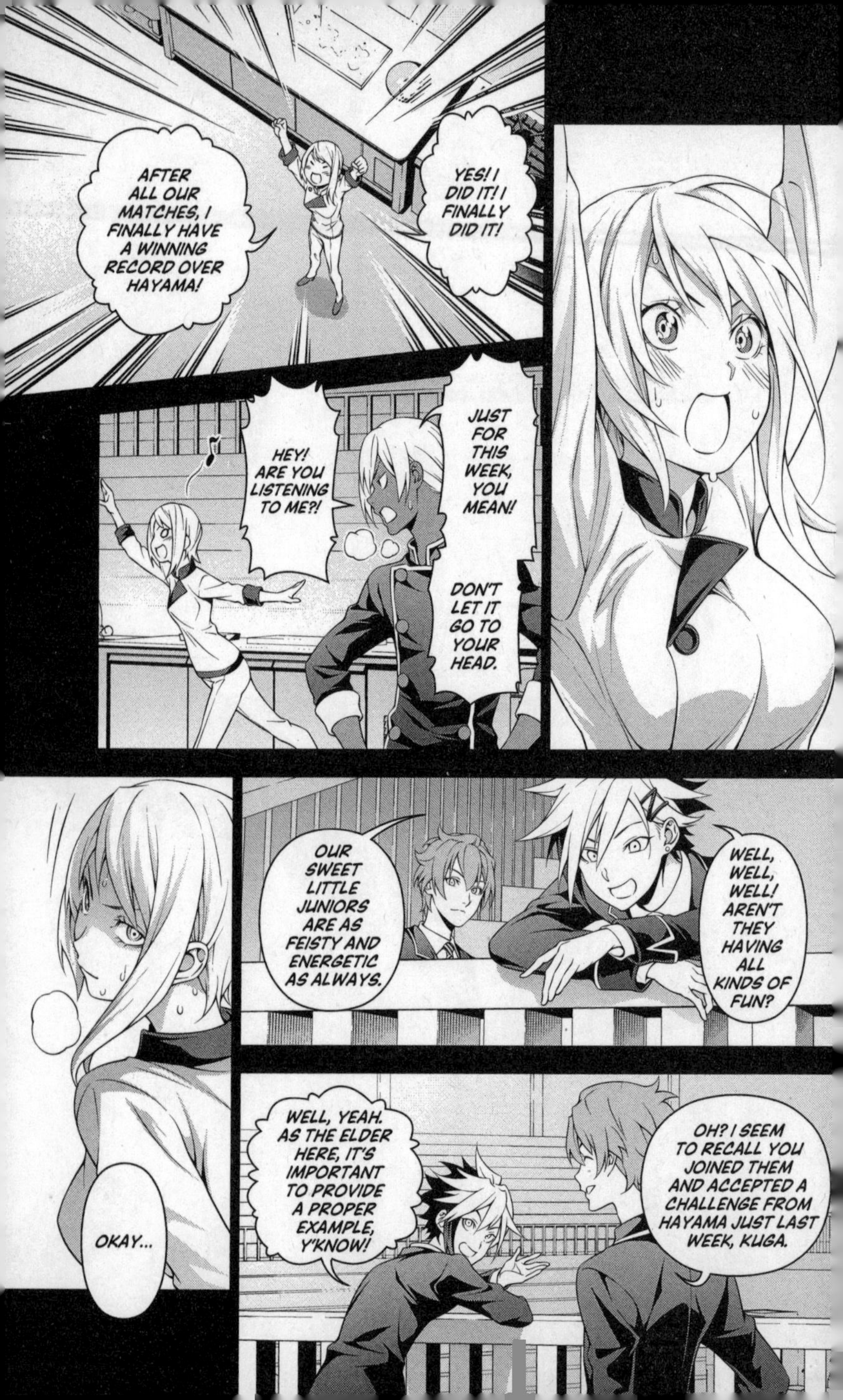
YES! I DID IT! I FINALLY DID IT!
AFTER ALL OUR MATCHES, I FINALLY HAVE A WINNING RECORD OVER HAYAMA!
JUST FOR THIS WEEK, YOU MEAN!
DON'T LET IT GO TO YOUR HEAD.
HEY! ARE YOU LISTENING TO ME?!
WELL, WELL, WELL! AREN'T THEY HAVING ALL KINDS OF FUN?
OUR SWEET LITTLE JUNIORS ARE AS FEISTY AND ENERGETIC AS ALWAYS.
OH? I SEEM TO RECALL YOU JOINED THEM AND ACCEPTED A CHALLENGE FROM HAYAMA JUST LAST WEEK, KUGA.
WELL, YEAH. AS THE ELDER HERE, IT'S IMPORTANT TO PROVIDE A PROPER EXAMPLE, Y'KNOW!
OKAY...

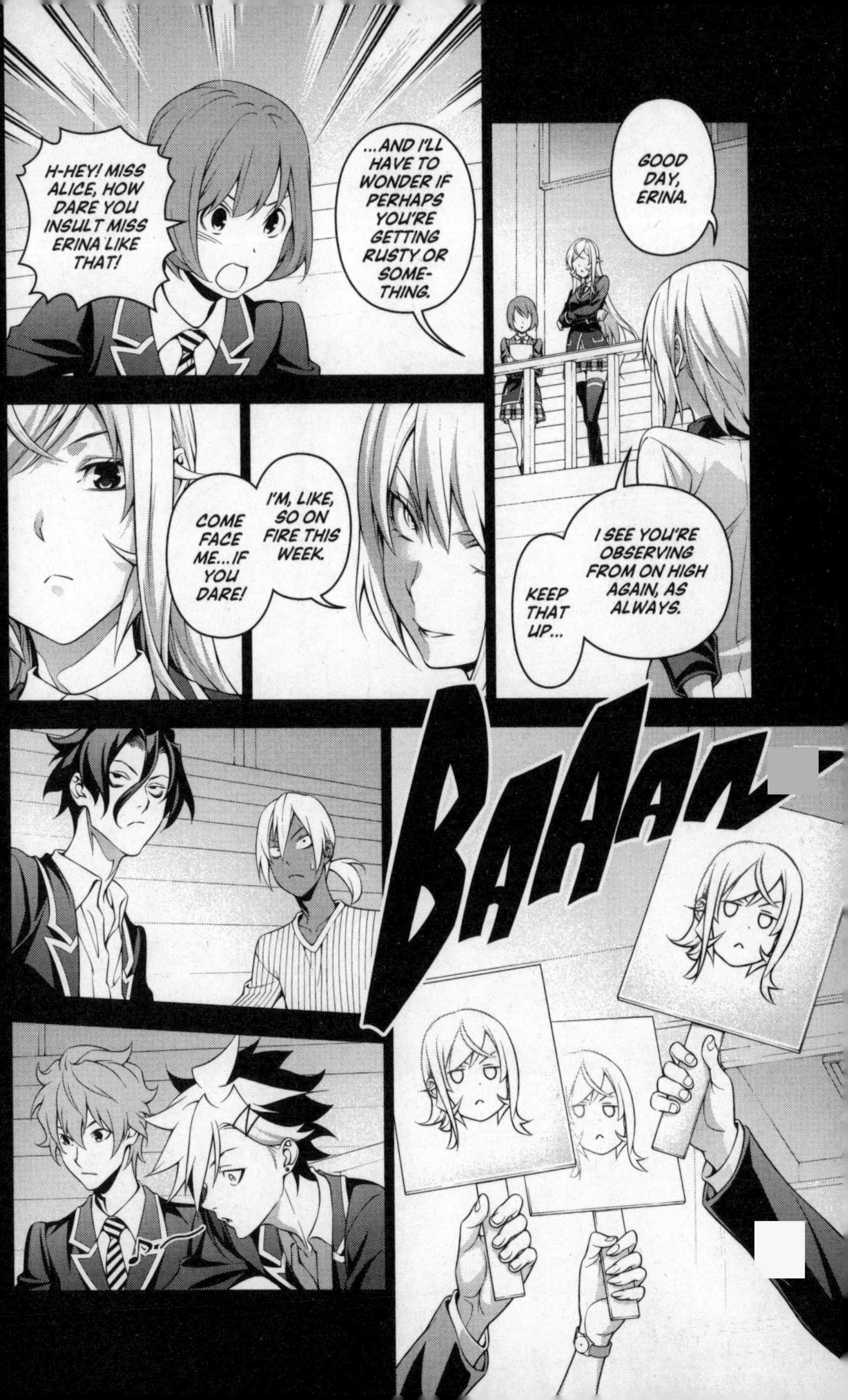
GOOD DAY, ERINA.
I SEE YOU'RE OBSERVING FROM ON HIGH AGAIN, AS ALWAYS.
KEEP THAT UP...
...AND I'LL HAVE TO WONDER IF PERHAPS YOU'RE GETTING RUSTY OR SOME-THING.
H-HEY! MISS ALICE, HOW DARE YOU INSULT MISS ERINA LIKE THAT!
I'M, LIKE, SO ON FIRE THIS WEEK.
COME FACE ME...IF YOU DARE!
BAAAN

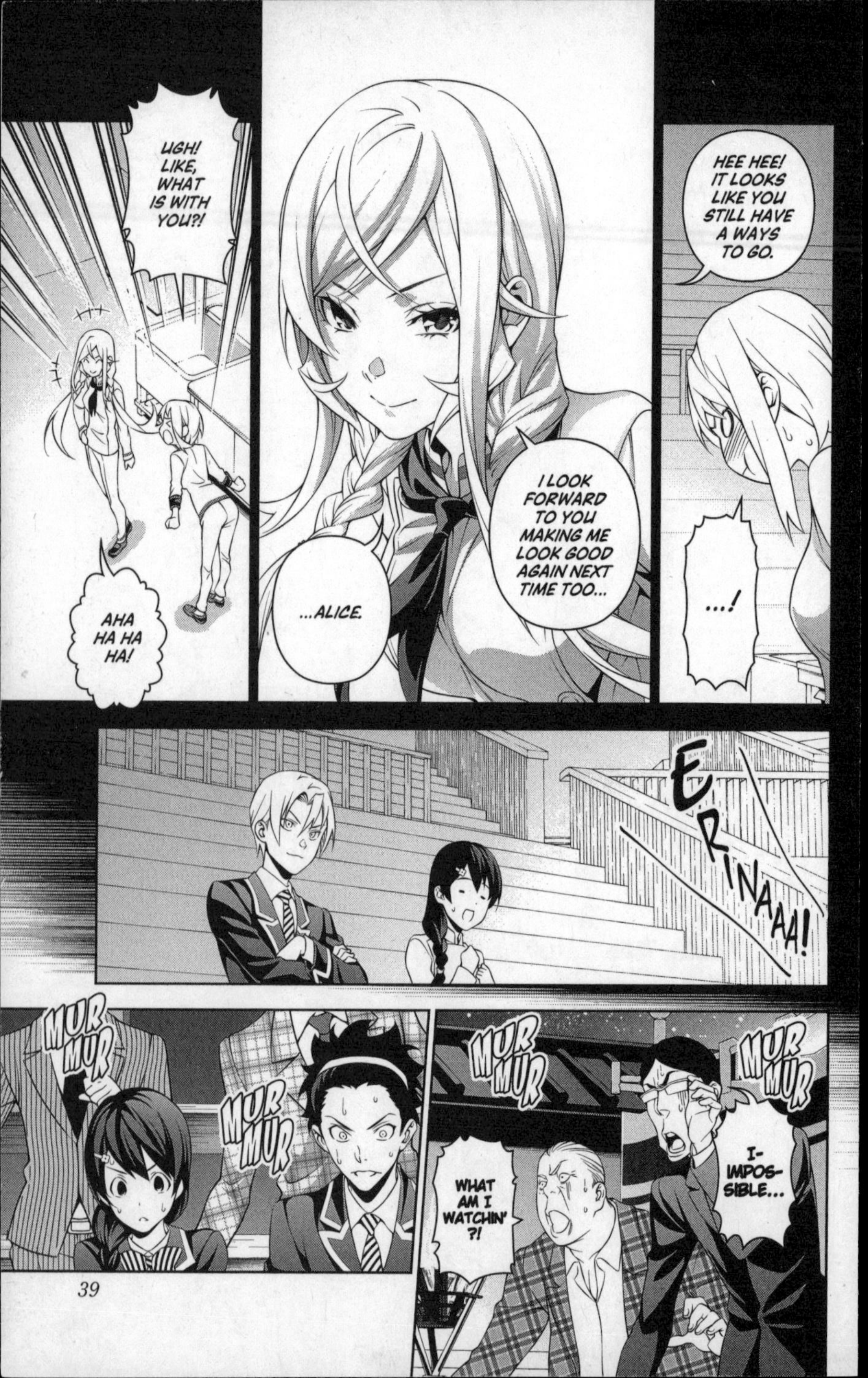
HEE HEE! IT LOOKS LIKE YOU STILL HAVE A WAYS TO GO.
...!
I LOOK FORWARD TO YOU MAKING ME LOOK GOOD AGAIN NEXT TIME TOO...
...ALICE.
UGH! LIKE, WHAT IS WITH YOU?!
AHA HA HA HA!
ERINAAAA!
MUR MUR
I-IMPOSSIBLE...
MUR MUR
WHAT AM I WATCHIN'?!
MUR MUR
MUR MUR

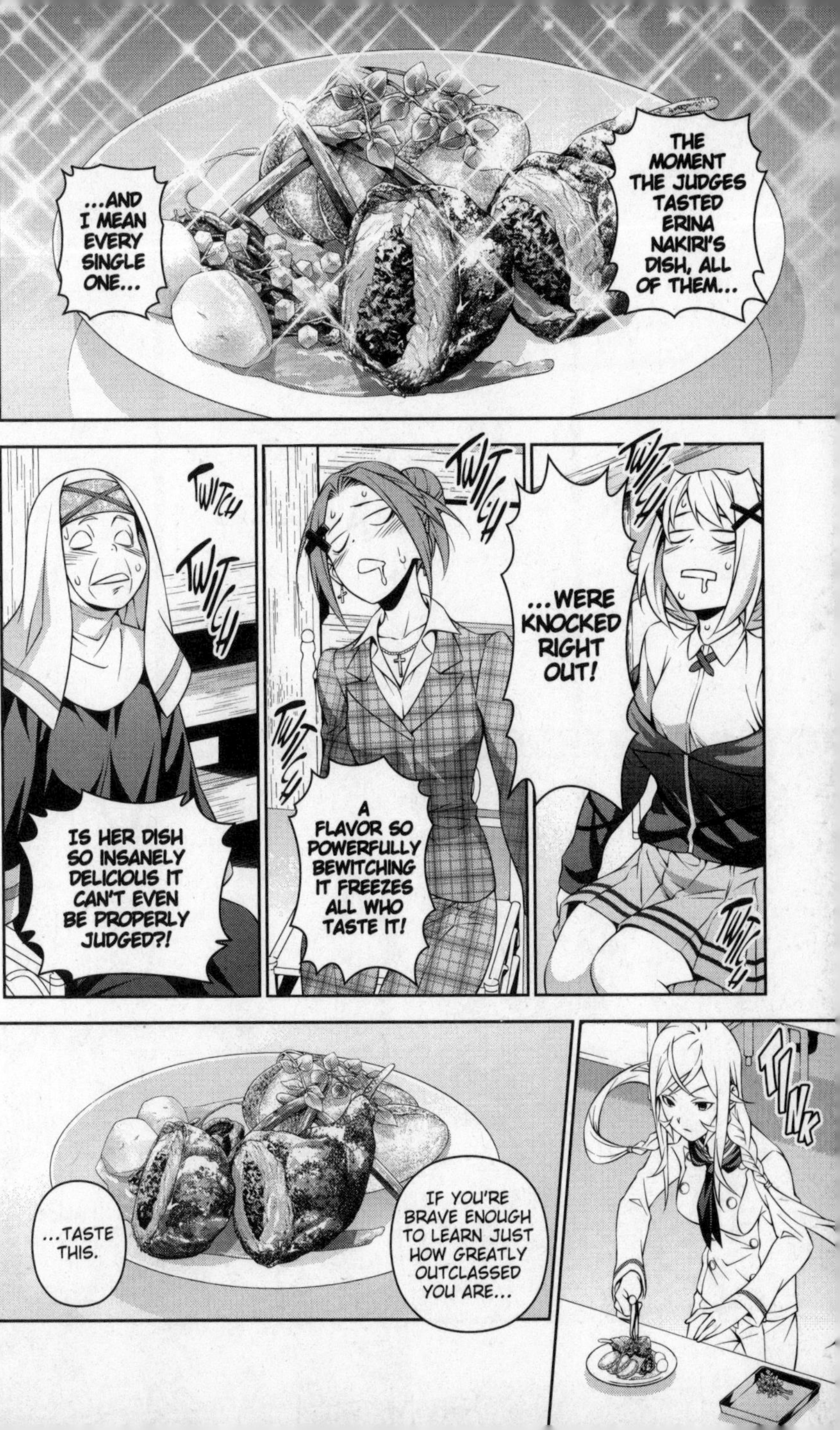
THE MOMENT THE JUDGES TASTED ERINA NAKIRI'S DISH, ALL OF THEM...
...AND I MEAN EVERY SINGLE ONE...
TWITCH
...WERE KNOCKED RIGHT OUT!
TWITCH
TWITCH
TWITCH
A FLAVOR SO POWERFULLY BEWITCHING IT FREEZES ALL WHO TASTE IT!
TWITCH
TWITCH
IS HER DISH SO INSANELY DELICIOUS IT CAN'T EVEN BE PROPERLY JUDGED?!
TINK
IF YOU'RE BRAVE ENOUGH TO LEARN JUST HOW GREATLY OUTCLASSED YOU ARE...
...TASTE THIS.

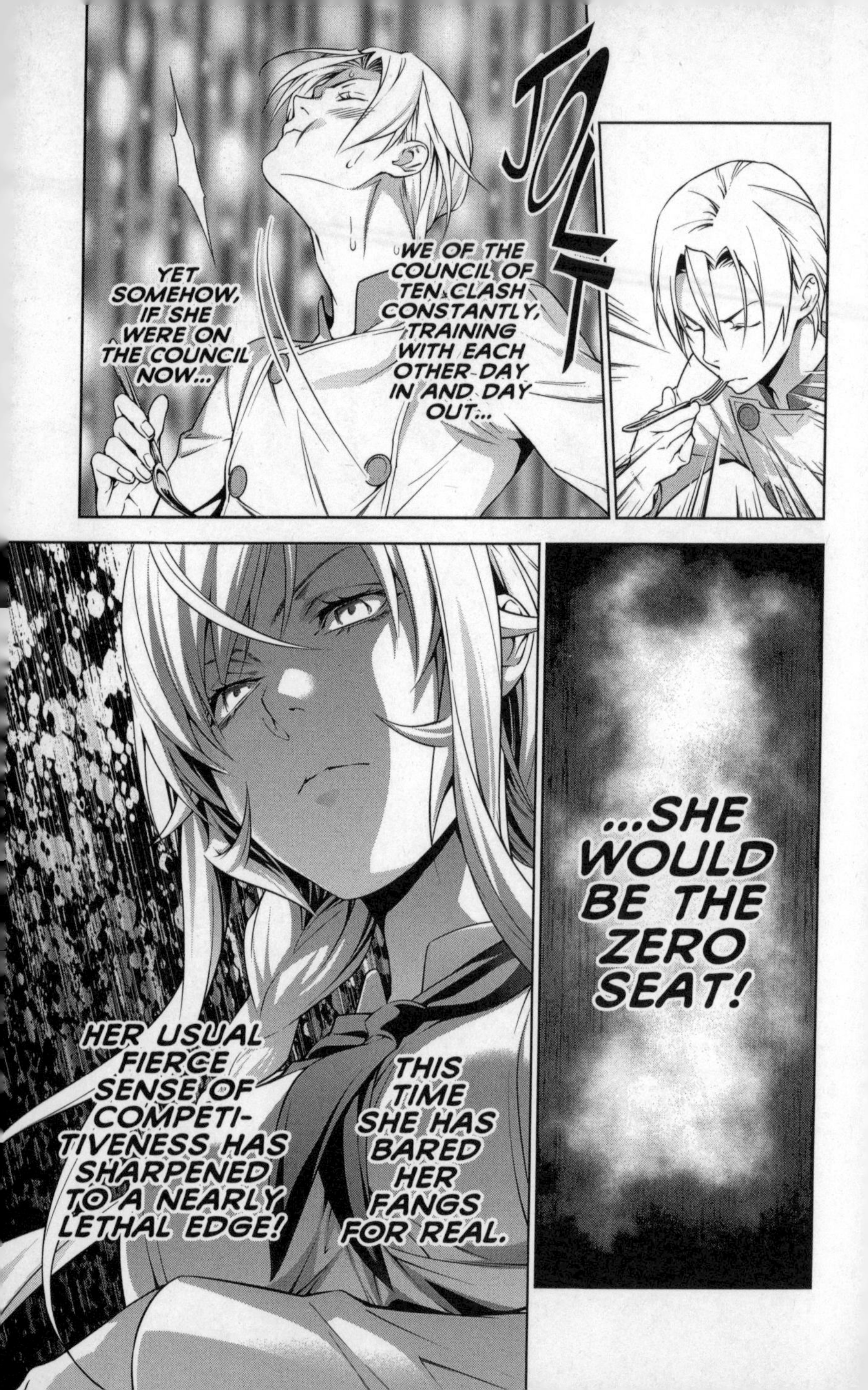
JOLT
WE OF THE COUNCIL OF TEN CLASH CONSTANTLY, TRAINING WITH EACH OTHER DAY IN AND DAY OUT...
YET SOMEHOW, IF SHE WERE ON THE COUNCIL NOW...
...SHE WOULD BE THE ZERO SEAT!
THIS TIME SHE HAS BARED HER FANGS FOR REAL.
HER USUAL FIERCE SENSE OF COMPETI-TIVENESS HAS SHARPENED TO A NEARLY LETHAL EDGE!

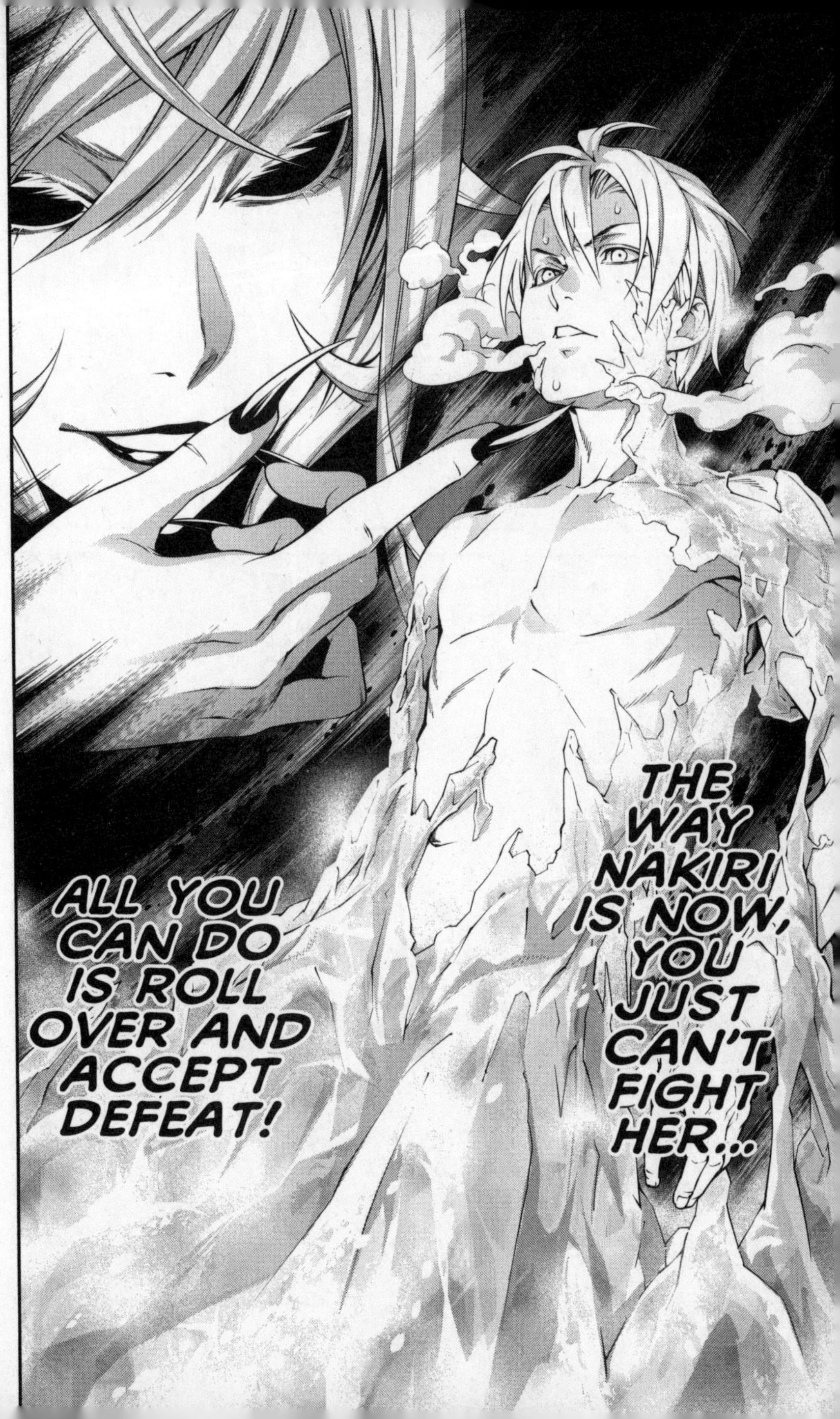
THE WAY NAKIRI IS NOW, YOU JUST CAN'T FIGHT HER...
ALL YOU CAN DO IS ROLL OVER AND ACCEPT DEFEAT!

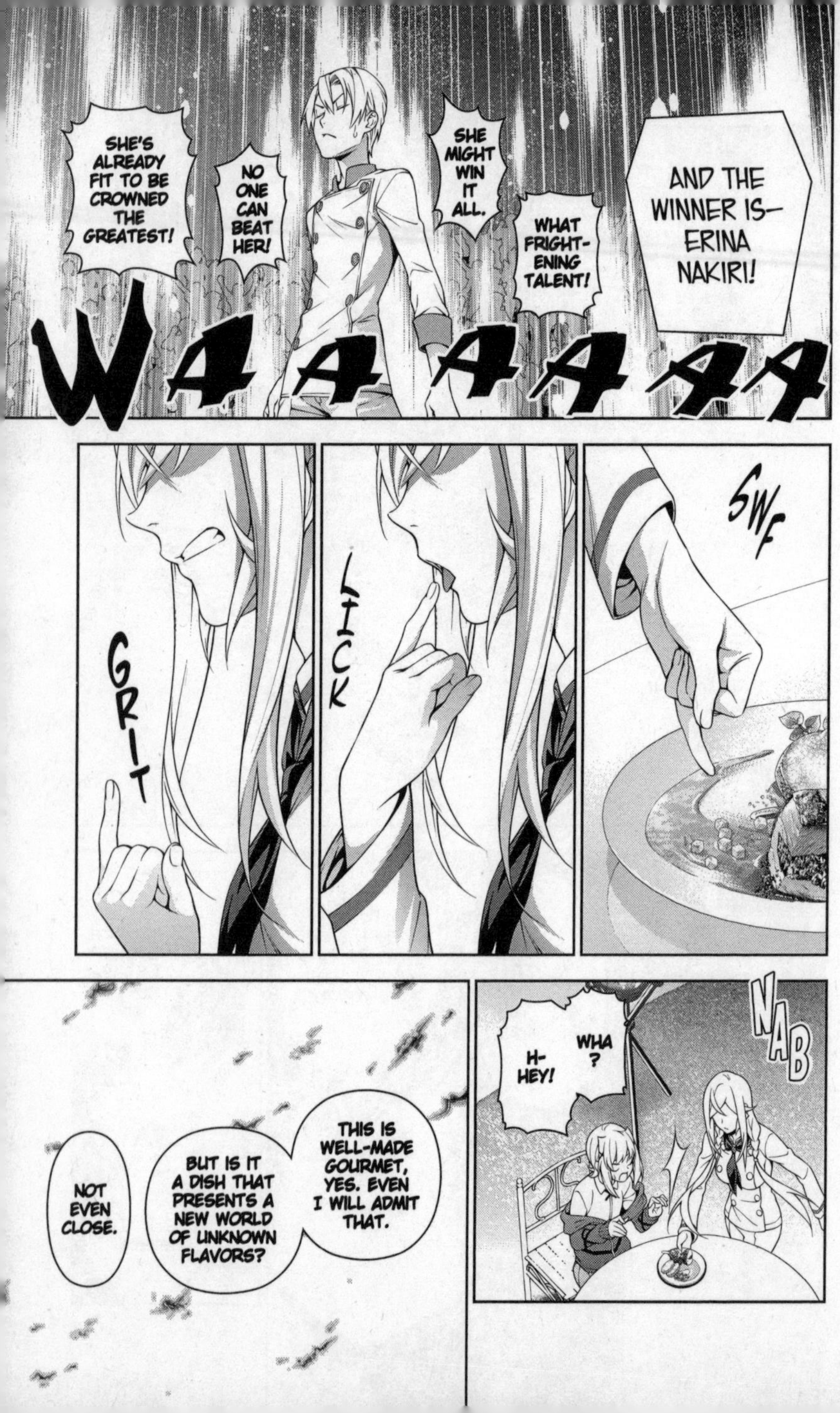
AND THE WINNER IS—ERINA NAKIRI!
WHAT FRIGHTENING TALENT!
SHE MIGHT WIN IT ALL.
NO ONE CAN BEAT HER!
SHE'S ALREADY FIT TO BE CROWNED THE GREATEST!
WAAAAAA
SWF
LICK
GRIT
NAB
WHA?
H-HEY!
THIS IS WELL-MADE GOURMET, YES. EVEN I WILL ADMIT THAT.
BUT IS IT A DISH THAT PRESENTS A NEW WORLD OF UNKNOWN FLAVORS?
NOT EVEN CLOSE.

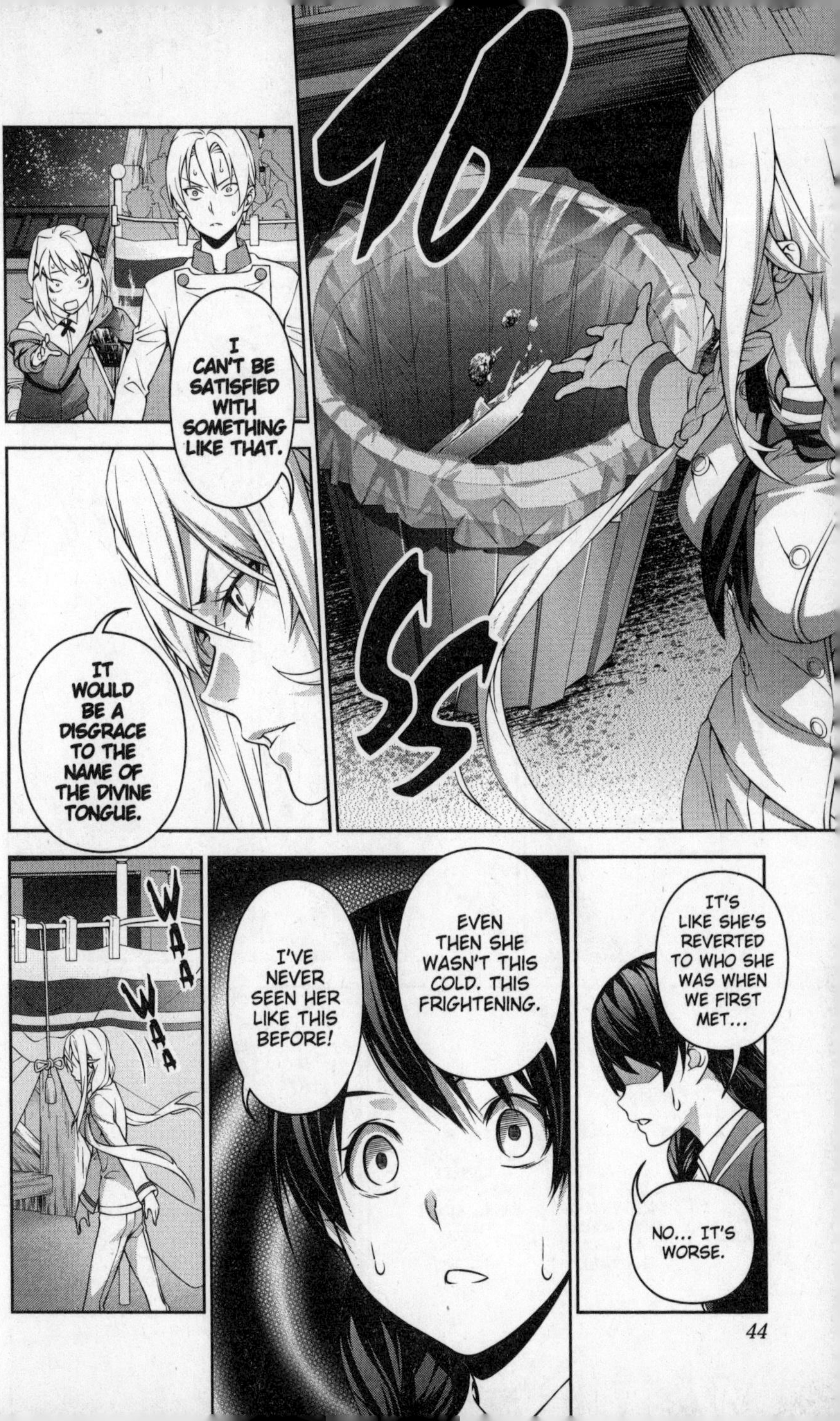
TO
SS
I CAN'T BE SATISFIED WITH SOMETHING LIKE THAT.
IT WOULD BE A DISGRACE TO THE NAME OF THE DIVINE TONGUE.
IT'S LIKE SHE'S REVERTED TO WHO SHE WAS WHEN WE FIRST MET...
NO... IT'S WORSE.
EVEN THEN SHE WASN'T THIS COLD. THIS FRIGHTENING.
I'VE NEVER SEEN HER LIKE THIS BEFORE!
WAA
WAA

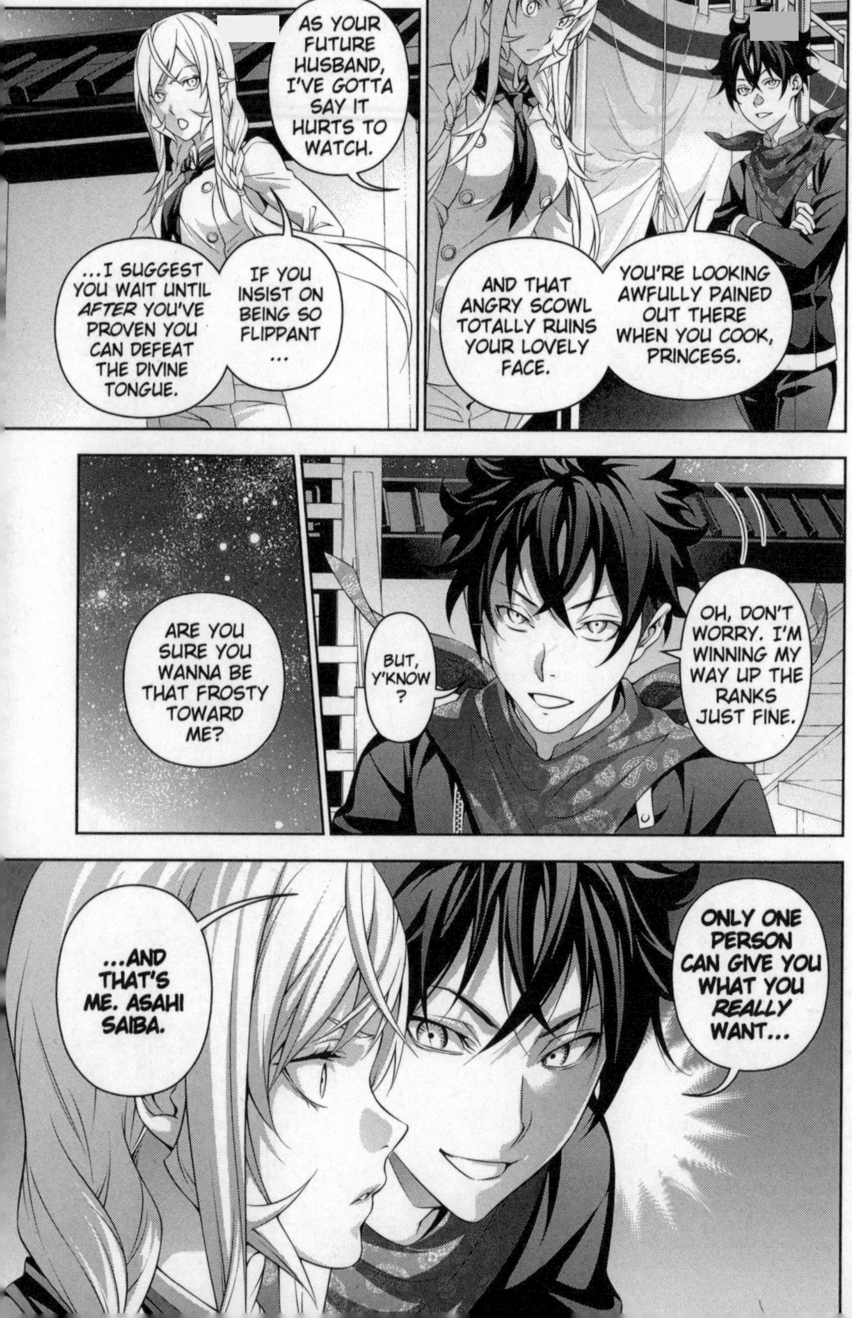
YOU'RE LOOKING AWFULLY PAINED OUT THERE WHEN YOU COOK, PRINCESS.
AND THAT ANGRY SCOWL TOTALLY RUINS YOUR LOVELY FACE.
AS YOUR FUTURE HUSBAND, I'VE GOTTA SAY IT HURTS TO WATCH.
IF YOU INSIST ON BEING SO FLIPPANT ...
...I SUGGEST YOU WAIT UNTIL *AFTER* YOU'VE PROVEN YOU CAN DEFEAT THE DIVINE TONGUE.
OH, DON'T WORRY. I'M WINNING MY WAY UP THE RANKS JUST FINE.
BUT, Y'KNOW?
ARE YOU SURE YOU WANNA BE THAT FROSTY TOWARD ME?
ONLY ONE PERSON CAN GIVE YOU WHAT YOU *REALLY* WANT...
...AND THAT'S ME. ASAHI SAIBA.

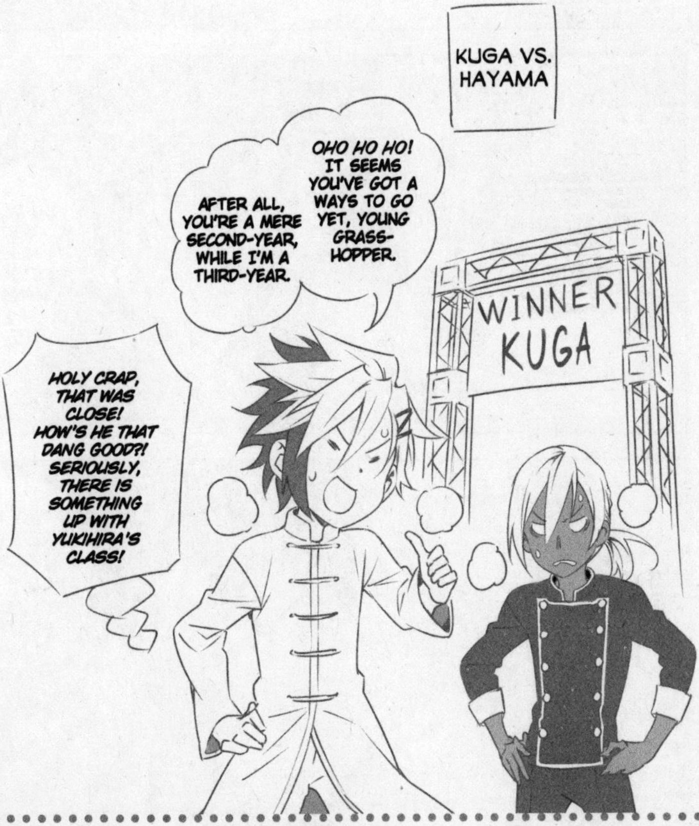
KUGA VS. HAYAMA
OHO HO HO! IT SEEMS YOU'VE GOT A WAYS TO GO YET, YOUNG GRASS-HOPPER.
AFTER ALL, YOU'RE A MERE SECOND-YEAR, WHILE I'M A THIRD-YEAR.
WINNER KUGA
HOLY CRAP, THAT WAS CLOSE! HOW'S HE THAT DANG GOOD?! SERIOUSLY, THERE IS SOMETHING UP WITH YUKIHIRA'S CLASS!

302 THE CLAWS OF EVIL

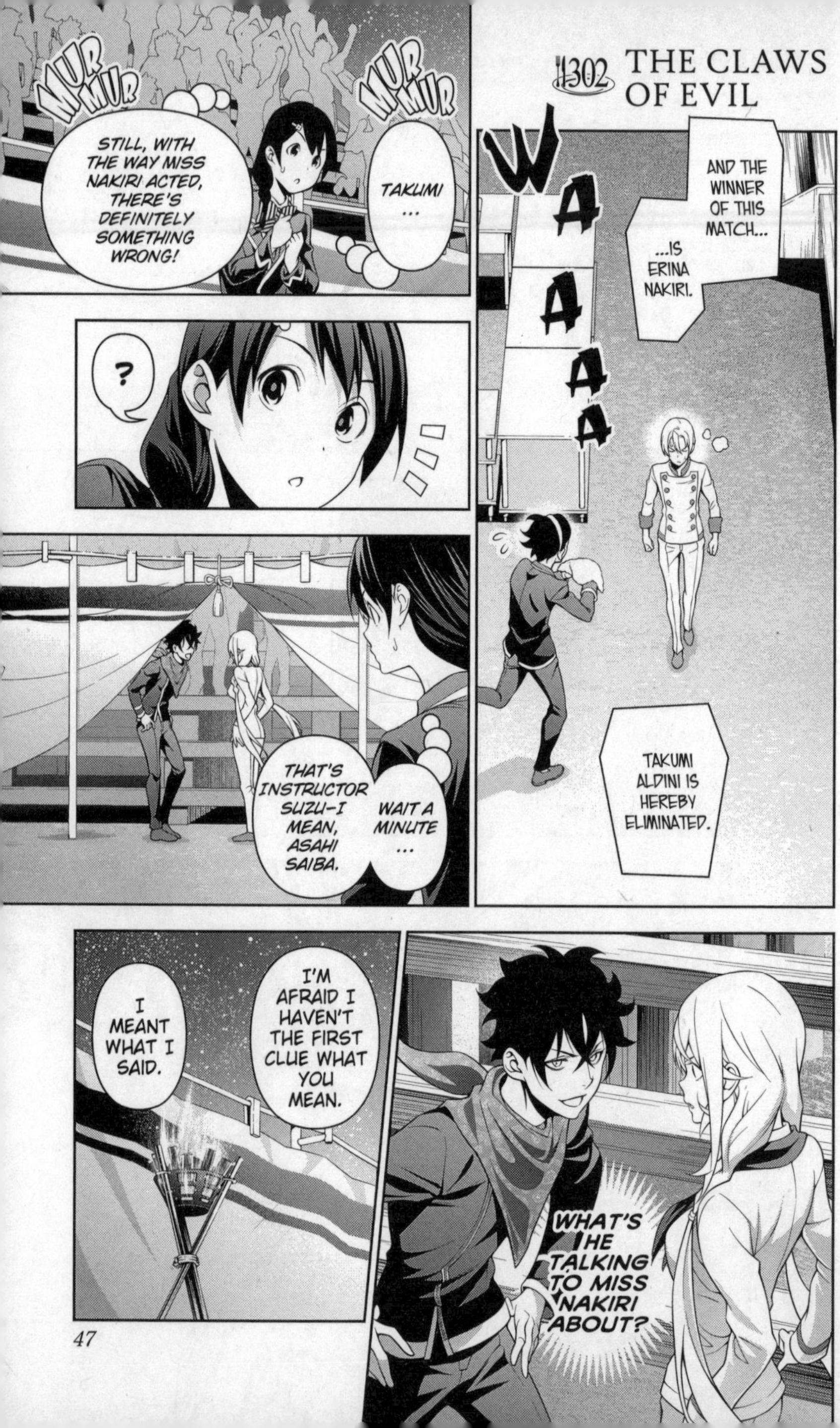
WAAAAA
AND THE WINNER OF THIS MATCH...
...IS ERINA NAKIRI.
TAKUMI ALDINI IS HEREBY ELIMINATED.
MUR MUR
MUR MUR
TAKUMI ...
STILL, WITH THE WAY MISS NAKIRI ACTED, THERE'S DEFINITELY SOMETHING WRONG!
?
WAIT A MINUTE ...
THAT'S INSTRUCTOR SUZU–I MEAN, ASAHI SAIBA.
WHAT'S HE TALKING TO MISS NAKIRI ABOUT?
I'M AFRAID I HAVEN'T THE FIRST CLUE WHAT YOU MEAN.
I MEANT WHAT I SAID.

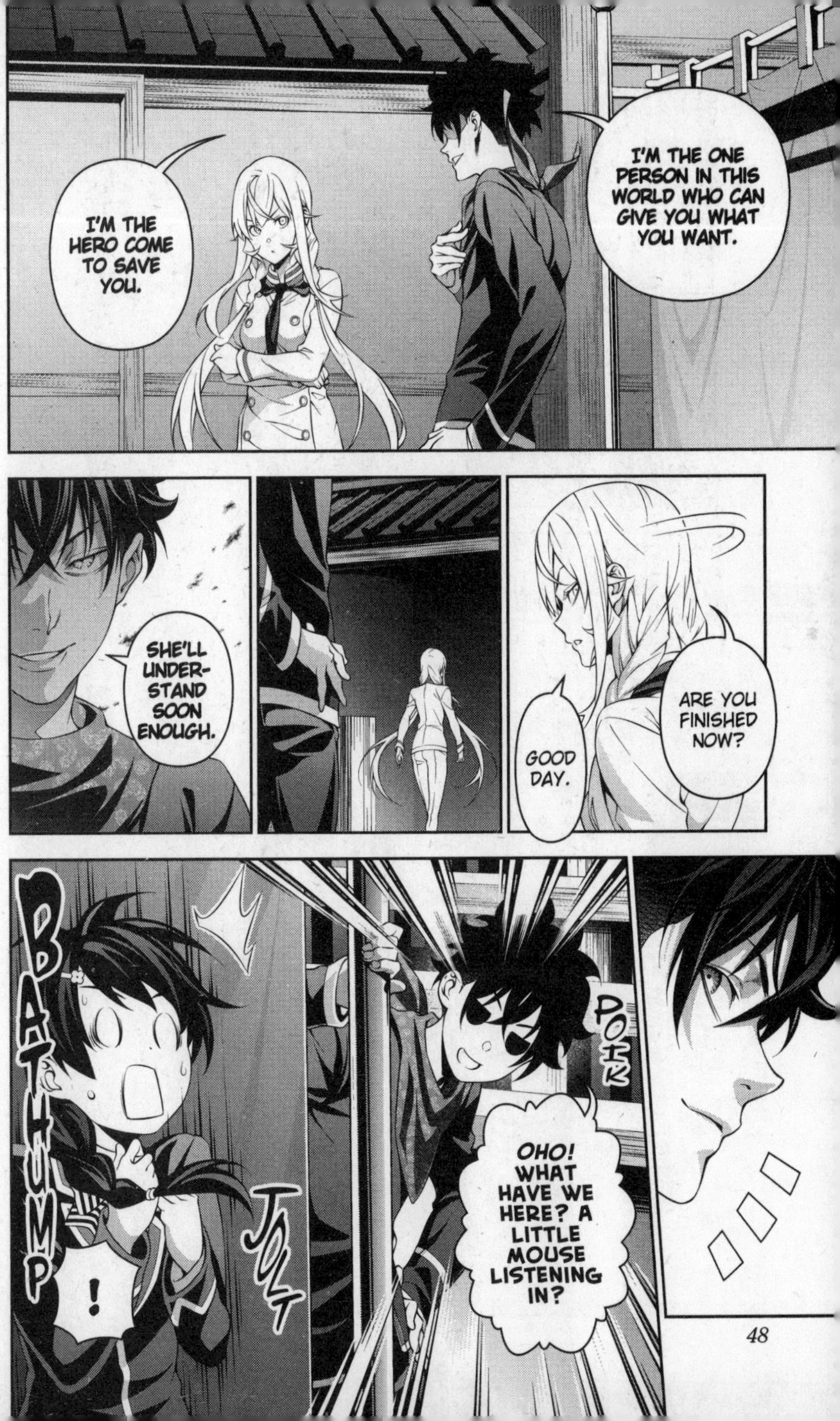

I'M THE ONE PERSON IN THIS WORLD WHO CAN GIVE YOU WHAT YOU WANT.
I'M THE HERO COME TO SAVE YOU.
ARE YOU FINISHED NOW?
GOOD DAY.
SHE'LL UNDER-STAND SOON ENOUGH.
POIK
OHO! WHAT HAVE WE HERE? A LITTLE MOUSE LISTENING IN?
JOLT
BATHUMP
!

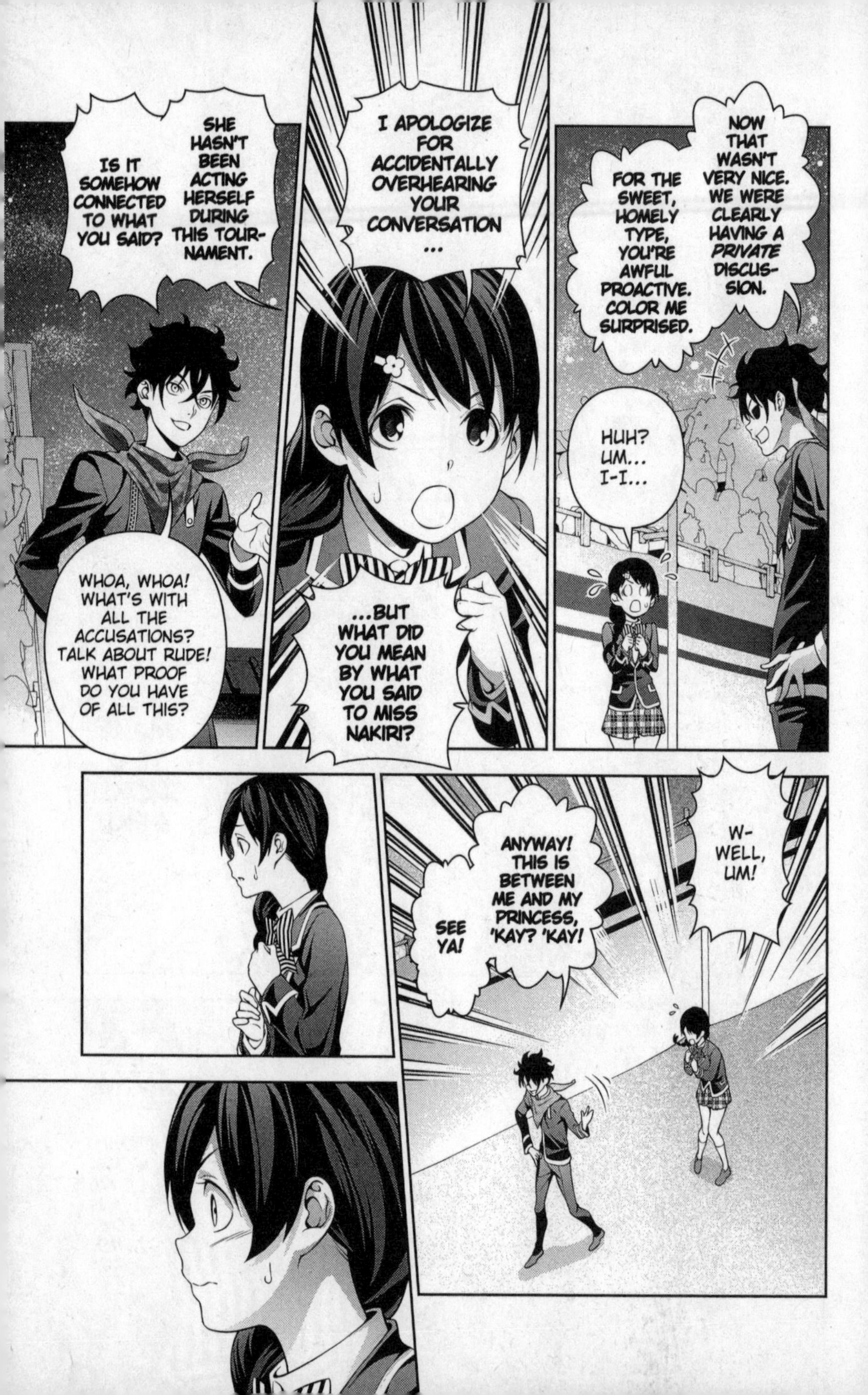
NOW THAT WASN'T VERY NICE. WE WERE CLEARLY HAVING A *PRIVATE* DISCUSSION.
FOR THE SWEET, HOMELY TYPE, YOU'RE AWFUL PROACTIVE. COLOR ME SURPRISED.
HUH? UM... I-I...
I APOLOGIZE FOR ACCIDENTALLY OVERHEARING YOUR CONVERSATION...
...BUT WHAT DID YOU MEAN BY WHAT YOU SAID TO MISS NAKIRI?
SHE HASN'T BEEN ACTING HERSELF DURING THIS TOURNAMENT.
IS IT SOMEHOW CONNECTED TO WHAT YOU SAID?
WHOA, WHOA! WHAT'S WITH ALL THE ACCUSATIONS? TALK ABOUT RUDE! WHAT PROOF DO YOU HAVE OF ALL THIS?
W-WELL, UM!
ANYWAY! THIS IS BETWEEN ME AND MY PRINCESS, 'KAY? 'KAY!
SEE YA!

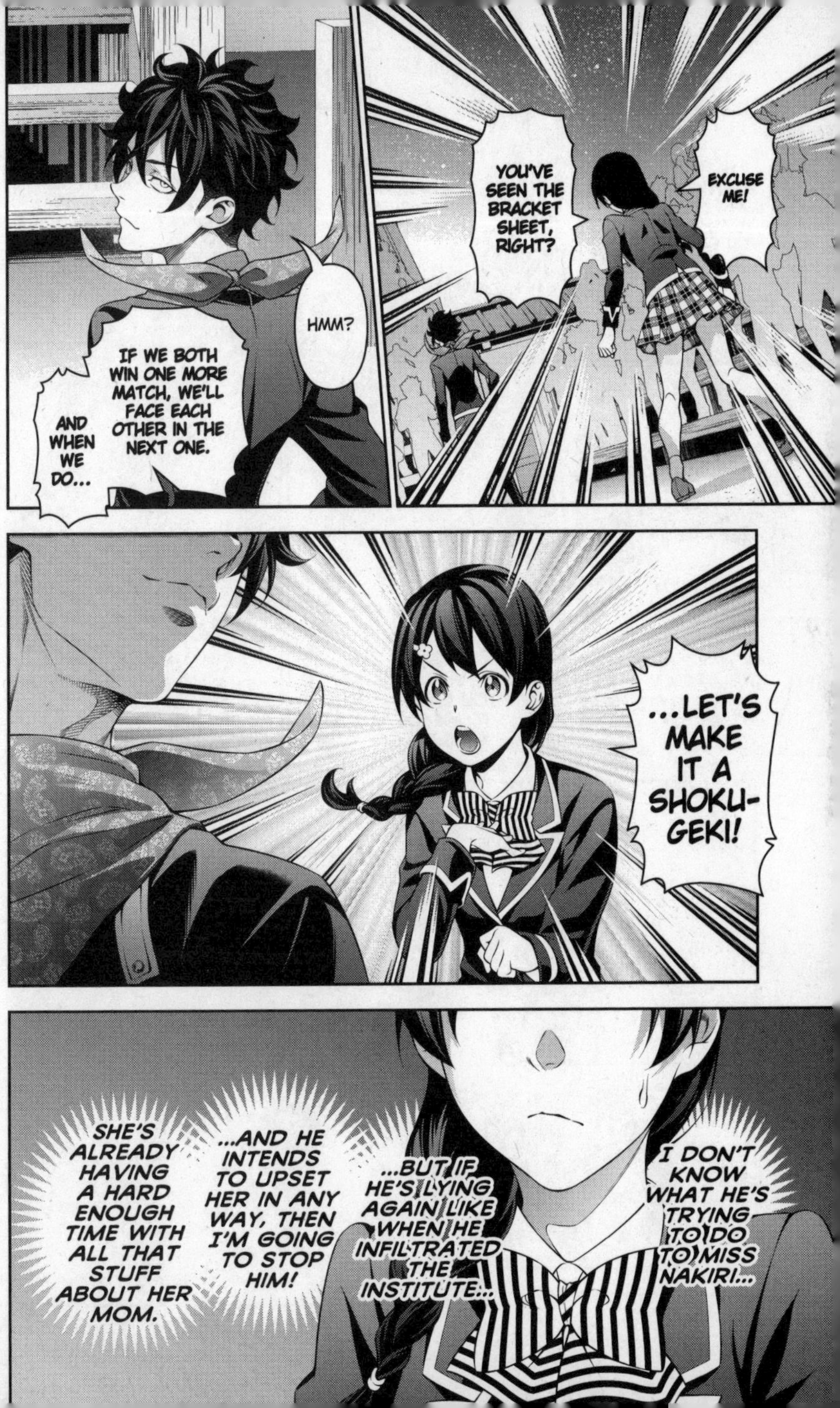
EXCUSE ME!
YOU'VE SEEN THE BRACKET SHEET, RIGHT?
HMM?
IF WE BOTH WIN ONE MORE MATCH, WE'LL FACE EACH OTHER IN THE NEXT ONE.
AND WHEN WE DO...
...LET'S MAKE IT A SHOKU-GEKI!
I DON'T KNOW WHAT HE'S TRYING TO DO TO MISS NAKIRI...
...BUT IF HE'S LYING AGAIN LIKE WHEN HE INFILTRATED THE INSTITUTE...
...AND HE INTENDS TO UPSET HER IN ANY WAY, THEN I'M GOING TO STOP HIM!
SHE'S ALREADY HAVING A HARD ENOUGH TIME WITH ALL THAT STUFF ABOUT HER MOM.

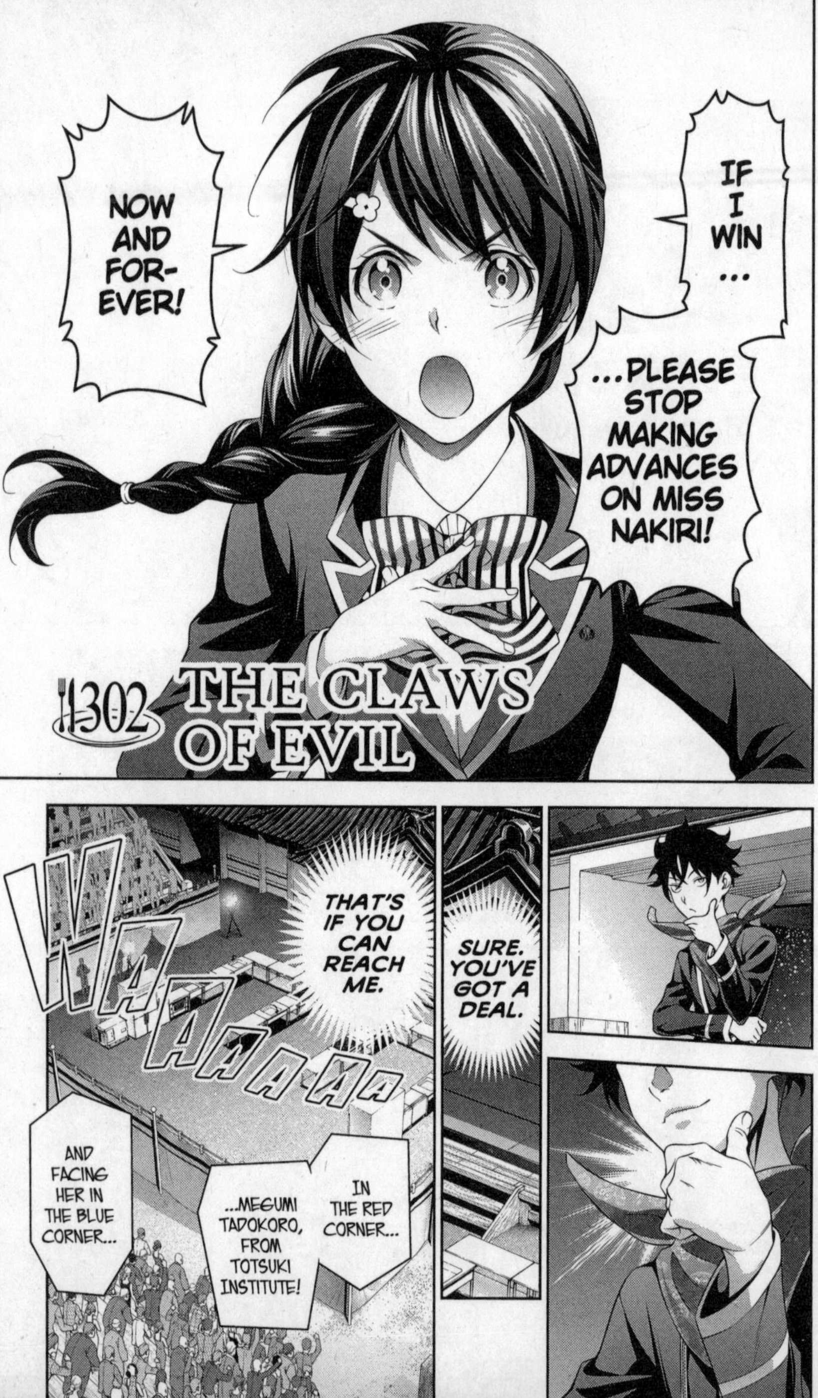
IF I WIN...
...PLEASE STOP MAKING ADVANCES ON MISS NAKIRI!
NOW AND FOR-EVER!
302 THE CLAWS OF EVIL
SURE. YOU'VE GOT A DEAL.
THAT'S IF YOU CAN REACH ME.
WAAAAAAA
IN THE RED CORNER...
...MEGUMI TADOKORO, FROM TOTSUKI INSTITUTE!
AND FACING HER IN THE BLUE CORNER...

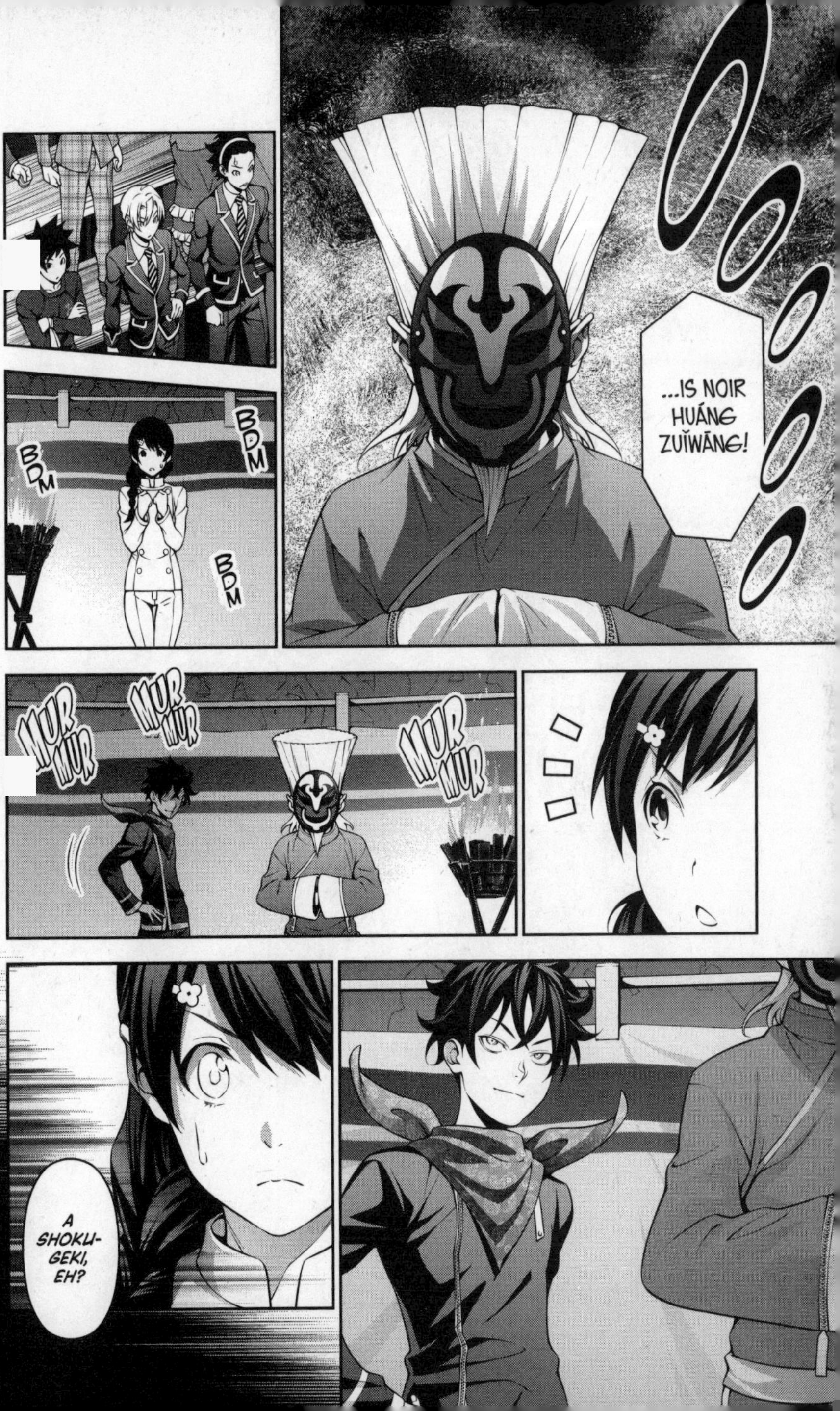
...IS NOIR HUÁNG ZUǏWĀNG!
BDM BDM
BDM
MUR MUR
MUR MUR
MUR MUR
A SHOKU-GEKI, EH?

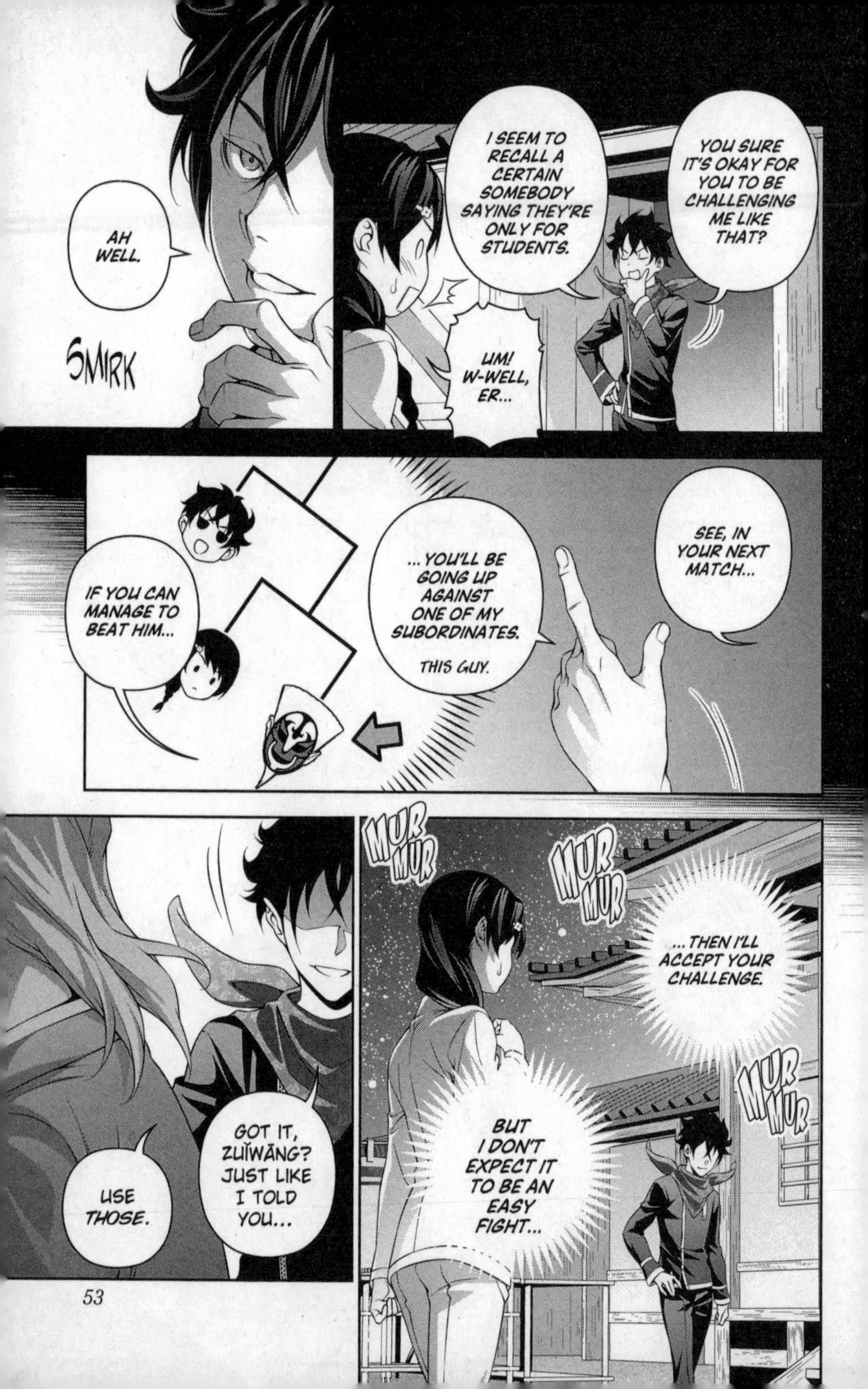
YOU SURE IT'S OKAY FOR YOU TO BE CHALLENGING ME LIKE THAT?
I SEEM TO RECALL A CERTAIN SOMEBODY SAYING THEY'RE ONLY FOR STUDENTS.
UM! W-WELL, ER...
AH WELL.
SMIRK
SEE, IN YOUR NEXT MATCH...
...YOU'LL BE GOING UP AGAINST ONE OF MY SUBORDINATES.
THIS GUY.
IF YOU CAN MANAGE TO BEAT HIM...
MUR MUR
MUR MUR
...THEN I'LL ACCEPT YOUR CHALLENGE.
MUR MUR
BUT I DON'T EXPECT IT TO BE AN EASY FIGHT...
GOT IT, ZUĬWĀNG? JUST LIKE I TOLD YOU...
USE THOSE.

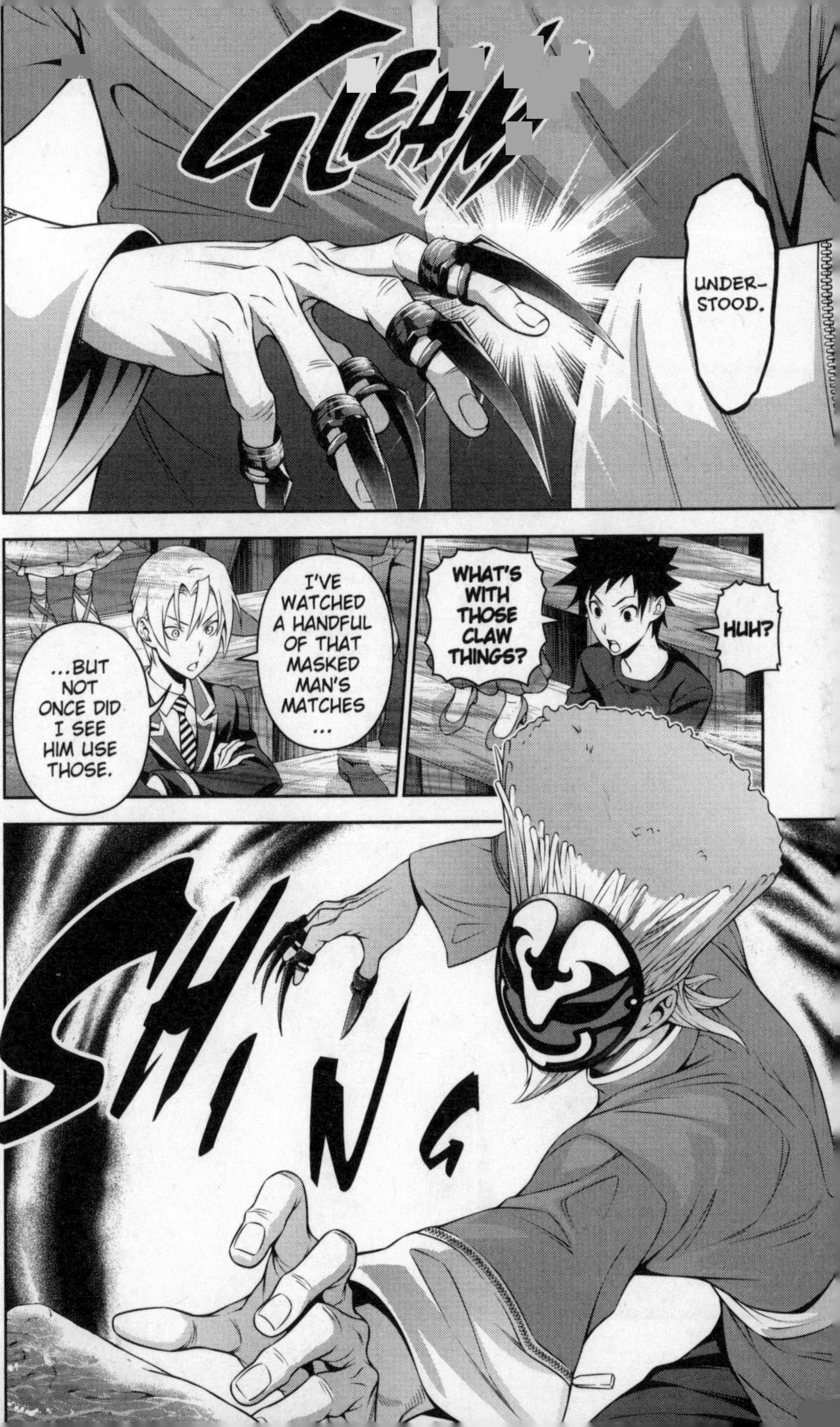
UNDER-STOOD.
GLEAM
HUH?
WHAT'S WITH THOSE CLAW THINGS?
I'VE WATCHED A HANDFUL OF THAT MASKED MAN'S MATCHES...
...BUT NOT ONCE DID I SEE HIM USE THOSE.
SHING

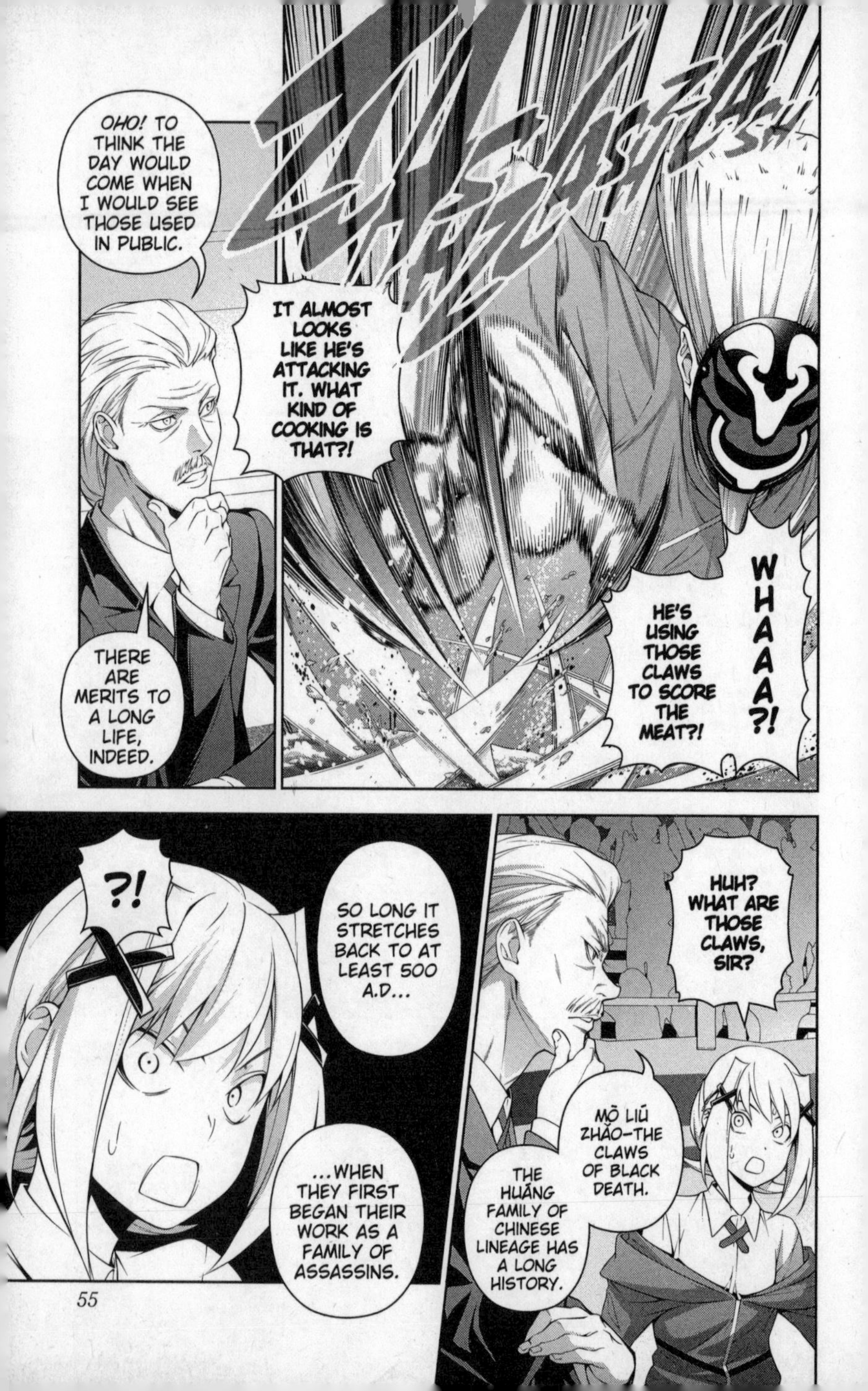
WHAAAA?!
HE'S USING THOSE CLAWS TO SCORE THE MEAT?!
IT ALMOST LOOKS LIKE HE'S ATTACKING IT. WHAT KIND OF COOKING IS THAT?!
OHO! TO THINK THE DAY WOULD COME WHEN I WOULD SEE THOSE USED IN PUBLIC.
THERE ARE MERITS TO A LONG LIFE, INDEED.
HUH? WHAT ARE THOSE CLAWS, SIR?
MÒ LIǓ ZHǍO—THE CLAWS OF BLACK DEATH.
THE HUÁNG FAMILY OF CHINESE LINEAGE HAS A LONG HISTORY.
?!
SO LONG IT STRETCHES BACK TO AT LEAST 500 A.D...
...WHEN THEY FIRST BEGAN THEIR WORK AS A FAMILY OF ASSASSINS.

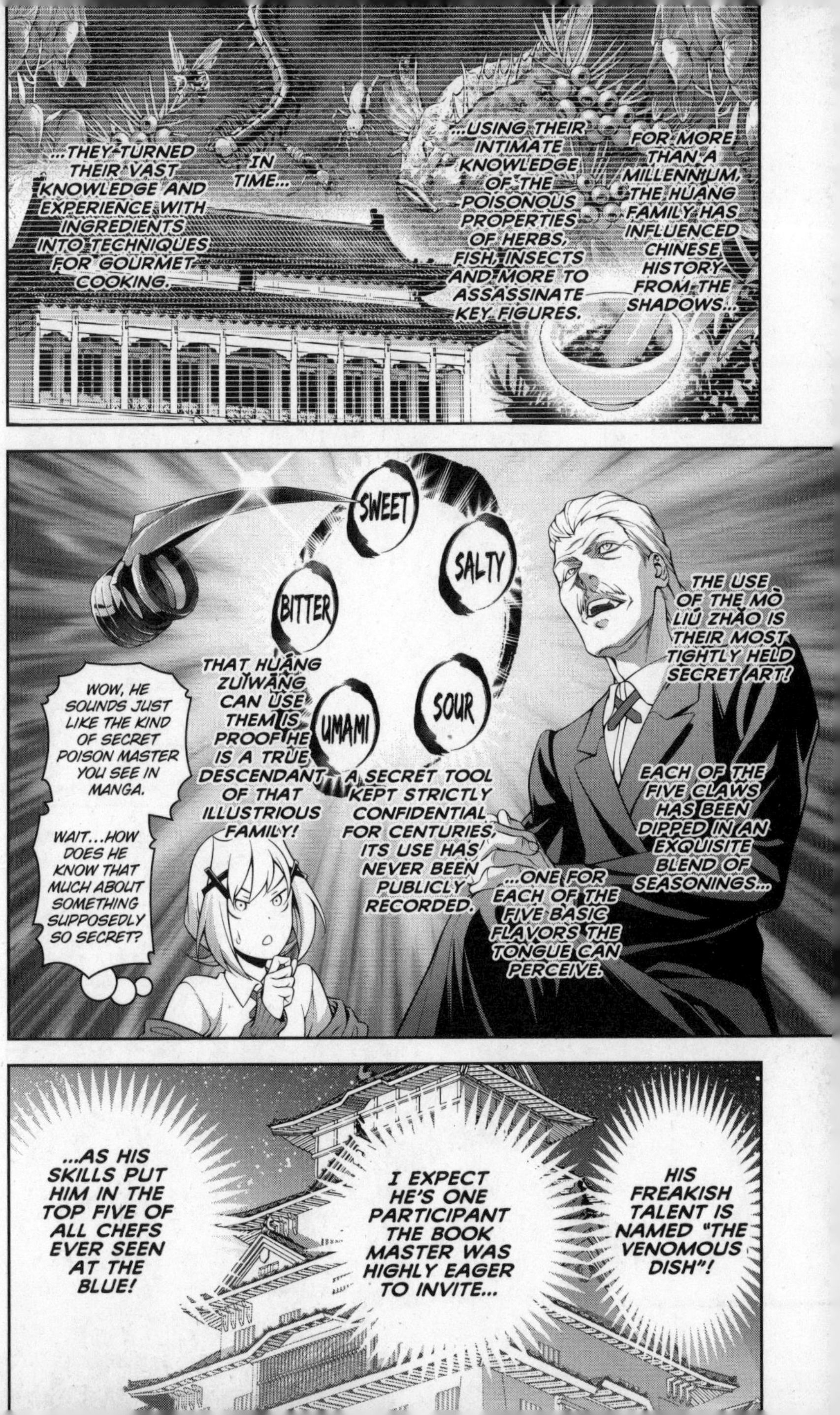
FOR MORE THAN A MILLENNIUM, THE HUÁNG FAMILY HAS INFLUENCED CHINESE HISTORY FROM THE SHADOWS...
...USING THEIR INTIMATE KNOWLEDGE OF THE POISONOUS PROPERTIES OF HERBS, FISH, INSECTS AND MORE TO ASSASSINATE KEY FIGURES.
IN TIME...
...THEY TURNED THEIR VAST KNOWLEDGE AND EXPERIENCE WITH INGREDIENTS INTO TECHNIQUES FOR GOURMET COOKING.
THE USE OF THE MÒ LIÚ ZHǍO IS THEIR MOST TIGHTLY HELD SECRET ART!
SWEET
SALTY
SOUR
UMAMI
BITTER
EACH OF THE FIVE CLAWS HAS BEEN DIPPED IN AN EXQUISITE BLEND OF SEASONINGS...
...ONE FOR EACH OF THE FIVE BASIC FLAVORS THE TONGUE CAN PERCEIVE.
A SECRET TOOL KEPT STRICTLY CONFIDENTIAL FOR CENTURIES, ITS USE HAS NEVER BEEN PUBLICLY RECORDED.
THAT HUÁNG ZUÌWĀNG CAN USE THEM IS PROOF HE IS A TRUE DESCENDANT OF THAT ILLUSTRIOUS FAMILY!
WOW, HE SOUNDS JUST LIKE THE KIND OF SECRET POISON MASTER YOU SEE IN MANGA.
WAIT...HOW DOES HE KNOW THAT MUCH ABOUT SOMETHING SUPPOSEDLY SO SECRET?
HIS FREAKISH TALENT IS NAMED "THE VENOMOUS DISH"!
I EXPECT HE'S ONE PARTICIPANT THE BOOK MASTER WAS HIGHLY EAGER TO INVITE...
...AS HIS SKILLS PUT HIM IN THE TOP FIVE OF ALL CHEFS EVER SEEN AT THE BLUE!

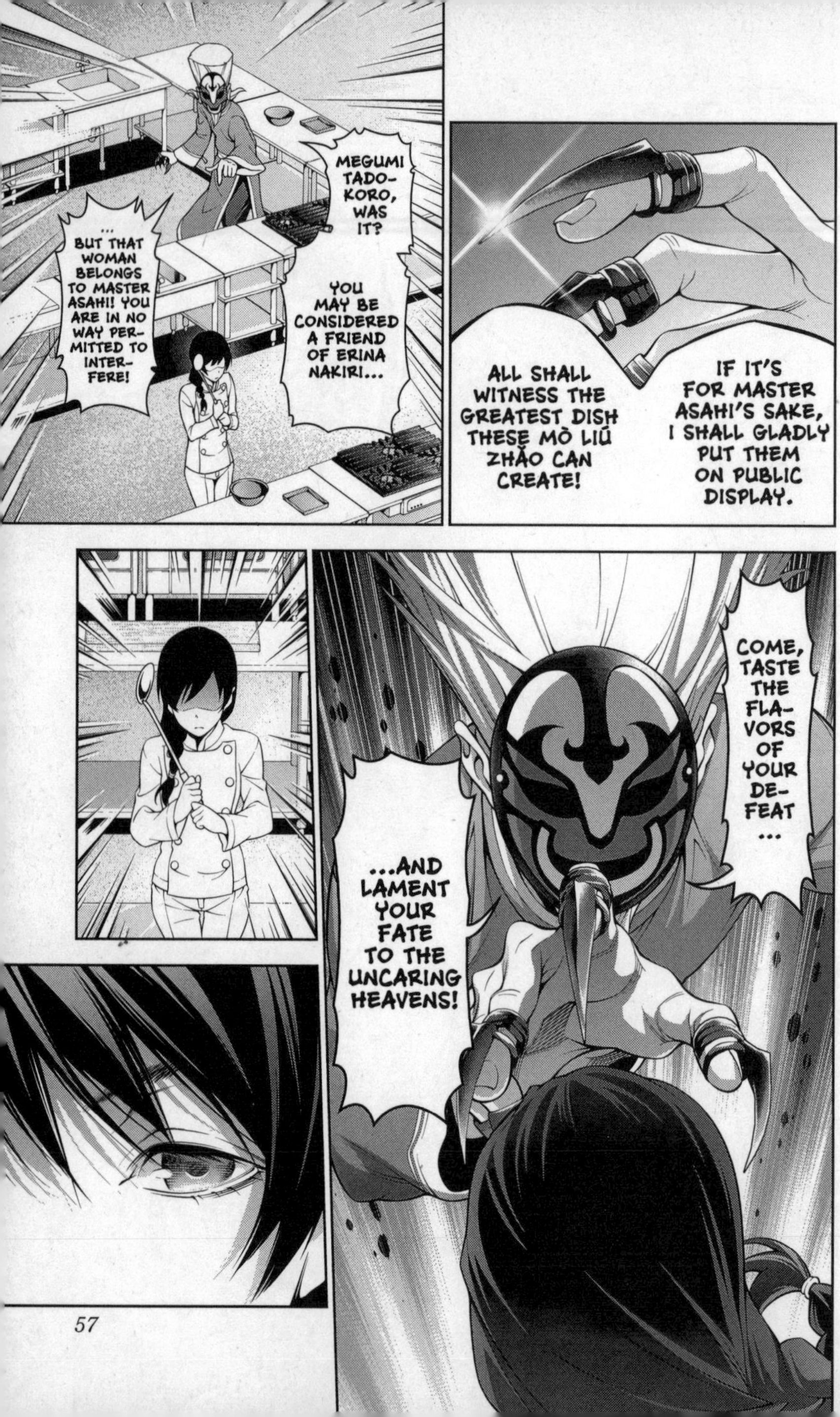
IF IT'S FOR MASTER ASAHI'S SAKE, I SHALL GLADLY PUT THEM ON PUBLIC DISPLAY.
ALL SHALL WITNESS THE GREATEST DISH THESE MÒ LIÚ ZHǍO CAN CREATE!
MEGUMI TADOKORO, WAS IT?
YOU MAY BE CONSIDERED A FRIEND OF ERINA NAKIRI...
... BUT THAT WOMAN BELONGS TO MASTER ASAHI! YOU ARE IN NO WAY PERMITTED TO INTERFERE!
COME, TASTE THE FLAVORS OF YOUR DEFEAT...
...AND LAMENT YOUR FATE TO THE UNCARING HEAVENS!

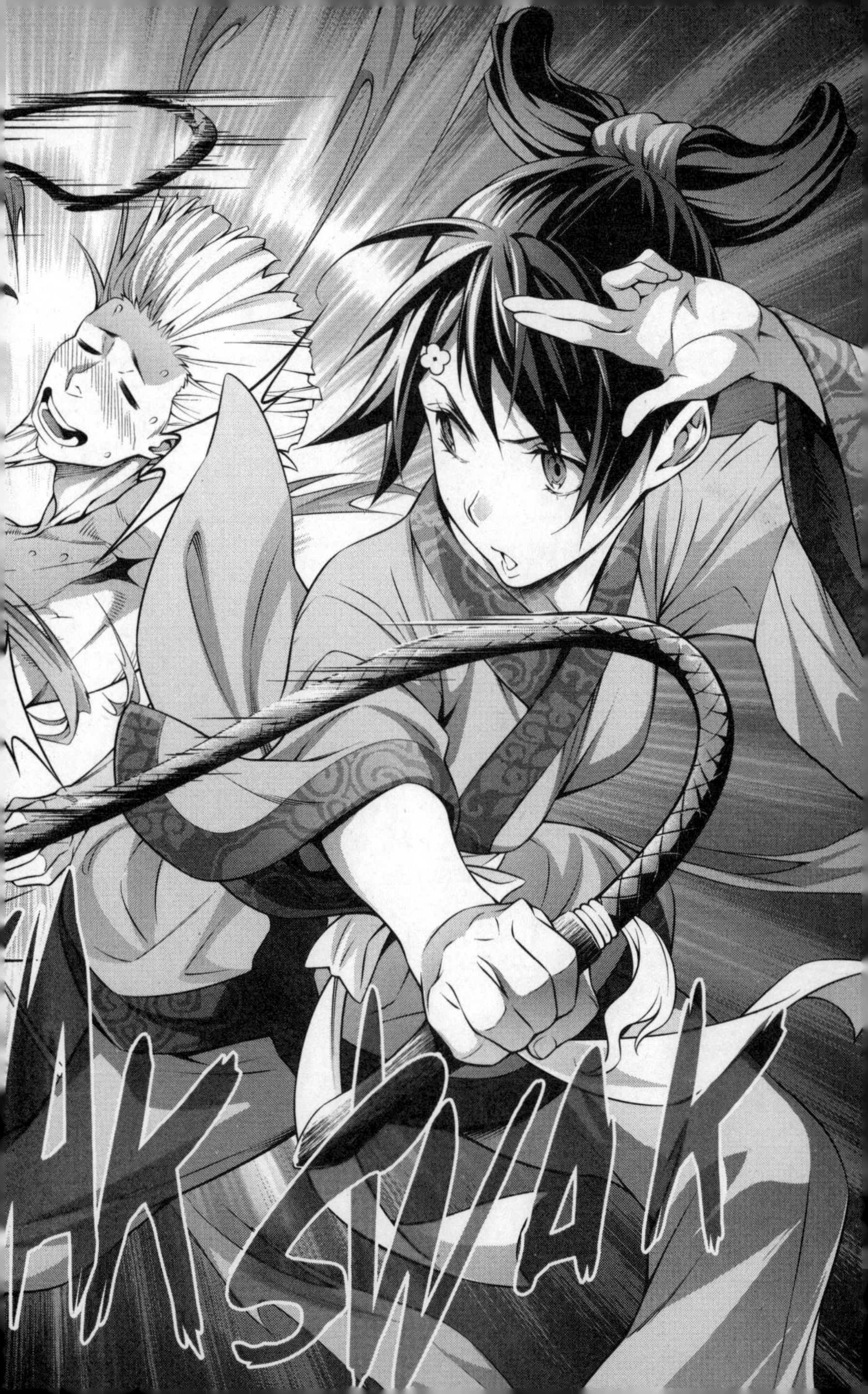
HK SWAK

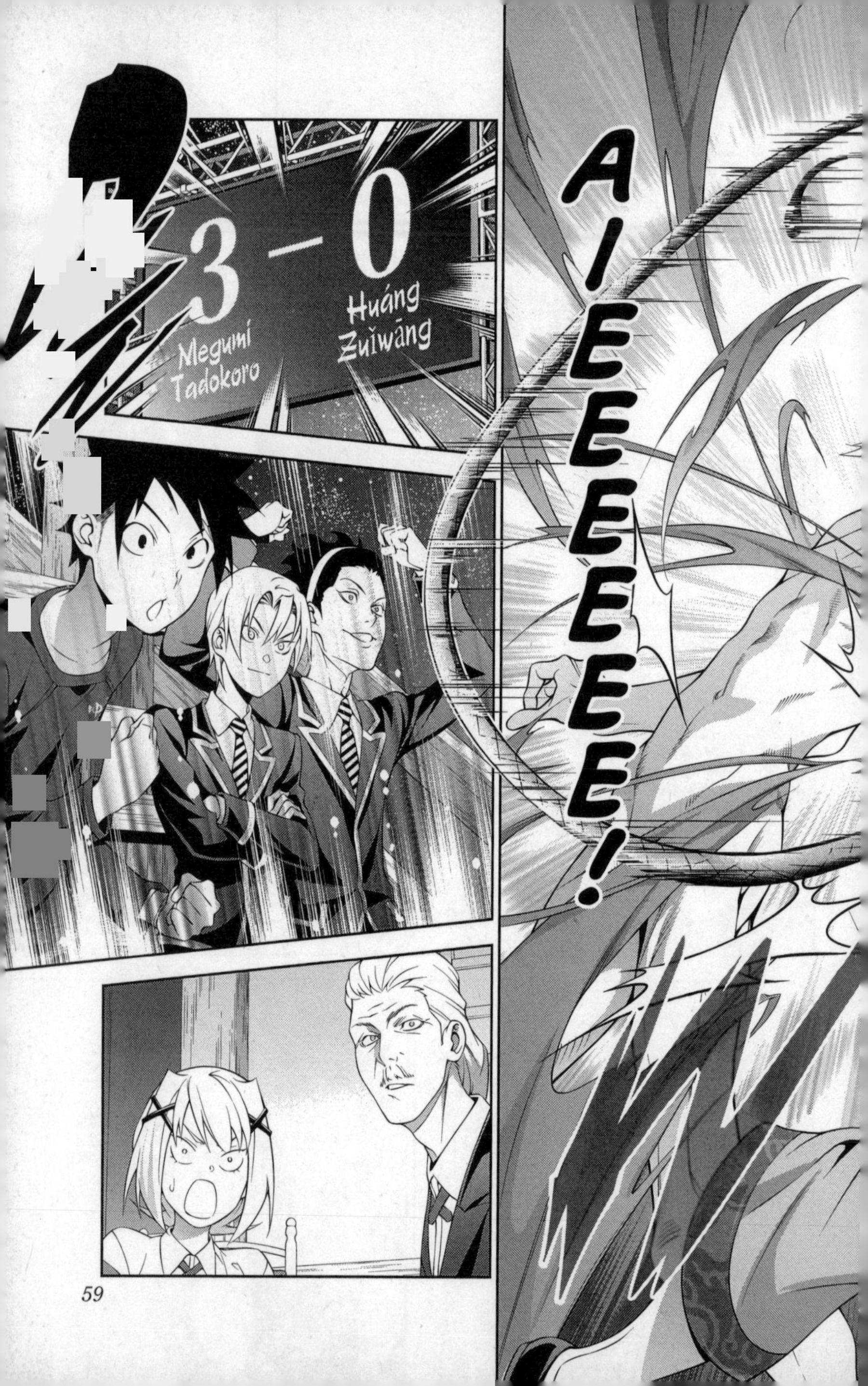
AIEEEEEE!
3 — 0
Megumi Tadokoro
Huáng Zuiwāng

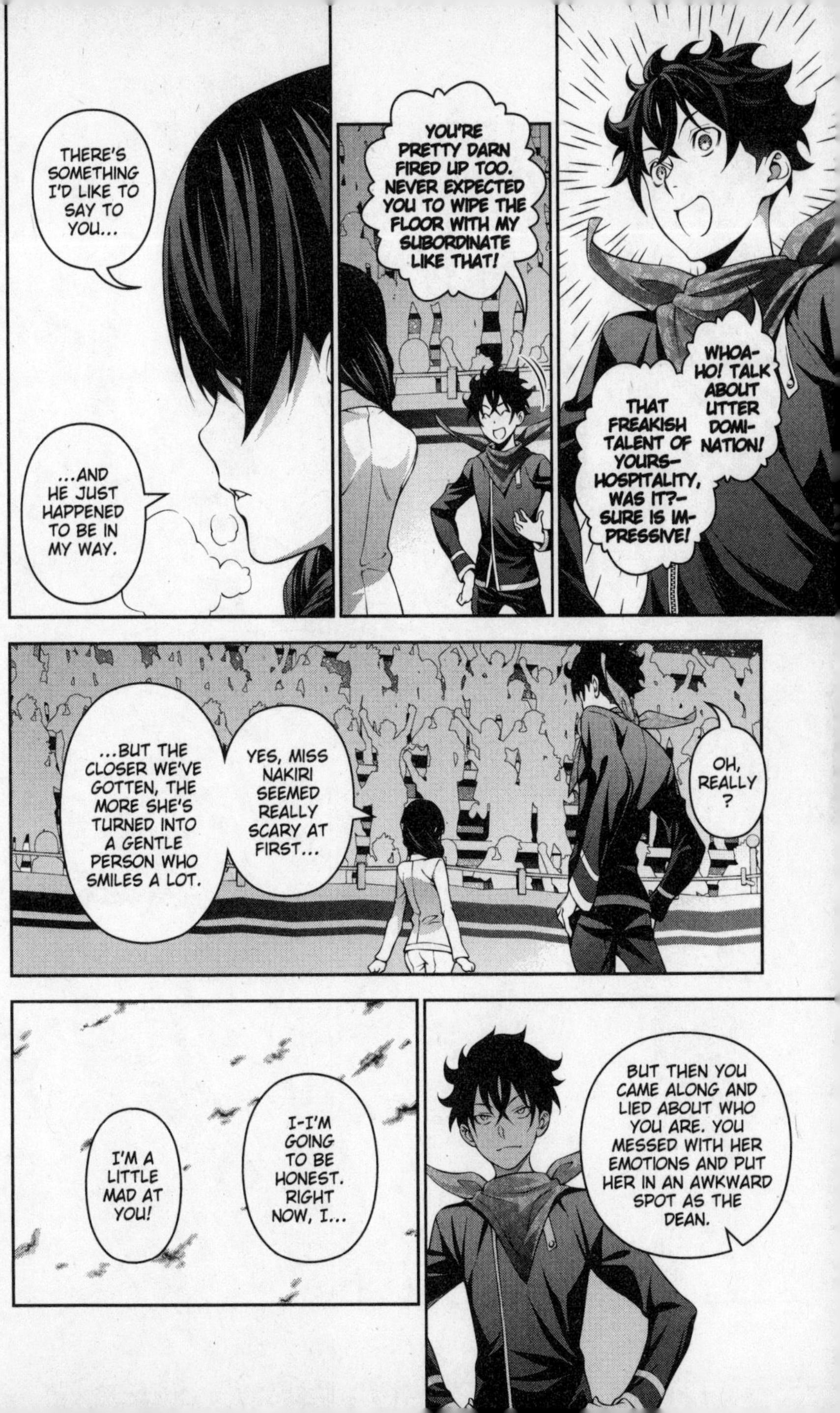
WHOA-HO! TALK ABOUT UTTER DOMINATION!
THAT FREAKISH TALENT OF YOURS—HOSPITALITY, WAS IT?—SURE IS IMPRESSIVE!
YOU'RE PRETTY DARN FIRED UP TOO. NEVER EXPECTED YOU TO WIPE THE FLOOR WITH MY SUBORDINATE LIKE THAT!
THERE'S SOMETHING I'D LIKE TO SAY TO YOU...
...AND HE JUST HAPPENED TO BE IN MY WAY.
OH, REALLY?
YES, MISS NAKIRI SEEMED REALLY SCARY AT FIRST...
...BUT THE CLOSER WE'VE GOTTEN, THE MORE SHE'S TURNED INTO A GENTLE PERSON WHO SMILES A LOT.
BUT THEN YOU CAME ALONG AND LIED ABOUT WHO YOU ARE. YOU MESSED WITH HER EMOTIONS AND PUT HER IN AN AWKWARD SPOT AS THE DEAN.
I-I'M GOING TO BE HONEST. RIGHT NOW, I...
I'M A LITTLE MAD AT YOU!

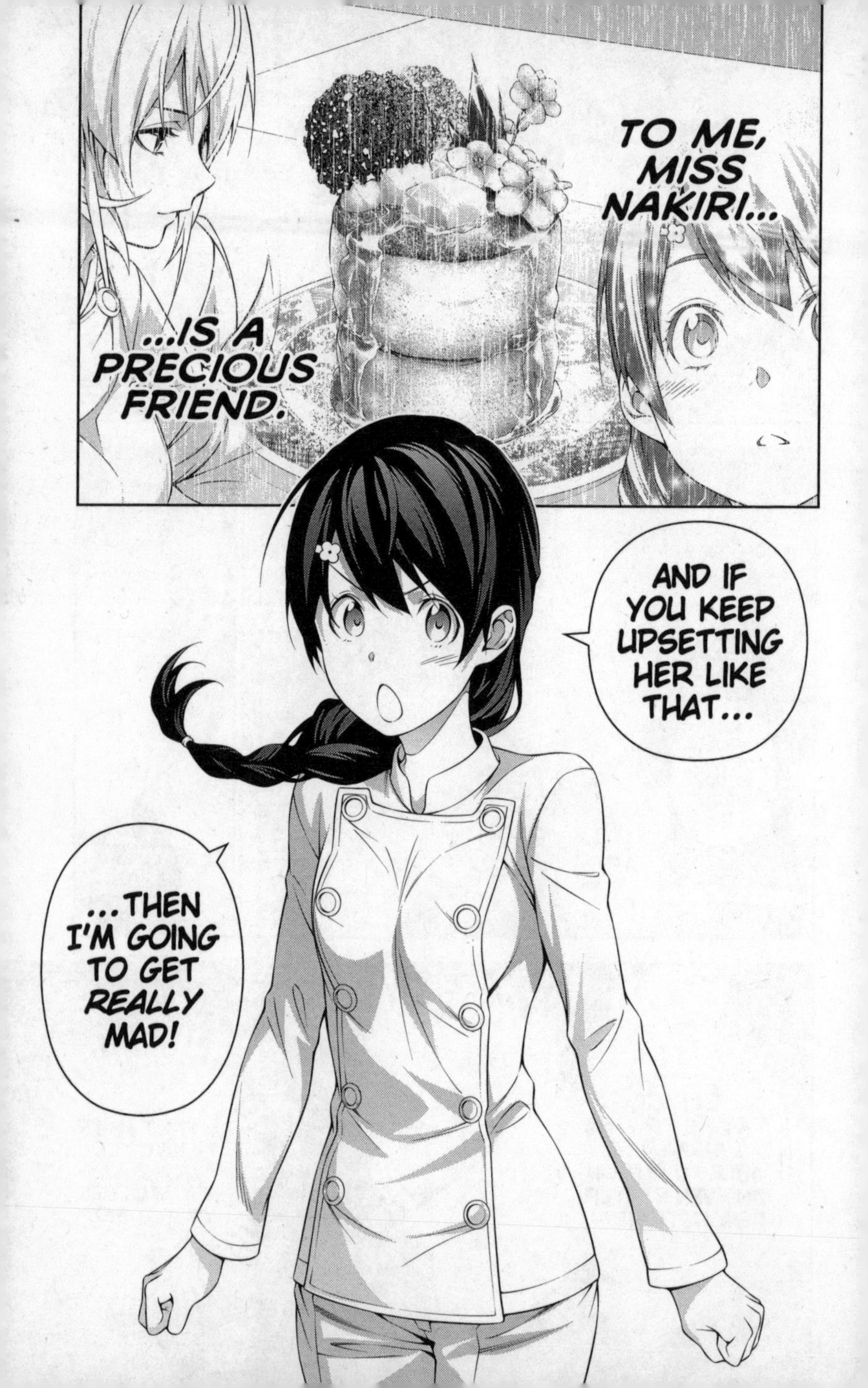
TO ME, MISS NAKIRI...
...IS A PRECIOUS FRIEND.
AND IF YOU KEEP UPSETTING HER LIKE THAT...
...THEN I'M GOING TO GET REALLY MAD!

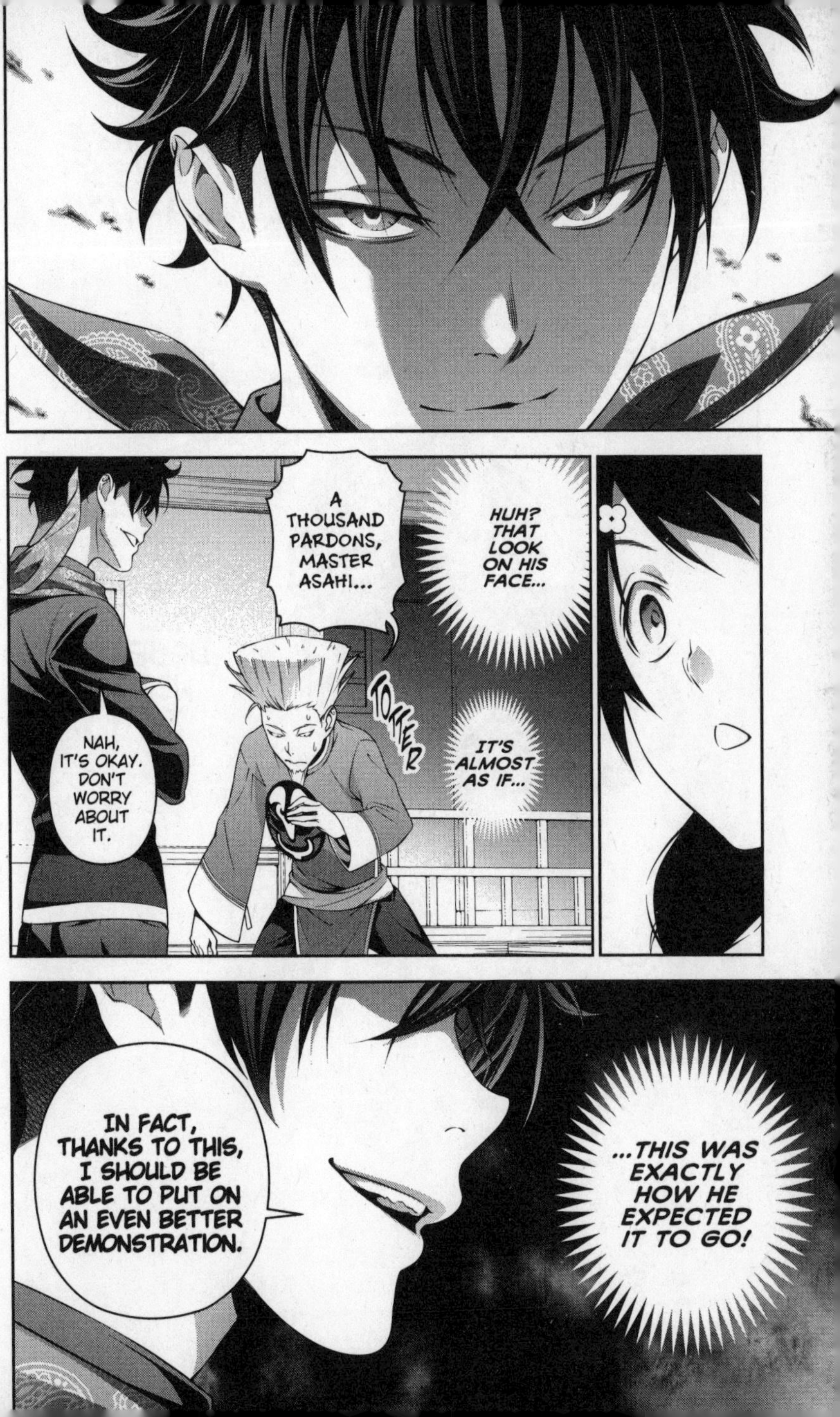
HUH? THAT LOOK ON HIS FACE...
IT'S ALMOST AS IF...
A THOUSAND PARDONS, MASTER ASAHI...
TOKKER
NAH, IT'S OKAY. DON'T WORRY ABOUT IT.
...THIS WAS EXACTLY HOW HE EXPECTED IT TO GO!
IN FACT, THANKS TO THIS, I SHOULD BE ABLE TO PUT ON AN EVEN BETTER DEMONSTRATION.

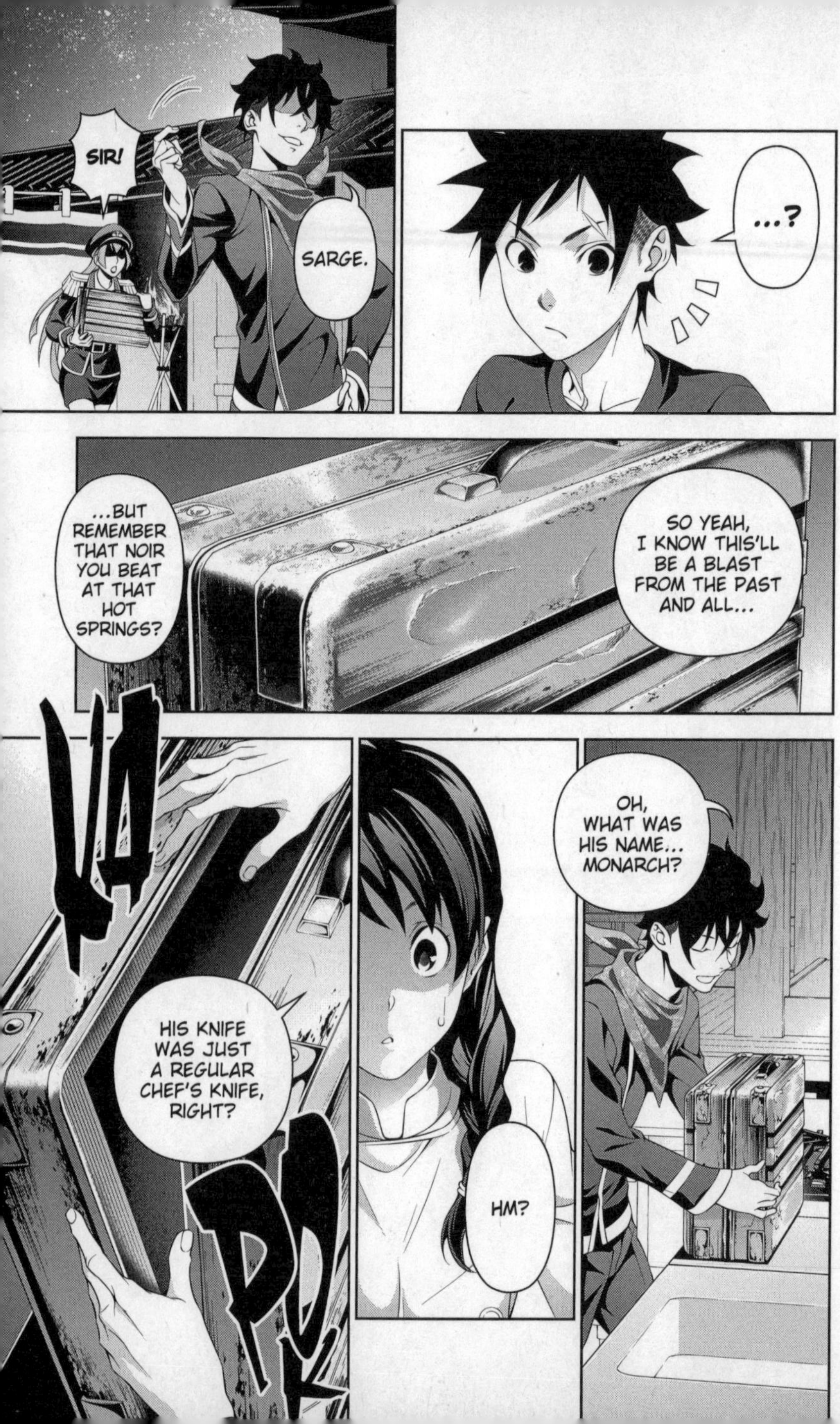
...?
SARGE.
SIR!
SO YEAH, I KNOW THIS'LL BE A BLAST FROM THE PAST AND ALL...
...BUT REMEMBER THAT NOIR YOU BEAT AT THAT HOT SPRINGS?
OH, WHAT WAS HIS NAME... MONARCH?
HM?
HIS KNIFE WAS JUST A REGULAR CHEF'S KNIFE, RIGHT?

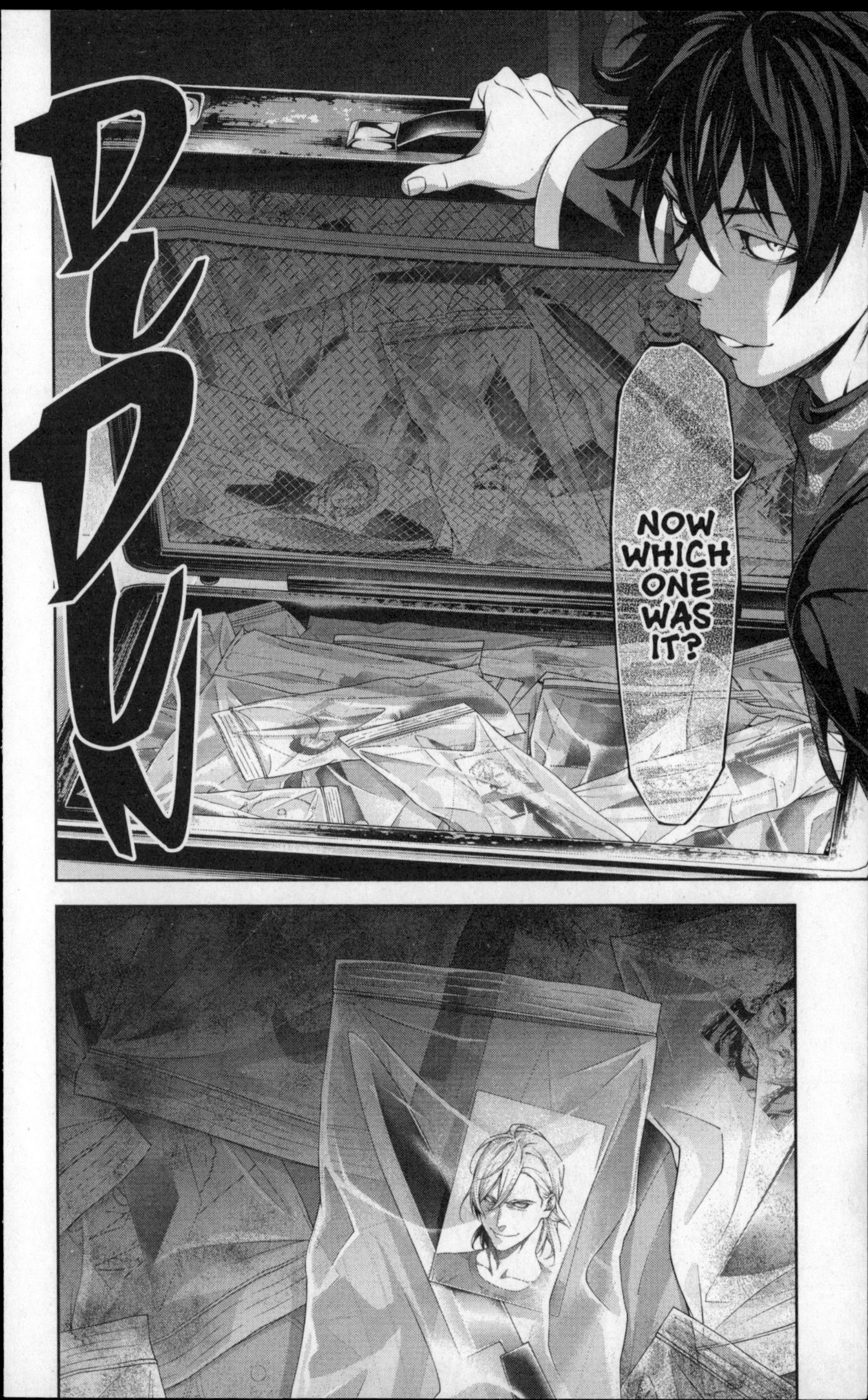
DUDUN
NOW WHICH ONE WAS IT?

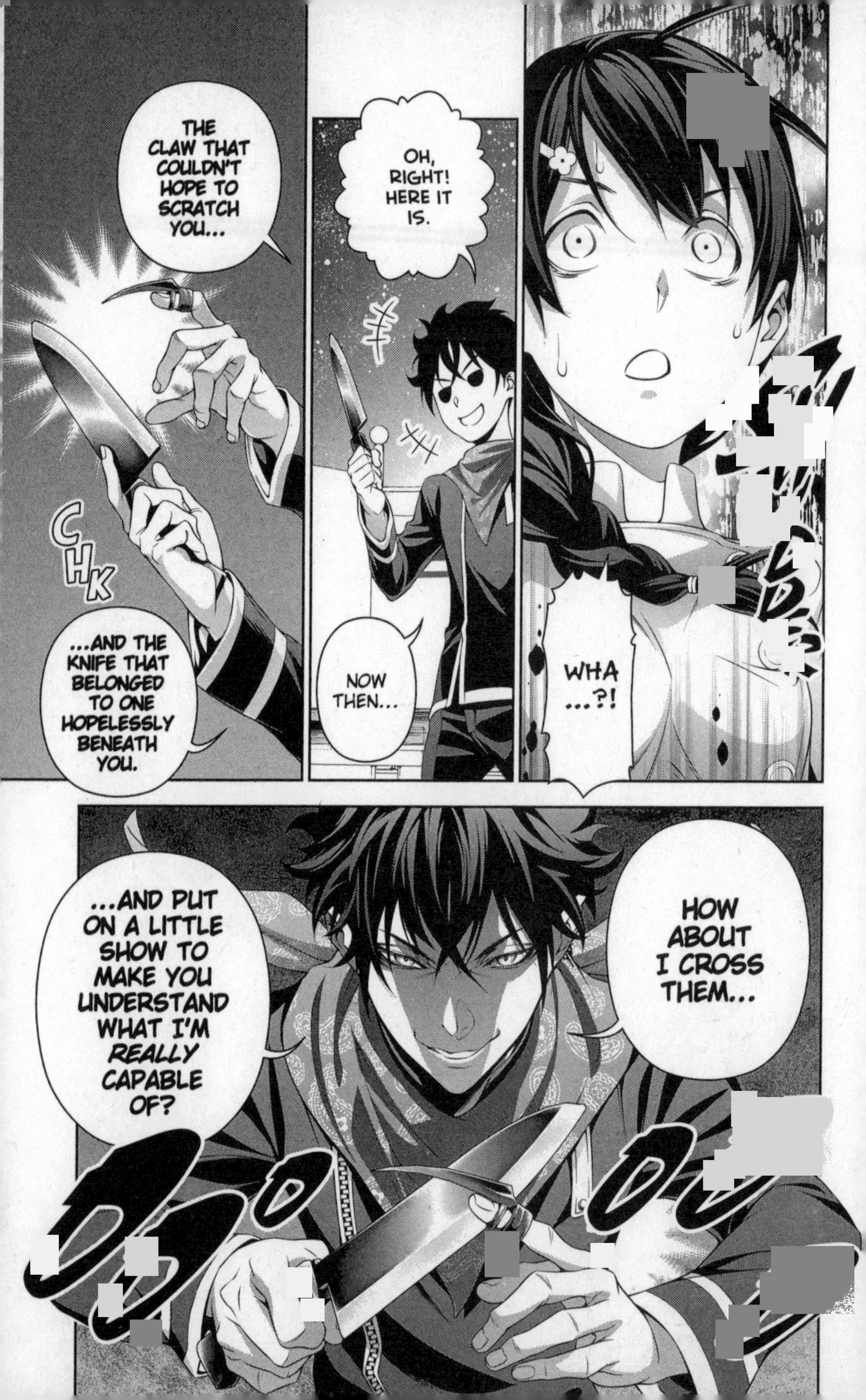
WHA ...?!
OH, RIGHT! HERE IT IS.
NOW THEN...
THE CLAW THAT COULDN'T HOPE TO SCRATCH YOU...
CHK
...AND THE KNIFE THAT BELONGED TO ONE HOPELESSLY BENEATH YOU.
HOW ABOUT I CROSS THEM...
...AND PUT ON A LITTLE SHOW TO MAKE YOU UNDERSTAND WHAT I'M *REALLY* CAPABLE OF?

IF YOU DON'T RECALL
WHO MONARCH IS, PLEASE
CHECK OUT VOLUME 31!

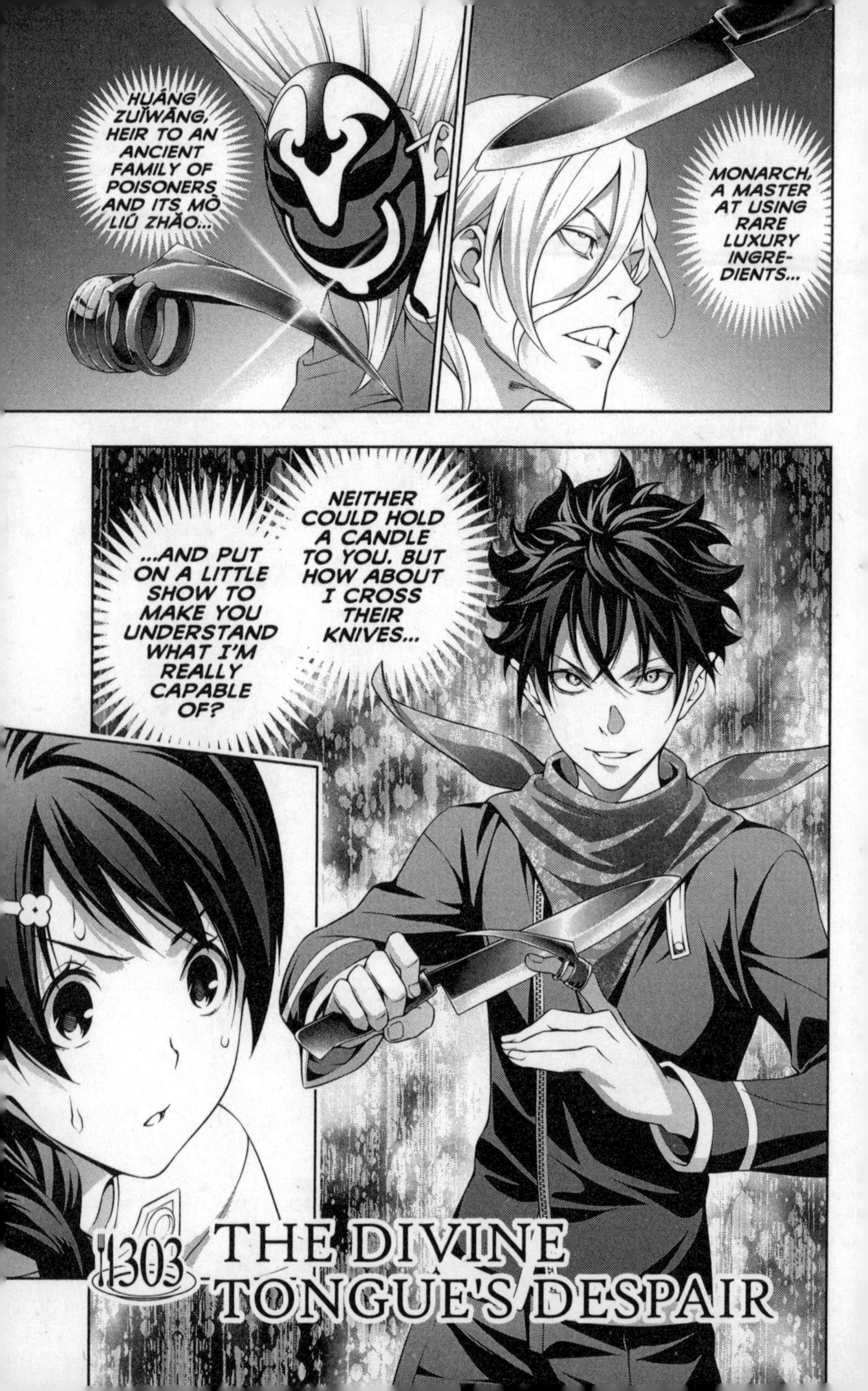
MONARCH, A MASTER AT USING RARE LUXURY INGREDIENTS...
HUÁNG ZUǏWĀNG, HEIR TO AN ANCIENT FAMILY OF POISONERS AND ITS MÒ LIÚ ZHǍO...
NEITHER COULD HOLD A CANDLE TO YOU. BUT HOW ABOUT I CROSS THEIR KNIVES...
...AND PUT ON A LITTLE SHOW TO MAKE YOU UNDERSTAND WHAT I'M REALLY CAPABLE OF?
303 THE DIVINE TONGUE'S DESPAIR

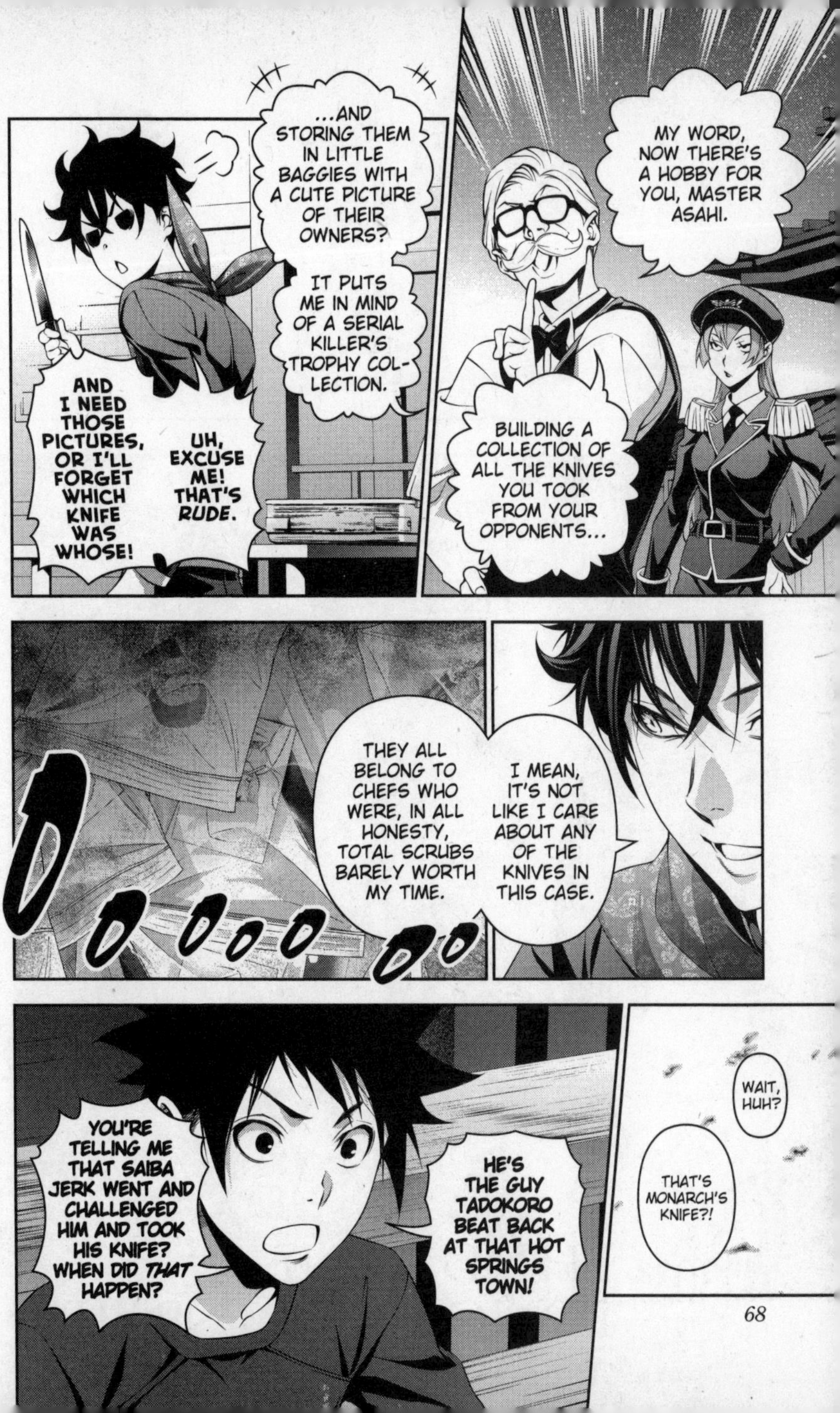
MY WORD, NOW THERE'S A HOBBY FOR YOU, MASTER ASAHI.
BUILDING A COLLECTION OF ALL THE KNIVES YOU TOOK FROM YOUR OPPONENTS...
...AND STORING THEM IN LITTLE BAGGIES WITH A CUTE PICTURE OF THEIR OWNERS?
IT PUTS ME IN MIND OF A SERIAL KILLER'S TROPHY COL-LECTION.
UH, EXCUSE ME! THAT'S *RUDE*.
AND I NEED THOSE PICTURES, OR I'LL FORGET WHICH KNIFE WAS WHOSE!
I MEAN, IT'S NOT LIKE I CARE ABOUT ANY OF THE KNIVES IN THIS CASE.
THEY ALL BELONG TO CHEFS WHO WERE, IN ALL HONESTY, TOTAL SCRUBS BARELY WORTH MY TIME.
DOOOOOO
WAIT, HUH?
THAT'S MONARCH'S KNIFE?!
HE'S THE GUY TADOKORO BEAT BACK AT THAT HOT SPRINGS TOWN!
YOU'RE TELLING ME THAT SAIBA JERK WENT AND CHALLENGED HIM AND TOOK HIS KNIFE? WHEN DID *THAT* HAPPEN?

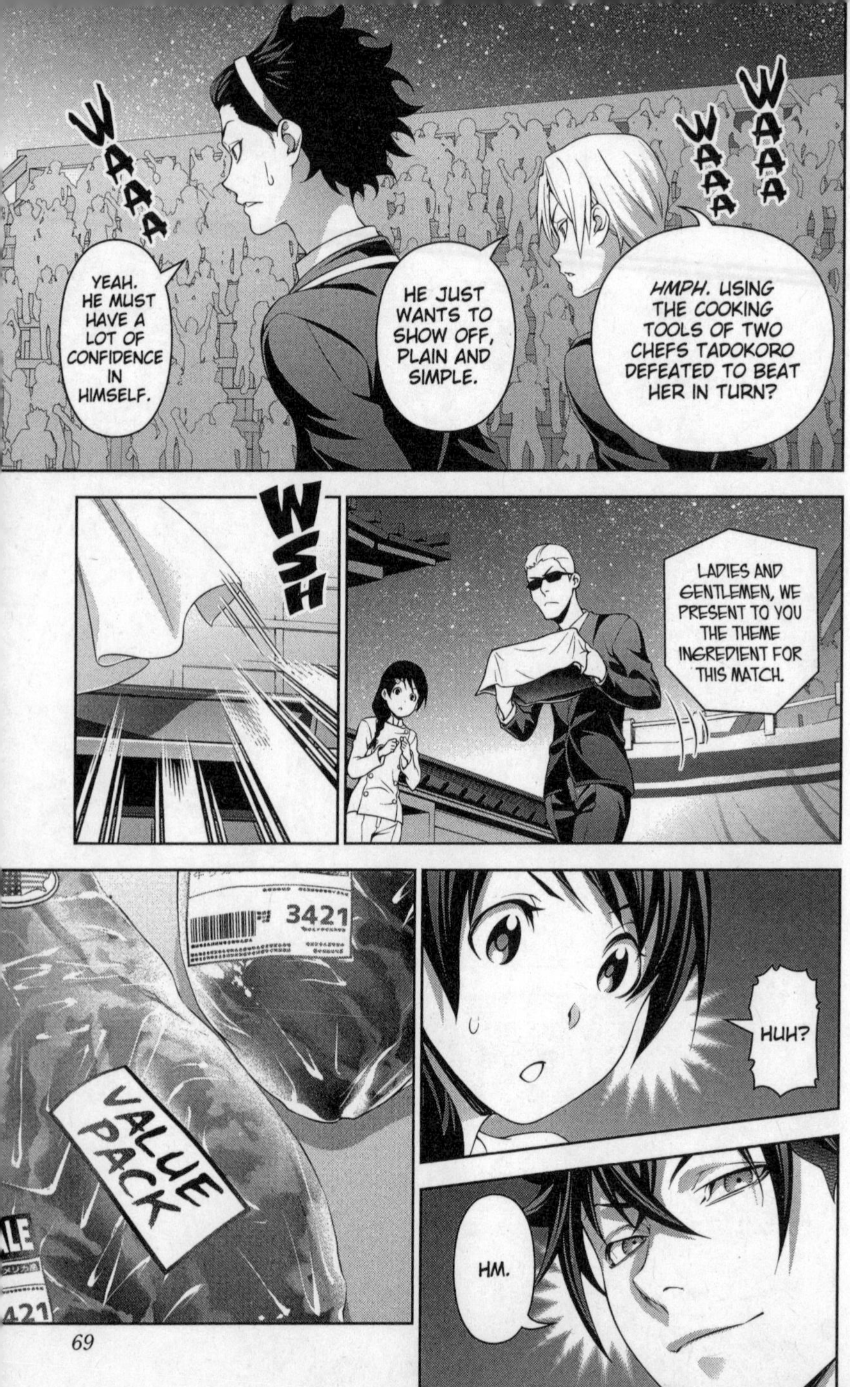
WAAA
WAAA
HMPH. USING THE COOKING TOOLS OF TWO CHEFS TADOKORO DEFEATED TO BEAT HER IN TURN?
HE JUST WANTS TO SHOW OFF, PLAIN AND SIMPLE.
WAAA
YEAH. HE MUST HAVE A LOT OF CONFIDENCE IN HIMSELF.
LADIES AND GENTLEMEN, WE PRESENT TO YOU THE THEME INGREDIENT FOR THIS MATCH.
WSH
HUH?
HM.
3421
VALUE PACK

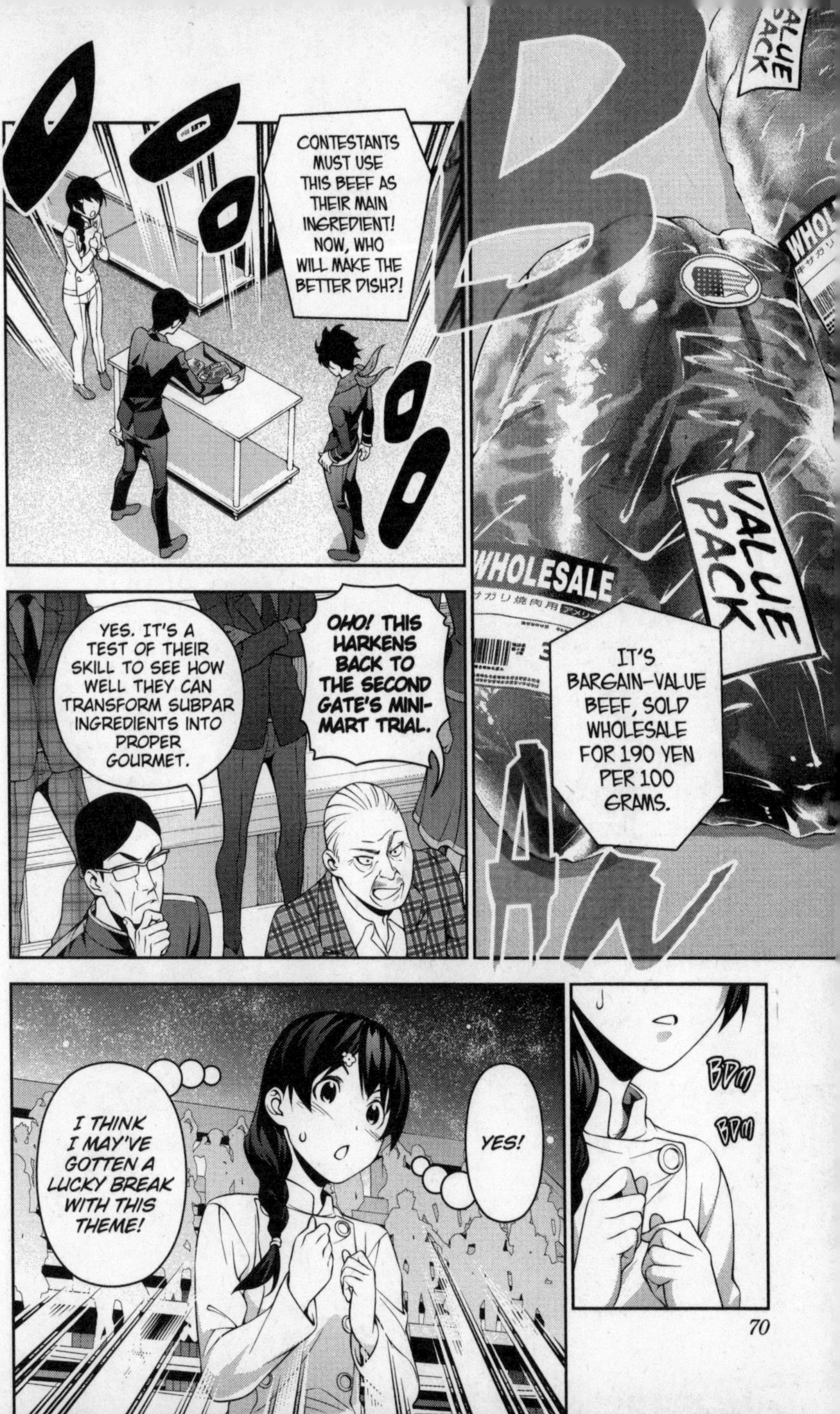
VALUE PACK
WHOLESALE
IT'S BARGAIN-VALUE BEEF, SOLD WHOLESALE FOR 190 YEN PER 100 GRAMS.
CONTESTANTS MUST USE THIS BEEF AS THEIR MAIN INGREDIENT! NOW, WHO WILL MAKE THE BETTER DISH?!
OHO! THIS HARKENS BACK TO THE SECOND GATE'S MINI-MART TRIAL.
YES. IT'S A TEST OF THEIR SKILL TO SEE HOW WELL THEY CAN TRANSFORM SUBPAR INGREDIENTS INTO PROPER GOURMET.
BDM
BDM
YES!
I THINK I MAY'VE GOTTEN A LUCKY BREAK WITH THIS THEME!

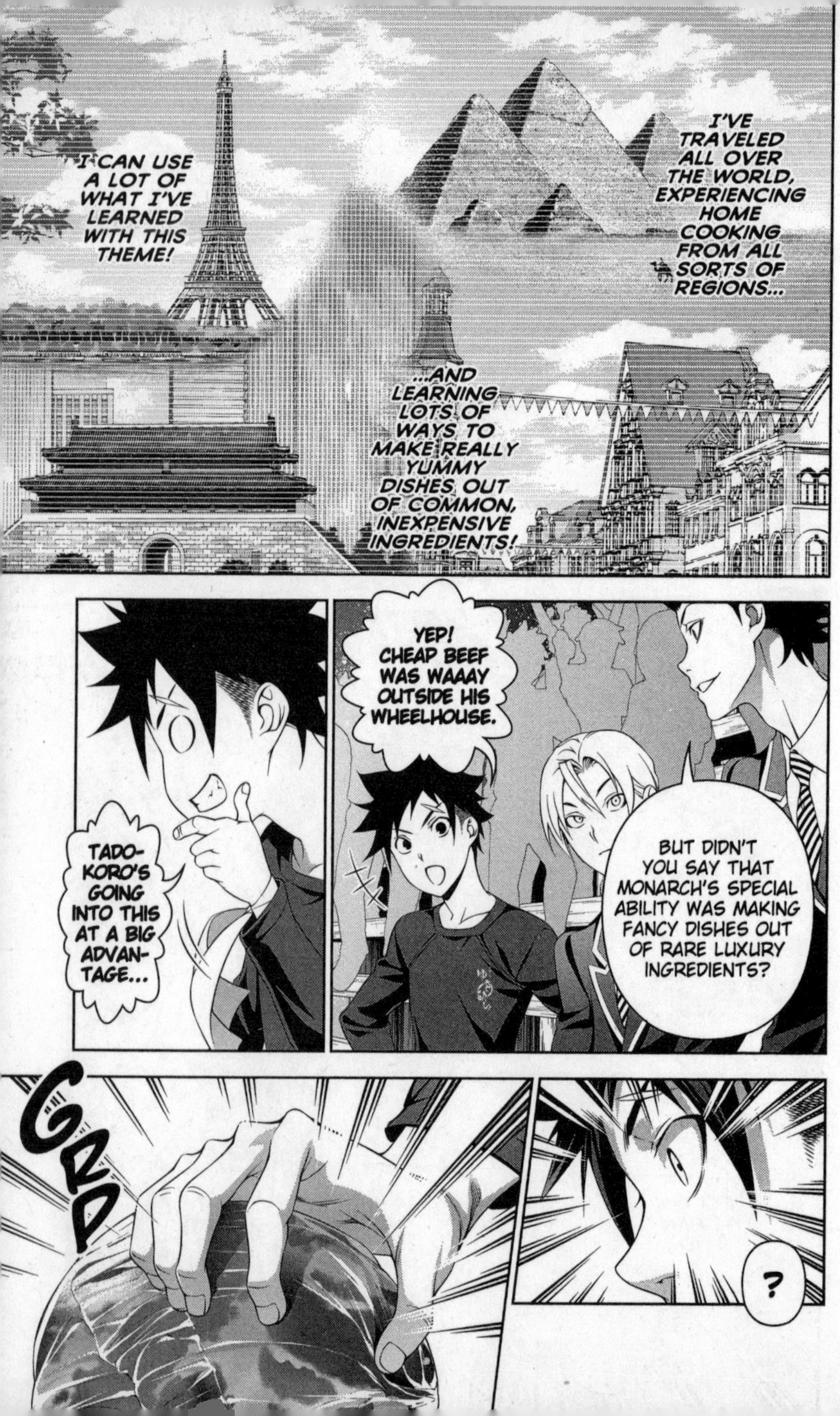

I'VE TRAVELED ALL OVER THE WORLD, EXPERIENCING HOME COOKING FROM ALL SORTS OF REGIONS...
...AND LEARNING LOTS OF WAYS TO MAKE REALLY YUMMY DISHES OUT OF COMMON, INEXPENSIVE INGREDIENTS!
I CAN USE A LOT OF WHAT I'VE LEARNED WITH THIS THEME!
BUT DIDN'T YOU SAY THAT MONARCH'S SPECIAL ABILITY WAS MAKING FANCY DISHES OUT OF RARE LUXURY INGREDIENTS?
YEP! CHEAP BEEF WAS WAAAY OUTSIDE HIS WHEELHOUSE.
TADO-KORO'S GOING INTO THIS AT A BIG ADVAN-TAGE...
?
GRP

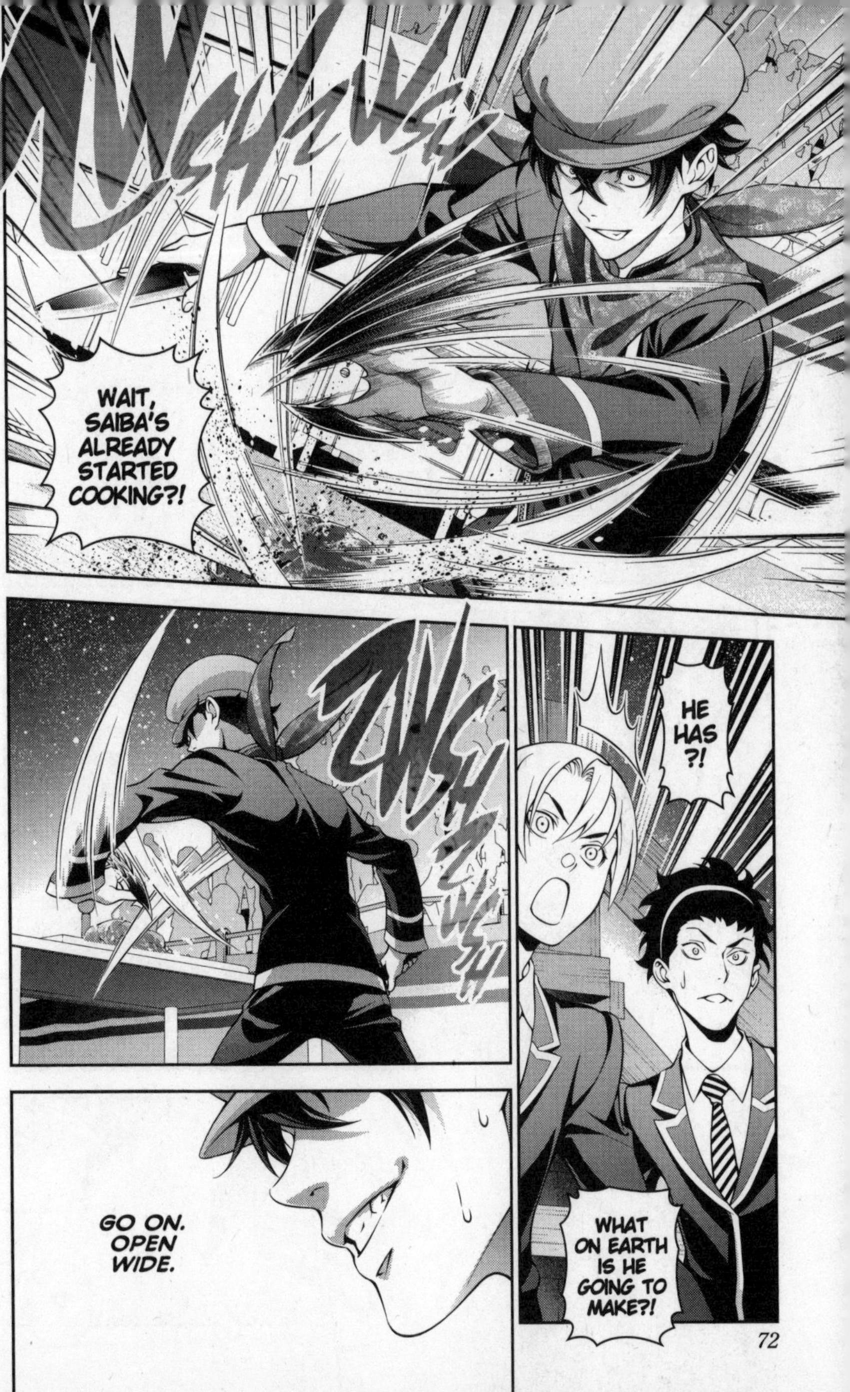
WAIT, SAIBA'S ALREADY STARTED COOKING?!
HE HAS?!
WHAT ON EARTH IS HE GOING TO MAKE?!
GO ON. OPEN WIDE.

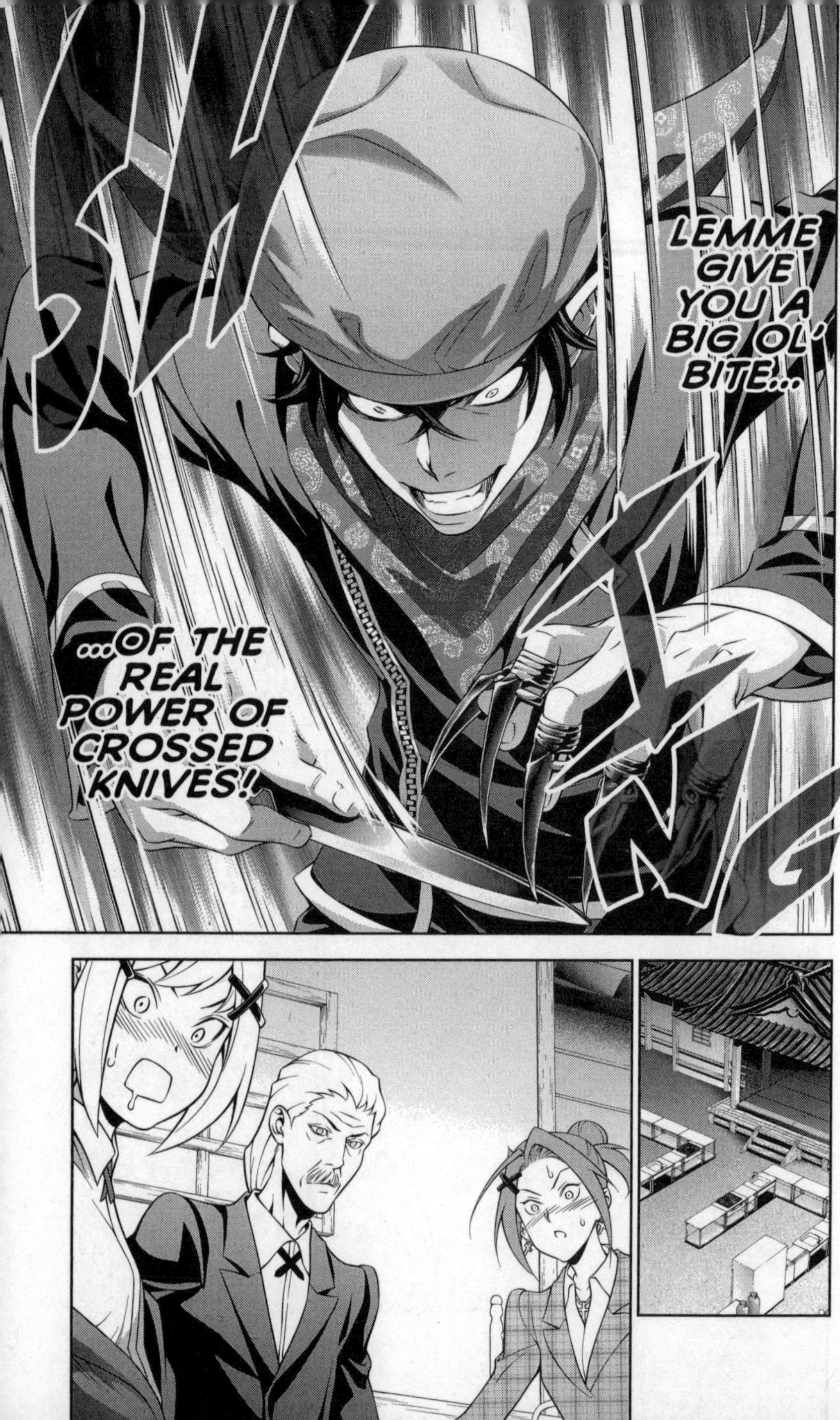
LEMME GIVE YOU A BIG OL' BITE...
...OF THE REAL POWER OF CROSSED KNIVES!!

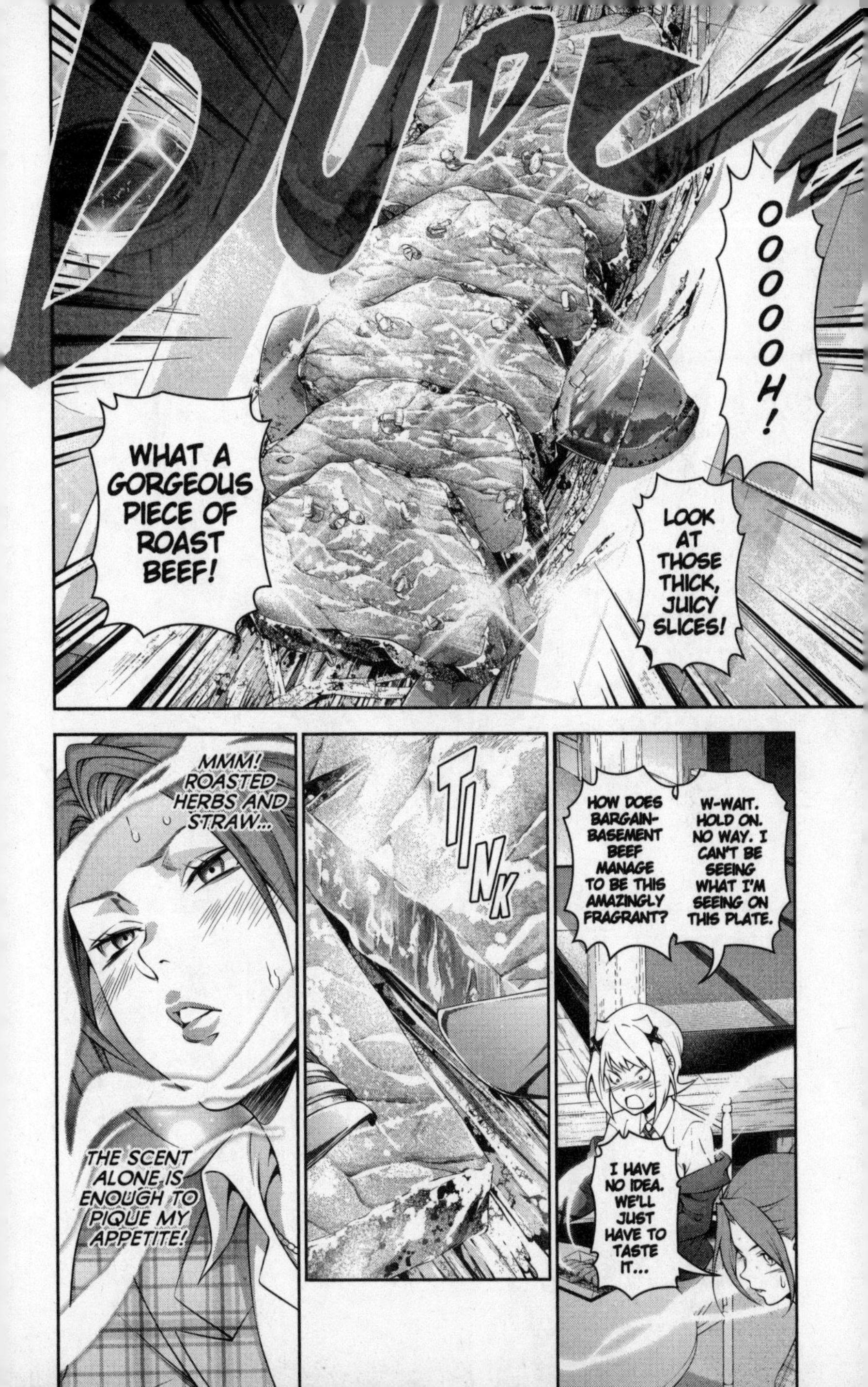
OOOOOOH!
LOOK AT THOSE THICK, JUICY SLICES!
WHAT A GORGEOUS PIECE OF ROAST BEEF!
W-WAIT. HOLD ON. NO WAY. I CAN'T BE SEEING WHAT I'M SEEING ON THIS PLATE.
HOW DOES BARGAIN-BASEMENT BEEF MANAGE TO BE THIS AMAZINGLY FRAGRANT?
I HAVE NO IDEA. WE'LL JUST HAVE TO TASTE IT...
TINK
MMM! ROASTED HERBS AND STRAW...
THE SCENT ALONE IS ENOUGH TO PIQUE MY APPETITE!

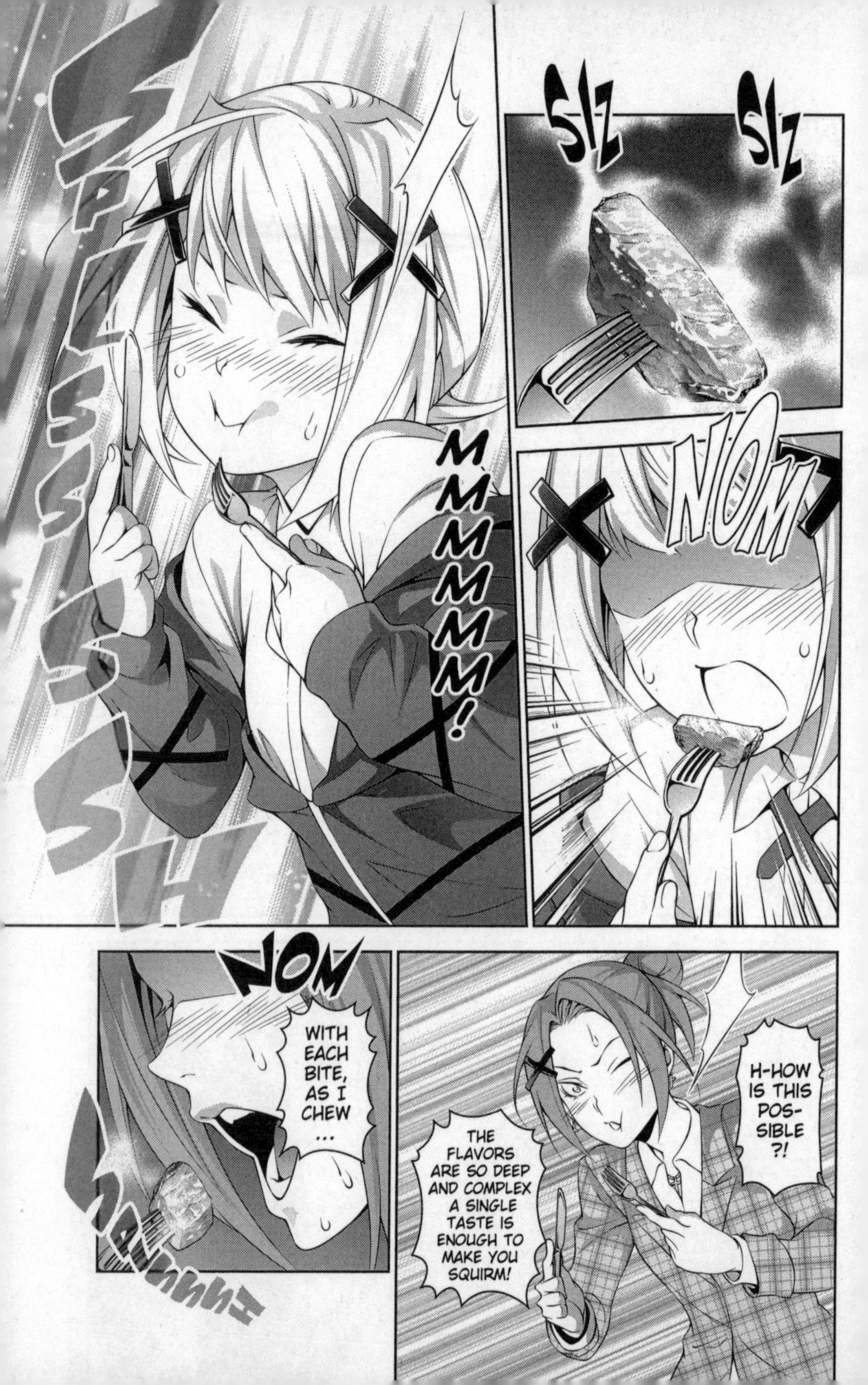
SIZ SIZ
NOM
MMMMMMM!
H-HOW IS THIS POS-SIBLE ?!
THE FLAVORS ARE SO DEEP AND COMPLEX A SINGLE TASTE IS ENOUGH TO MAKE YOU SQUIRM!
NOM
WITH EACH BITE, AS I CHEW ...

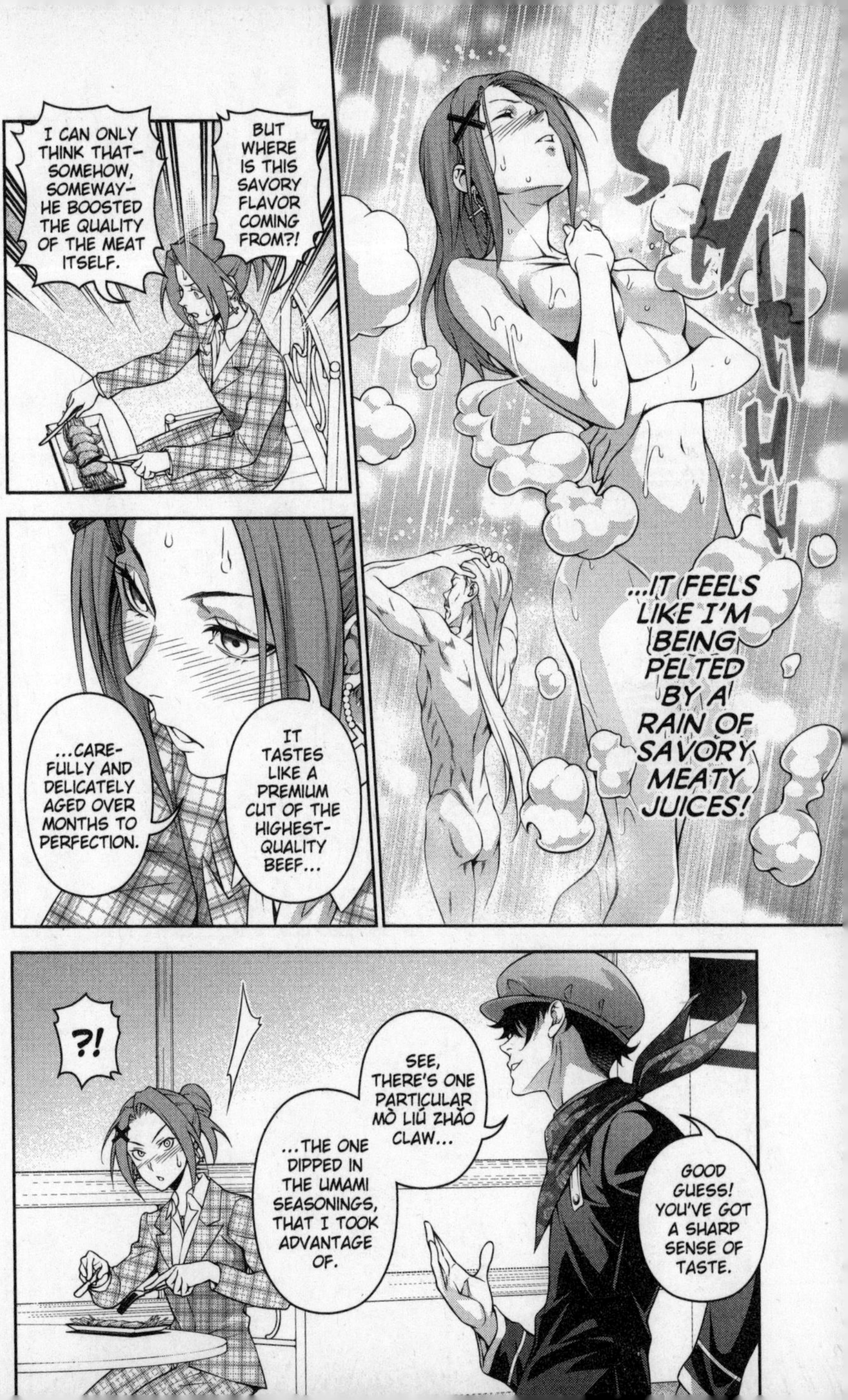
SHHHH
...IT FEELS LIKE I'M BEING PELTED BY A RAIN OF SAVORY MEATY JUICES!
BUT WHERE IS THIS SAVORY FLAVOR COMING FROM?!
I CAN ONLY THINK THAT—SOMEHOW, SOMEWAY—HE BOOSTED THE QUALITY OF THE MEAT ITSELF.
IT TASTES LIKE A PREMIUM CUT OF THE HIGHEST-QUALITY BEEF...
...CAREFULLY AND DELICATELY AGED OVER MONTHS TO PERFECTION.
GOOD GUESS! YOU'VE GOT A SHARP SENSE OF TASTE.
SEE, THERE'S ONE PARTICULAR MÒ LIÚ ZHǍO CLAW...
...THE ONE DIPPED IN THE UMAMI SEASONINGS, THAT I TOOK ADVANTAGE OF.
?!

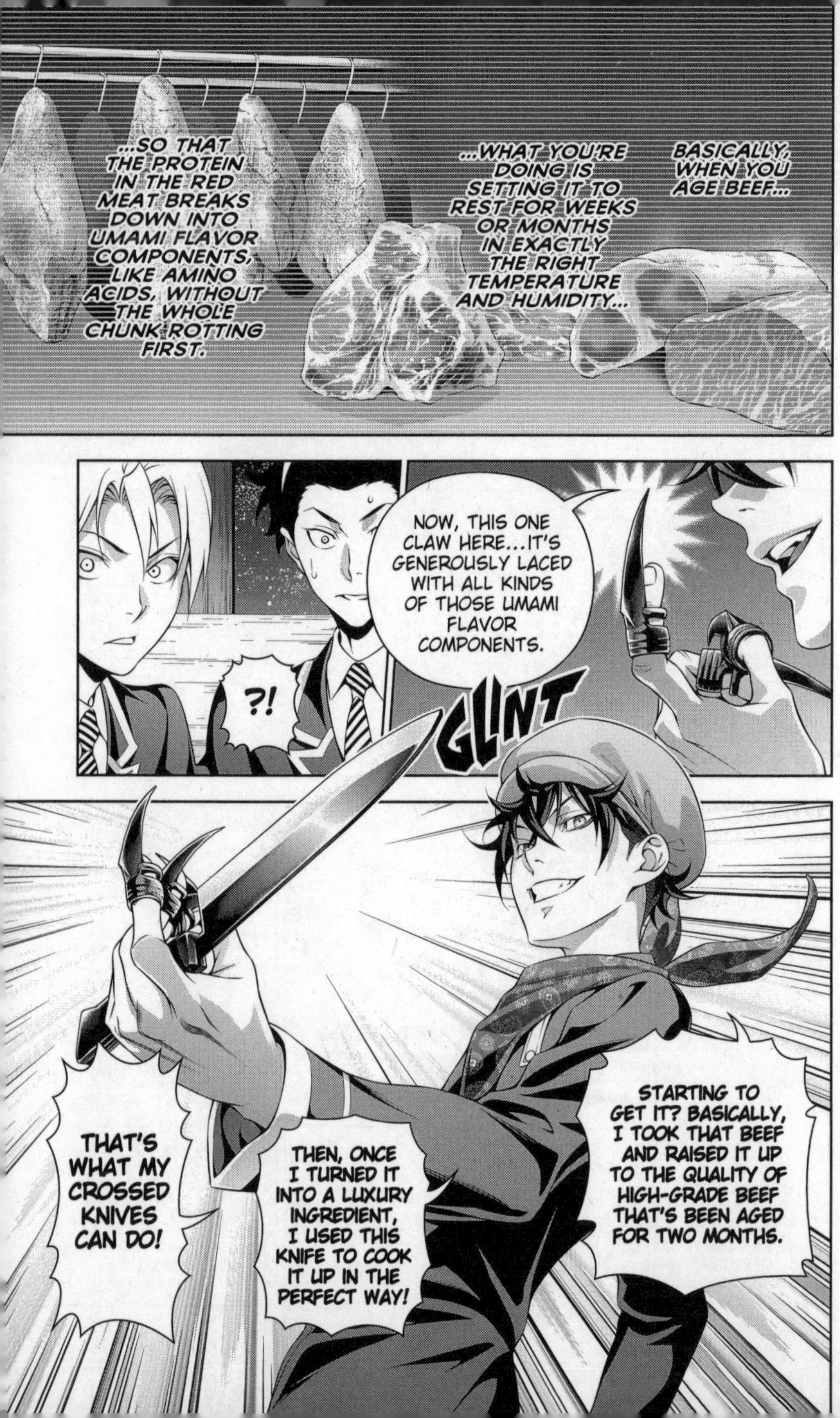
BASICALLY, WHEN YOU AGE BEEF...
...WHAT YOU'RE DOING IS SETTING IT TO REST FOR WEEKS OR MONTHS IN EXACTLY THE RIGHT TEMPERATURE AND HUMIDITY...
...SO THAT THE PROTEIN IN THE RED MEAT BREAKS DOWN INTO UMAMI FLAVOR COMPONENTS, LIKE AMINO ACIDS, WITHOUT THE WHOLE CHUNK ROTTING FIRST.
NOW, THIS ONE CLAW HERE...IT'S GENEROUSLY LACED WITH ALL KINDS OF THOSE UMAMI FLAVOR COMPONENTS.
GLINT
?!
STARTING TO GET IT? BASICALLY, I TOOK THAT BEEF AND RAISED IT UP TO THE QUALITY OF HIGH-GRADE BEEF THAT'S BEEN AGED FOR TWO MONTHS.
THEN, ONCE I TURNED IT INTO A LUXURY INGREDIENT, I USED THIS KNIFE TO COOK IT UP IN THE PERFECT WAY!
THAT'S WHAT MY CROSSED KNIVES CAN DO!

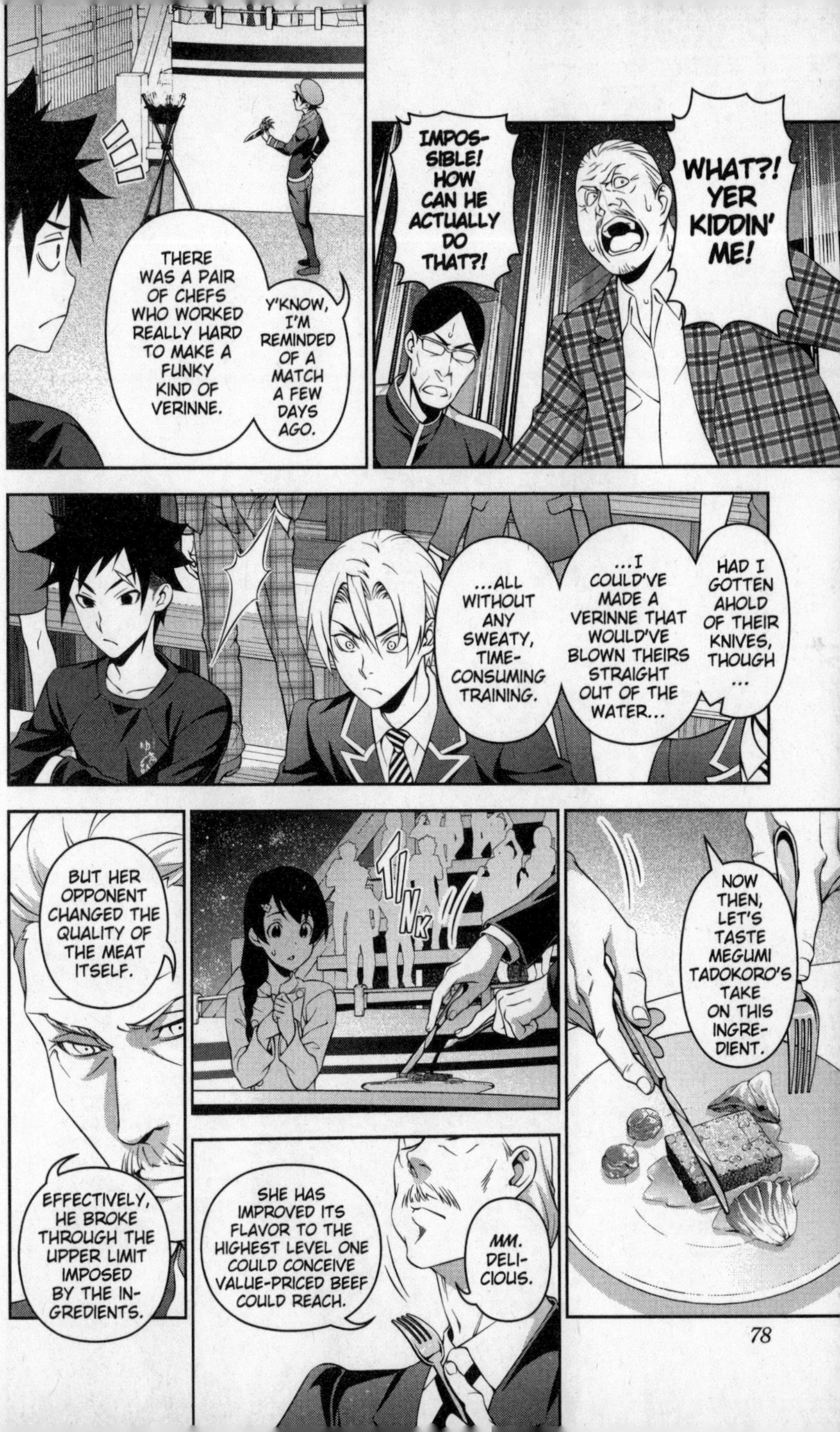
WHAT?! YER KIDDIN' ME!
IMPOSSIBLE! HOW CAN HE ACTUALLY DO THAT?!
Y'KNOW, I'M REMINDED OF A MATCH A FEW DAYS AGO.
THERE WAS A PAIR OF CHEFS WHO WORKED REALLY HARD TO MAKE A FUNKY KIND OF VERINNE.
HAD I GOTTEN AHOLD OF THEIR KNIVES, THOUGH ...
...I COULD'VE MADE A VERINNE THAT WOULD'VE BLOWN THEIRS STRAIGHT OUT OF THE WATER...
...ALL WITHOUT ANY SWEATY, TIME-CONSUMING TRAINING.
NOW THEN, LET'S TASTE MEGUMI TADOKORO'S TAKE ON THIS INGREDIENT.
TINK
MM. DELICIOUS.
SHE HAS IMPROVED ITS FLAVOR TO THE HIGHEST LEVEL ONE COULD CONCEIVE VALUE-PRICED BEEF COULD REACH.
BUT HER OPPONENT CHANGED THE QUALITY OF THE MEAT ITSELF.
EFFECTIVELY, HE BROKE THROUGH THE UPPER LIMIT IMPOSED BY THE INGREDIENTS.

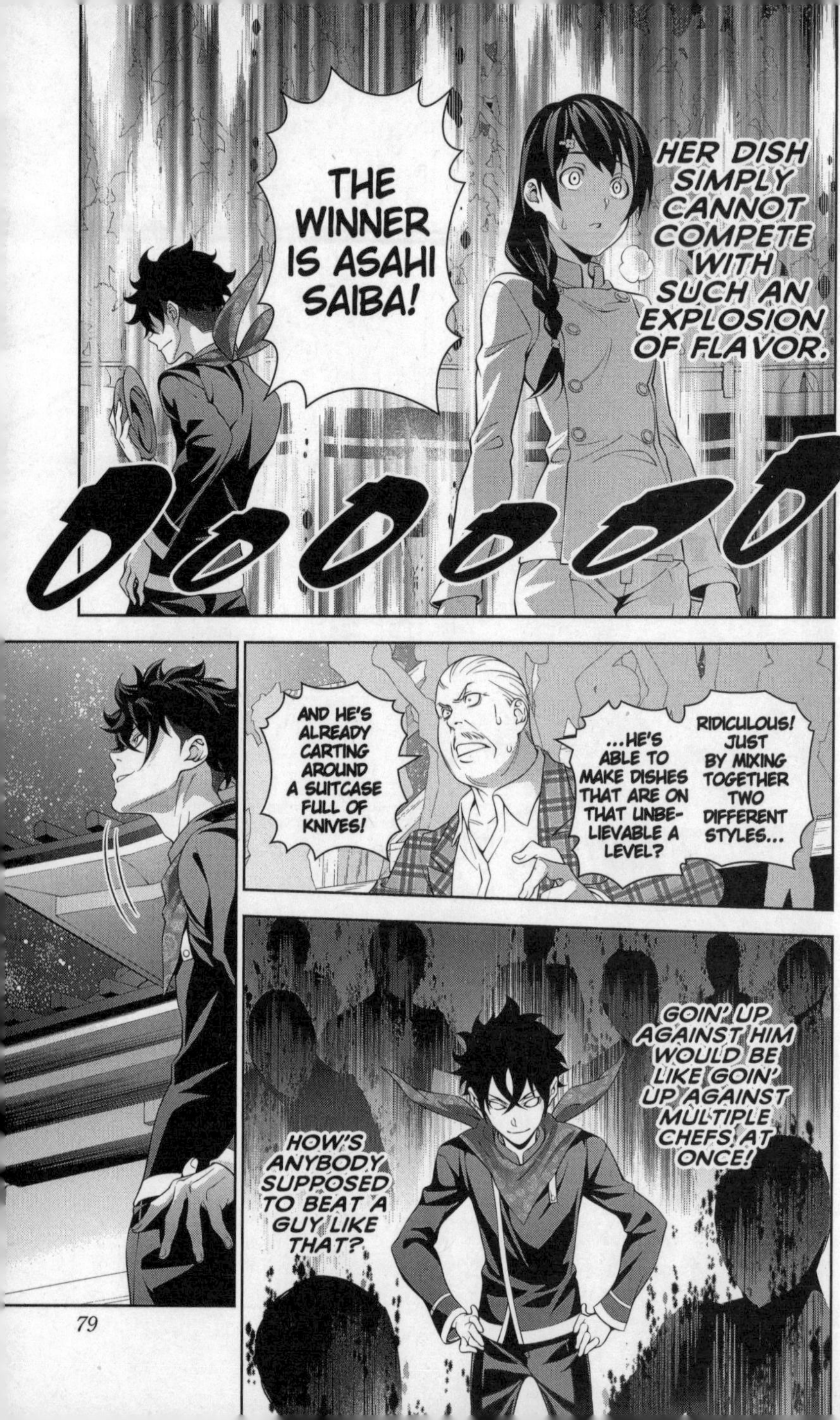
HER DISH SIMPLY CANNOT COMPETE WITH SUCH AN EXPLOSION OF FLAVOR.
THE WINNER IS ASAHI SAIBA!
RIDICULOUS! JUST BY MIXING TOGETHER TWO DIFFERENT STYLES...
...HE'S ABLE TO MAKE DISHES THAT ARE ON THAT UNBE-LIEVABLE A LEVEL?
AND HE'S ALREADY CARTING AROUND A SUITCASE FULL OF KNIVES!
GOIN' UP AGAINST HIM WOULD BE LIKE GOIN' UP AGAINST MULTIPLE CHEFS AT ONCE!
HOW'S ANYBODY SUPPOSED TO BEAT A GUY LIKE THAT?

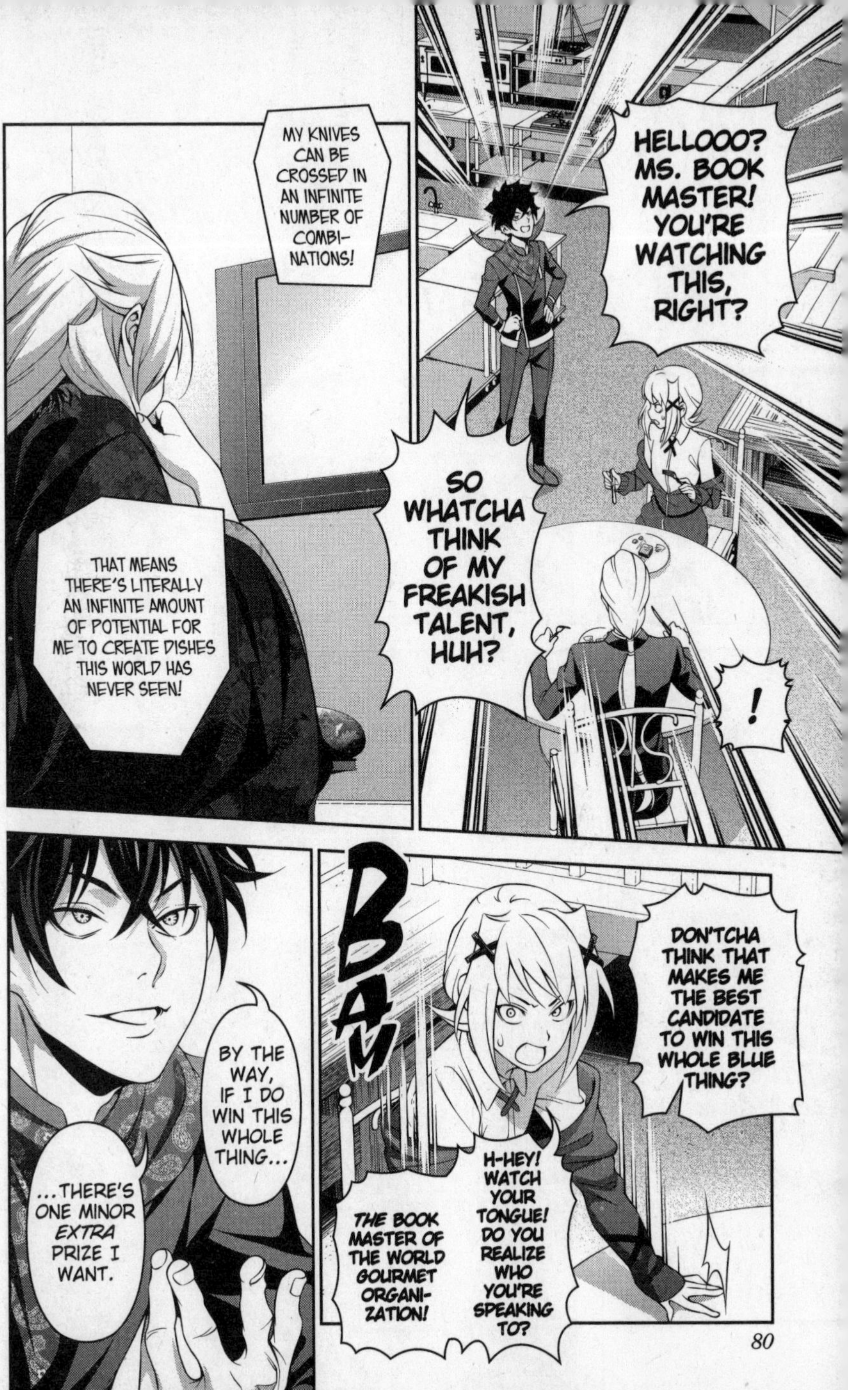
HELLOOO? MS. BOOK MASTER! YOU'RE WATCHING THIS, RIGHT?
SO WHATCHA THINK OF MY FREAKISH TALENT, HUH?
!
MY KNIVES CAN BE CROSSED IN AN INFINITE NUMBER OF COMBI-NATIONS!
THAT MEANS THERE'S LITERALLY AN INFINITE AMOUNT OF POTENTIAL FOR ME TO CREATE DISHES THIS WORLD HAS NEVER SEEN!
DON'TCHA THINK THAT MAKES ME THE BEST CANDIDATE TO WIN THIS WHOLE BLUE THING?
BAM
H-HEY! WATCH YOUR TONGUE! DO YOU REALIZE WHO YOU'RE SPEAKING TO?
THE BOOK MASTER OF THE WORLD GOURMET ORGANI-ZATION!
BY THE WAY, IF I DO WIN THIS WHOLE THING...
...THERE'S ONE MINOR *EXTRA* PRIZE I WANT.

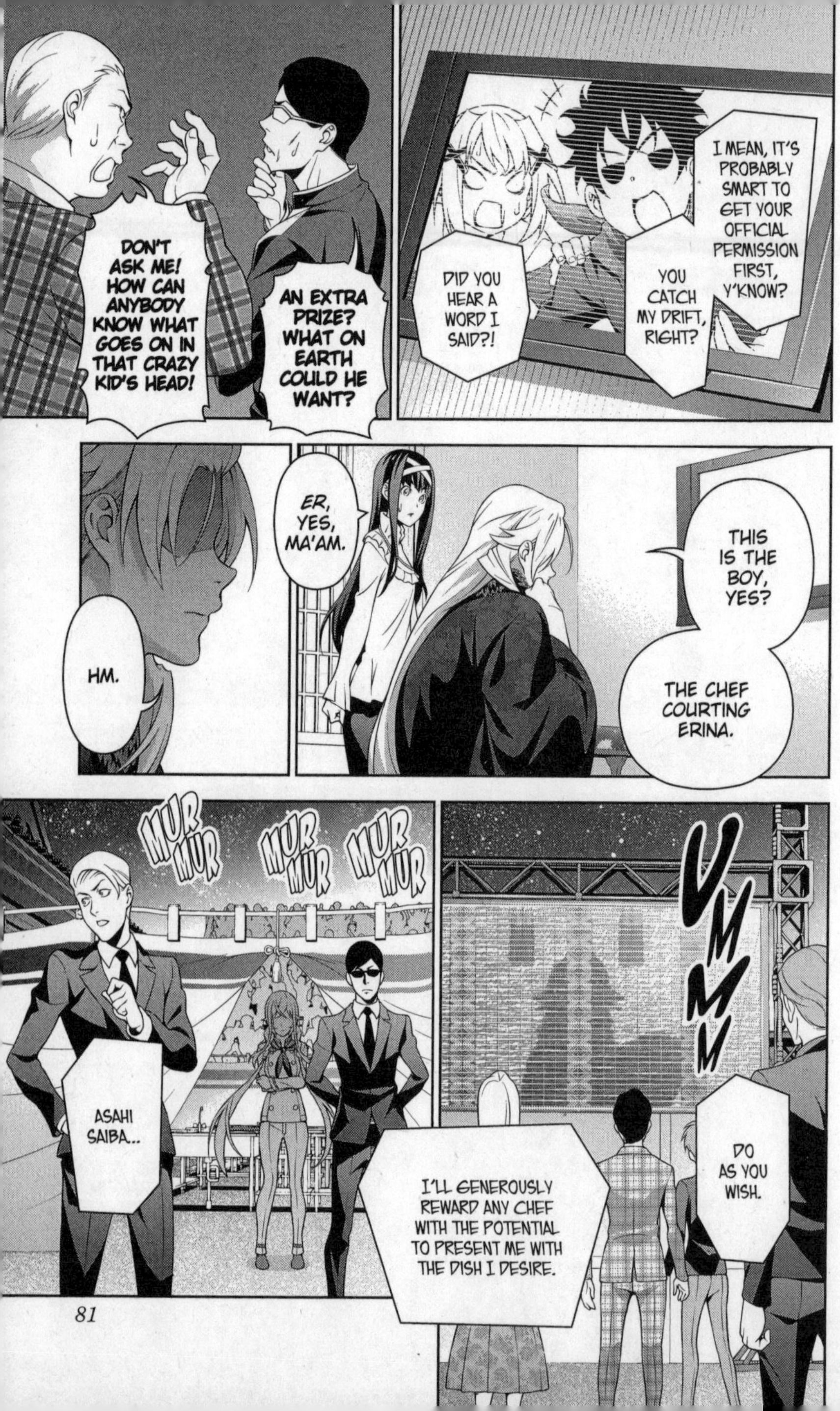
I MEAN, IT'S PROBABLY SMART TO GET YOUR OFFICIAL PERMISSION FIRST, Y'KNOW?
YOU CATCH MY DRIFT, RIGHT?
DID YOU HEAR A WORD I SAID?!
AN EXTRA PRIZE? WHAT ON EARTH COULD HE WANT?
DON'T ASK ME! HOW CAN ANYBODY KNOW WHAT GOES ON IN THAT CRAZY KID'S HEAD!
THIS IS THE BOY, YES?
THE CHEF COURTING ERINA.
ER, YES, MA'AM.
HM.
VMMM
DO AS YOU WISH.
I'LL GENEROUSLY REWARD ANY CHEF WITH THE POTENTIAL TO PRESENT ME WITH THE DISH I DESIRE.
MUR MUR
MUR MUR
MUR MUR
ASAHI SAIBA...

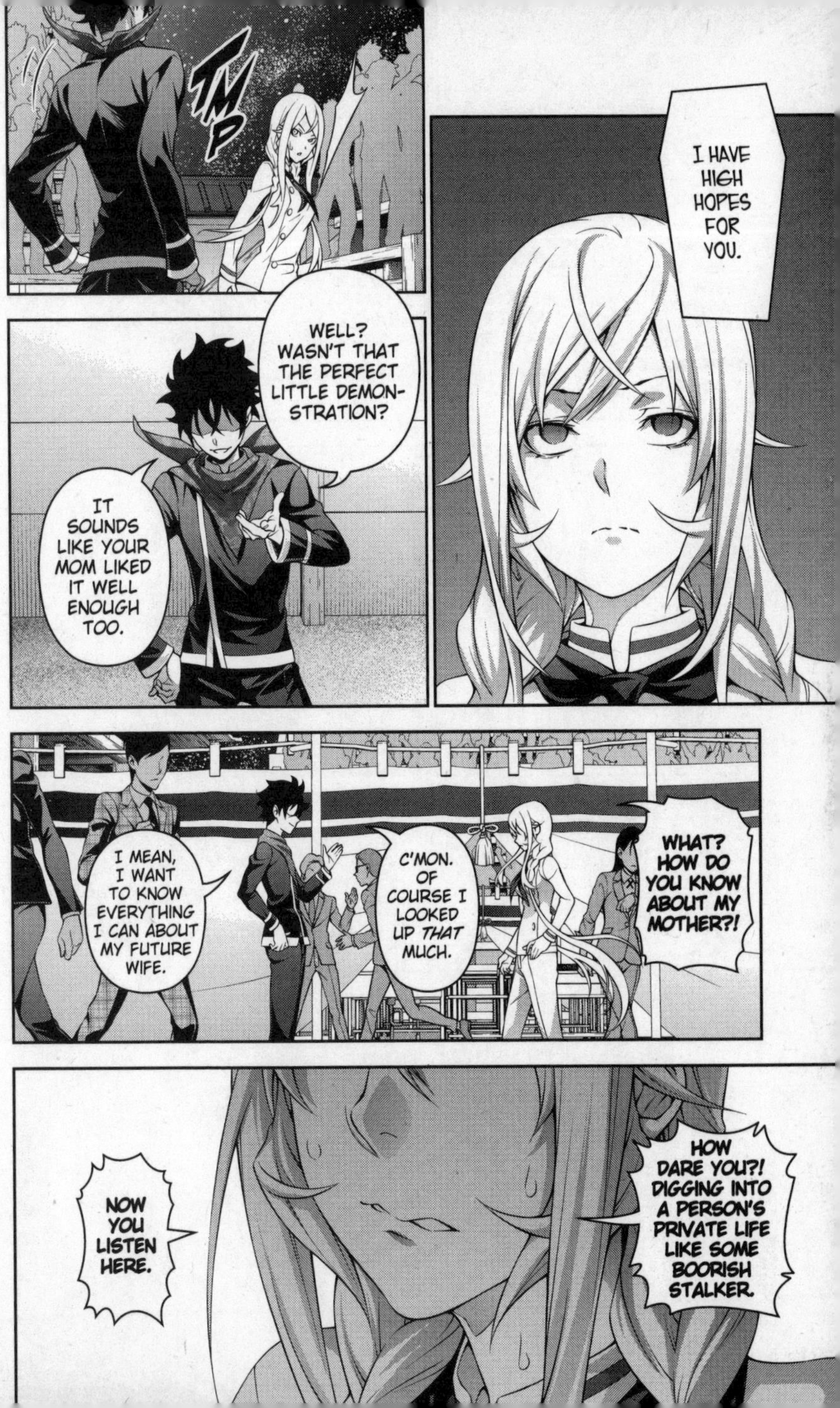
I HAVE HIGH HOPES FOR YOU.
TMP
WELL? WASN'T THAT THE PERFECT LITTLE DEMON-STRATION?
IT SOUNDS LIKE YOUR MOM LIKED IT WELL ENOUGH TOO.
WHAT? HOW DO YOU KNOW ABOUT MY MOTHER?!
C'MON. OF COURSE I LOOKED UP *THAT* MUCH.
I MEAN, I WANT TO KNOW EVERYTHING I CAN ABOUT MY FUTURE WIFE.
HOW DARE YOU?! DIGGING INTO A PERSON'S PRIVATE LIFE LIKE SOME BOORISH STALKER.
NOW YOU LISTEN HERE.

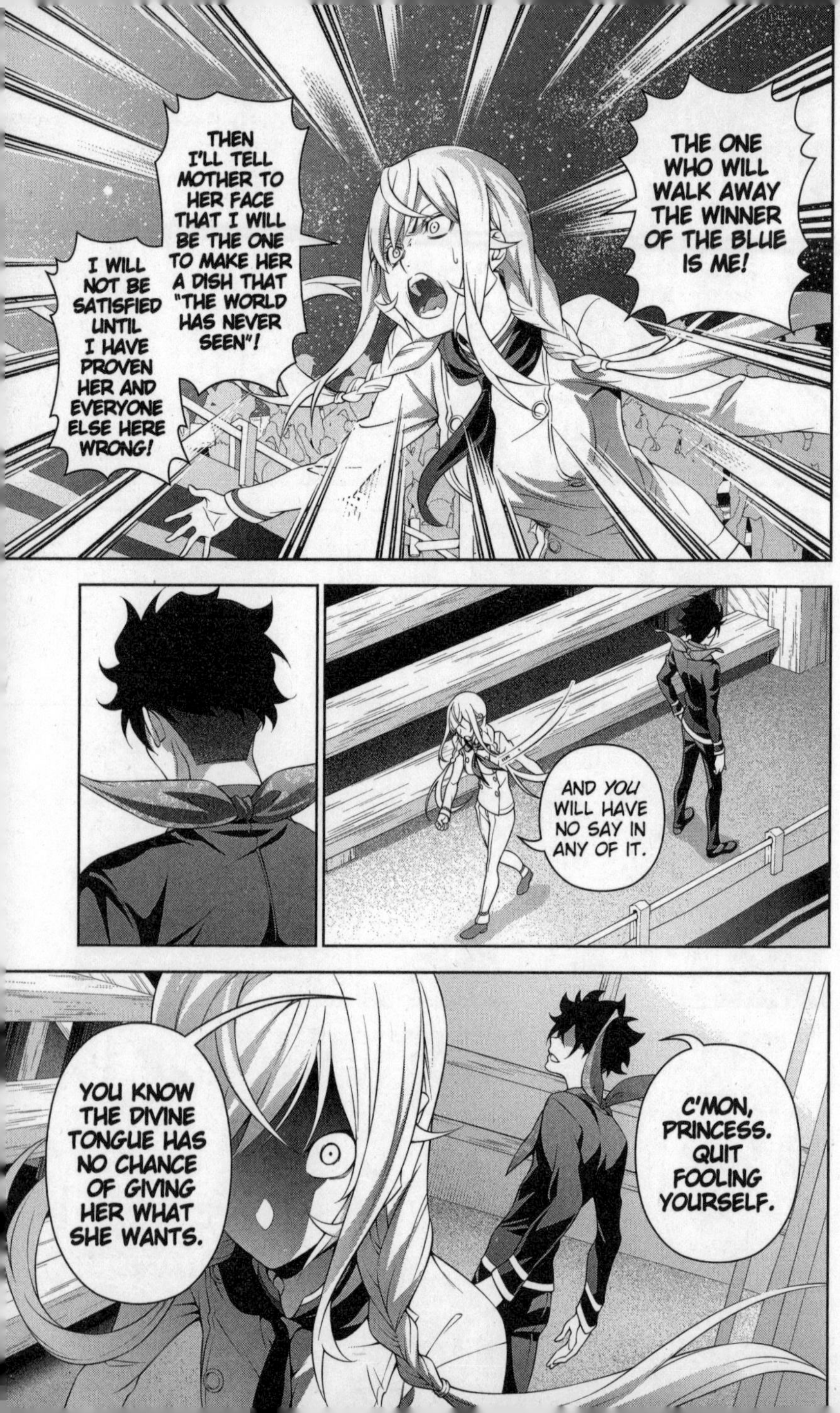
THE ONE WHO WILL WALK AWAY THE WINNER OF THE BLUE IS ME!
THEN I'LL TELL MOTHER TO HER FACE THAT I WILL BE THE ONE TO MAKE HER A DISH THAT "THE WORLD HAS NEVER SEEN"!
I WILL NOT BE SATISFIED UNTIL I HAVE PROVEN HER AND EVERYONE ELSE HERE WRONG!
AND YOU WILL HAVE NO SAY IN ANY OF IT.
C'MON, PRINCESS. QUIT FOOLING YOURSELF.
YOU KNOW THE DIVINE TONGUE HAS NO CHANCE OF GIVING HER WHAT SHE WANTS.

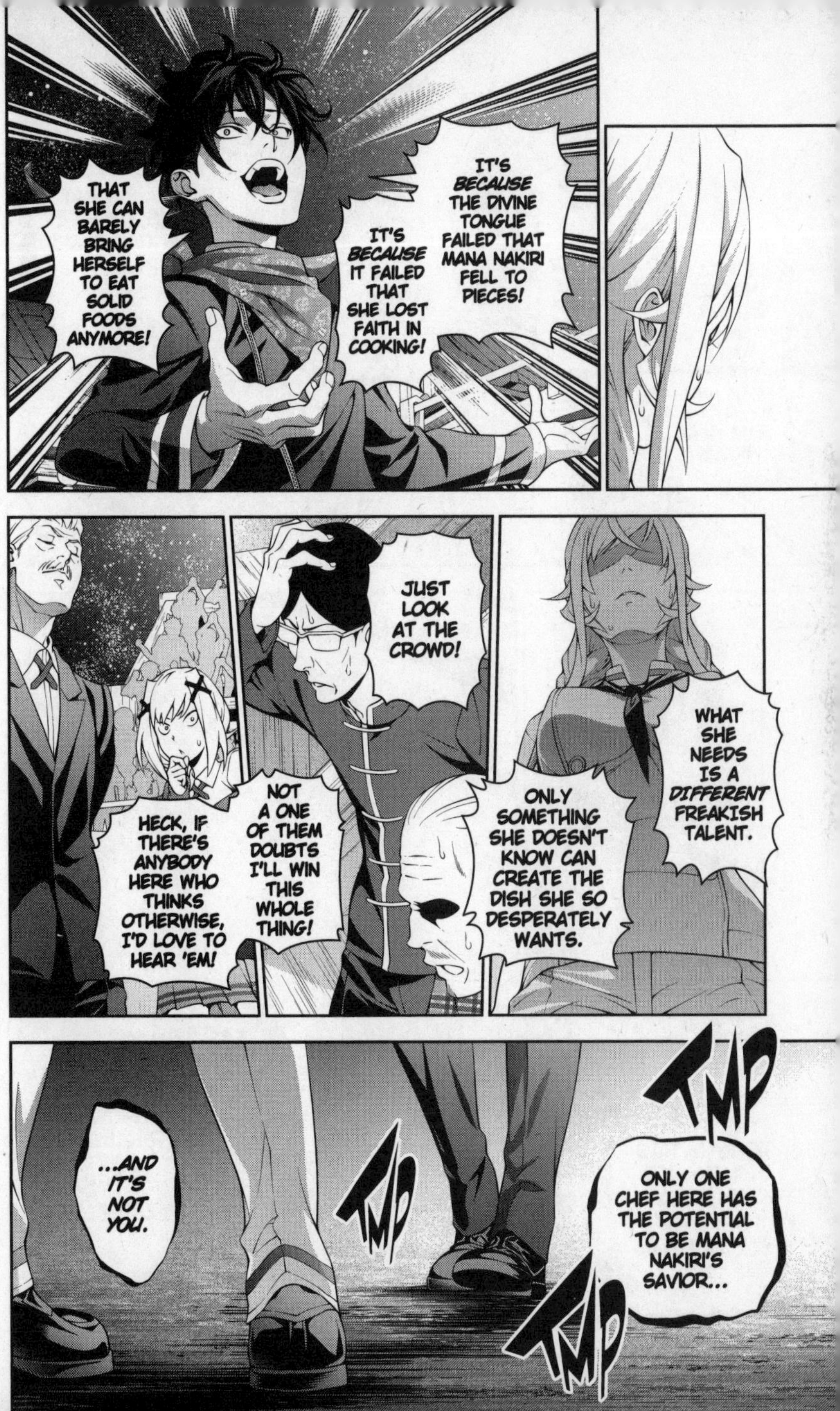
IT'S BECAUSE THE DIVINE TONGUE FAILED THAT MANA NAKIRI FELL TO PIECES!
IT'S BECAUSE IT FAILED THAT SHE LOST FAITH IN COOKING!
THAT SHE CAN BARELY BRING HERSELF TO EAT SOLID FOODS ANYMORE!
WHAT SHE NEEDS IS A DIFFERENT FREAKISH TALENT.
ONLY SOMETHING SHE DOESN'T KNOW CAN CREATE THE DISH SHE SO DESPERATELY WANTS.
JUST LOOK AT THE CROWD!
NOT A ONE OF THEM DOUBTS I'LL WIN THIS WHOLE THING!
HECK, IF THERE'S ANYBODY HERE WHO THINKS OTHERWISE, I'D LOVE TO HEAR 'EM!
TMP
ONLY ONE CHEF HERE HAS THE POTENTIAL TO BE MANA NAKIRI'S SAVIOR...
TMP
TMP
...AND IT'S NOT YOU.

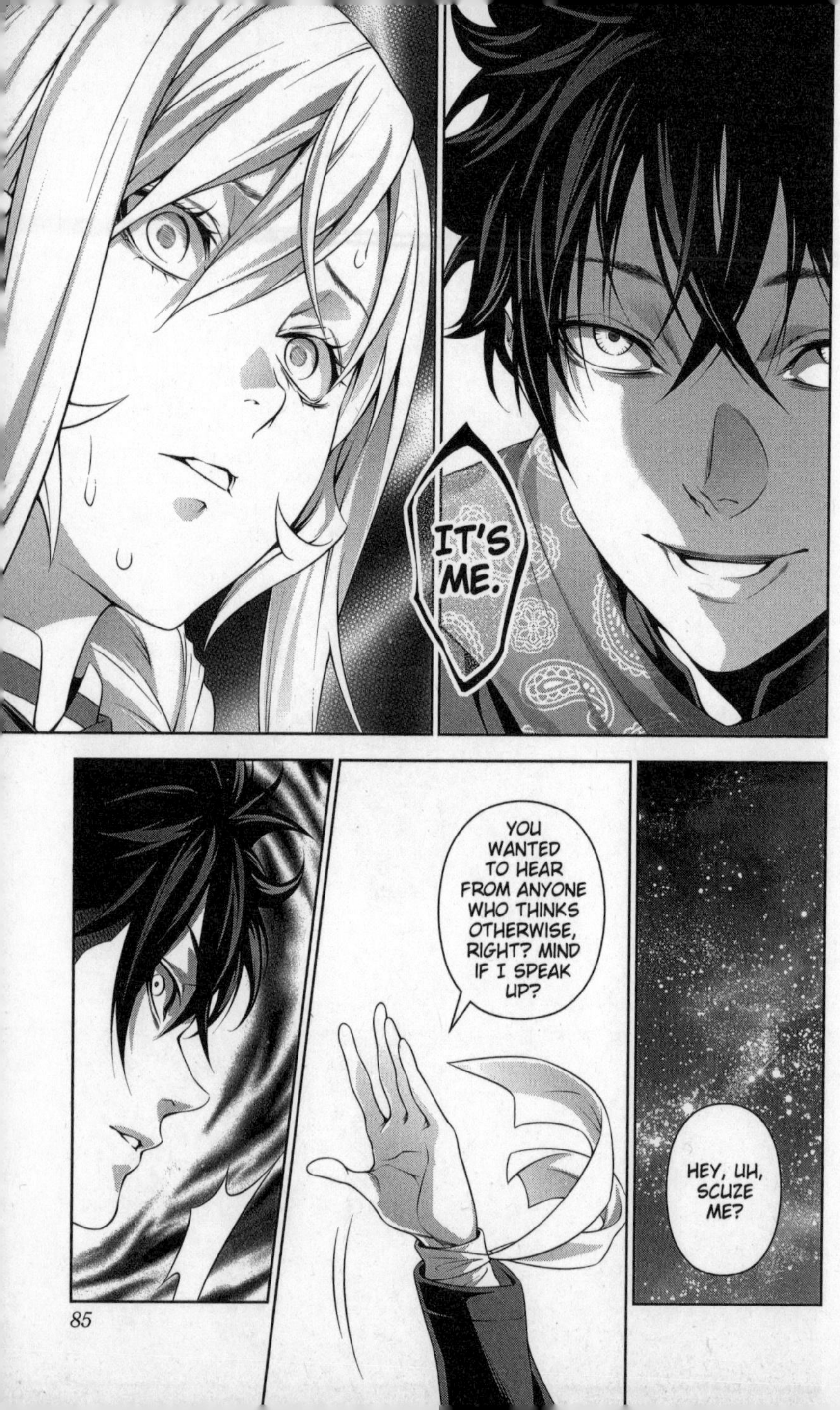
IT'S ME.
HEY, UH, SCUZE ME?
YOU WANTED TO HEAR FROM ANYONE WHO THINKS OTHERWISE, RIGHT? MIND IF I SPEAK UP?

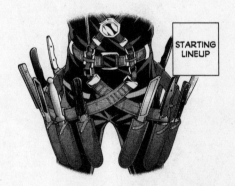

STARTING
LINEUP

RESERVES

304 THE CURSE OF THE DIVINE TONGUE

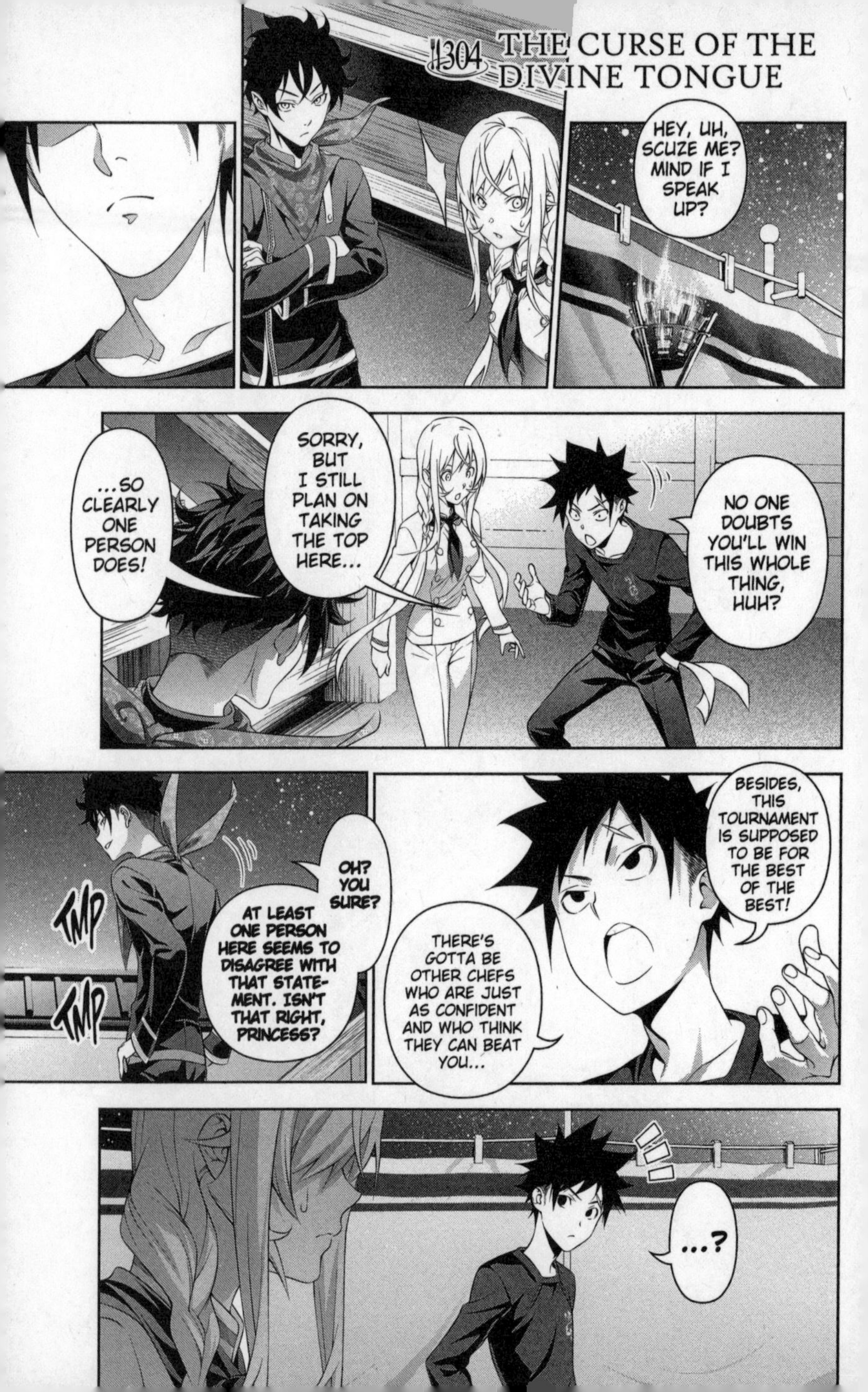
HEY, UH, SCUZE ME? MIND IF I SPEAK UP?
NO ONE DOUBTS YOU'LL WIN THIS WHOLE THING, HUH?
SORRY, BUT I STILL PLAN ON TAKING THE TOP HERE...
...SO CLEARLY ONE PERSON DOES!
BESIDES, THIS TOURNAMENT IS SUPPOSED TO BE FOR THE BEST OF THE BEST!
THERE'S GOTTA BE OTHER CHEFS WHO ARE JUST AS CONFIDENT AND WHO THINK THEY CAN BEAT YOU...
OH? YOU SURE?
AT LEAST ONE PERSON HERE SEEMS TO DISAGREE WITH THAT STATEMENT. ISN'T THAT RIGHT, PRINCESS?
TMP
TMP
...?

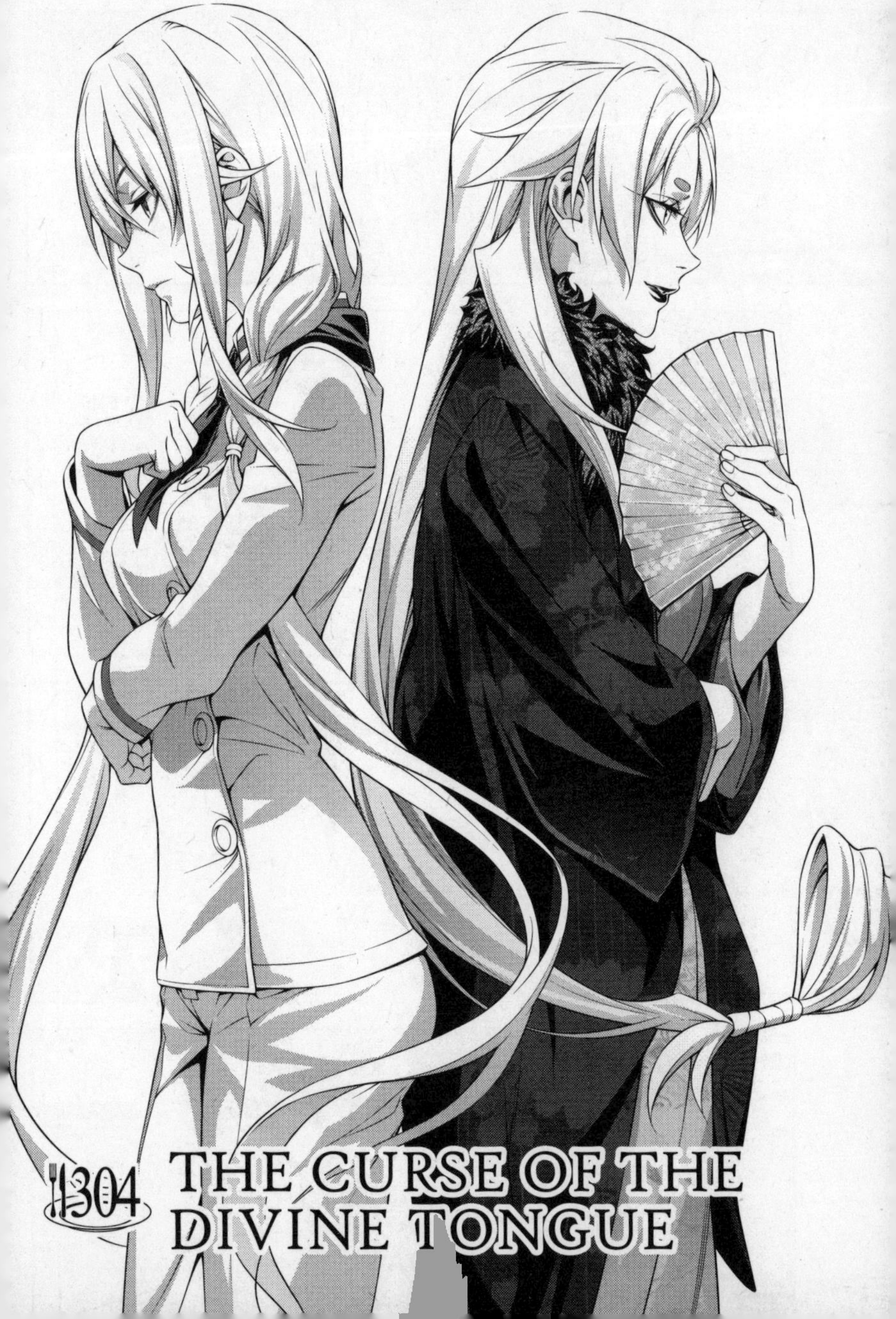

304 THE CURSE OF THE DIVINE TONGUE

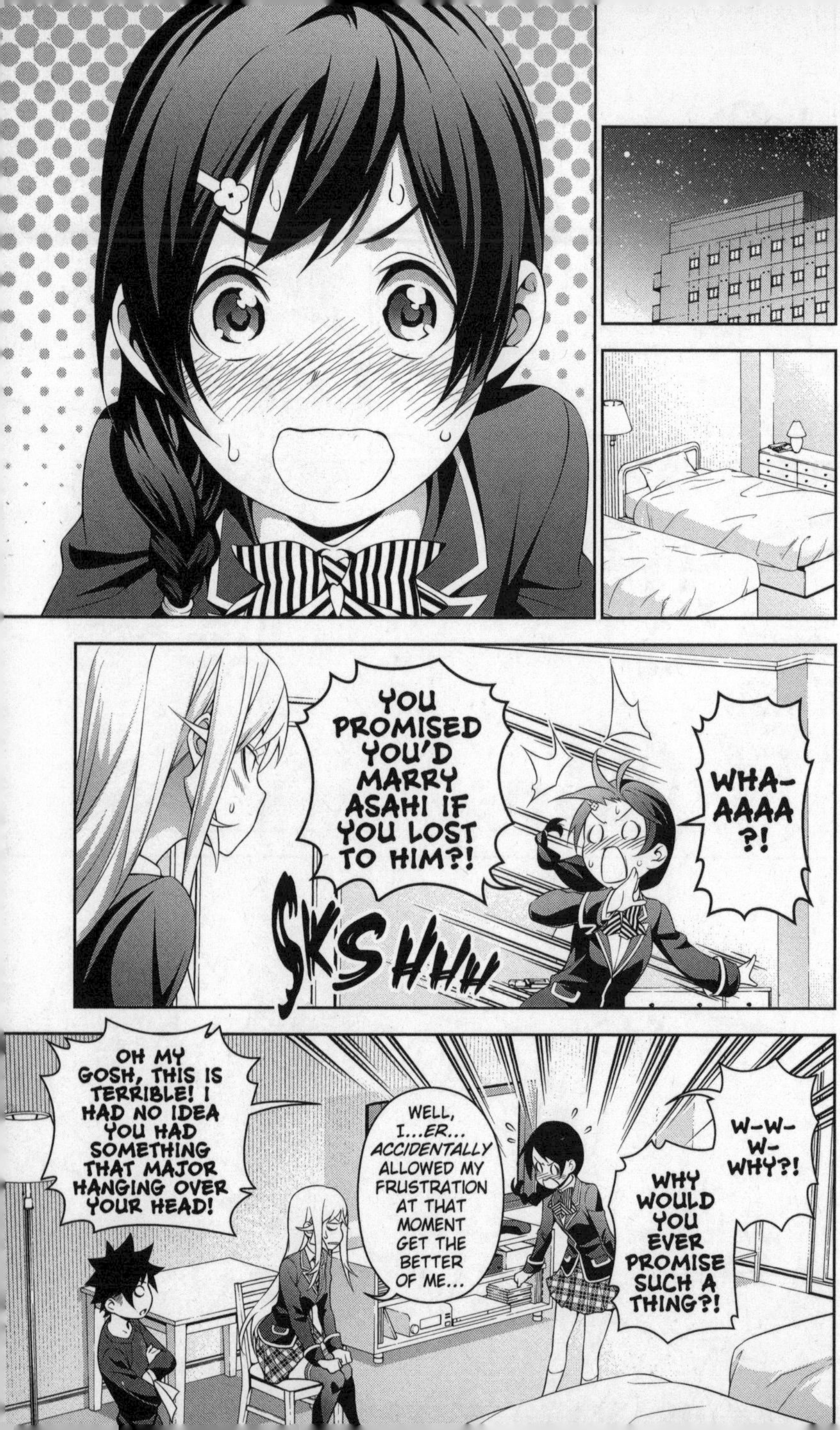
WHA-AAAA?!
YOU PROMISED YOU'D MARRY ASAHI IF YOU LOST TO HIM?!
SKSHHH
W-W-W-WHY?!
WHY WOULD YOU EVER PROMISE SUCH A THING?!
WELL, I...ER... *ACCIDENTALLY* ALLOWED MY FRUSTRATION AT THAT MOMENT GET THE BETTER OF ME...
OH MY GOSH, THIS IS TERRIBLE! I HAD NO IDEA YOU HAD SOMETHING THAT MAJOR HANGING OVER YOUR HEAD!

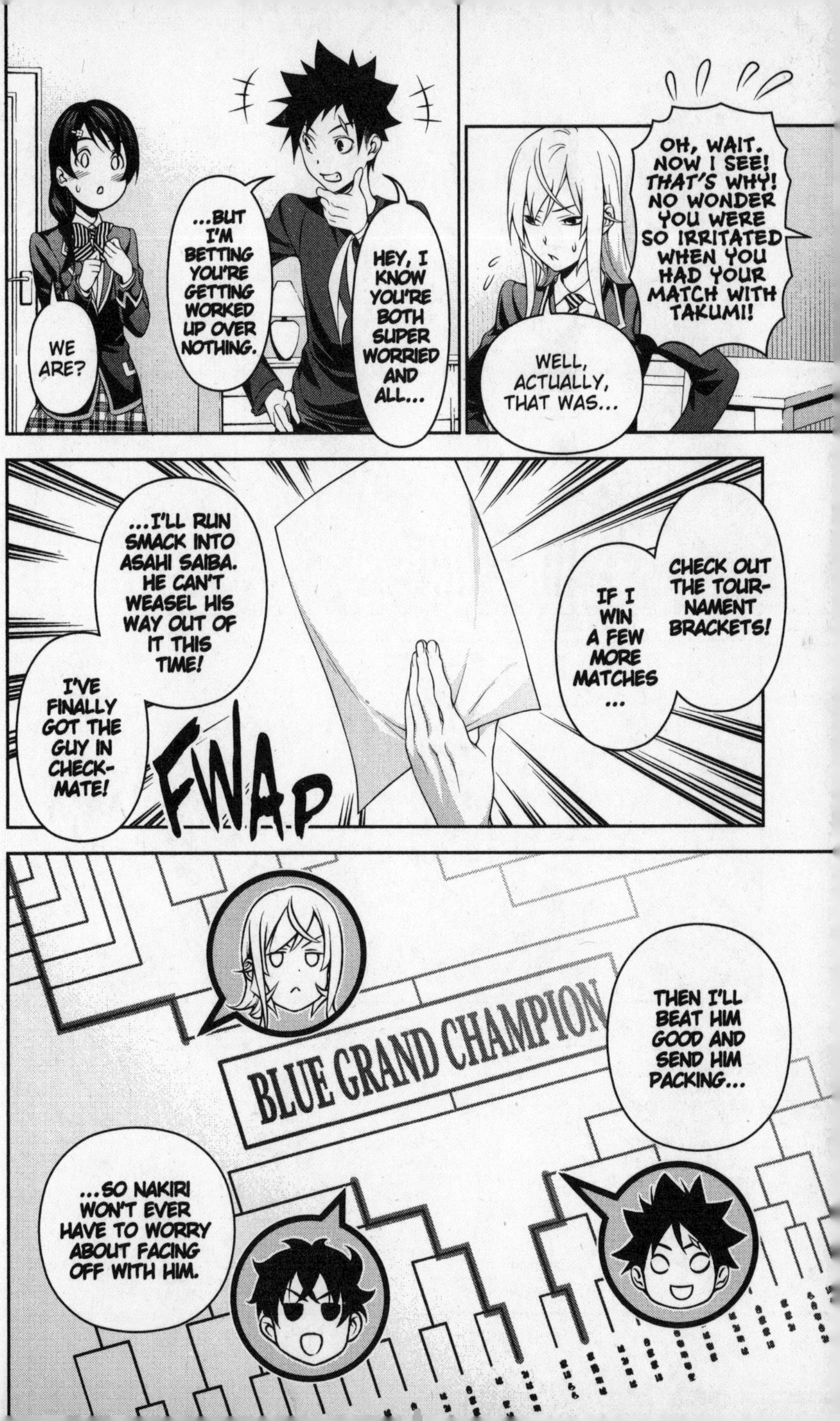
OH, WAIT. NOW I SEE! THAT'S WHY! NO WONDER YOU WERE SO IRRITATED WHEN YOU HAD YOUR MATCH WITH TAKUMI!
WELL, ACTUALLY, THAT WAS...
HEY, I KNOW YOU'RE BOTH SUPER WORRIED AND ALL...
...BUT I'M BETTING YOU'RE GETTING WORKED UP OVER NOTHING.
WE ARE?
CHECK OUT THE TOUR-NAMENT BRACKETS!
IF I WIN A FEW MORE MATCHES...
...I'LL RUN SMACK INTO ASAHI SAIBA. HE CAN'T WEASEL HIS WAY OUT OF IT THIS TIME!
I'VE FINALLY GOT THE GUY IN CHECK-MATE!
FWAP
BLUE GRAND CHAMPION
THEN I'LL BEAT HIM GOOD AND SEND HIM PACKING...
...SO NAKIRI WON'T EVER HAVE TO WORRY ABOUT FACING OFF WITH HIM.

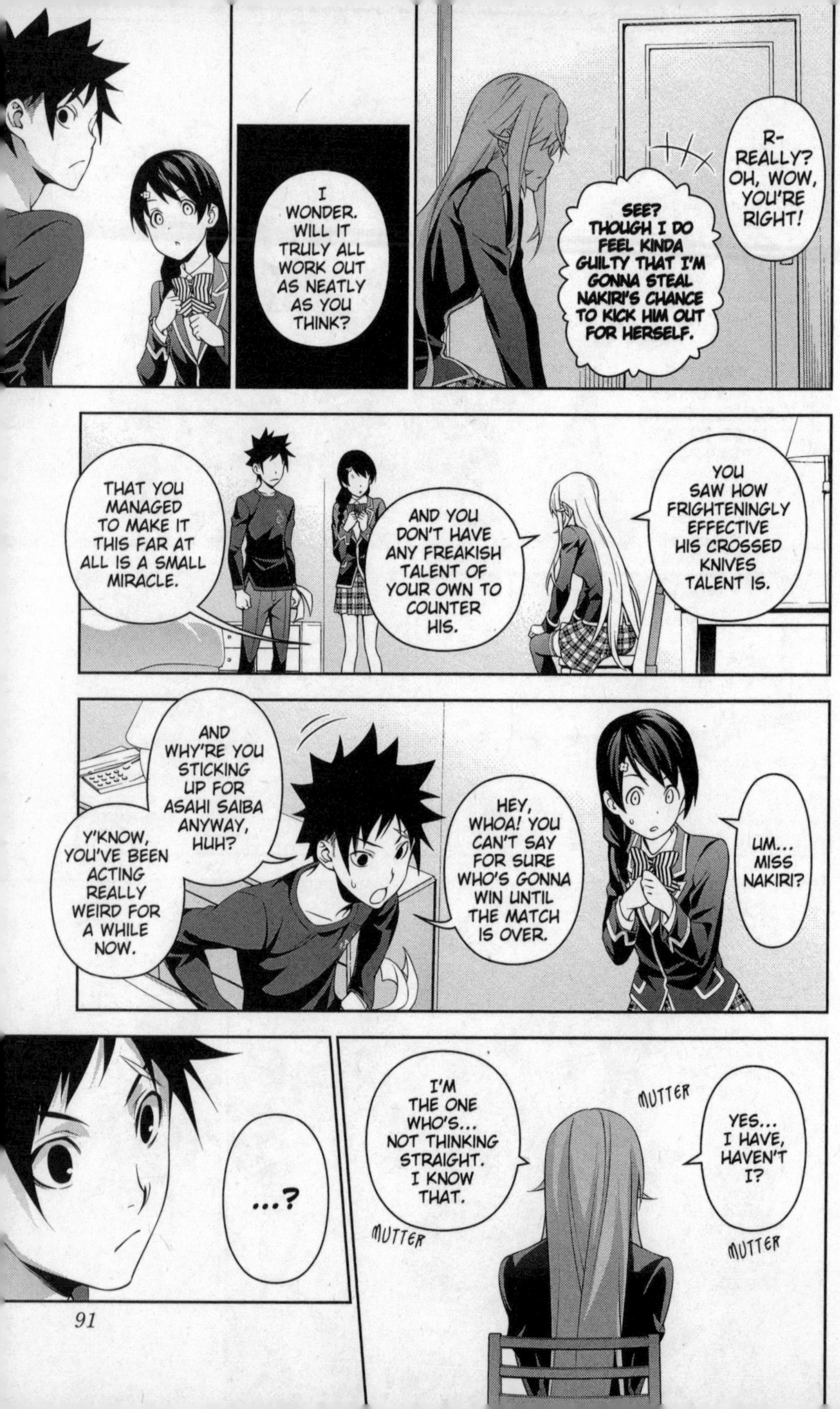
R-REALLY? OH, WOW, YOU'RE RIGHT!
SEE? THOUGH I DO FEEL KINDA GUILTY THAT I'M GONNA STEAL NAKIRI'S CHANCE TO KICK HIM OUT FOR HERSELF.
I WONDER. WILL IT TRULY ALL WORK OUT AS NEATLY AS YOU THINK?
YOU SAW HOW FRIGHTENINGLY EFFECTIVE HIS CROSSED KNIVES TALENT IS.
AND YOU DON'T HAVE ANY FREAKISH TALENT OF YOUR OWN TO COUNTER HIS.
THAT YOU MANAGED TO MAKE IT THIS FAR AT ALL IS A SMALL MIRACLE.
UM... MISS NAKIRI?
HEY, WHOA! YOU CAN'T SAY FOR SURE WHO'S GONNA WIN UNTIL THE MATCH IS OVER.
AND WHY'RE YOU STICKING UP FOR ASAHI SAIBA ANYWAY, HUH?
Y'KNOW, YOU'VE BEEN ACTING REALLY WEIRD FOR A WHILE NOW.
YES... I HAVE, HAVEN'T I?
MUTTER
I'M THE ONE WHO'S... NOT THINKING STRAIGHT. I KNOW THAT.
MUTTER
MUTTER
...?

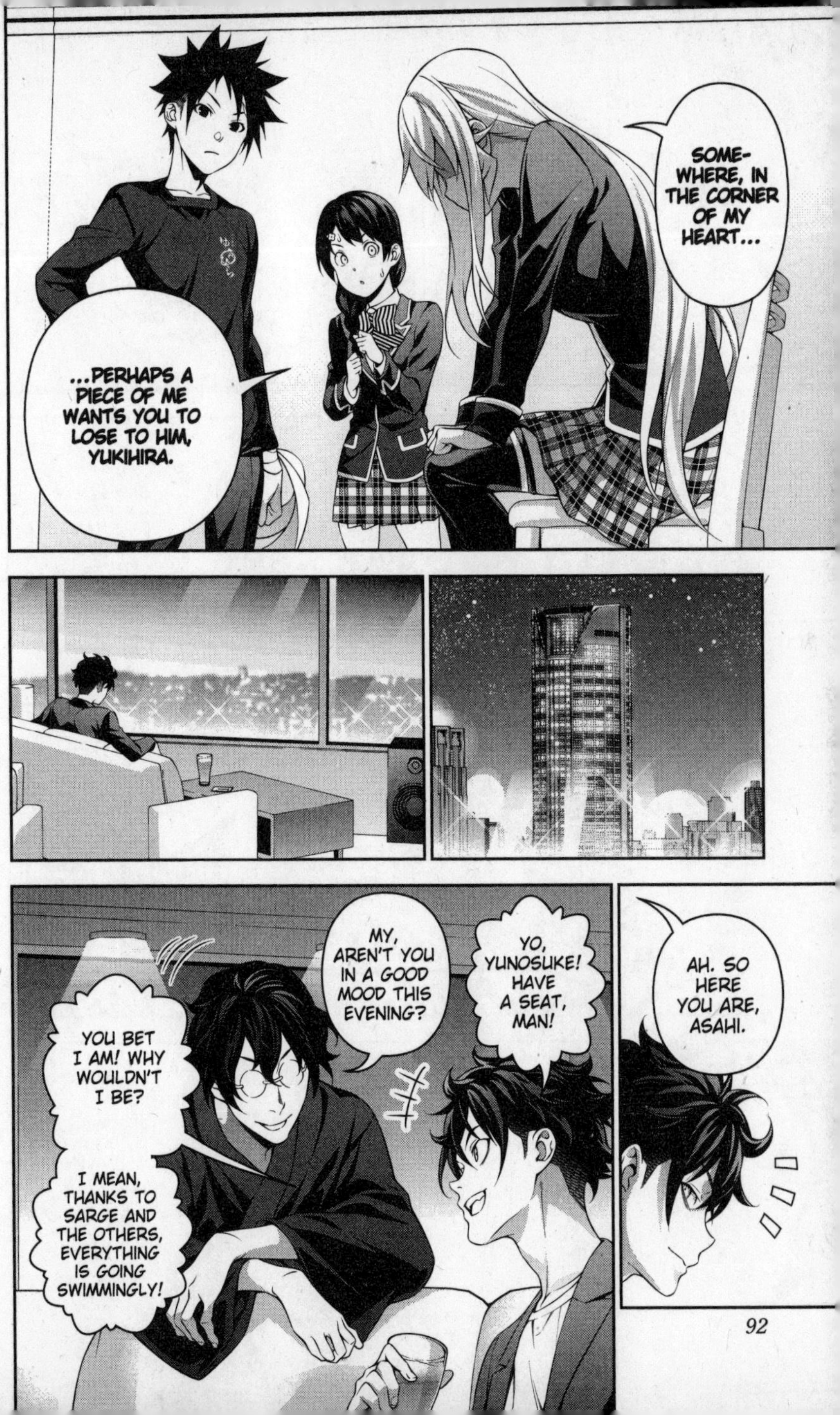
SOMEWHERE, IN THE CORNER OF MY HEART...
...PERHAPS A PIECE OF ME WANTS YOU TO LOSE TO HIM, YUKIHIRA.
AH. SO HERE YOU ARE, ASAHI.
YO, YUNOSUKE! HAVE A SEAT, MAN!
MY, AREN'T YOU IN A GOOD MOOD THIS EVENING?
YOU BET I AM! WHY WOULDN'T I BE?
I MEAN, THANKS TO SARGE AND THE OTHERS, EVERYTHING IS GOING SWIMMINGLY!

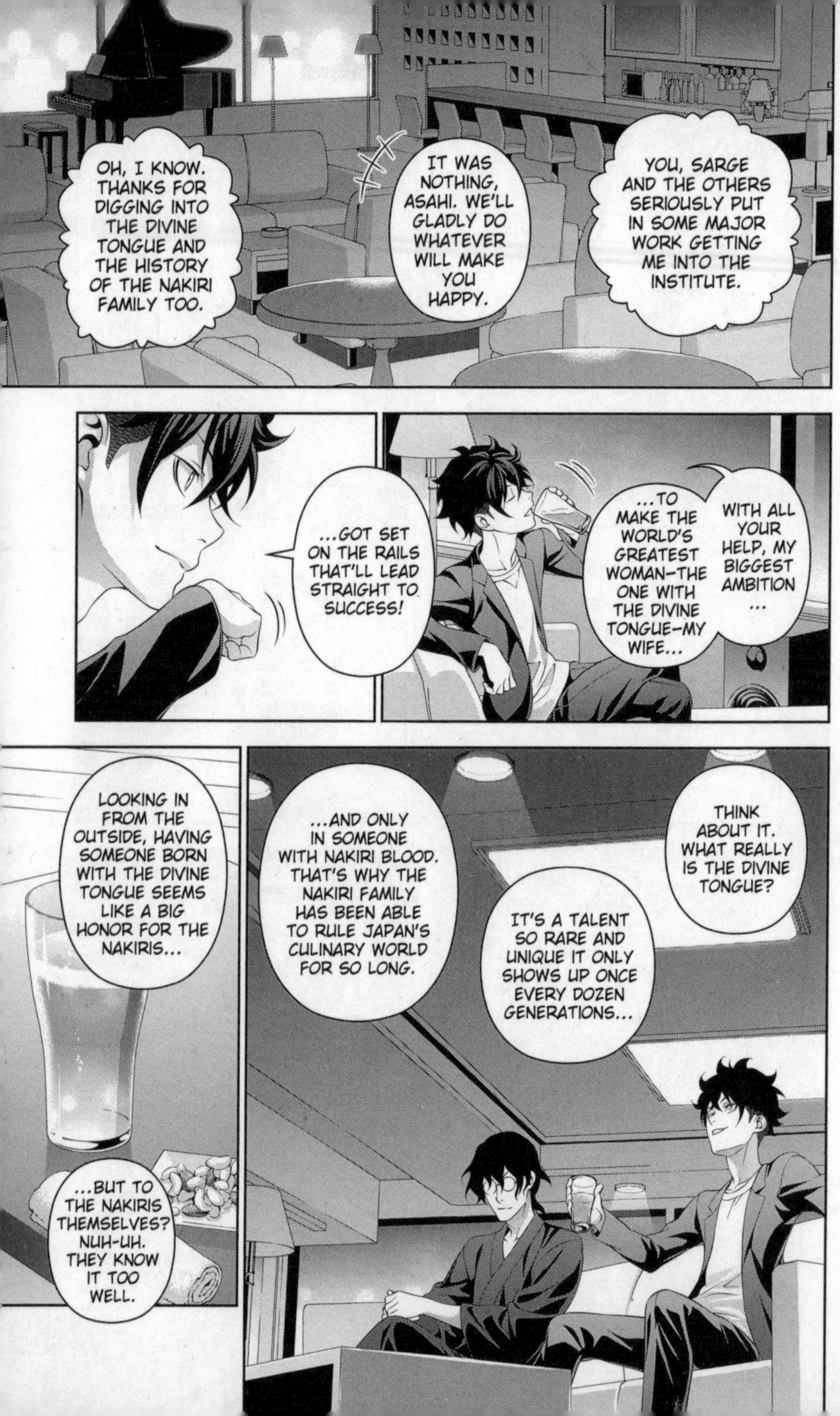
YOU, SARGE AND THE OTHERS SERIOUSLY PUT IN SOME MAJOR WORK GETTING ME INTO THE INSTITUTE.
IT WAS NOTHING, ASAHI. WE'LL GLADLY DO WHATEVER WILL MAKE YOU HAPPY.
OH, I KNOW. THANKS FOR DIGGING INTO THE DIVINE TONGUE AND THE HISTORY OF THE NAKIRI FAMILY TOO.
WITH ALL YOUR HELP, MY BIGGEST AMBITION...
...TO MAKE THE WORLD'S GREATEST WOMAN—THE ONE WITH THE DIVINE TONGUE—MY WIFE...
...GOT SET ON THE RAILS THAT'LL LEAD STRAIGHT TO SUCCESS!
THINK ABOUT IT. WHAT REALLY IS THE DIVINE TONGUE?
IT'S A TALENT SO RARE AND UNIQUE IT ONLY SHOWS UP ONCE EVERY DOZEN GENERATIONS...
...AND ONLY IN SOMEONE WITH NAKIRI BLOOD. THAT'S WHY THE NAKIRI FAMILY HAS BEEN ABLE TO RULE JAPAN'S CULINARY WORLD FOR SO LONG.
LOOKING IN FROM THE OUTSIDE, HAVING SOMEONE BORN WITH THE DIVINE TONGUE SEEMS LIKE A BIG HONOR FOR THE NAKIRIS...
...BUT TO THE NAKIRIS THEMSELVES? NUH-UH. THEY KNOW IT TOO WELL.

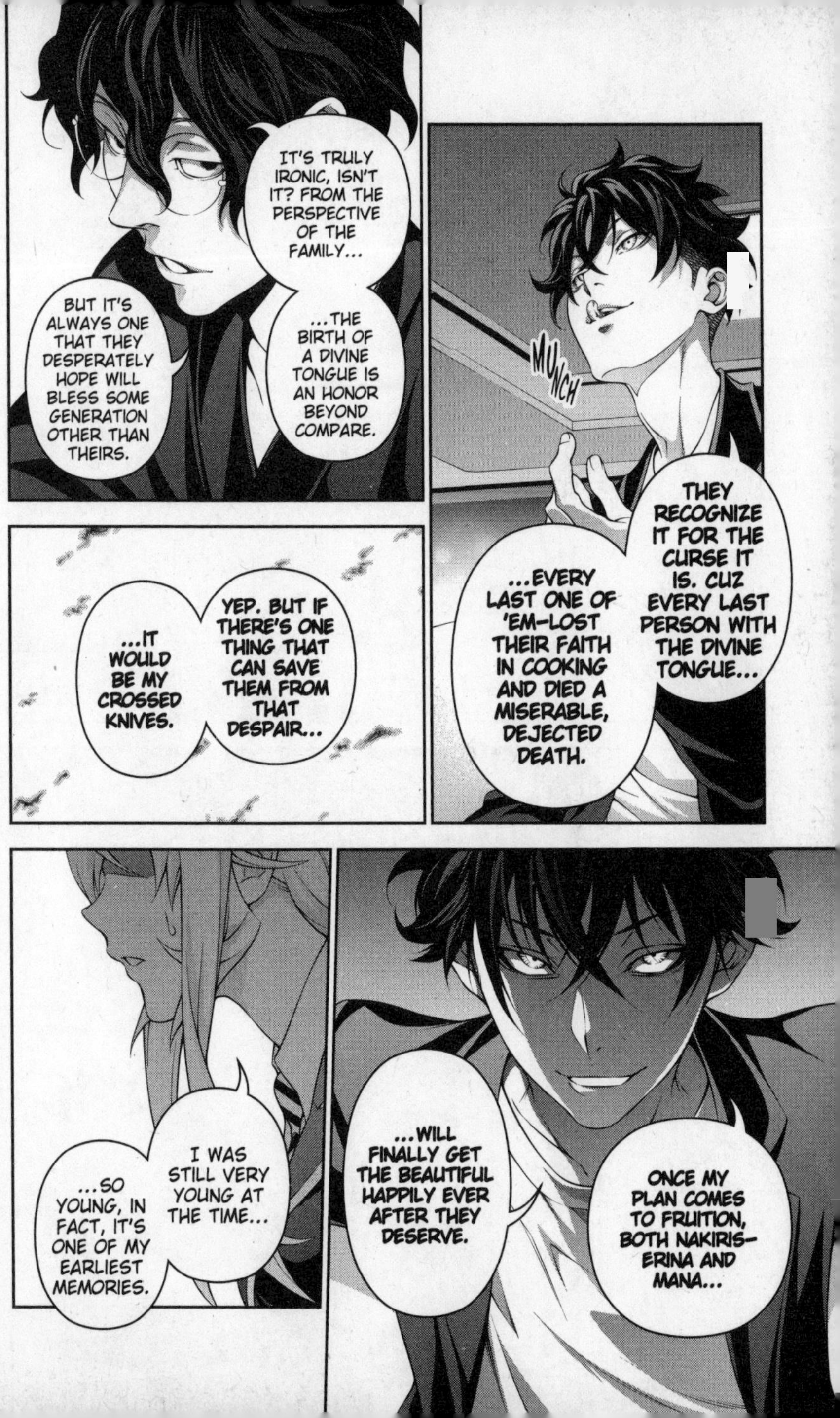
MUNCH
THEY RECOGNIZE IT FOR THE CURSE IT IS. CUZ EVERY LAST PERSON WITH THE DIVINE TONGUE...
...EVERY LAST ONE OF 'EM—LOST THEIR FAITH IN COOKING AND DIED A MISERABLE, DEJECTED DEATH.
IT'S TRULY IRONIC, ISN'T IT? FROM THE PERSPECTIVE OF THE FAMILY...
...THE BIRTH OF A DIVINE TONGUE IS AN HONOR BEYOND COMPARE.
BUT IT'S ALWAYS ONE THAT THEY DESPERATELY HOPE WILL BLESS SOME GENERATION OTHER THAN THEIRS.
YEP. BUT IF THERE'S ONE THING THAT CAN SAVE THEM FROM THAT DESPAIR...
...IT WOULD BE MY CROSSED KNIVES.
ONCE MY PLAN COMES TO FRUITION, BOTH NAKIRIS—ERINA AND MANA...
...WILL FINALLY GET THE BEAUTIFUL HAPPILY EVER AFTER THEY DESERVE.
I WAS STILL VERY YOUNG AT THE TIME...
...SO YOUNG, IN FACT, IT'S ONE OF MY EARLIEST MEMORIES.

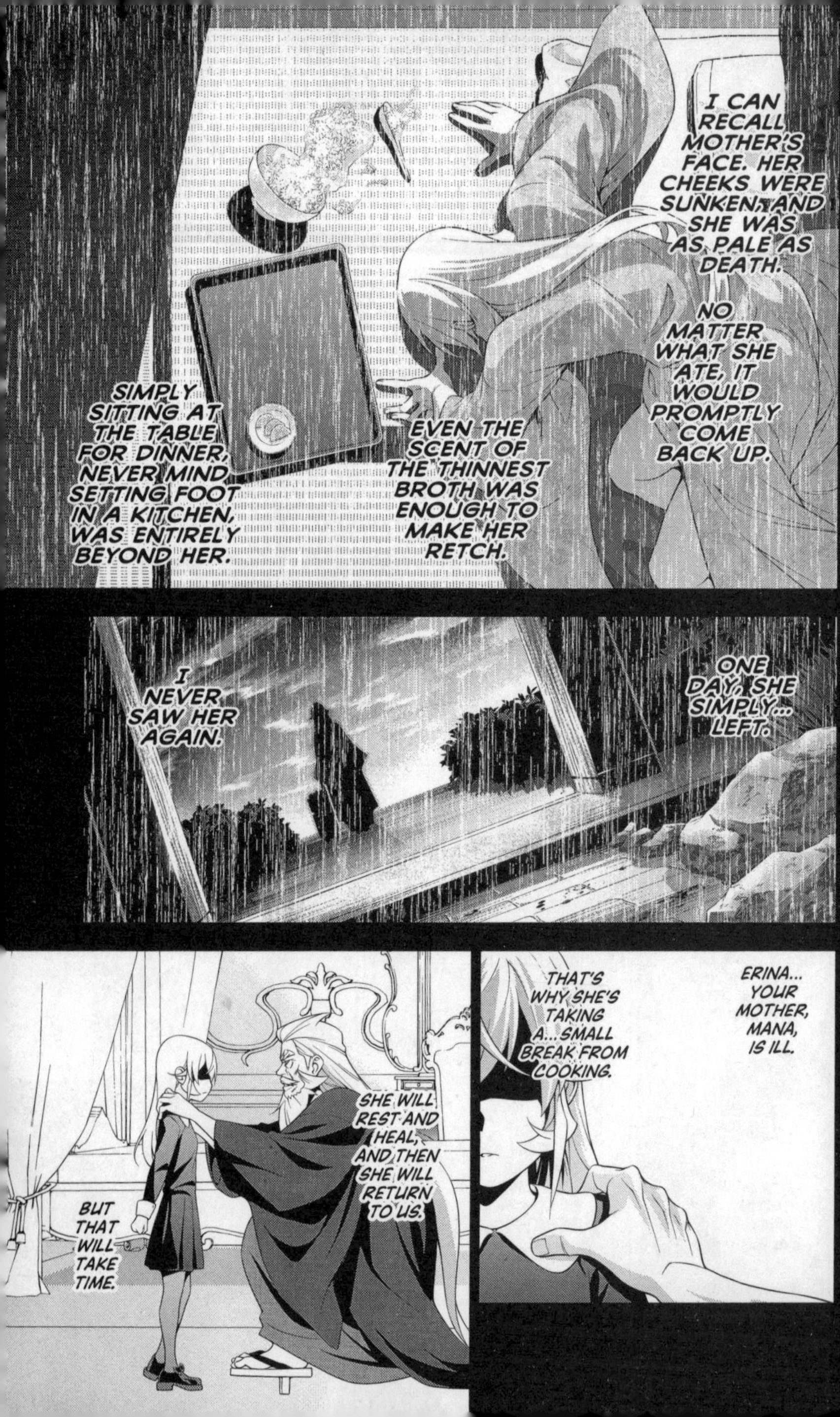
I CAN RECALL MOTHER'S FACE. HER CHEEKS WERE SUNKEN, AND SHE WAS AS PALE AS DEATH.
NO MATTER WHAT SHE ATE, IT WOULD PROMPTLY COME BACK UP.
EVEN THE SCENT OF THE THINNEST BROTH WAS ENOUGH TO MAKE HER RETCH.
SIMPLY SITTING AT THE TABLE FOR DINNER, NEVER MIND SETTING FOOT IN A KITCHEN, WAS ENTIRELY BEYOND HER.
ONE DAY, SHE SIMPLY... LEFT.
I NEVER SAW HER AGAIN.
ERINA... YOUR MOTHER, MANA, IS ILL.
THAT'S WHY SHE'S TAKING A... SMALL BREAK FROM COOKING.
SHE WILL REST AND HEAL, AND THEN SHE WILL RETURN TO US.
BUT THAT WILL TAKE TIME.

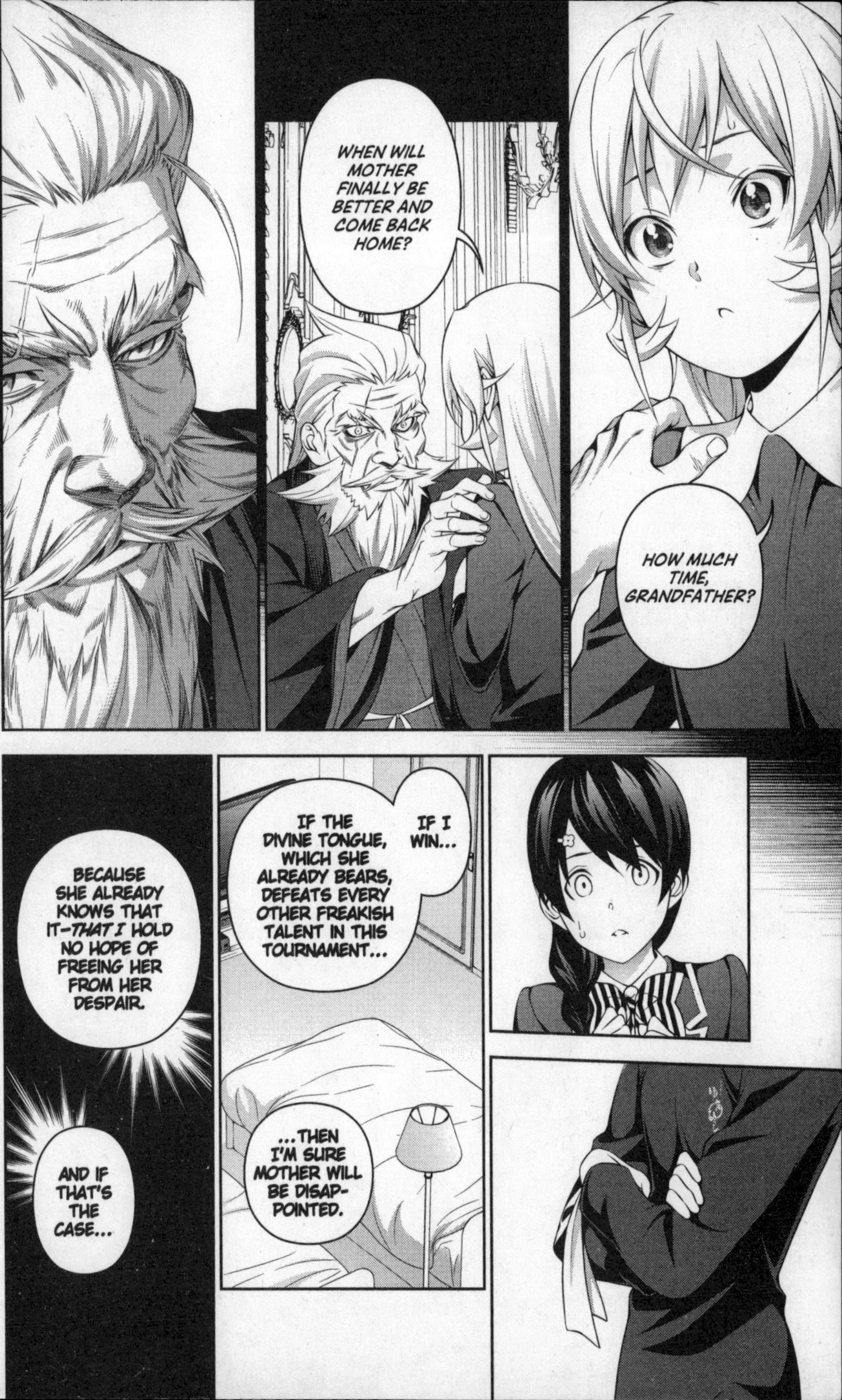
HOW MUCH TIME, GRANDFATHER?
WHEN WILL MOTHER FINALLY BE BETTER AND COME BACK HOME?
IF I WIN...
IF THE DIVINE TONGUE, WHICH SHE ALREADY BEARS, DEFEATS EVERY OTHER FREAKISH TALENT IN THIS TOURNAMENT...
...THEN I'M SURE MOTHER WILL BE DISAPPOINTED.
BECAUSE SHE ALREADY KNOWS THAT IT-THAT I HOLD NO HOPE OF FREEING HER FROM HER DESPAIR.
AND IF THAT'S THE CASE...

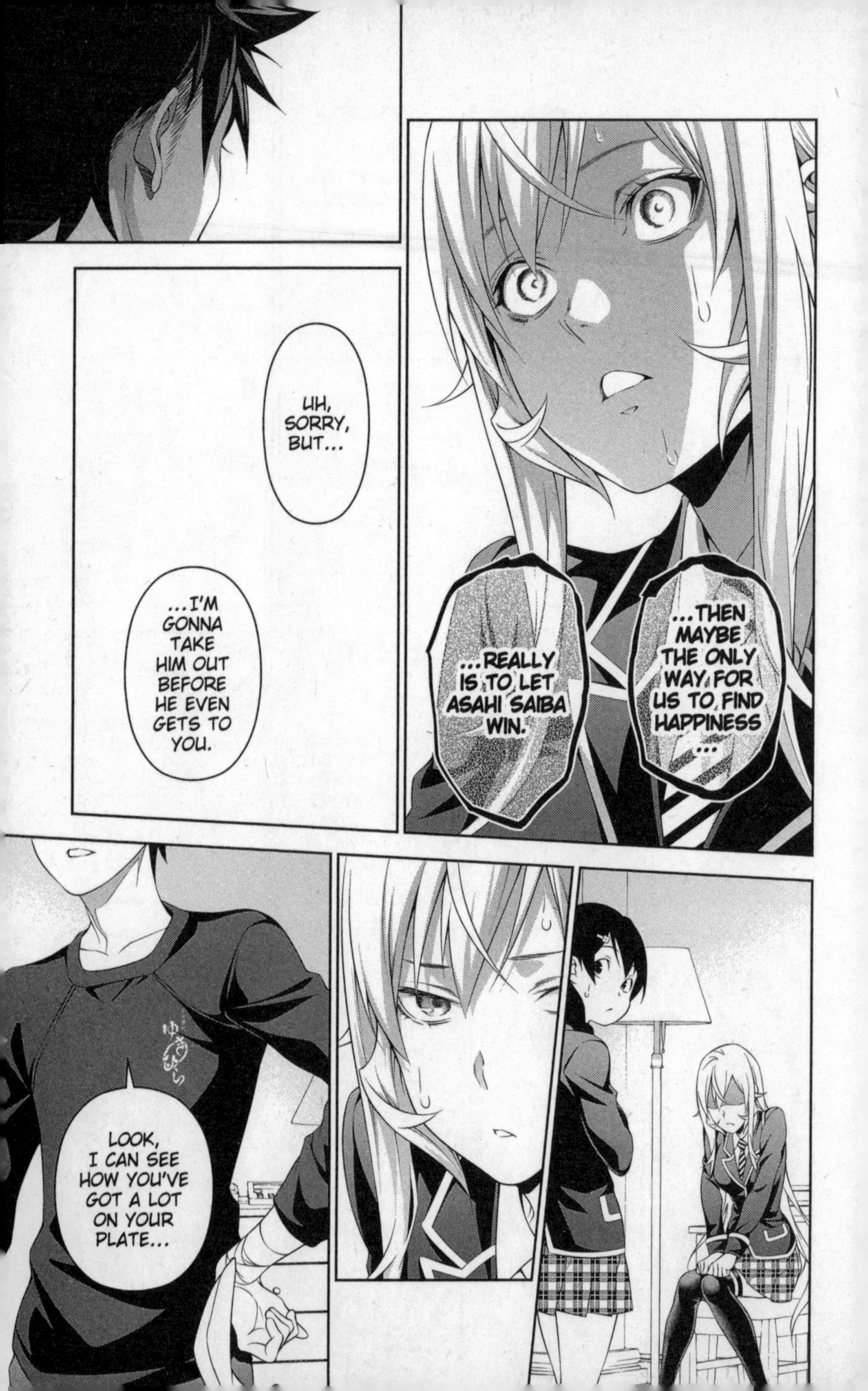
...THEN MAYBE THE ONLY WAY FOR US TO FIND HAPPINESS...
...REALLY IS TO LET ASAHI SAIBA WIN.
UH, SORRY, BUT...
...I'M GONNA TAKE HIM OUT BEFORE HE EVEN GETS TO YOU.
LOOK, I CAN SEE HOW YOU'VE GOT A LOT ON YOUR PLATE...

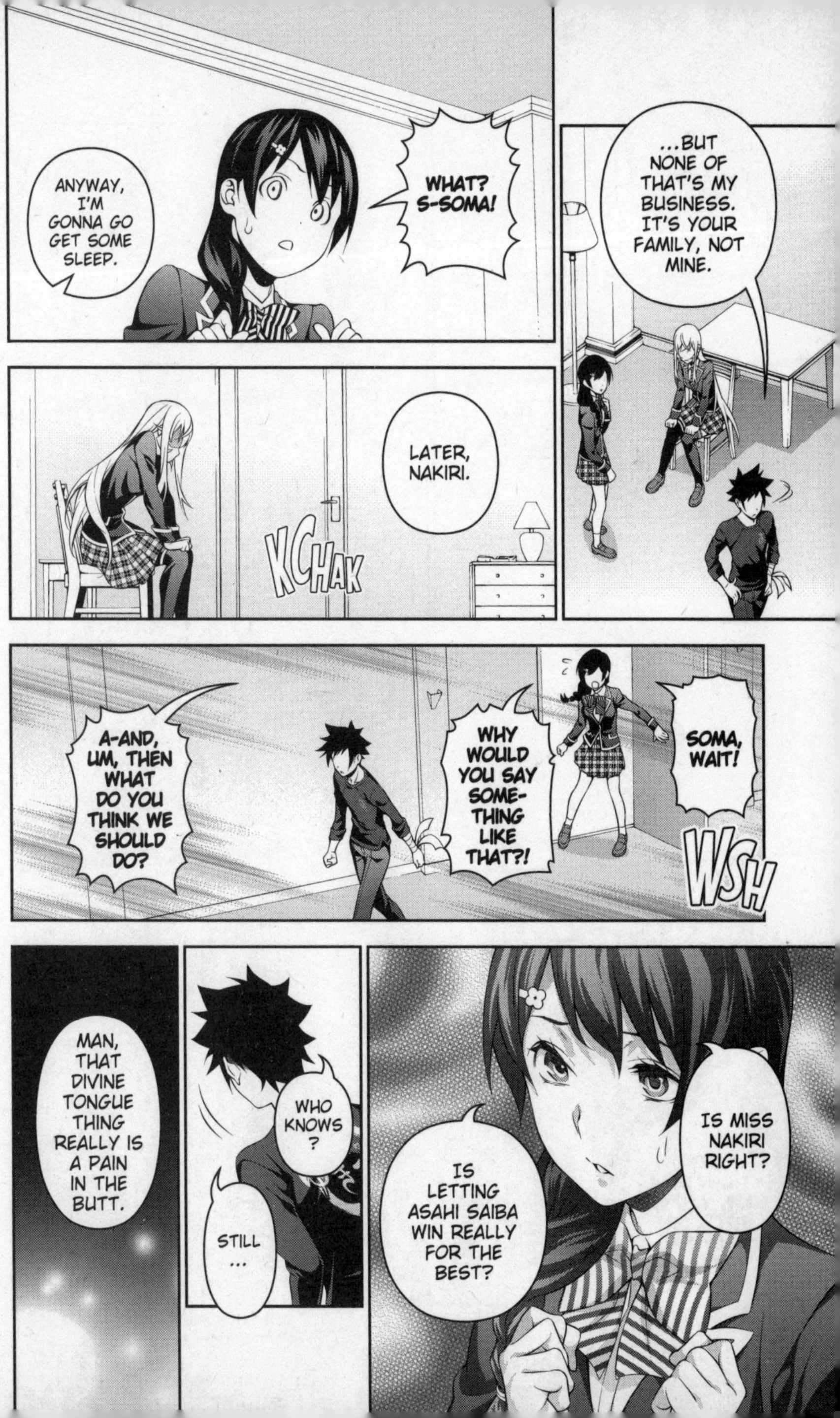
...BUT NONE OF THAT'S MY BUSINESS. IT'S YOUR FAMILY, NOT MINE.
ANYWAY, I'M GONNA GO GET SOME SLEEP.
WHAT? S-SOMA!
LATER, NAKIRI.
KCHAK
SOMA, WAIT!
WSH
WHY WOULD YOU SAY SOME-THING LIKE THAT?!
A-AND, UM, THEN WHAT DO YOU THINK WE SHOULD DO?
IS MISS NAKIRI RIGHT?
IS LETTING ASAHI SAIBA WIN REALLY FOR THE BEST?
WHO KNOWS?
STILL...
MAN, THAT DIVINE TONGUE THING REALLY IS A PAIN IN THE BUTT.

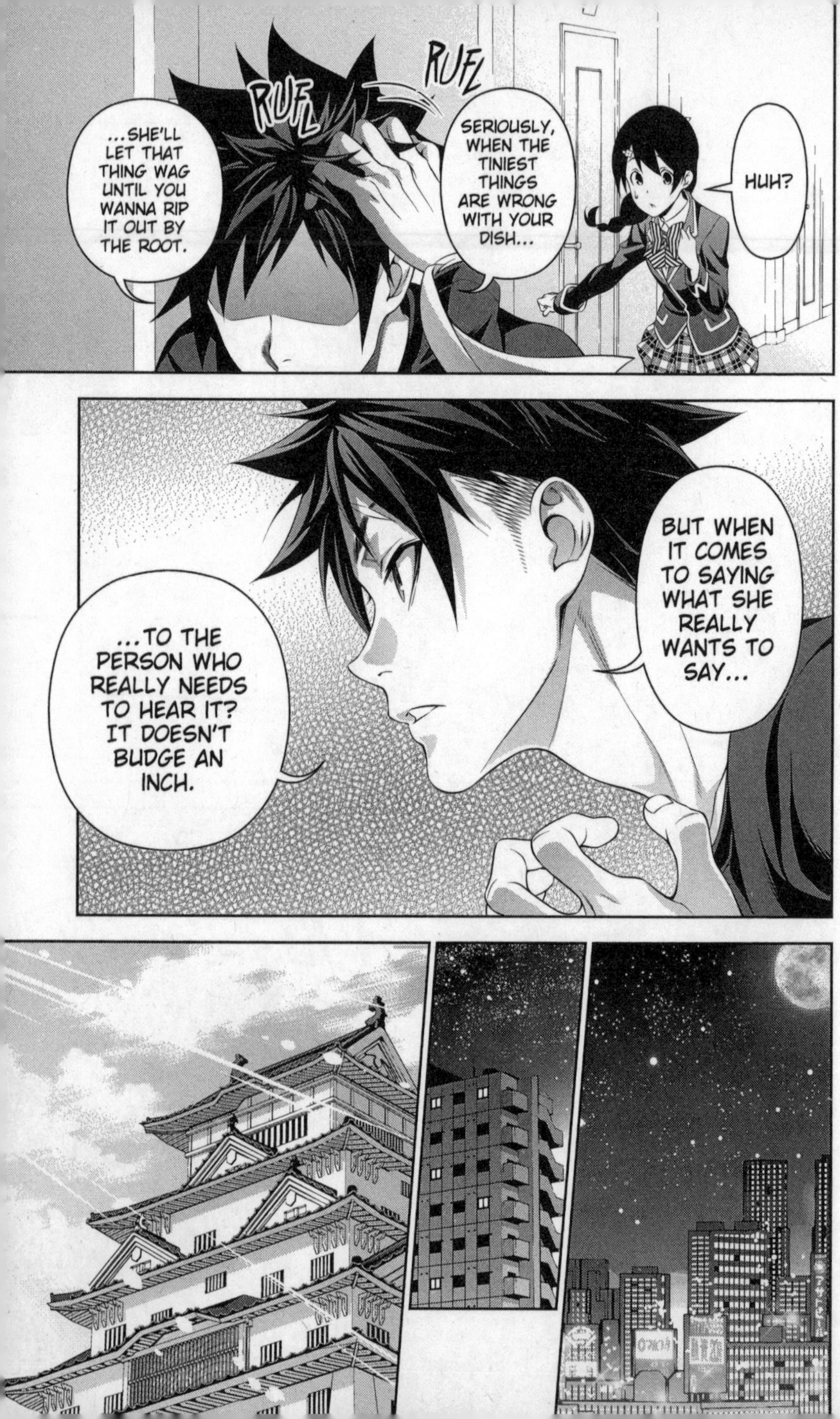
HUH?
RUFL
SERIOUSLY, WHEN THE TINIEST THINGS ARE WRONG WITH YOUR DISH...
RUFL
...SHE'LL LET THAT THING WAG UNTIL YOU WANNA RIP IT OUT BY THE ROOT.
BUT WHEN IT COMES TO SAYING WHAT SHE REALLY WANTS TO SAY...
...TO THE PERSON WHO REALLY NEEDS TO HEAR IT? IT DOESN'T BUDGE AN INCH.

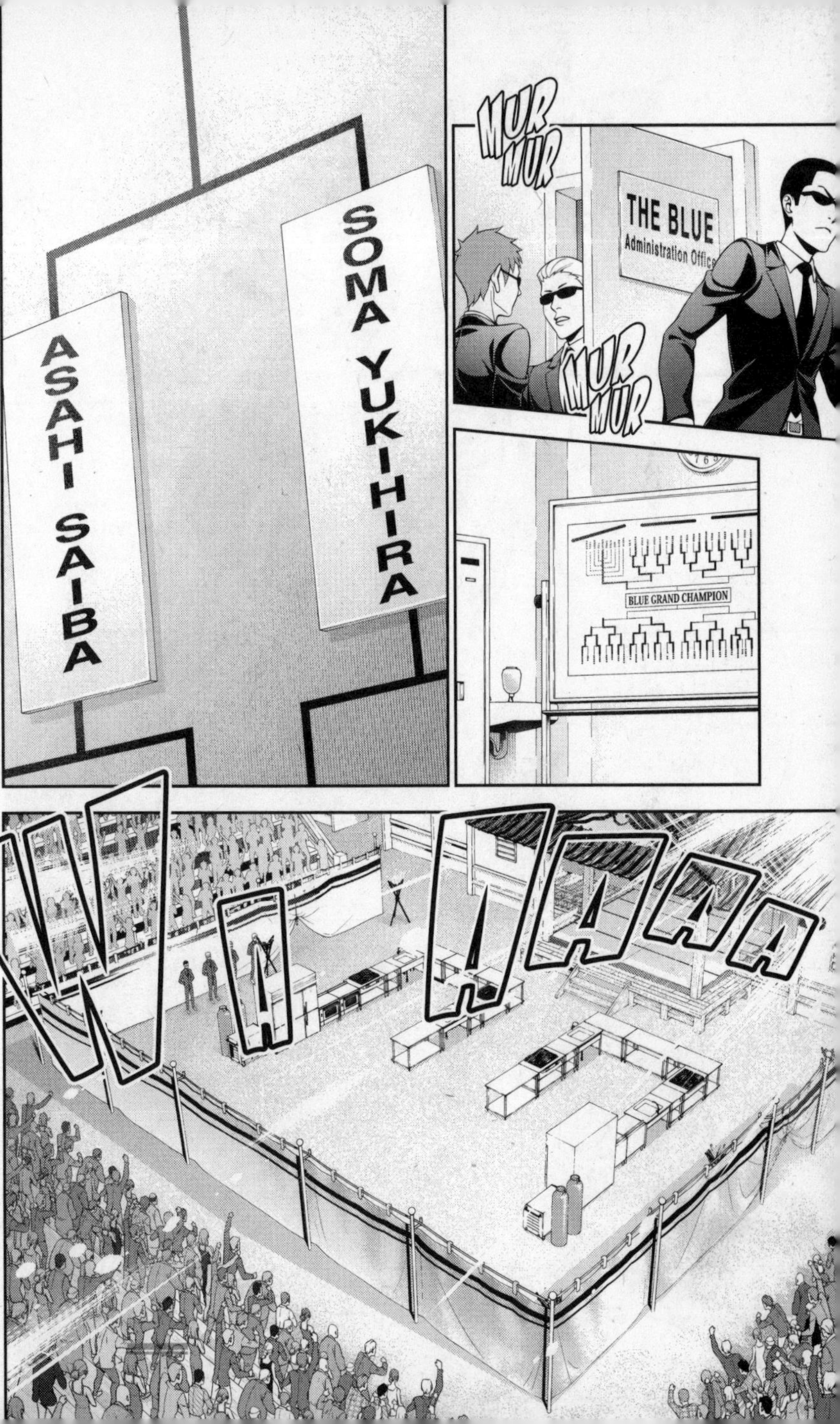
MUR MUR
THE BLUE
Administration Offic
MUR MUR
BLUE GRAND CHAMPION
SOMA YUKIHIRA
ASAHI SAIBA
WAAAAA

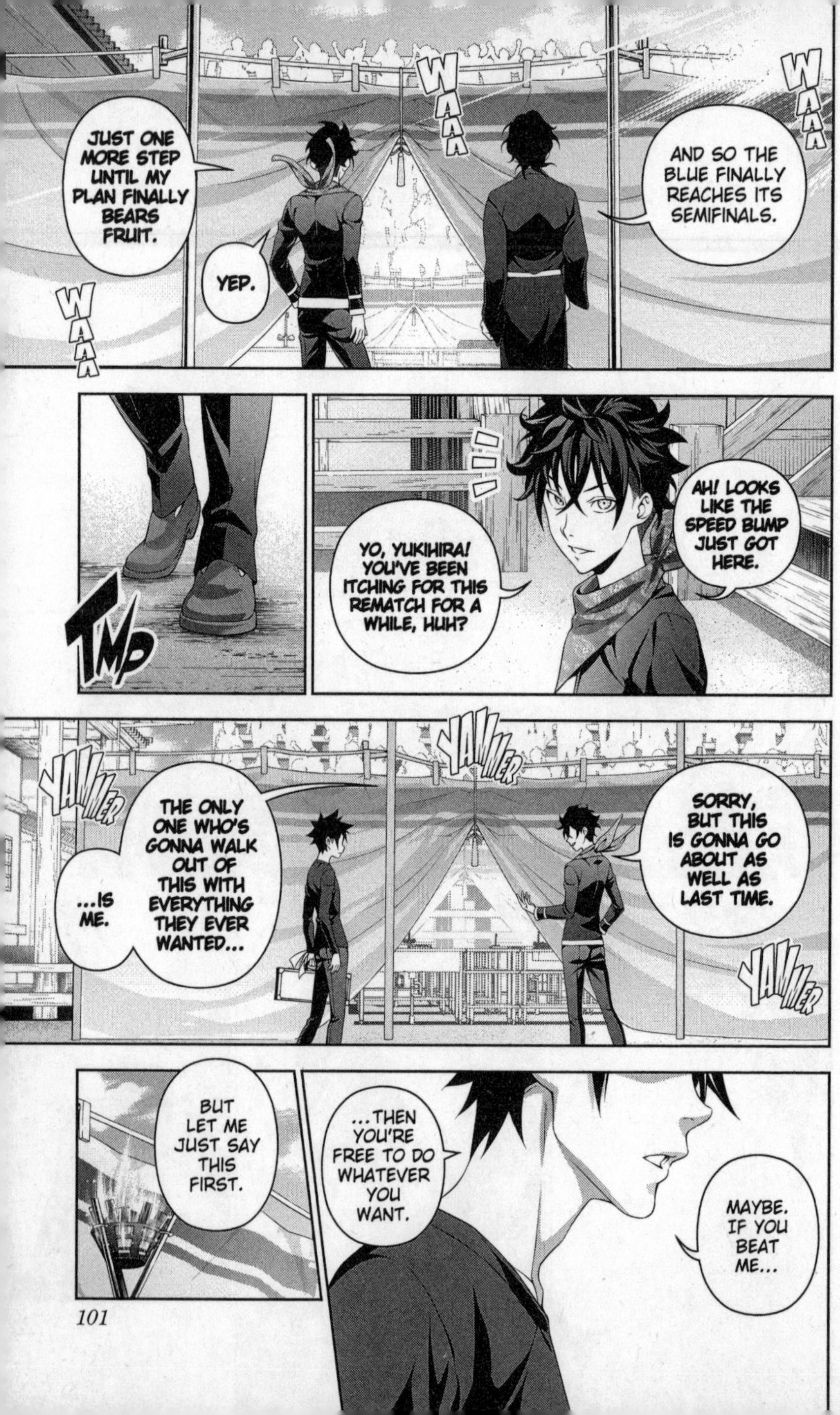
WAAA
AND SO THE BLUE FINALLY REACHES ITS SEMIFINALS.
WAAA
YEP.
JUST ONE MORE STEP UNTIL MY PLAN FINALLY BEARS FRUIT.
WAAA
!!
AH! LOOKS LIKE THE SPEED BUMP JUST GOT HERE.
YO, YUKIHIRA! YOU'VE BEEN ITCHING FOR THIS REMATCH FOR A WHILE, HUH?
TMP
YAMMER
SORRY, BUT THIS IS GONNA GO ABOUT AS WELL AS LAST TIME.
YAMMER
THE ONLY ONE WHO'S GONNA WALK OUT OF THIS WITH EVERYTHING THEY EVER WANTED...
...IS ME.
YAMMER
MAYBE. IF YOU BEAT ME...
...THEN YOU'RE FREE TO DO WHATEVER YOU WANT.
BUT LET ME JUST SAY THIS FIRST.

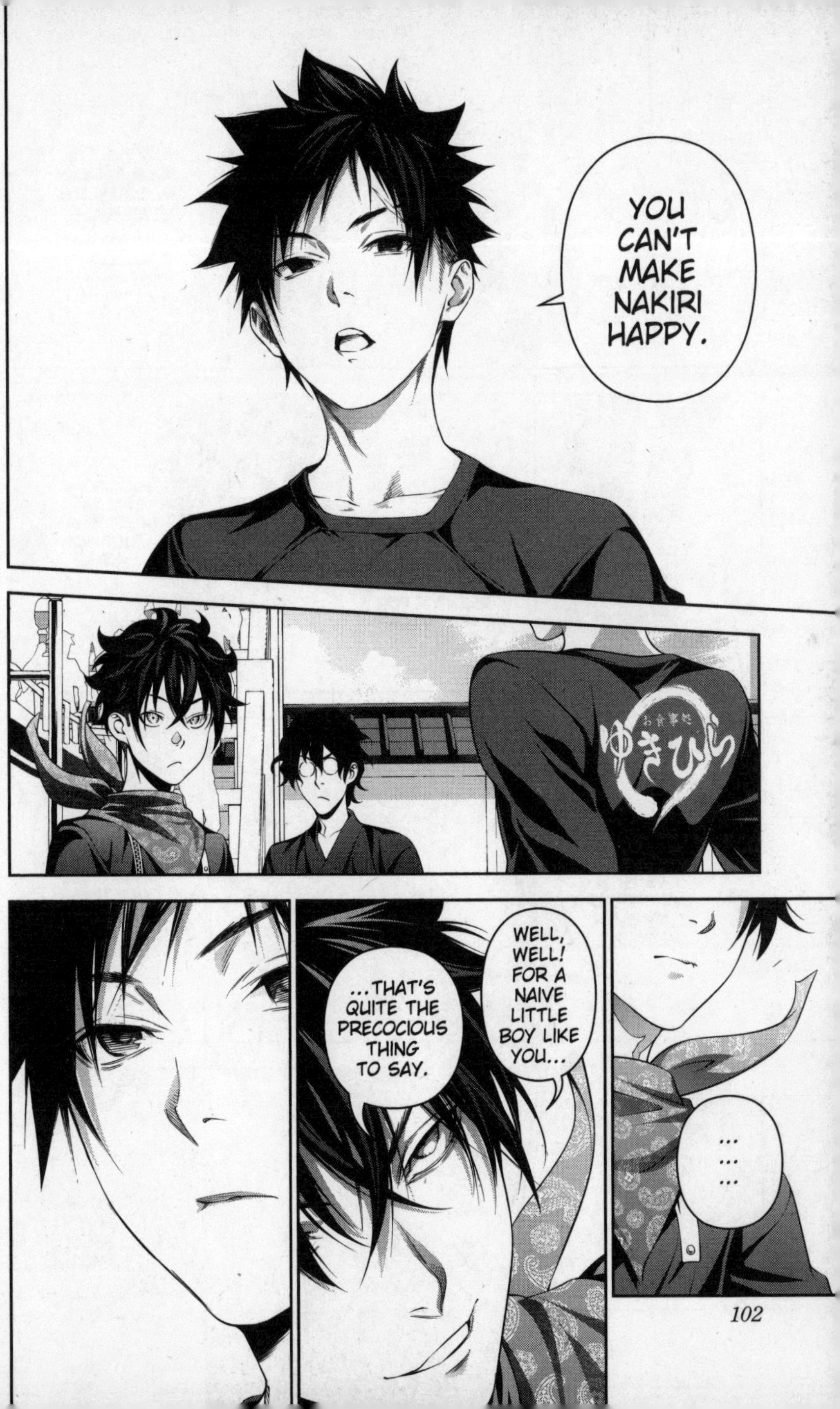
YOU CAN'T MAKE NAKIRI HAPPY.
ゆきひら
...
...
...
WELL, WELL! FOR A NAIVE LITTLE BOY LIKE YOU...
...THAT'S QUITE THE PRECOCIOUS THING TO SAY.

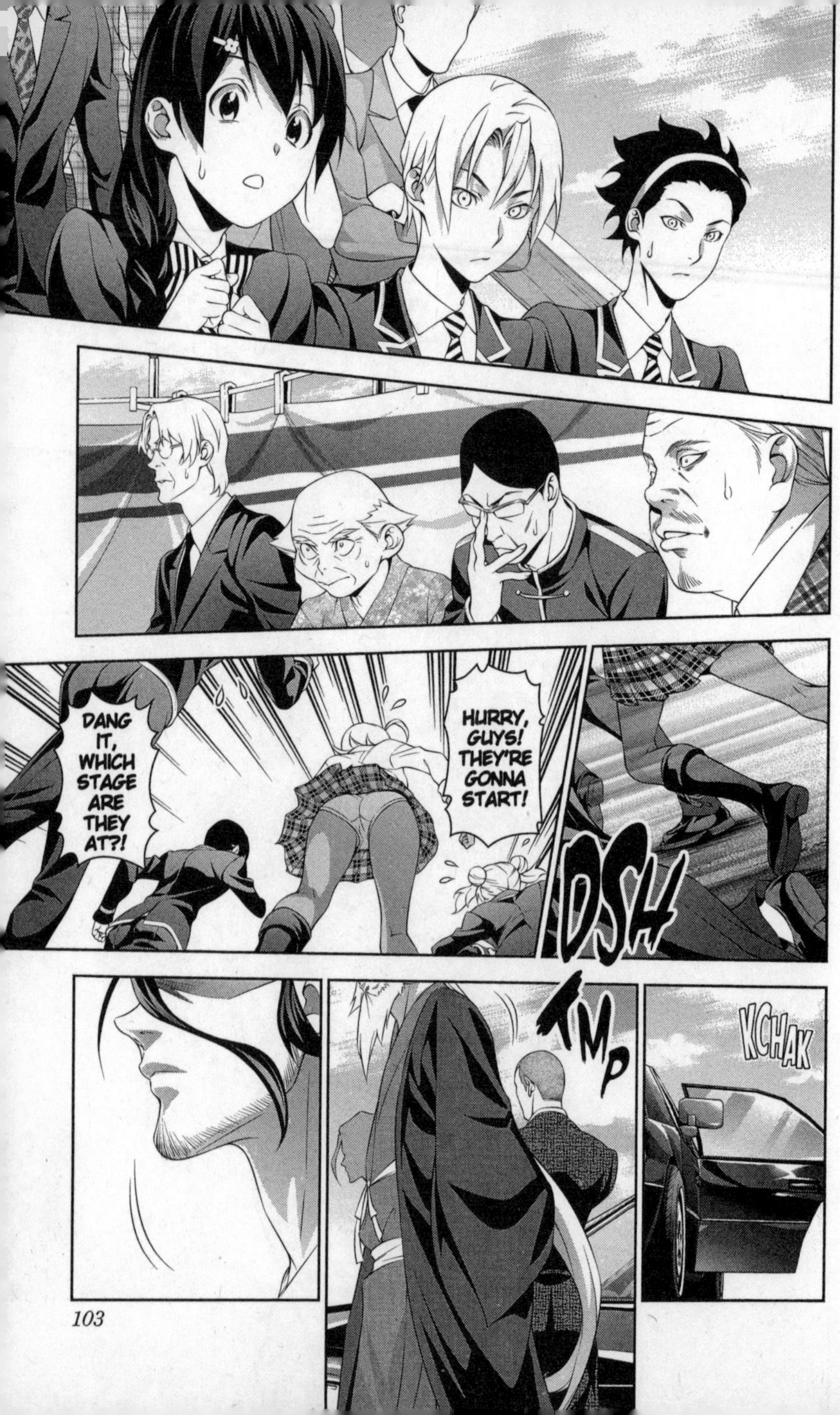
DSH
HURRY, GUYS! THEY'RE GONNA START!
DANG IT, WHICH STAGE ARE THEY AT?!
KCHAK
TMP

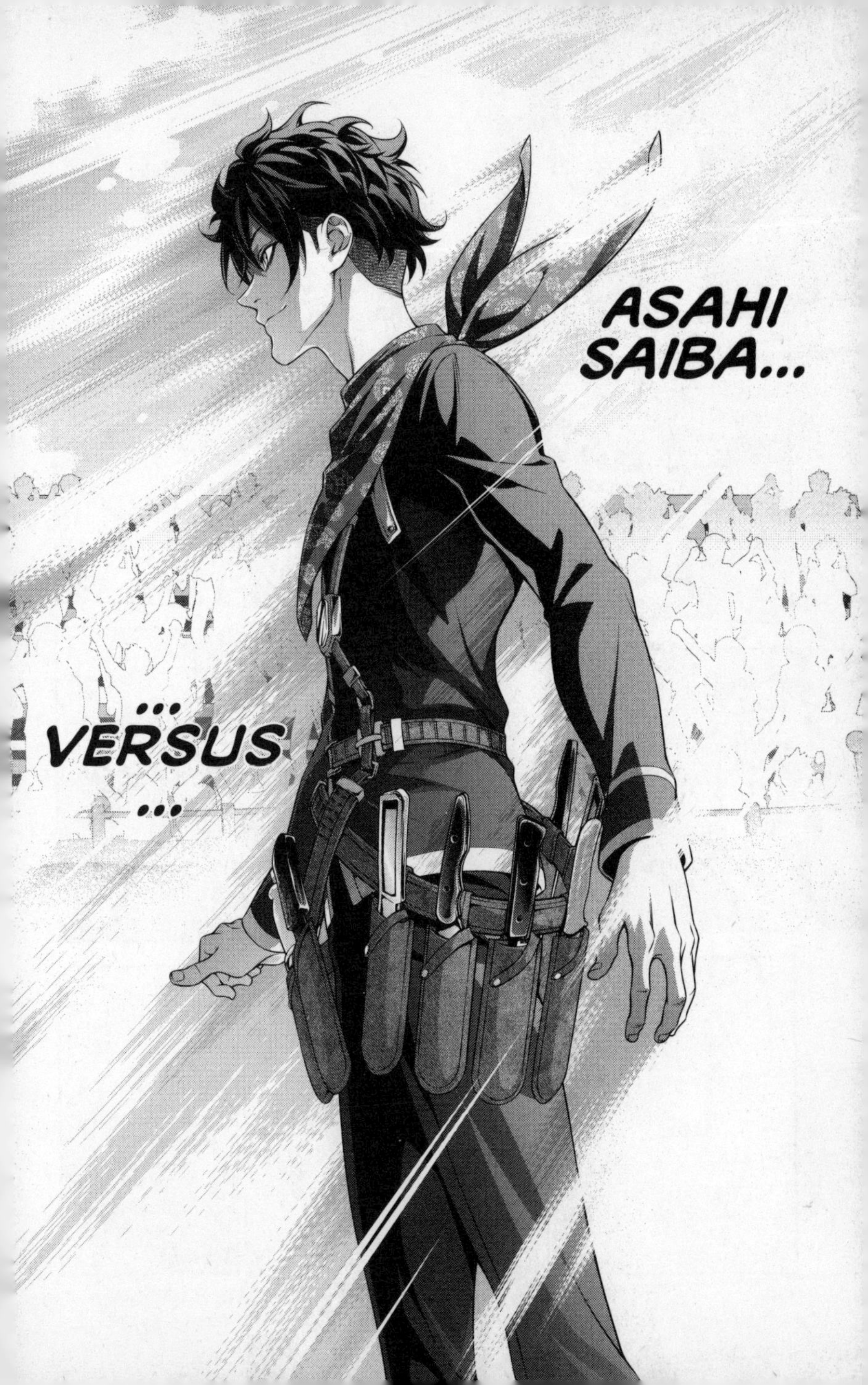
ASAHI SAIBA...
... VERSUS ...

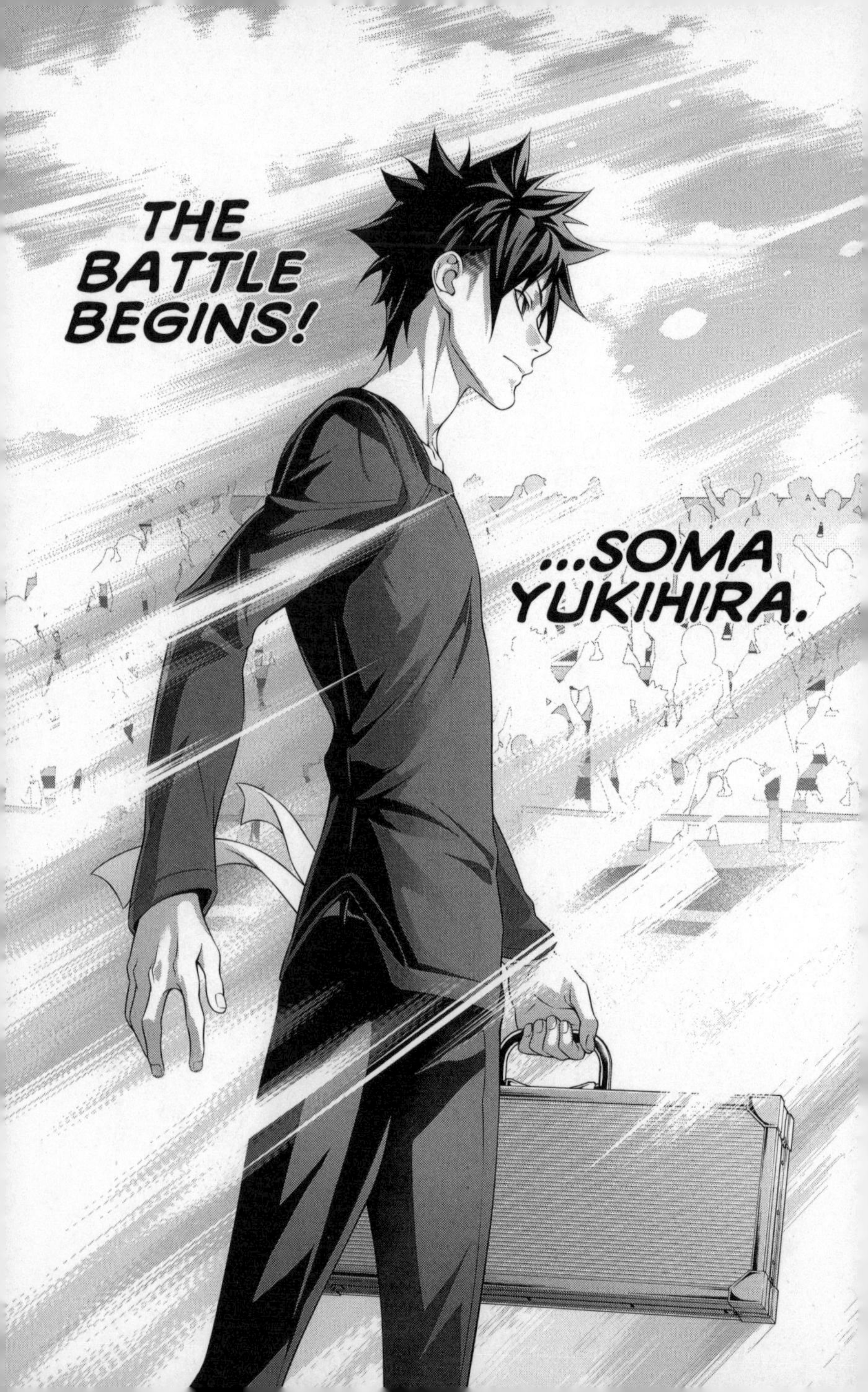
THE BATTLE BEGINS!
...SOMA YUKIHIRA.

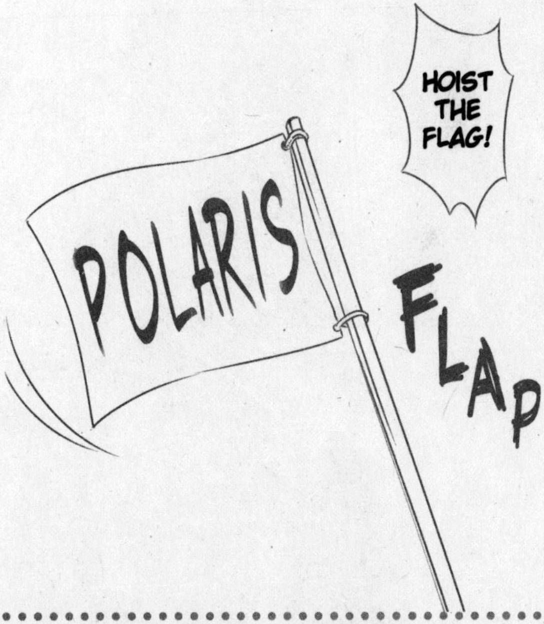
HOIST THE FLAG!
POLARIS
FLAP

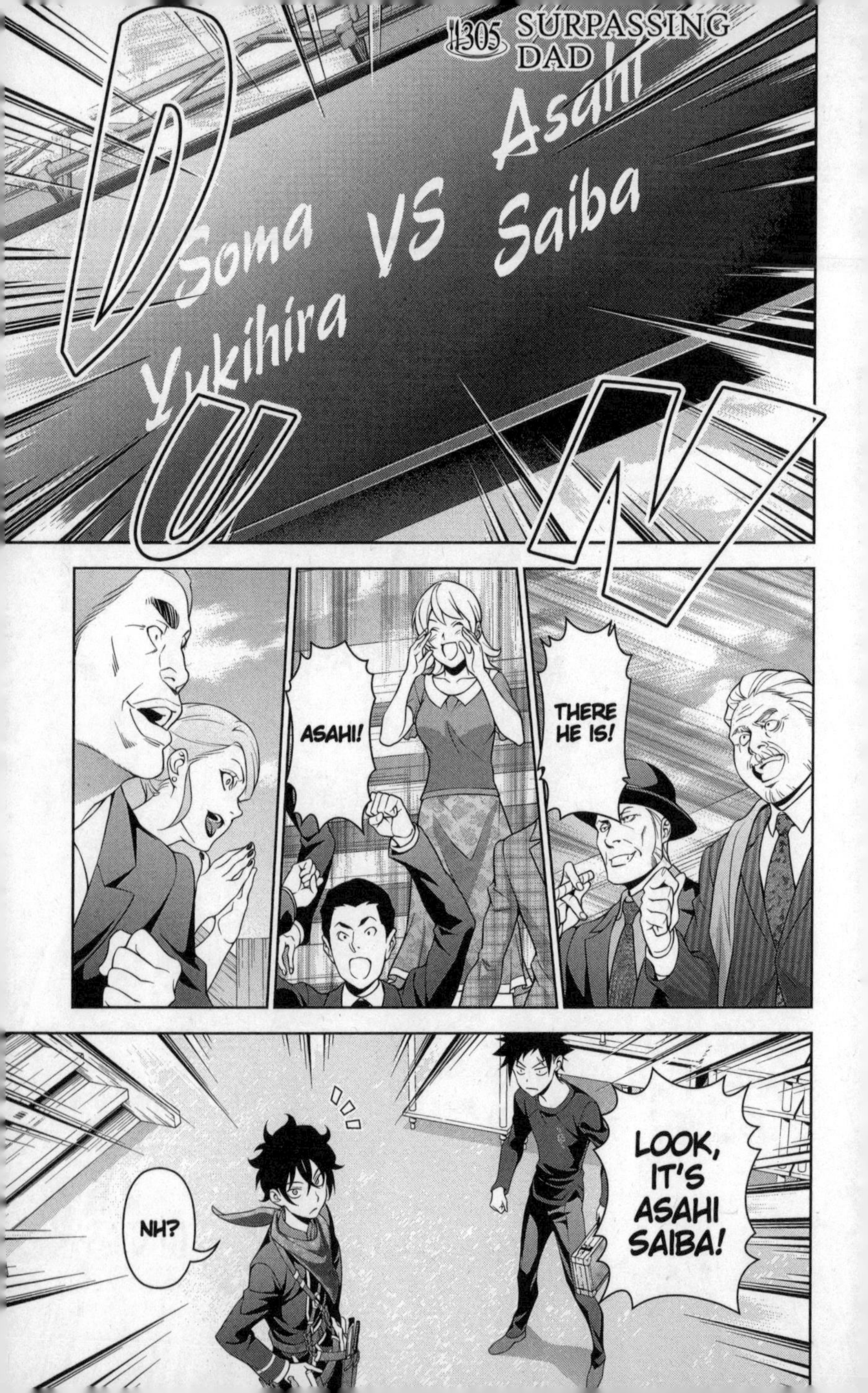
#305 SURPASSING DAD!
DUN
Soma Yukihira VS Asahi Saiba
THERE HE IS!
ASAHI!
LOOK, IT'S ASAHI SAIBA!
NH?

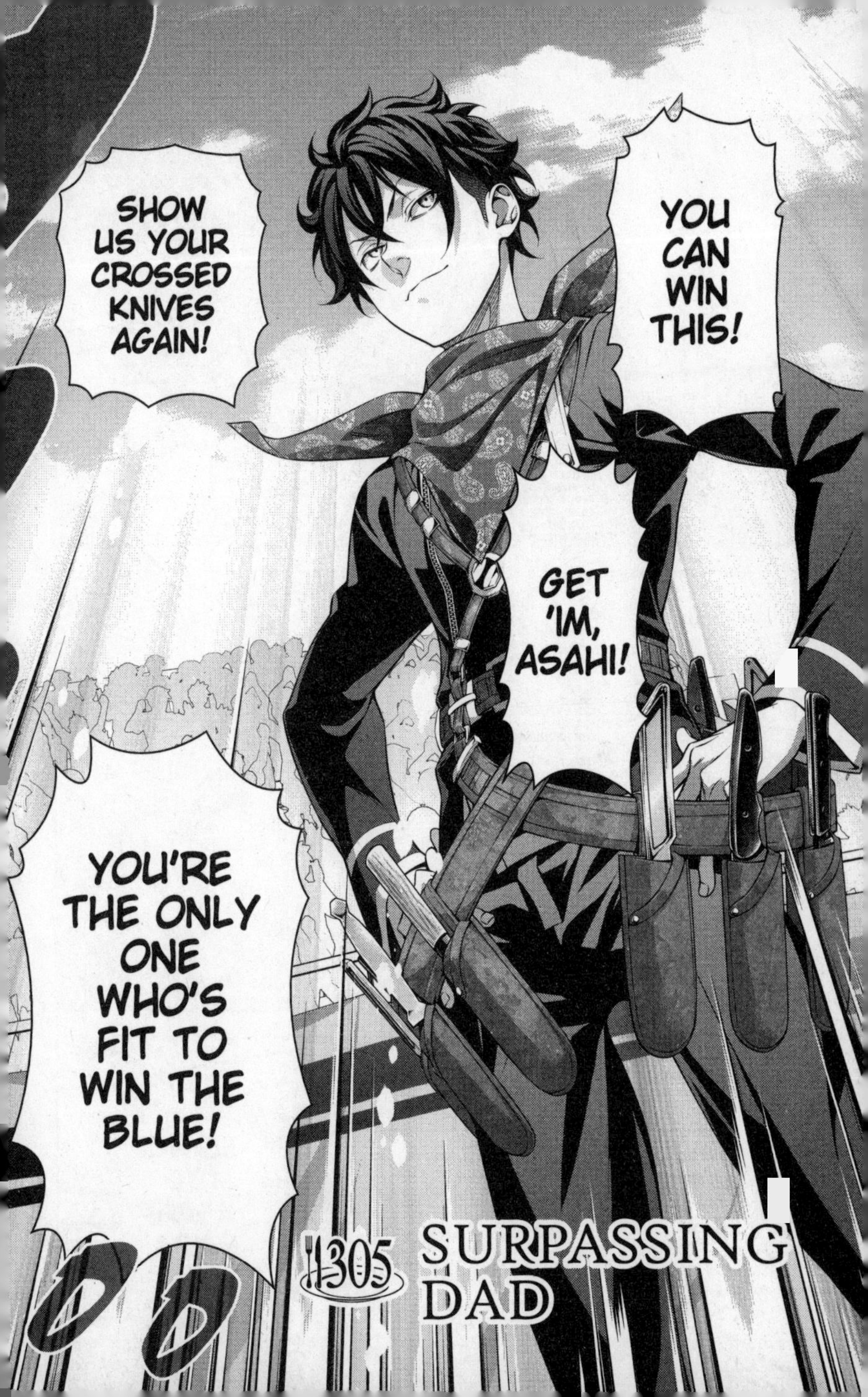
YOU CAN WIN THIS!
SHOW US YOUR CROSSED KNIVES AGAIN!
GET 'IM, ASAHI!
YOU'RE THE ONLY ONE WHO'S FIT TO WIN THE BLUE!
305
SURPASSING DAD

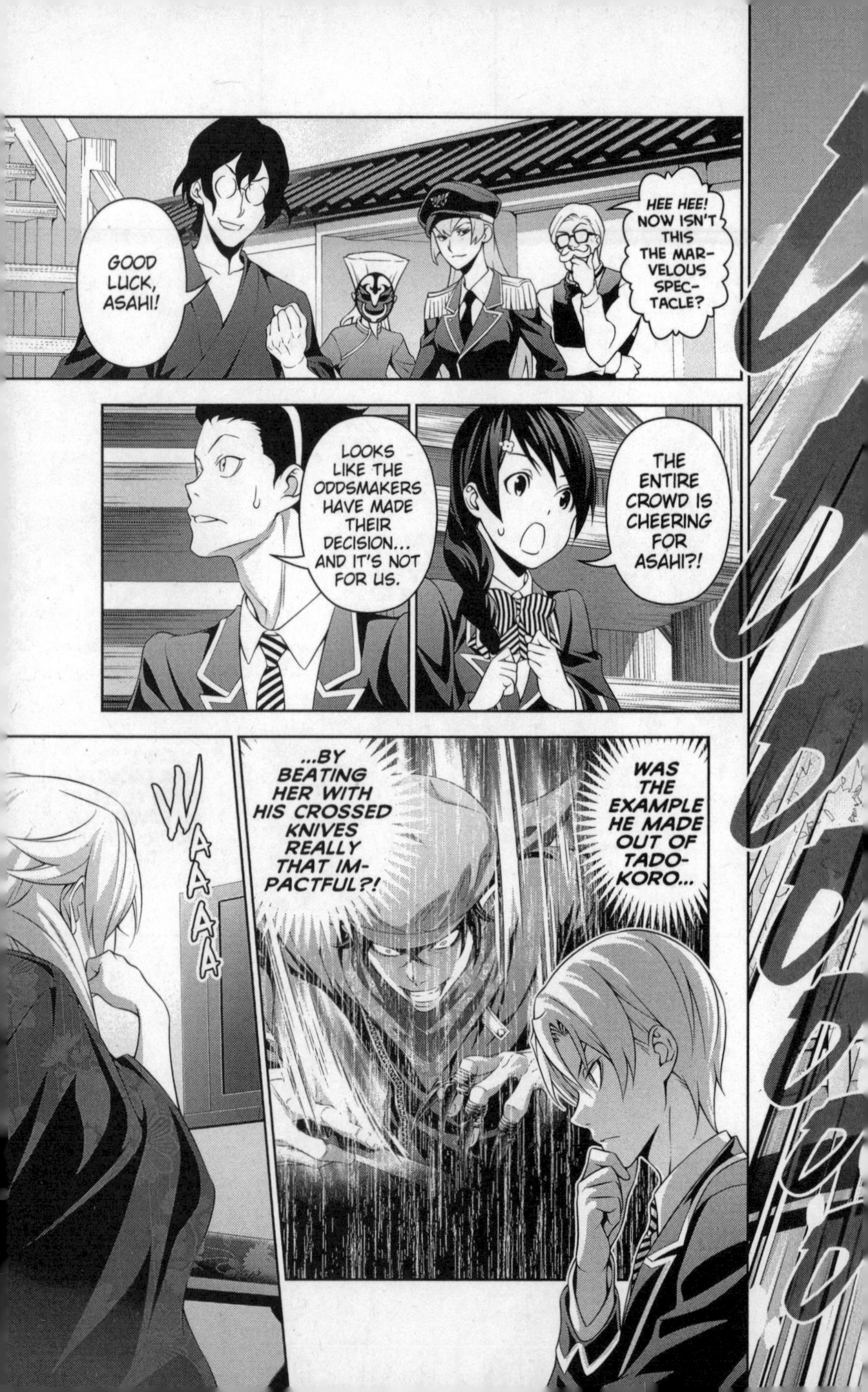
HEE HEE! NOW ISN'T THIS THE MAR-VELOUS SPEC-TACLE?
GOOD LUCK, ASAHI!
THE ENTIRE CROWD IS CHEERING FOR ASAHI?!
LOOKS LIKE THE ODDSMAKERS HAVE MADE THEIR DECISION... AND IT'S NOT FOR US.
WAS THE EXAMPLE HE MADE OUT OF TADO-KORO...
...BY BEATING HER WITH HIS CROSSED KNIVES REALLY THAT IM-PACTFUL?!
WAAAAA

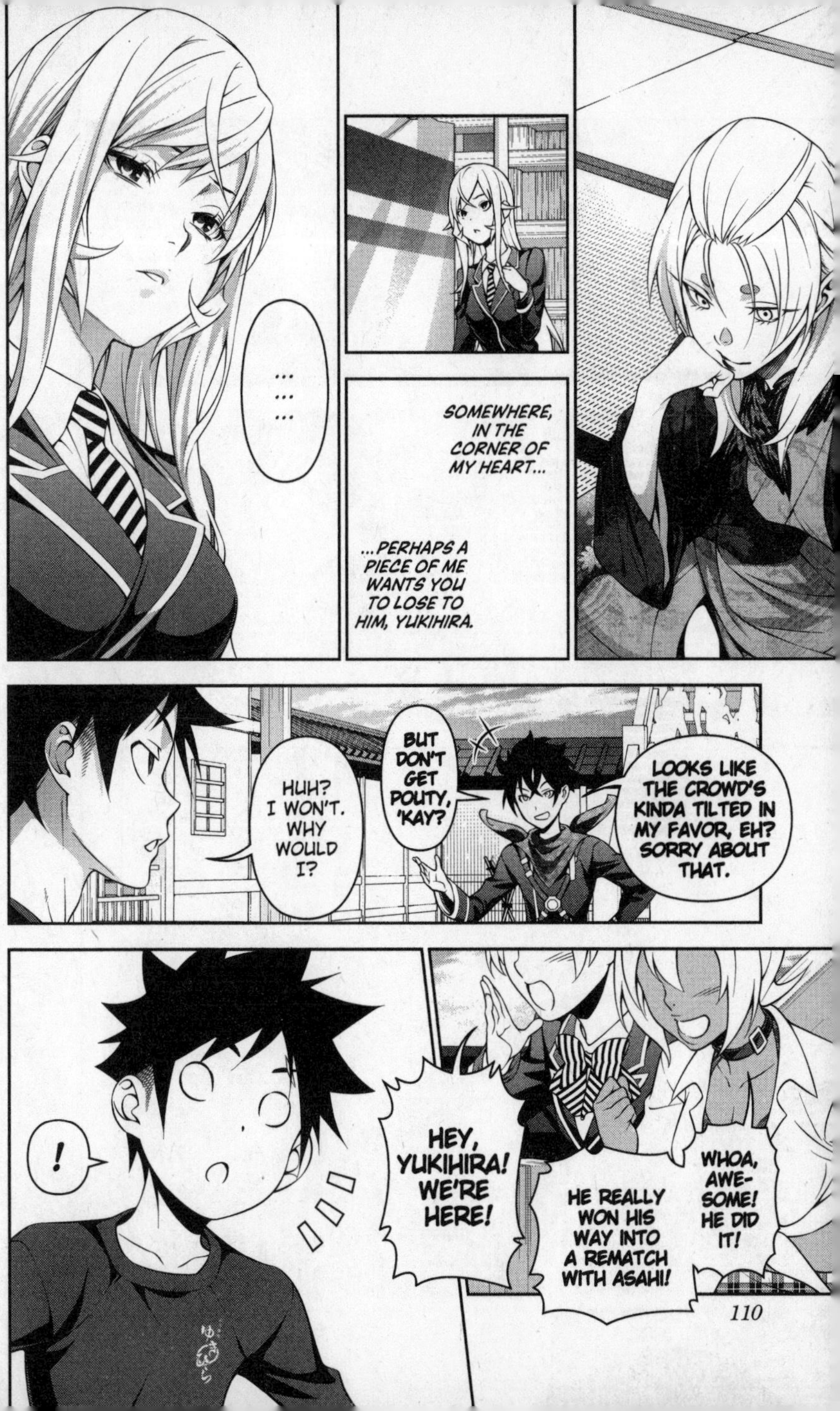
SOMEWHERE, IN THE CORNER OF MY HEART...
...PERHAPS A PIECE OF ME WANTS YOU TO LOSE TO HIM, YUKIHIRA.
... ...
LOOKS LIKE THE CROWD'S KINDA TILTED IN MY FAVOR, EH? SORRY ABOUT THAT.
BUT DON'T GET POUTY, 'KAY?
HUH? I WON'T. WHY WOULD I?
WHOA, AWE-SOME! HE DID IT!
HE REALLY WON HIS WAY INTO A REMATCH WITH ASAHI!
HEY, YUKIHIRA! WE'RE HERE!
!

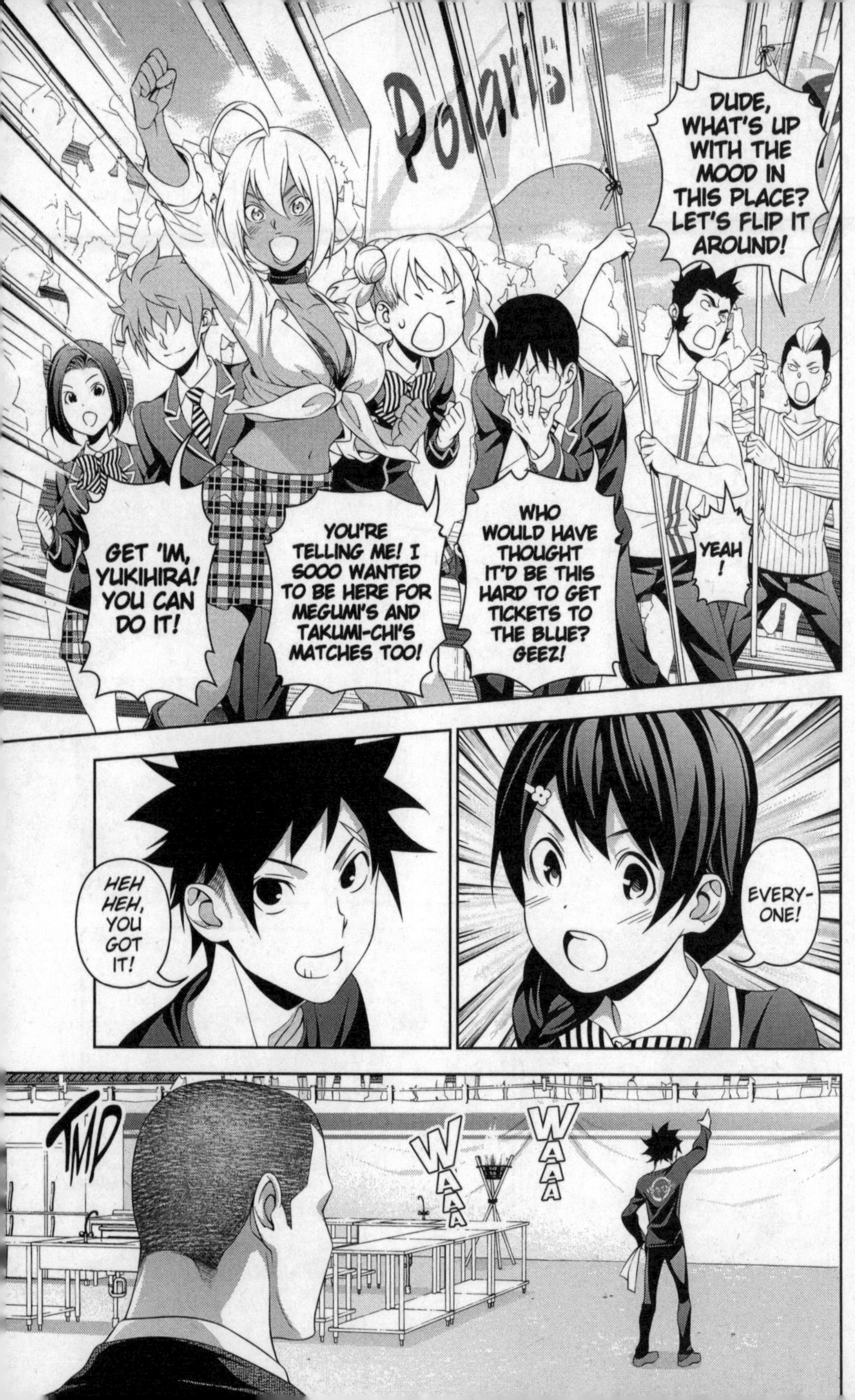
Polaris
DUDE, WHAT'S UP WITH THE MOOD IN THIS PLACE? LET'S FLIP IT AROUND!
YEAH!
WHO WOULD HAVE THOUGHT IT'D BE THIS HARD TO GET TICKETS TO THE BLUE? GEEZ!
YOU'RE TELLING ME! I SOOO WANTED TO BE HERE FOR MEGUMI'S AND TAKUMI-CHI'S MATCHES TOO!
GET 'IM, YUKIHIRA! YOU CAN DO IT!
EVERY-ONE!
HEH HEH, YOU GOT IT!
WAAA
WAAA
TMP

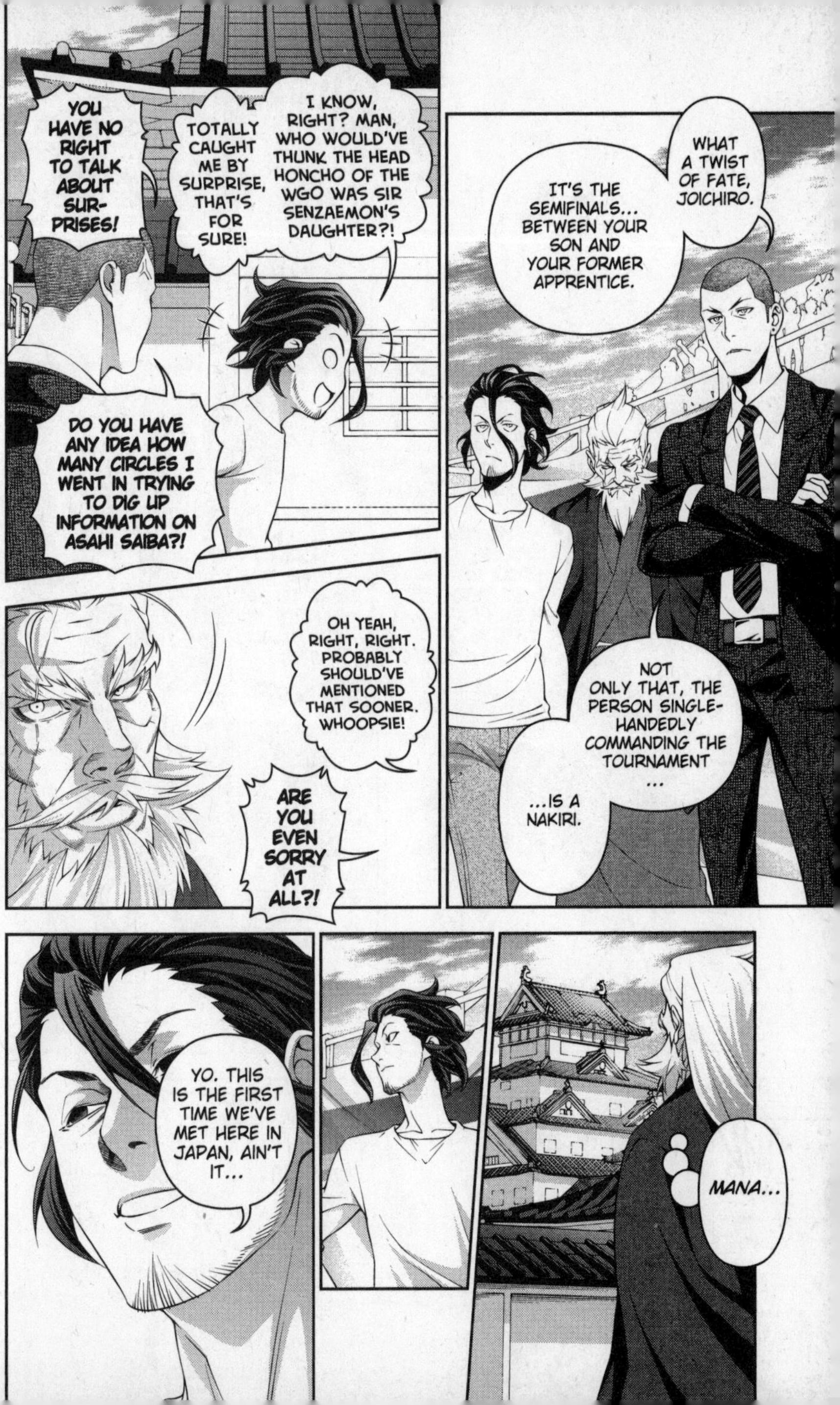
WHAT A TWIST OF FATE, JOICHIRO.
IT'S THE SEMIFINALS... BETWEEN YOUR SON AND YOUR FORMER APPRENTICE.
NOT ONLY THAT, THE PERSON SINGLE-HANDEDLY COMMANDING THE TOURNAMENT...
...IS A NAKIRI.
I KNOW, RIGHT? MAN, WHO WOULD'VE THUNK THE HEAD HONCHO OF THE WGO WAS SIR SENZAEMON'S DAUGHTER?!
TOTALLY CAUGHT ME BY SURPRISE, THAT'S FOR SURE!
YOU HAVE NO RIGHT TO TALK ABOUT SUR-PRISES!
DO YOU HAVE ANY IDEA HOW MANY CIRCLES I WENT IN TRYING TO DIG UP INFORMATION ON ASAHI SAIBA?!
OH YEAH, RIGHT, RIGHT. PROBABLY SHOULD'VE MENTIONED THAT SOONER. WHOOPSIE!
ARE YOU EVEN SORRY AT ALL?!
MANA...
YO. THIS IS THE FIRST TIME WE'VE MET HERE IN JAPAN, AIN'T IT...

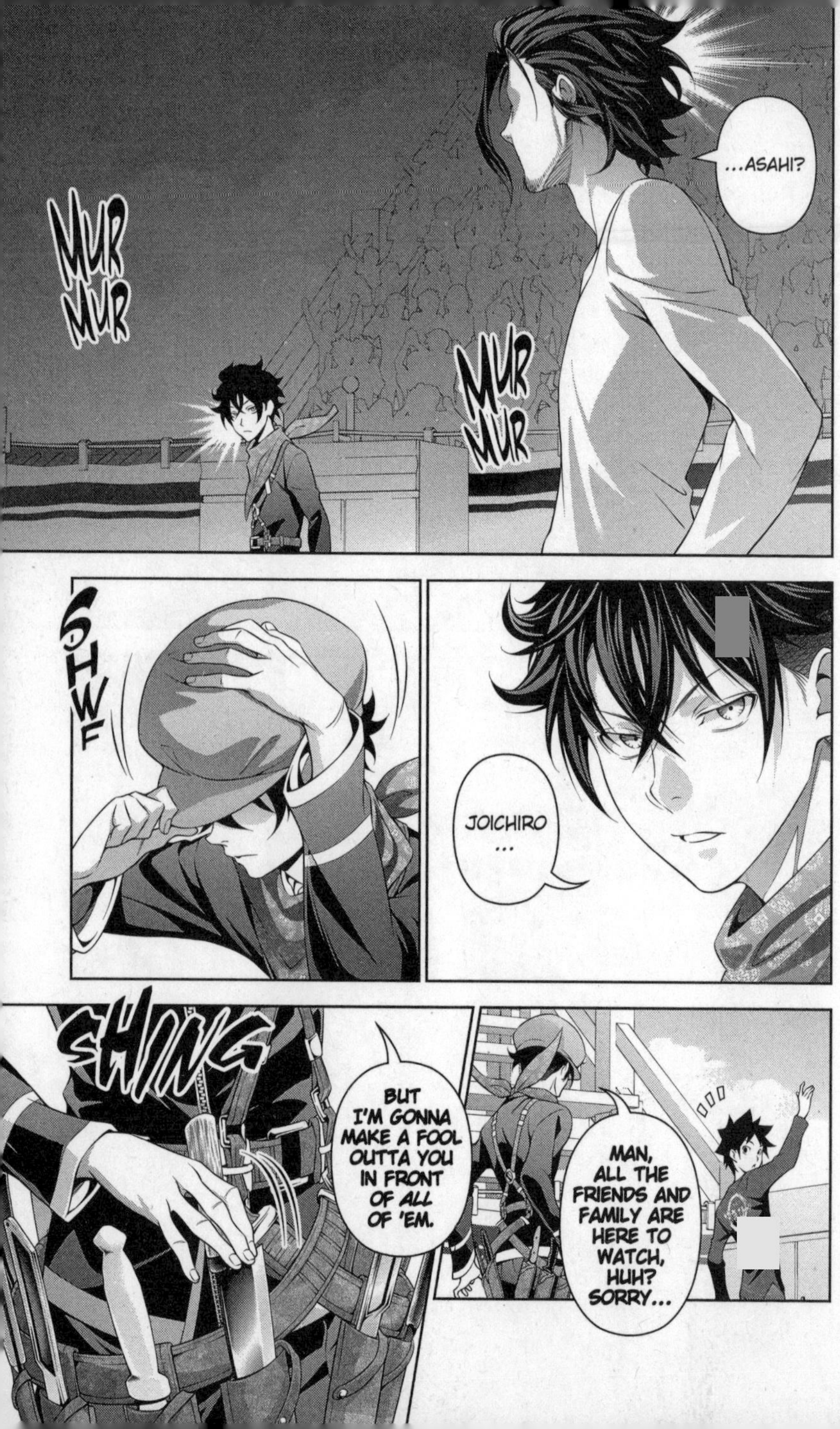
...ASAHI?
MUR MUR
MUR MUR
JOICHIRO ...
SHWF
MAN, ALL THE FRIENDS AND FAMILY ARE HERE TO WATCH, HUH? SORRY...
SHING
BUT I'M GONNA MAKE A FOOL OUTTA YOU IN FRONT OF ALL OF 'EM.

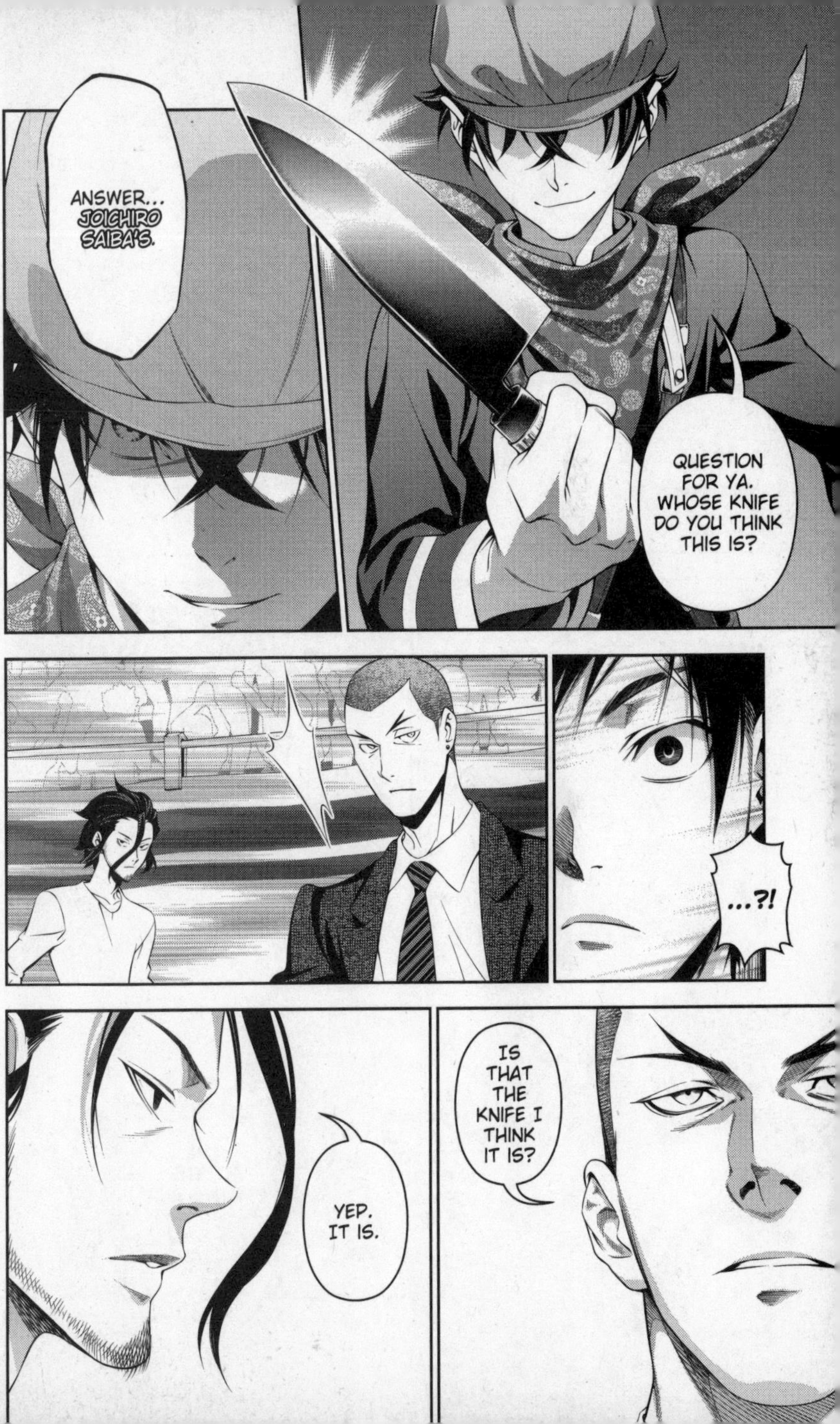
QUESTION FOR YA. WHOSE KNIFE DO YOU THINK THIS IS?
ANSWER... JOICHIRO SAIBA'S.
...?!
IS THAT THE KNIFE I THINK IT IS?
YEP. IT IS.

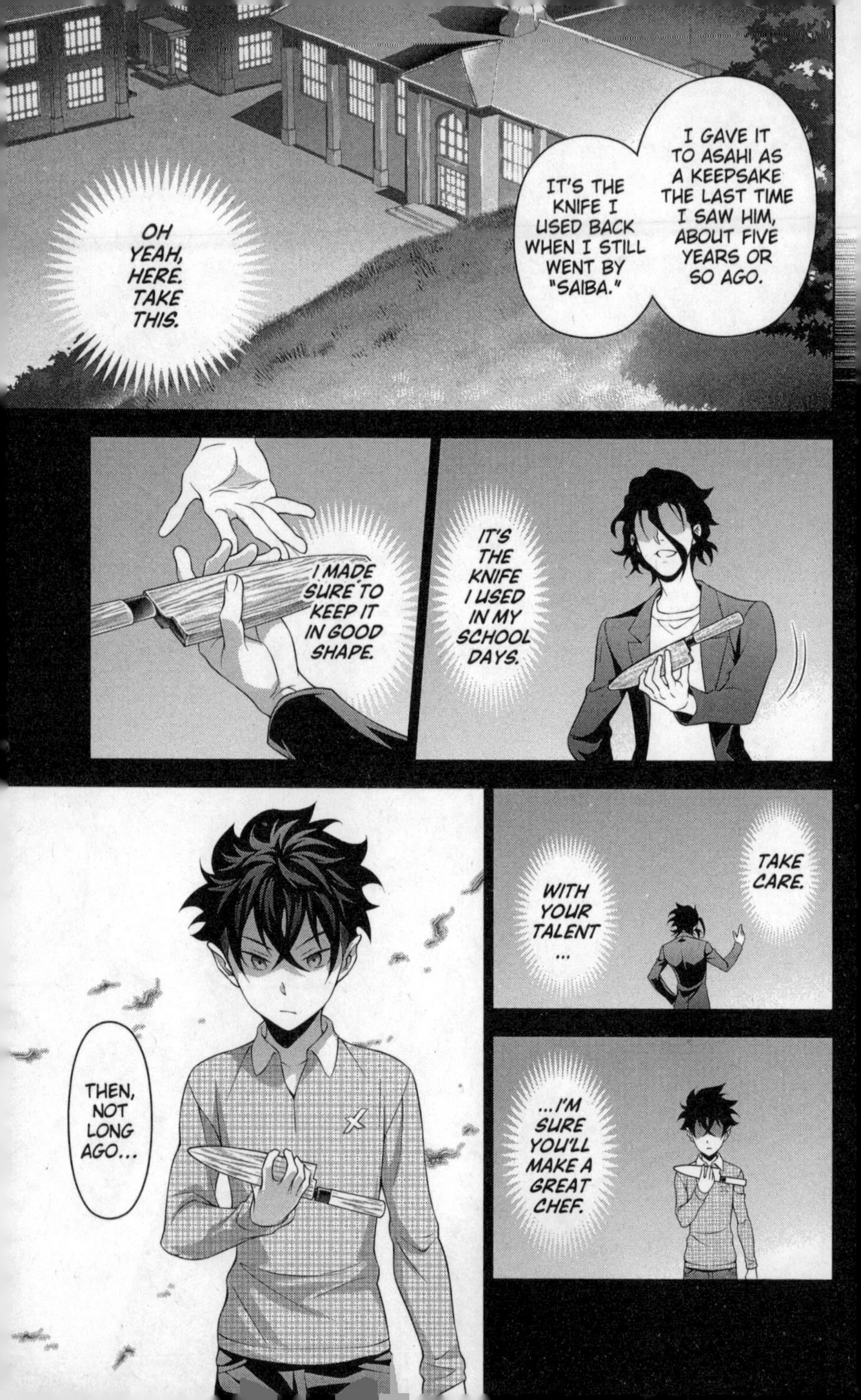
I GAVE IT TO ASAHI AS A KEEPSAKE THE LAST TIME I SAW HIM, ABOUT FIVE YEARS OR SO AGO.
IT'S THE KNIFE I USED BACK WHEN I STILL WENT BY "SAIBA."
OH YEAH, HERE. TAKE THIS.
IT'S THE KNIFE I USED IN MY SCHOOL DAYS.
I MADE SURE TO KEEP IT IN GOOD SHAPE.
TAKE CARE.
WITH YOUR TALENT...
...I'M SURE YOU'LL MAKE A GREAT CHEF.
THEN, NOT LONG AGO...

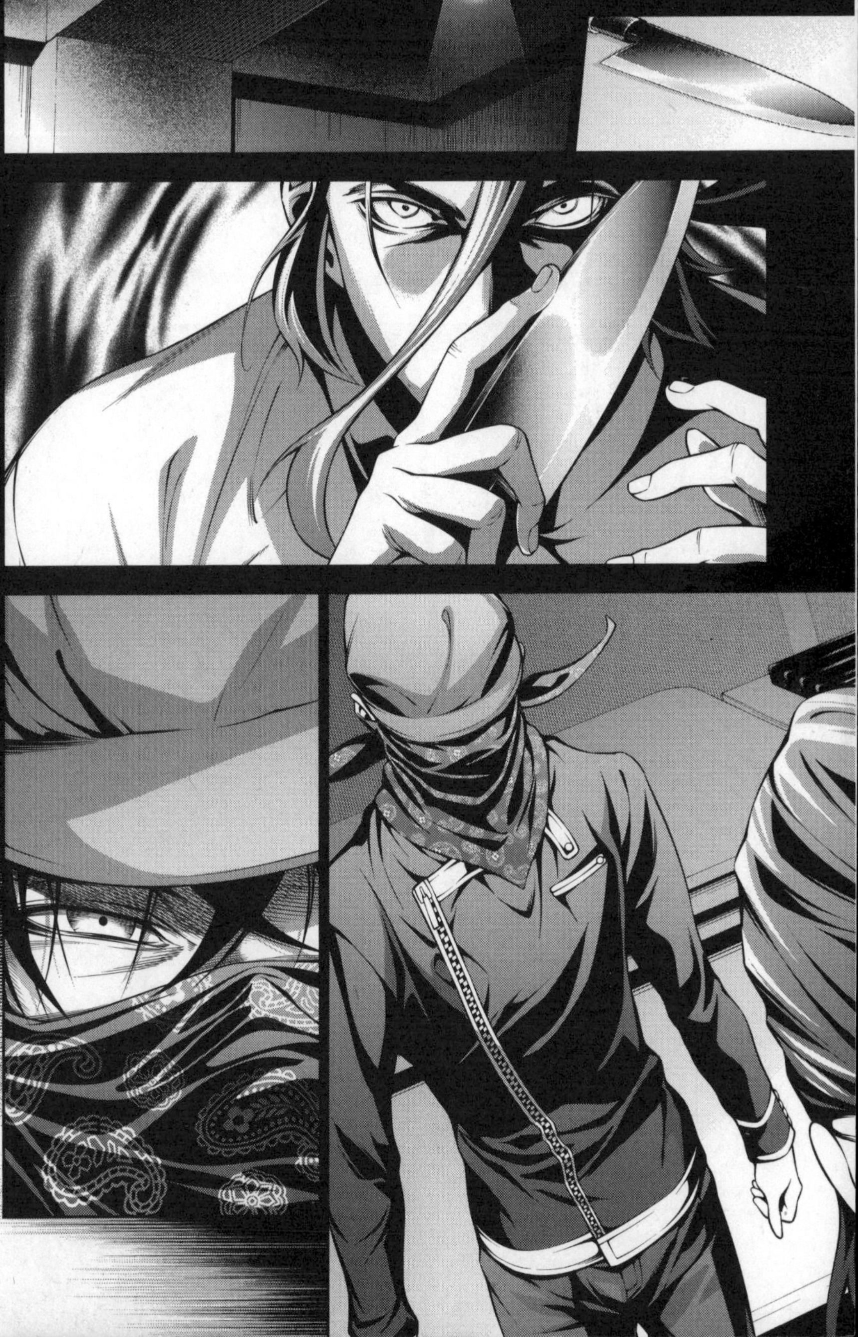

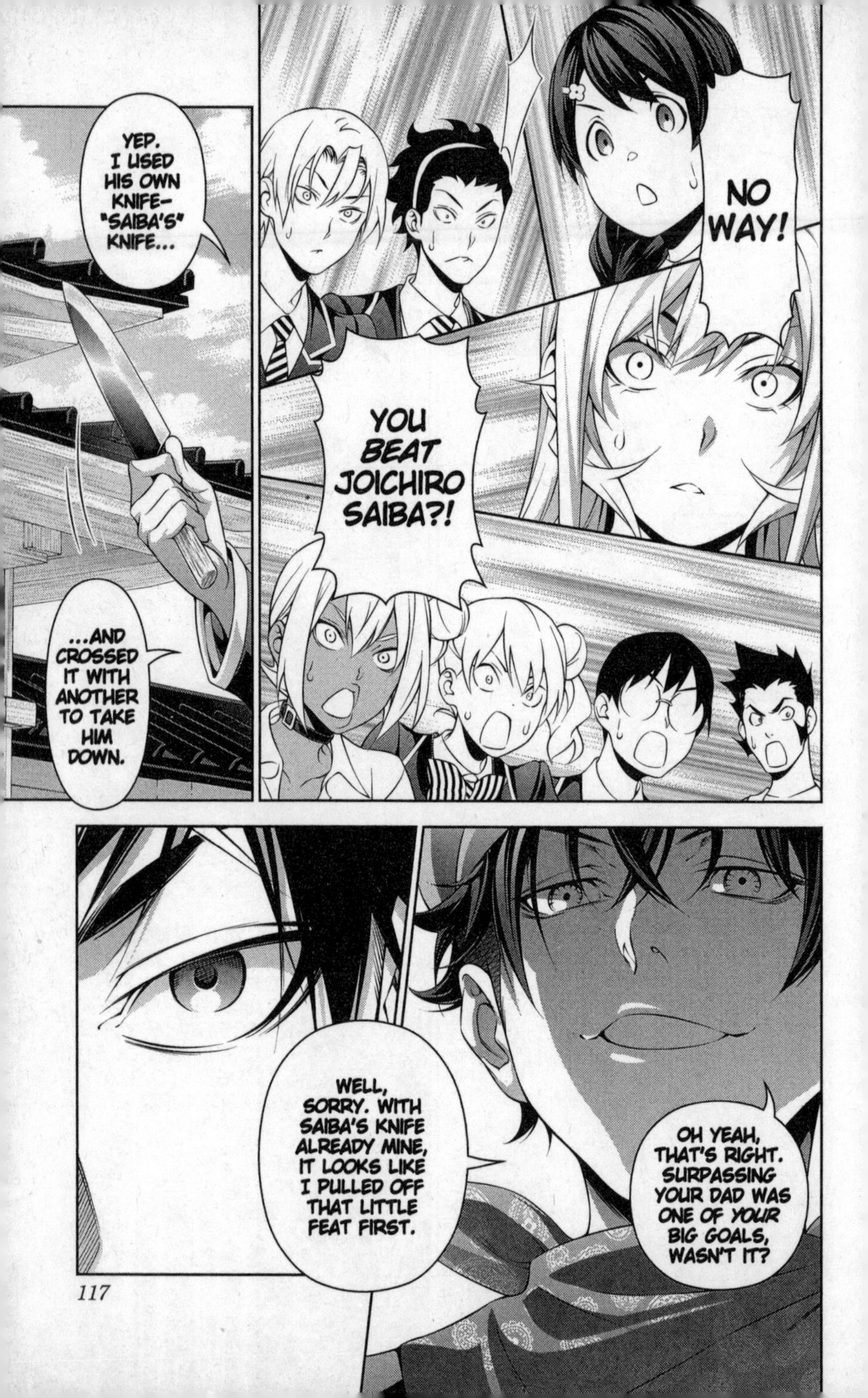
NO WAY!
YOU BEAT JOICHIRO SAIBA?!
YEP. I USED HIS OWN KNIFE— "SAIBA'S" KNIFE...
...AND CROSSED IT WITH ANOTHER TO TAKE HIM DOWN.
OH YEAH, THAT'S RIGHT. SURPASSING YOUR DAD WAS ONE OF *YOUR* BIG GOALS, WASN'T IT?
WELL, SORRY. WITH SAIBA'S KNIFE ALREADY MINE, IT LOOKS LIKE I PULLED OFF THAT LITTLE FEAT FIRST.

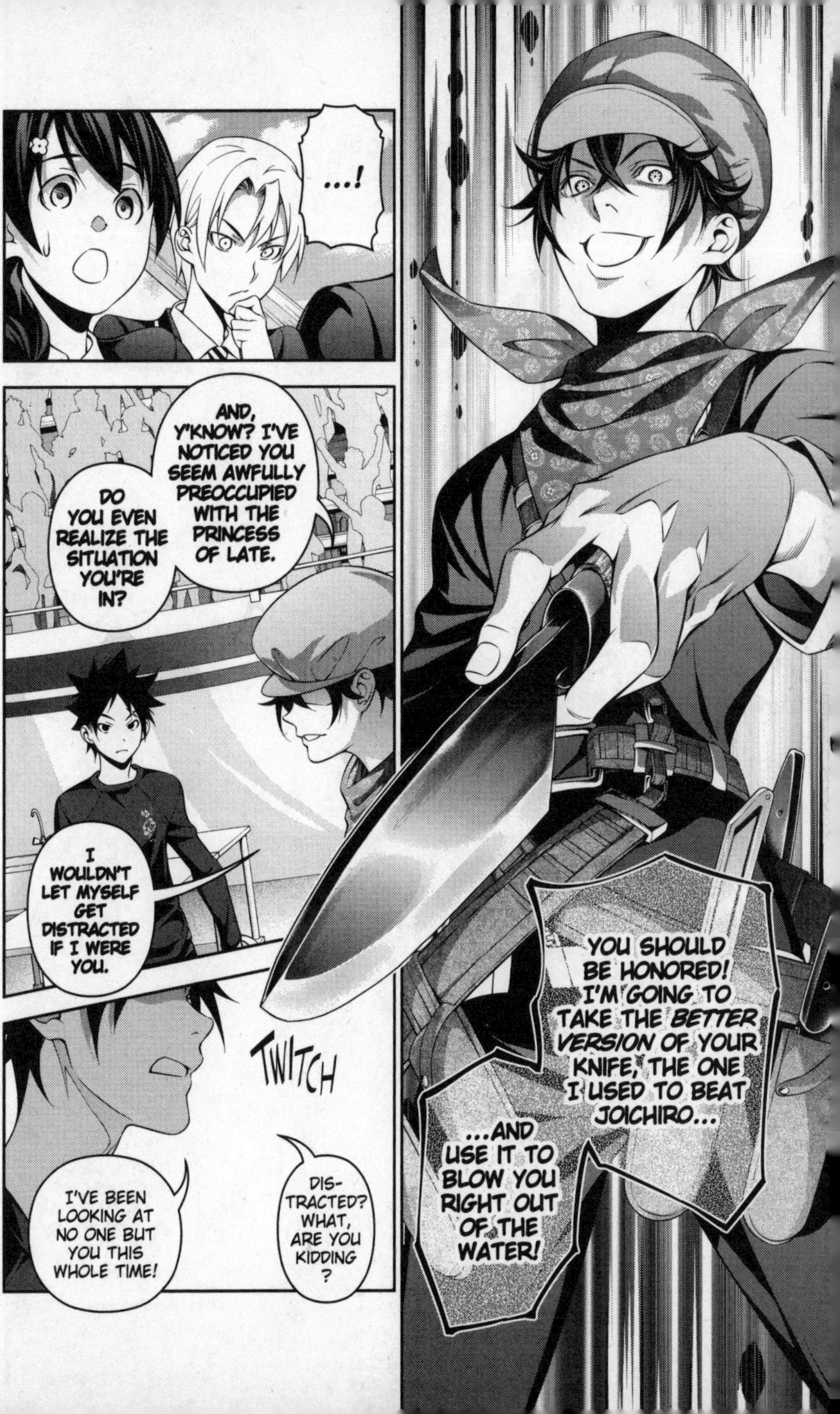
YOU SHOULD BE HONORED! I'M GOING TO TAKE THE *BETTER VERSION* OF YOUR KNIFE, THE ONE I USED TO BEAT JOICHIRO...
...AND USE IT TO BLOW YOU RIGHT OUT OF THE WATER!
...!
AND, Y'KNOW? I'VE NOTICED YOU SEEM AWFULLY PREOCCUPIED WITH THE PRINCESS OF LATE.
DO YOU EVEN REALIZE THE SITUATION YOU'RE IN?
I WOULDN'T LET MYSELF GET DISTRACTED IF I WERE YOU.
TWITCH
DIS-TRACTED? WHAT, ARE YOU KIDDING?
I'VE BEEN LOOKING AT NO ONE BUT YOU THIS WHOLE TIME!

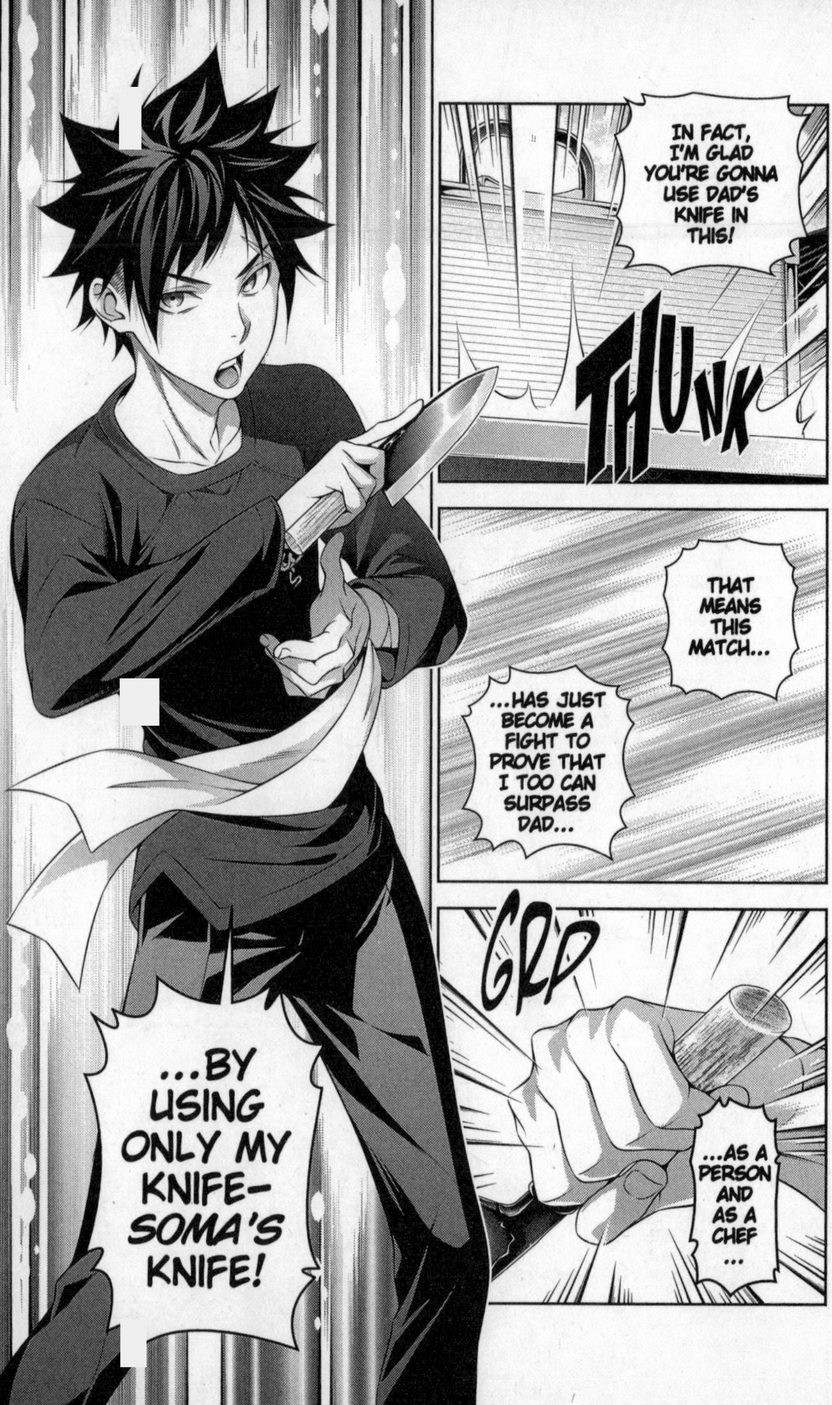
IN FACT, I'M GLAD YOU'RE GONNA USE DAD'S KNIFE IN THIS!
THUNK
THAT MEANS THIS MATCH...
...HAS JUST BECOME A FIGHT TO PROVE THAT I TOO CAN SURPASS DAD...
GRP
...AS A PERSON AND AS A CHEF...
...BY USING ONLY MY KNIFE—SOMA'S KNIFE!

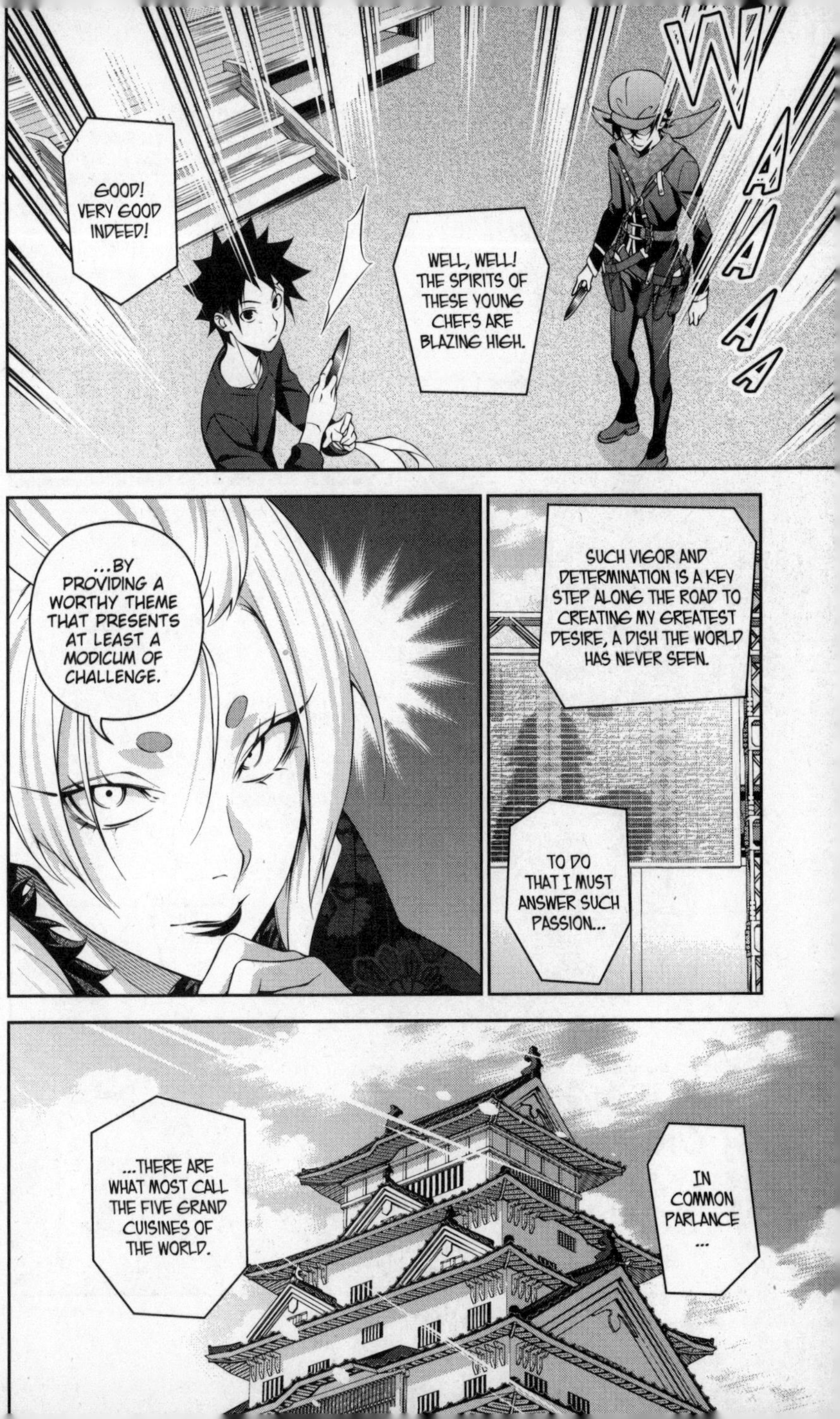
WAAAAA
WELL, WELL! THE SPIRITS OF THESE YOUNG CHEFS ARE BLAZING HIGH.
GOOD! VERY GOOD INDEED!
SUCH VIGOR AND DETERMINATION IS A KEY STEP ALONG THE ROAD TO CREATING MY GREATEST DESIRE, A DISH THE WORLD HAS NEVER SEEN.
TO DO THAT I MUST ANSWER SUCH PASSION...
...BY PROVIDING A WORTHY THEME THAT PRESENTS AT LEAST A MODICUM OF CHALLENGE.
IN COMMON PARLANCE ...
...THERE ARE WHAT MOST CALL THE FIVE GRAND CUISINES OF THE WORLD.

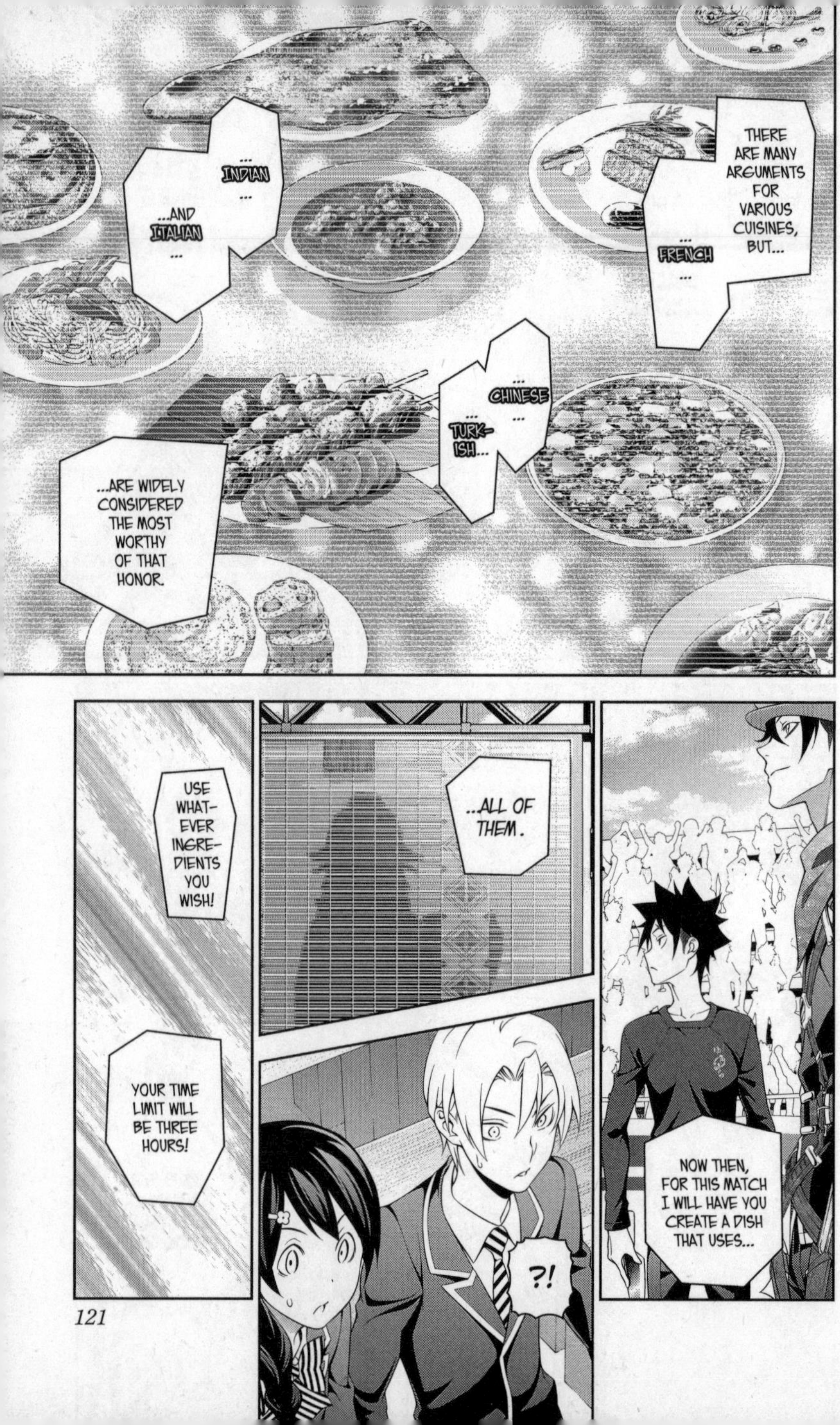
THERE ARE MANY ARGUMENTS FOR VARIOUS CUISINES, BUT...
...FRENCH...
...INDIAN...
...AND ITALIAN...
...CHINESE...
...TURKISH...
...ARE WIDELY CONSIDERED THE MOST WORTHY OF THAT HONOR.
NOW THEN, FOR THIS MATCH I WILL HAVE YOU CREATE A DISH THAT USES...
...ALL OF THEM.
?!
USE WHATEVER INGREDIENTS YOU WISH!
YOUR TIME LIMIT WILL BE THREE HOURS!

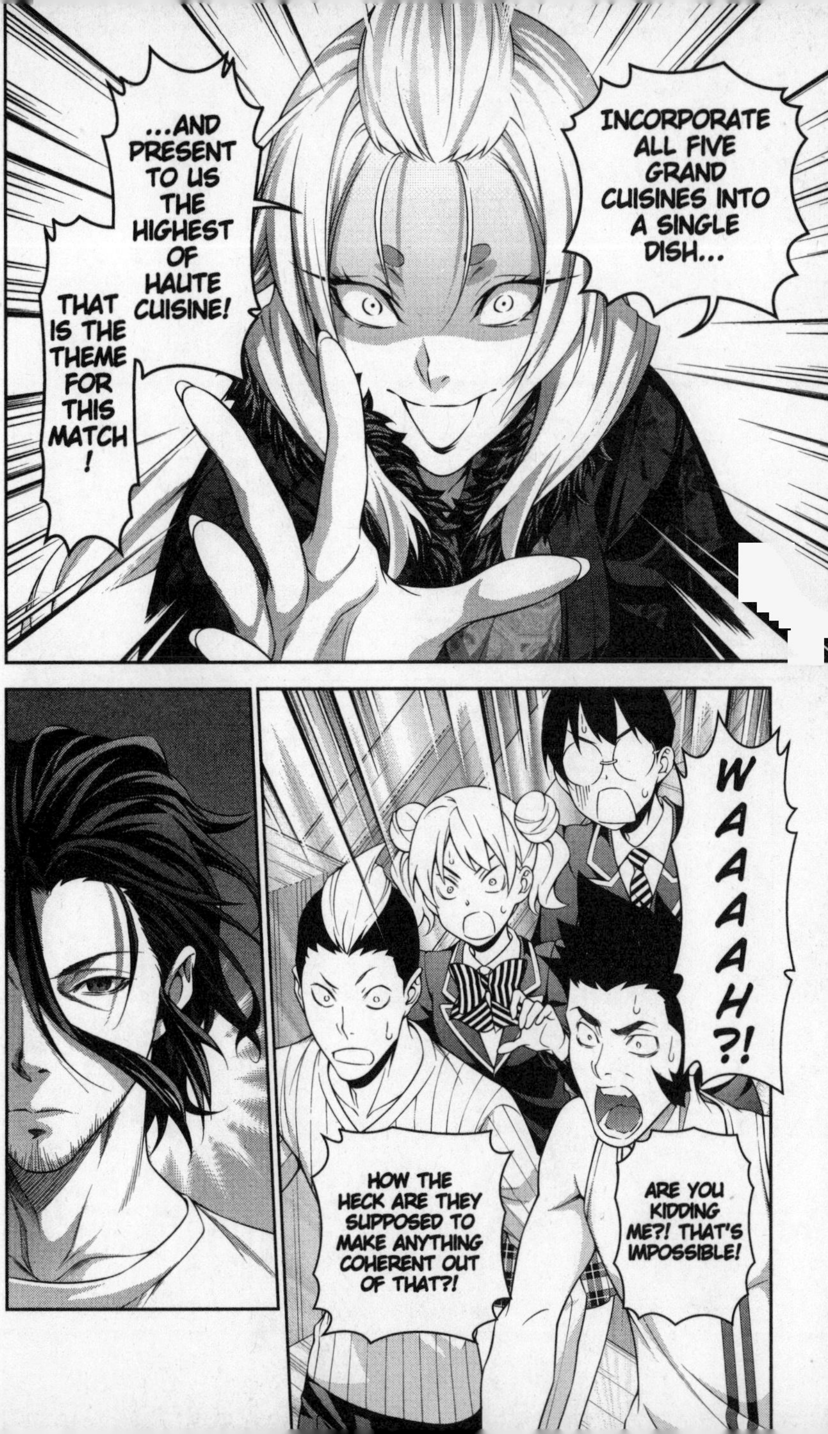
INCORPORATE ALL FIVE GRAND CUISINES INTO A SINGLE DISH...
...AND PRESENT TO US THE HIGHEST OF HAUTE CUISINE!
THAT IS THE THEME FOR THIS MATCH!
WAAAAAH?!
ARE YOU KIDDING ME?! THAT'S IMPOSSIBLE!
HOW THE HECK ARE THEY SUPPOSED TO MAKE ANYTHING COHERENT OUT OF THAT?!

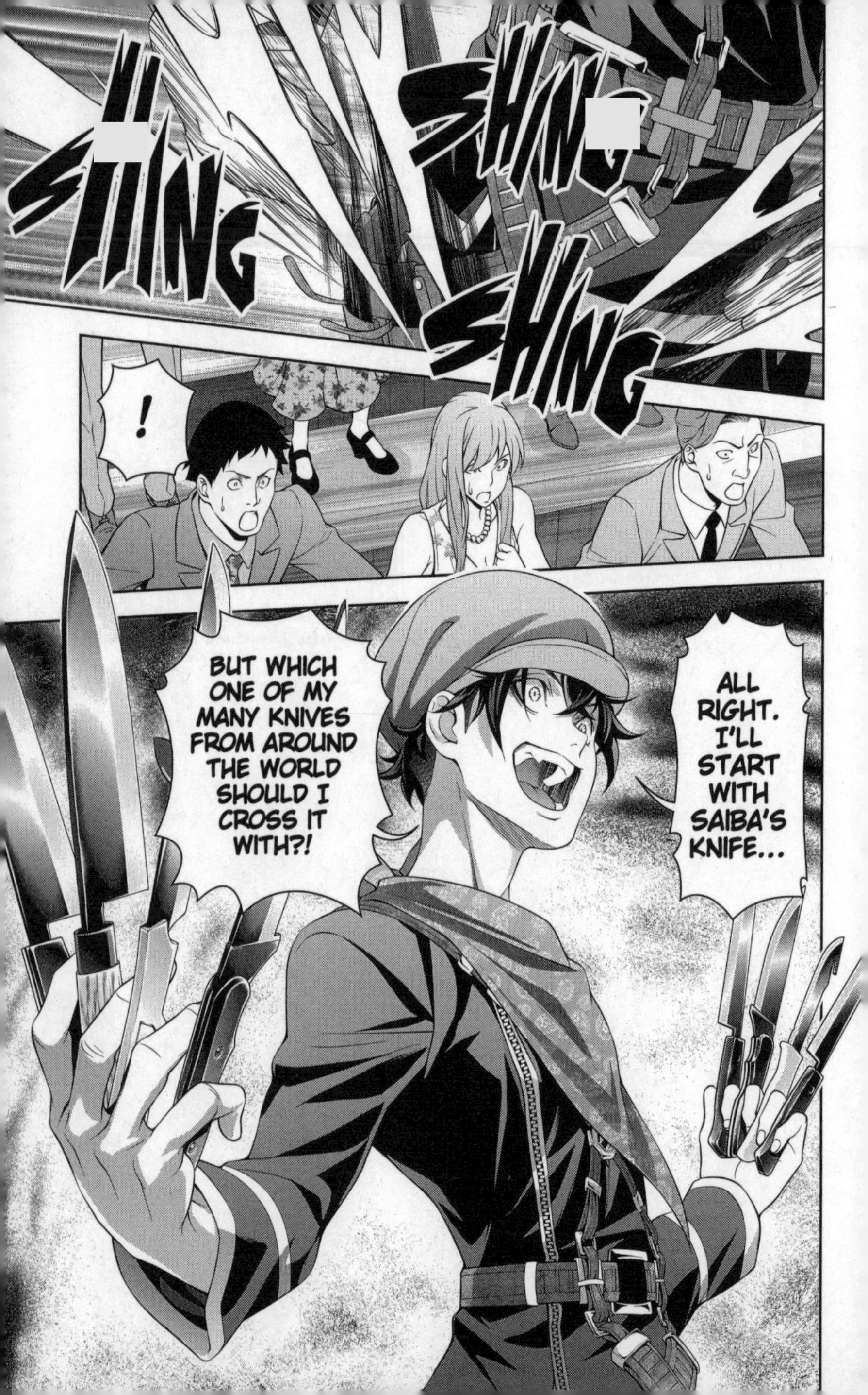
SHING
SHING
SHING
!
ALL RIGHT. I'LL START WITH SAIBA'S KNIFE...
BUT WHICH ONE OF MY MANY KNIVES FROM AROUND THE WORLD SHOULD I CROSS IT WITH?!

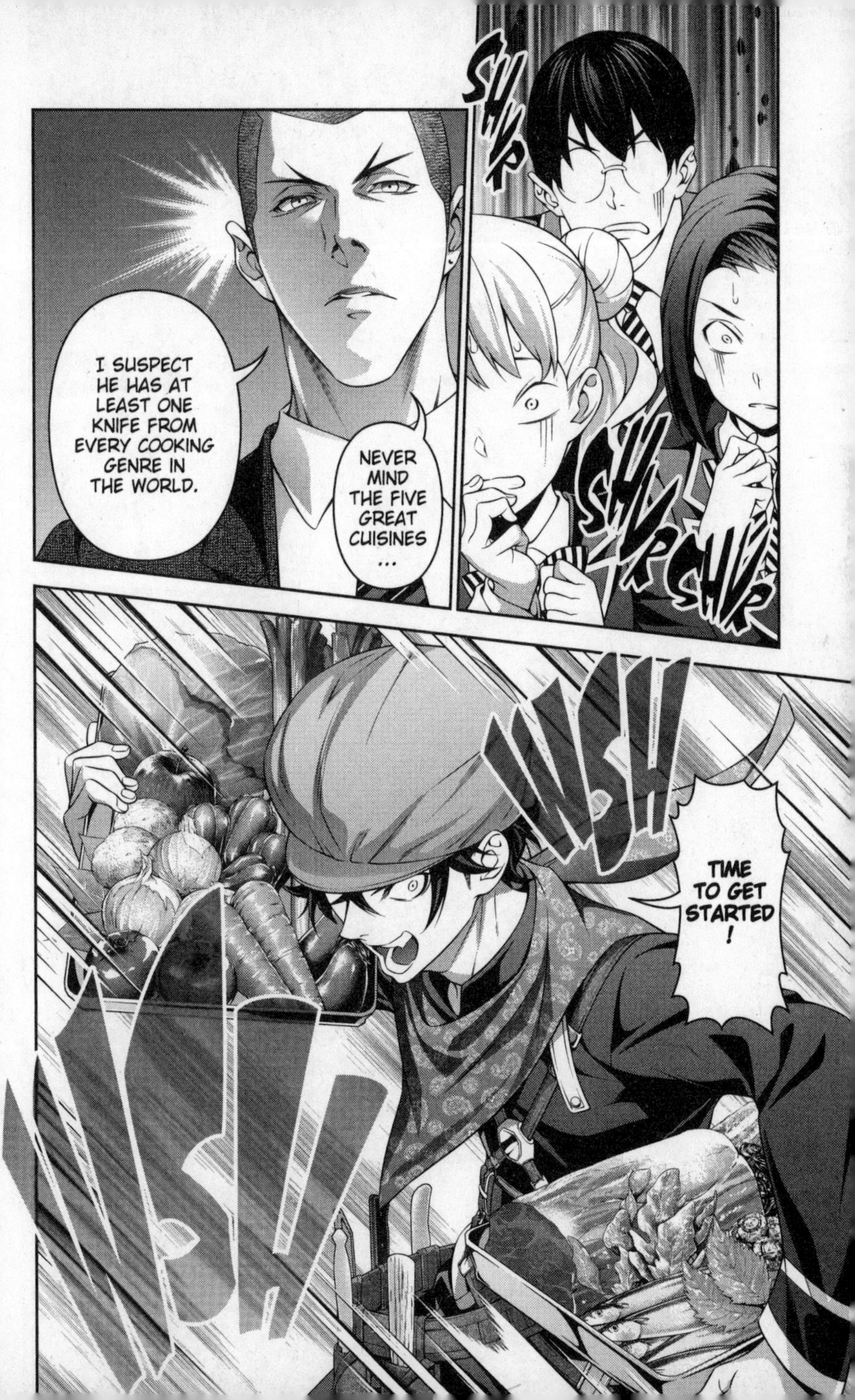
SHUP
SHUP
SHUP SHUP
NEVER MIND THE FIVE GREAT CUISINES...
I SUSPECT HE HAS AT LEAST ONE KNIFE FROM EVERY COOKING GENRE IN THE WORLD.
WHSH
TIME TO GET STARTED!

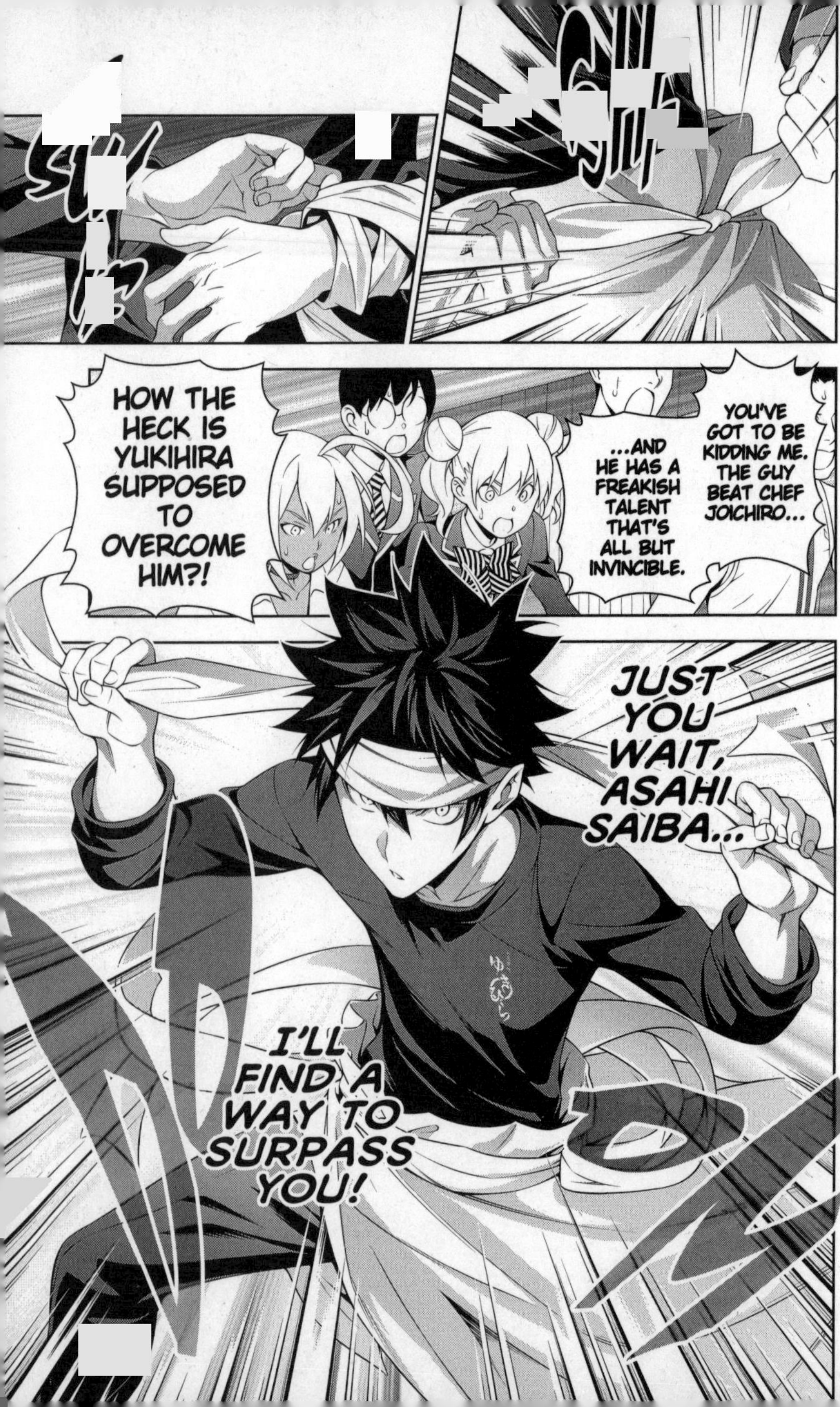
YOU'VE GOT TO BE KIDDING ME. THE GUY BEAT CHEF JOICHIRO...
...AND HE HAS A FREAKISH TALENT THAT'S ALL BUT INVINCIBLE.
HOW THE HECK IS YUKIHIRA SUPPOSED TO OVERCOME HIM?!
JUST YOU WAIT, ASAHI SAIBA...
I'LL FIND A WAY TO SURPASS YOU!

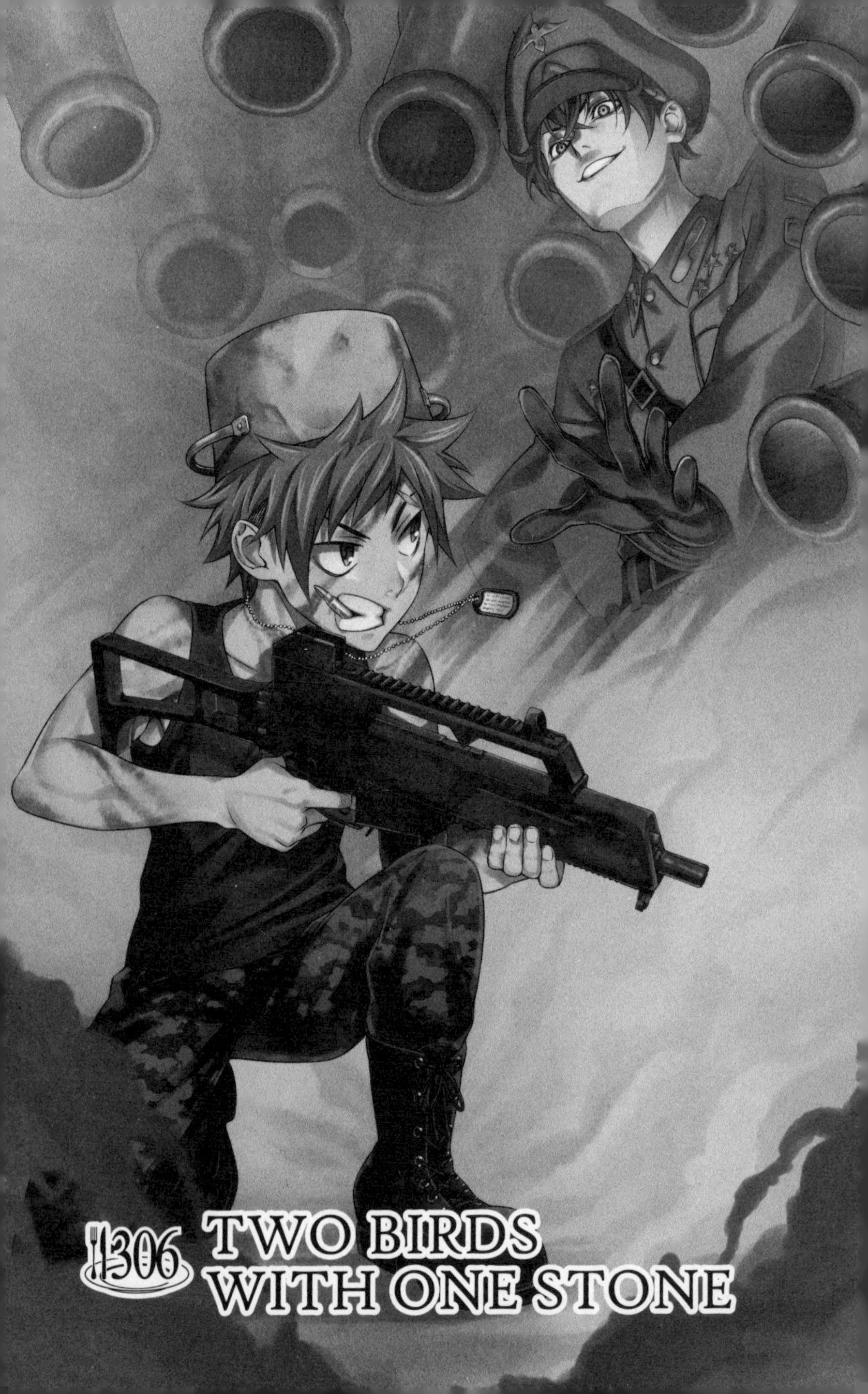

306
TWO BIRDS WITH ONE STONE

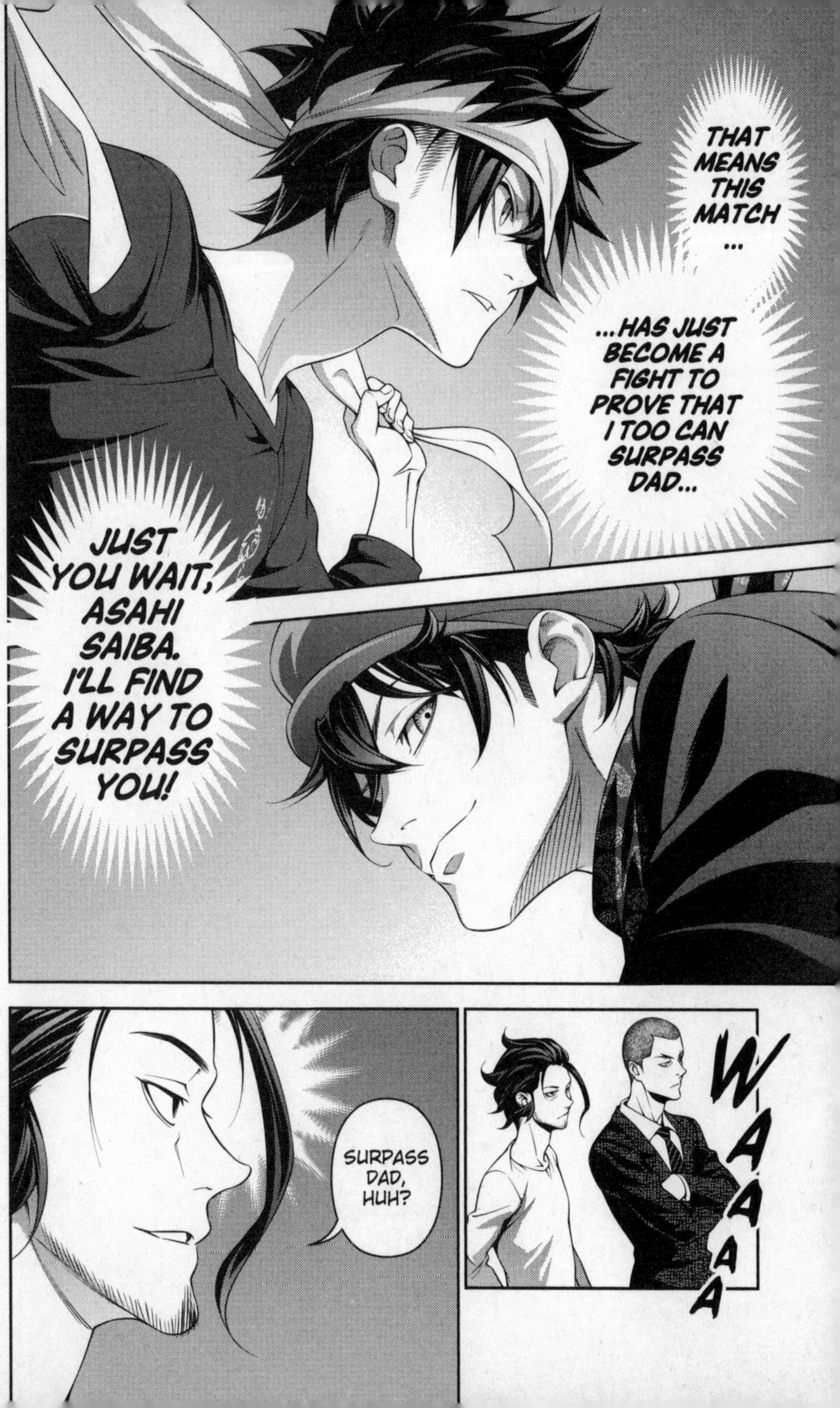
THAT MEANS THIS MATCH ...
...HAS JUST BECOME A FIGHT TO PROVE THAT I TOO CAN SURPASS DAD...
JUST YOU WAIT, ASAHI SAIBA. I'LL FIND A WAY TO SURPASS YOU!
WAAAAA
SURPASS DAD, HUH?

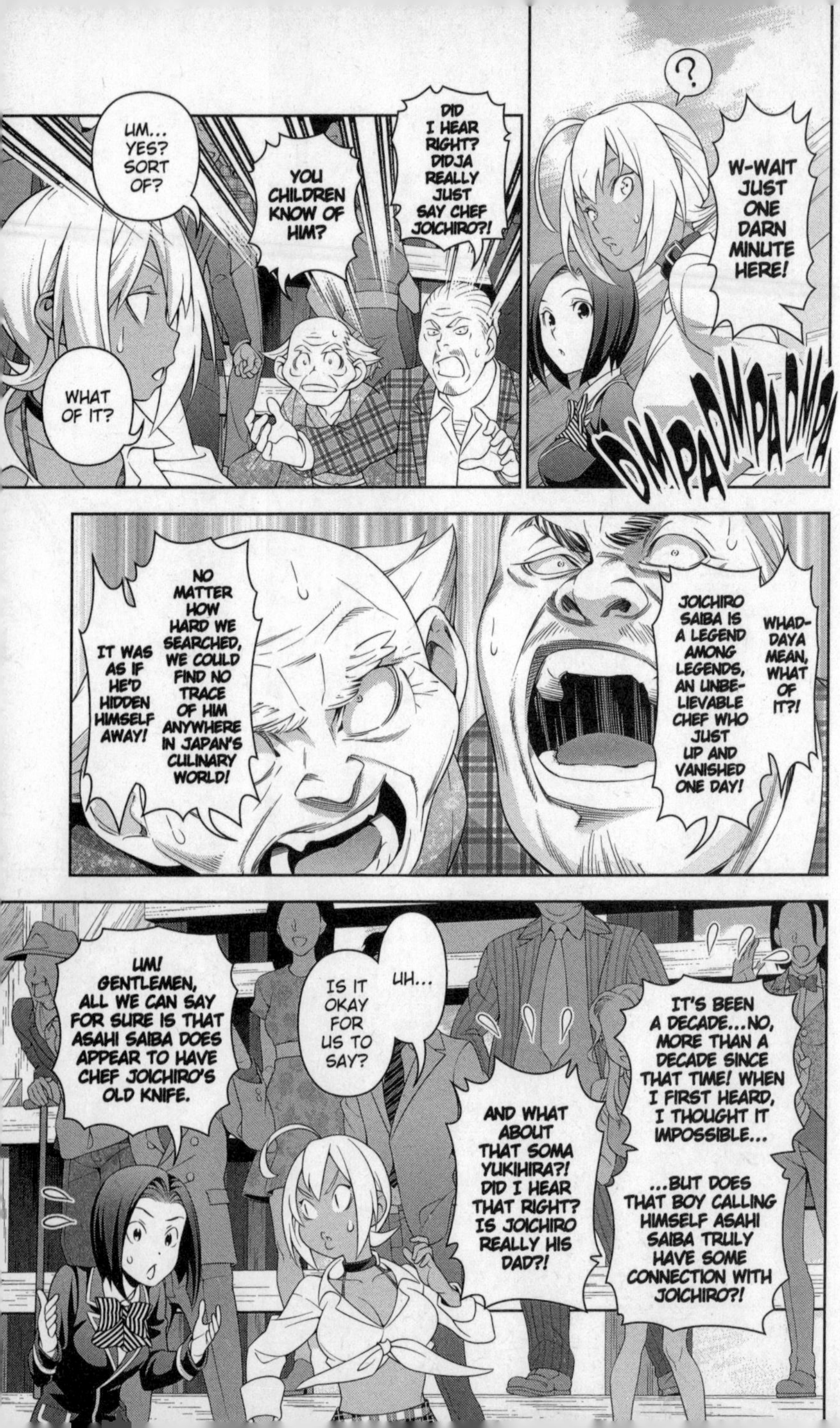
?
W-WAIT JUST ONE DARN MINUTE HERE!
DMPADMPADMPA
DID I HEAR RIGHT? DIDJA REALLY JUST SAY CHEF JOICHIRO?!
YOU CHILDREN KNOW OF HIM?
UM... YES? SORT OF?
WHAT OF IT?
WHAD-DAYA MEAN, WHAT OF IT?!
JOICHIRO SAIBA IS A LEGEND AMONG LEGENDS, AN UNBE-LIEVABLE CHEF WHO JUST UP AND VANISHED ONE DAY!
NO MATTER HOW HARD WE SEARCHED, WE COULD FIND NO TRACE OF HIM ANYWHERE IN JAPAN'S CULINARY WORLD!
IT WAS AS IF HE'D HIDDEN HIMSELF AWAY!
IT'S BEEN A DECADE...NO, MORE THAN A DECADE SINCE THAT TIME! WHEN I FIRST HEARD, I THOUGHT IT IMPOSSIBLE...
...BUT DOES THAT BOY CALLING HIMSELF ASAHI SAIBA TRULY HAVE SOME CONNECTION WITH JOICHIRO?!
AND WHAT ABOUT THAT SOMA YUKIHIRA?! DID I HEAR THAT RIGHT? IS JOICHIRO REALLY HIS DAD?!
UH...
IS IT OKAY FOR US TO SAY?
UM! GENTLEMEN, ALL WE CAN SAY FOR SURE IS THAT ASAHI SAIBA DOES APPEAR TO HAVE CHEF JOICHIRO'S OLD KNIFE.

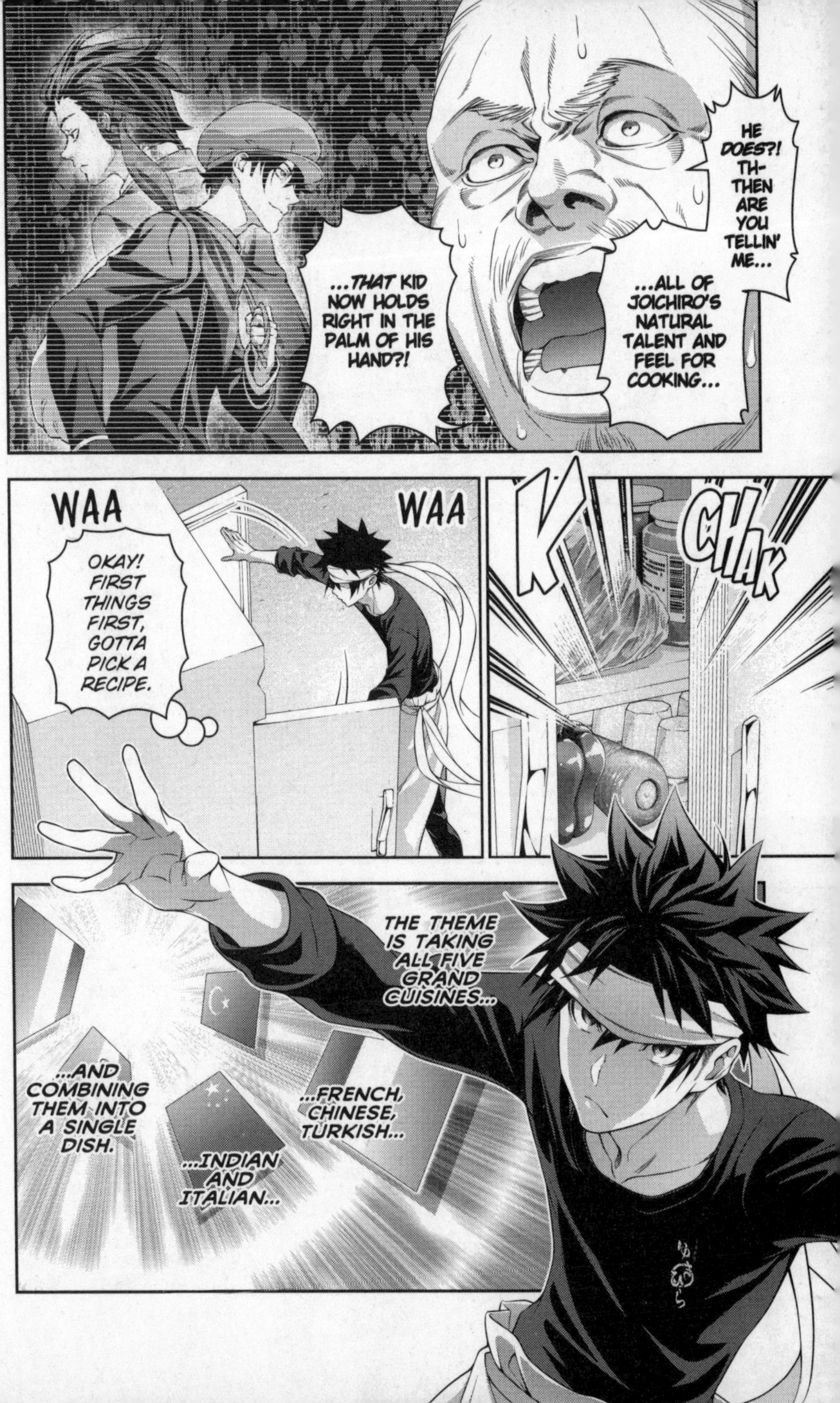
HE DOES?! TH-THEN ARE YOU TELLIN' ME...
...ALL OF JOICHIRO'S NATURAL TALENT AND FEEL FOR COOKING...
...THAT KID NOW HOLDS RIGHT IN THE PALM OF HIS HAND?!
K
CHAK
WAA
WAA
OKAY! FIRST THINGS FIRST, GOTTA PICK A RECIPE.
THE THEME IS TAKING ALL FIVE GRAND CUISINES...
...FRENCH, CHINESE, TURKISH...
...INDIAN AND ITALIAN...
...AND COMBINING THEM INTO A SINGLE DISH.

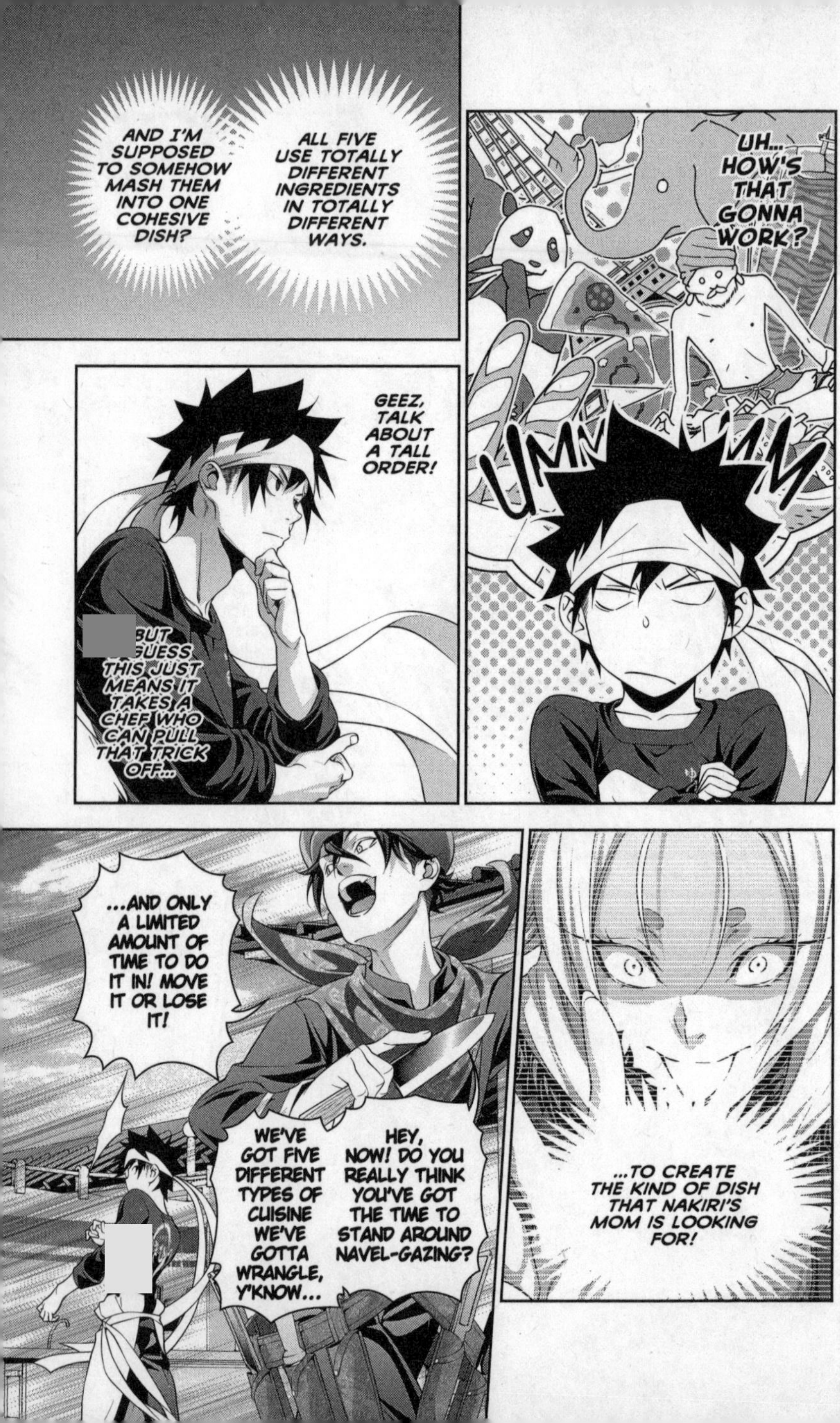
ALL FIVE USE TOTALLY DIFFERENT INGREDIENTS IN TOTALLY DIFFERENT WAYS.
AND I'M SUPPOSED TO SOMEHOW MASH THEM INTO ONE COHESIVE DISH?
UH... HOW'S THAT GONNA WORK?
UMMMM
GEEZ, TALK ABOUT A TALL ORDER!
BUT GUESS THIS JUST MEANS IT TAKES A CHEF WHO CAN PULL THAT TRICK OFF...
...TO CREATE THE KIND OF DISH THAT NAKIRI'S MOM IS LOOKING FOR!
HEY, NOW! DO YOU REALLY THINK YOU'VE GOT THE TIME TO STAND AROUND NAVEL-GAZING?
WE'VE GOT FIVE DIFFERENT TYPES OF CUISINE WE'VE GOTTA WRANGLE, Y'KNOW...
...AND ONLY A LIMITED AMOUNT OF TIME TO DO IT IN! MOVE IT OR LOSE IT!

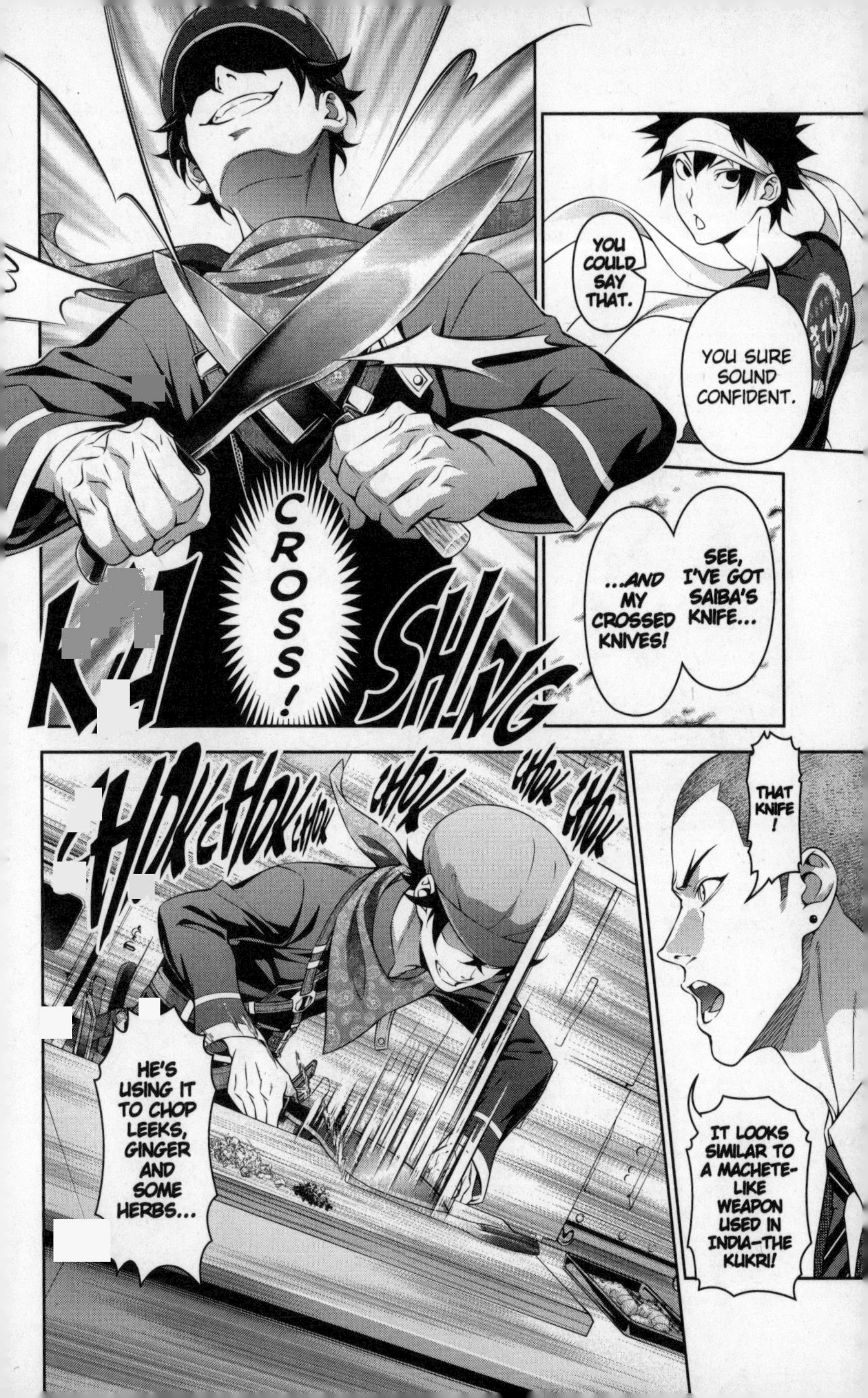
YOU SURE SOUND CONFIDENT.
YOU COULD SAY THAT.
SEE, I'VE GOT SAIBA'S KNIFE...
...AND MY CROSSED KNIVES!
CROSS!
SHING
THAT KNIFE!
IT LOOKS SIMILAR TO A MACHETE-LIKE WEAPON USED IN INDIA—THE KUKRI!
HE'S USING IT TO CHOP LEEKS, GINGER AND SOME HERBS...

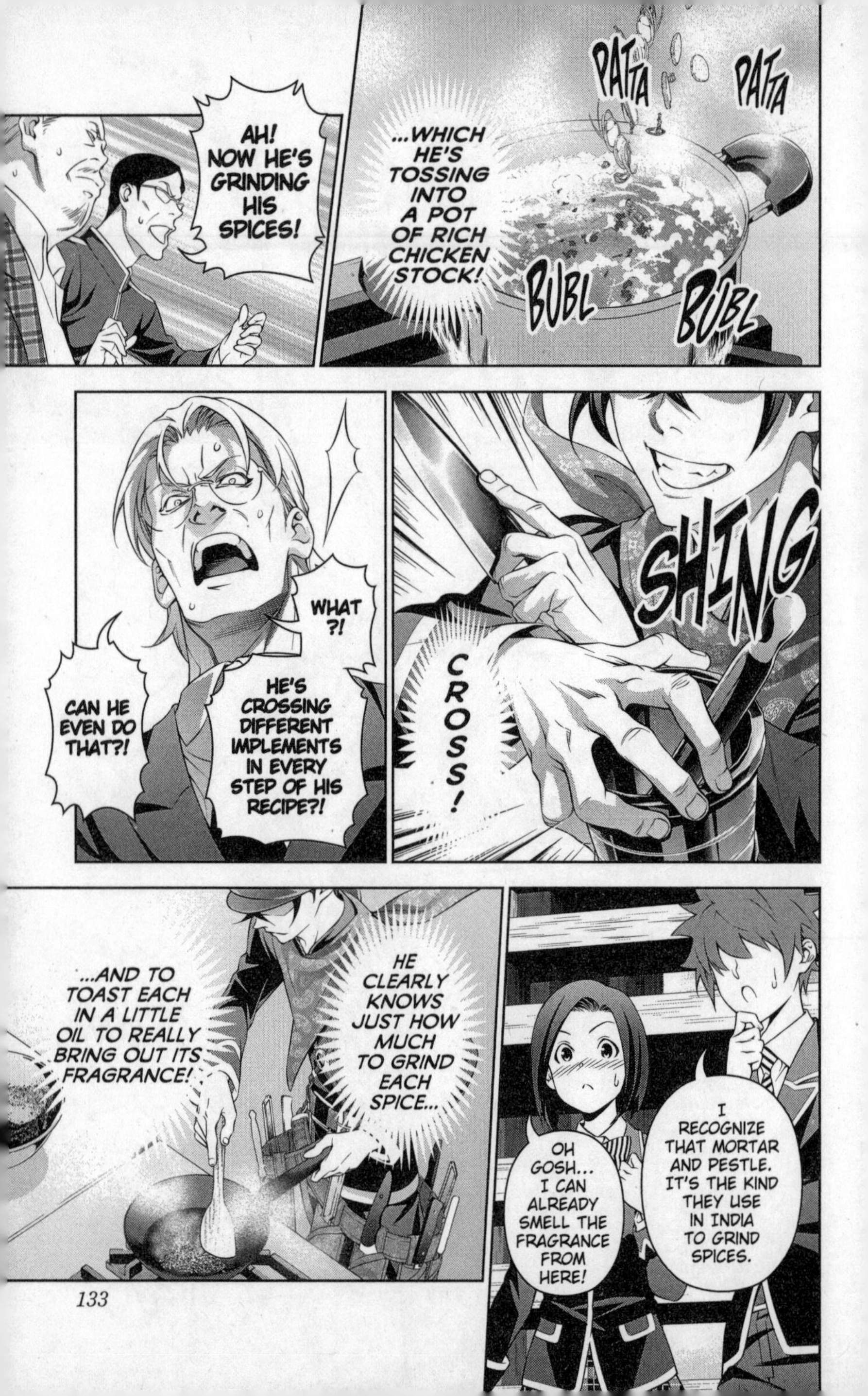
PATTA
PATTA
...WHICH HE'S TOSSING INTO A POT OF RICH CHICKEN STOCK!
BUBL
BUBL
AH! NOW HE'S GRINDING HIS SPICES!
SHING
CROSS!
WHAT?!
HE'S CROSSING DIFFERENT IMPLEMENTS IN EVERY STEP OF HIS RECIPE?!
CAN HE EVEN DO THAT?!
I RECOGNIZE THAT MORTAR AND PESTLE. IT'S THE KIND THEY USE IN INDIA TO GRIND SPICES.
OH GOSH... I CAN ALREADY SMELL THE FRAGRANCE FROM HERE!
HE CLEARLY KNOWS JUST HOW MUCH TO GRIND EACH SPICE...
...AND TO TOAST EACH IN A LITTLE OIL TO REALLY BRING OUT ITS FRAGRANCE!

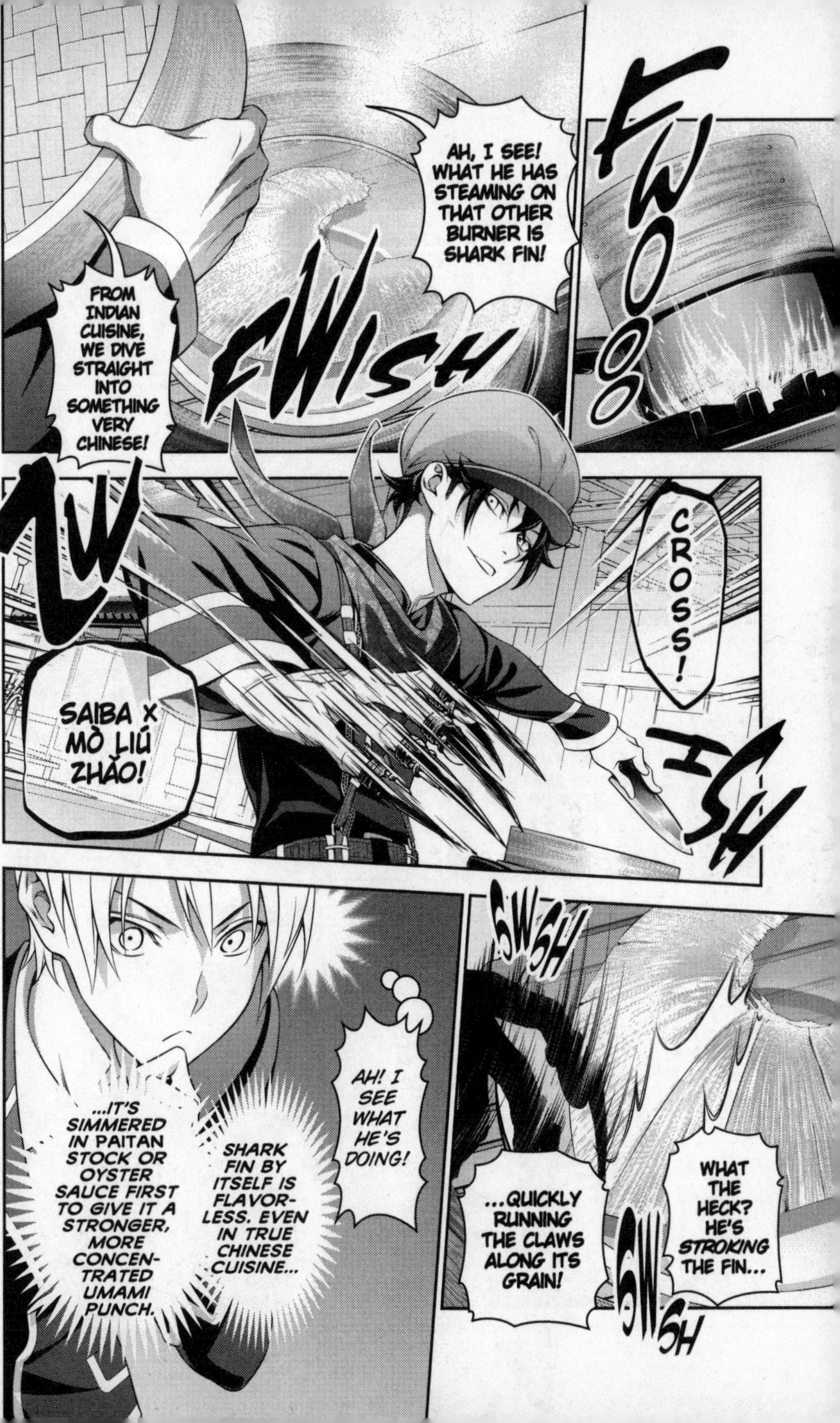
FWOOO
AH, I SEE! WHAT HE HAS STEAMING ON THAT OTHER BURNER IS SHARK FIN!
CWISH
FROM INDIAN CUISINE, WE DIVE STRAIGHT INTO SOMETHING VERY CHINESE!
CROSS!
FSH
SAIBA x MÒ LIÚ ZHǍO!
ZW
WHAT THE HECK? HE'S STROKING THE FIN...
SWSH
...QUICKLY RUNNING THE CLAWS ALONG ITS GRAIN!
SWSH
AH! I SEE WHAT HE'S DOING!
SHARK FIN BY ITSELF IS FLAVOR-LESS. EVEN IN TRUE CHINESE CUISINE...
...IT'S SIMMERED IN PAITAN STOCK OR OYSTER SAUCE FIRST TO GIVE IT A STRONGER, MORE CONCEN-TRATED UMAMI PUNCH.

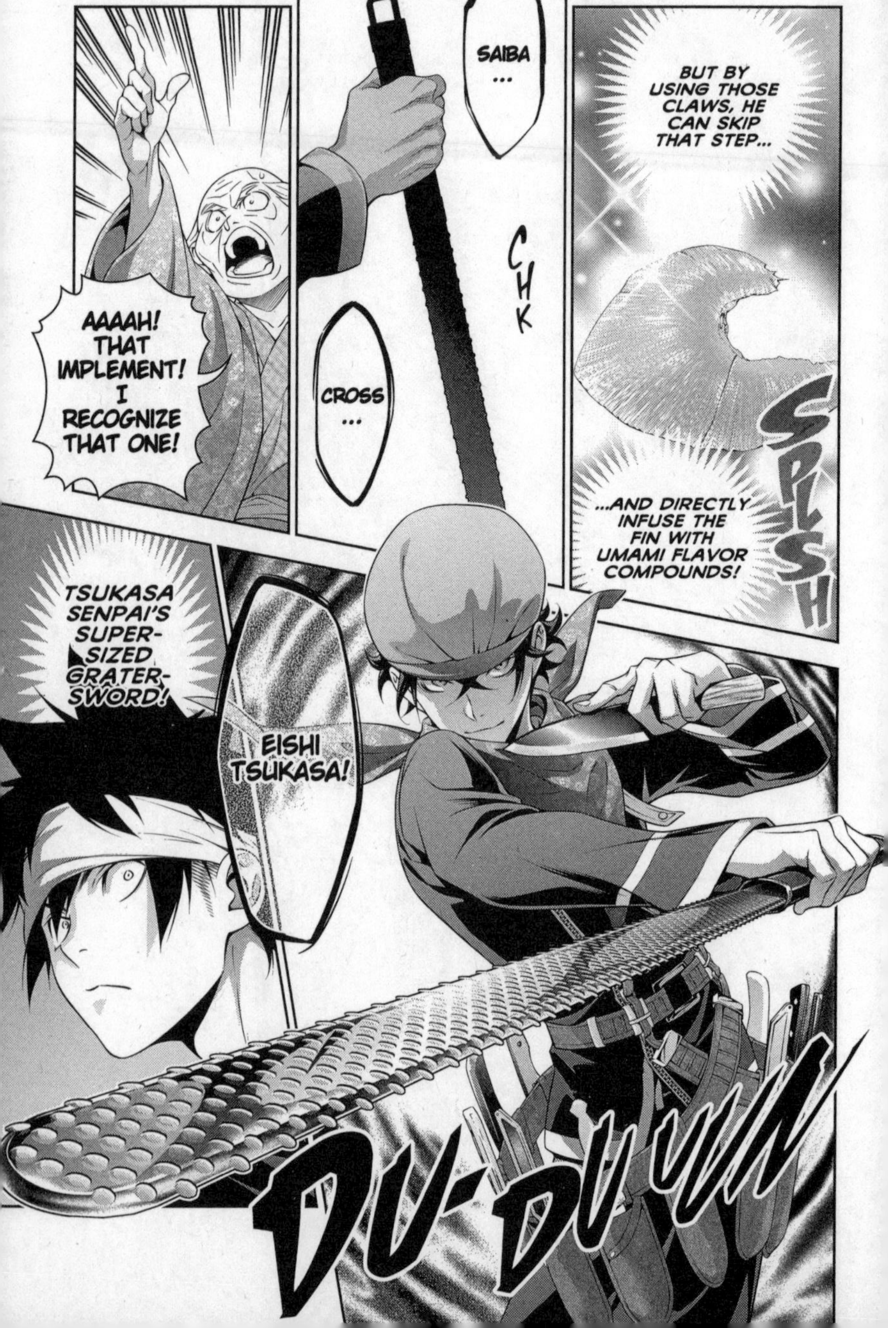
BUT BY USING THOSE CLAWS, HE CAN SKIP THAT STEP...
SPLSH
...AND DIRECTLY INFUSE THE FIN WITH UMAMI FLAVOR COMPOUNDS!
SAIBA ...
CHK
CROSS ...
AAAAH! THAT IMPLEMENT! I RECOGNIZE THAT ONE!
EISHI TSUKASA!
TSUKASA SENPAI'S SUPER-SIZED GRATER-SWORD!
DU-DU-UUN

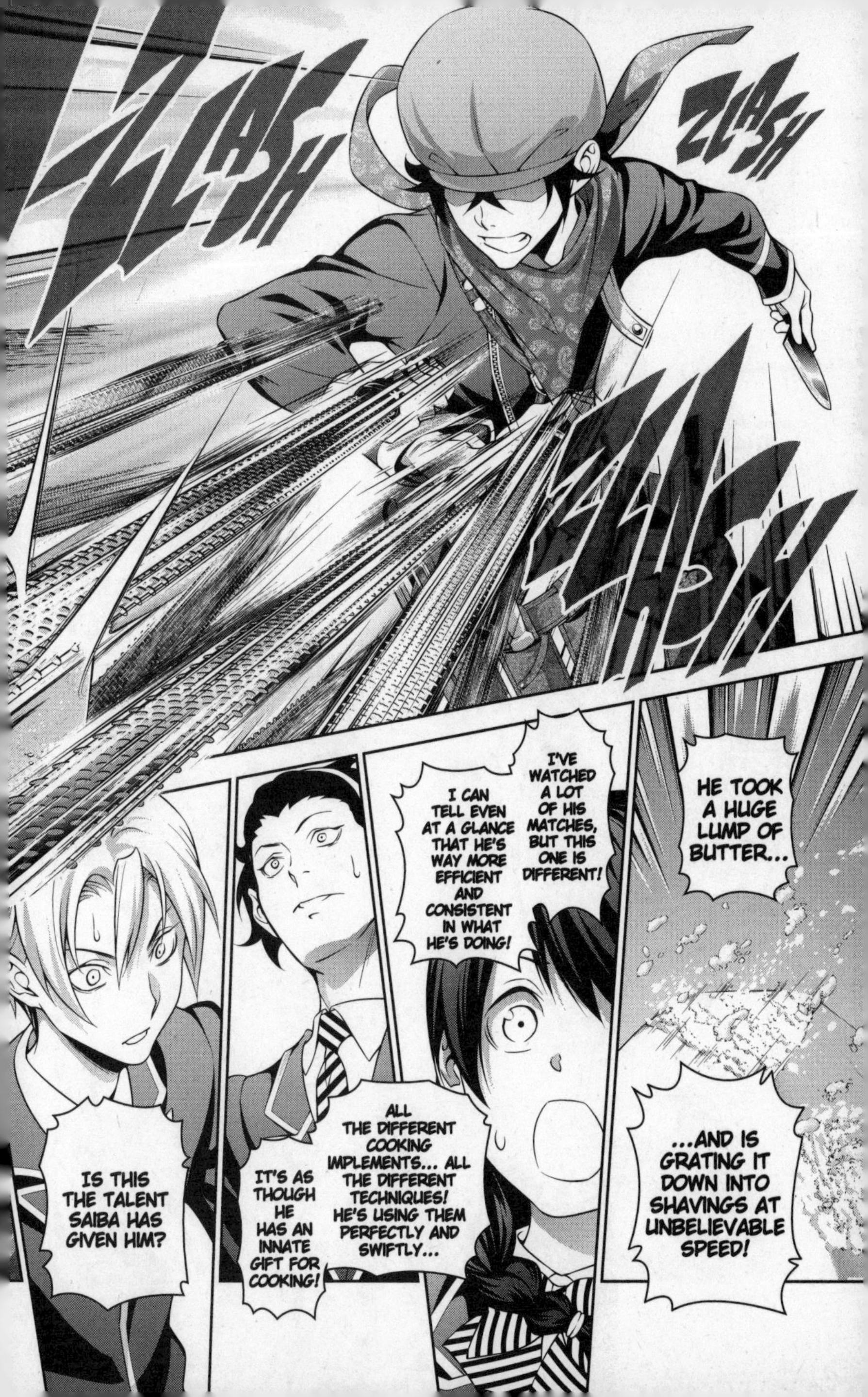
ZLASH
HE TOOK A HUGE LUMP OF BUTTER...
...AND IS GRATING IT DOWN INTO SHAVINGS AT UNBELIEVABLE SPEED!
I'VE WATCHED A LOT OF HIS MATCHES, BUT THIS ONE IS DIFFERENT!
I CAN TELL EVEN AT A GLANCE THAT HE'S WAY MORE EFFICIENT AND CONSISTENT IN WHAT HE'S DOING!
ALL THE DIFFERENT COOKING IMPLEMENTS... ALL THE DIFFERENT TECHNIQUES! HE'S USING THEM PERFECTLY AND SWIFTLY...
IT'S AS THOUGH HE HAS AN INNATE GIFT FOR COOKING!
IS THIS THE TALENT SAIBA HAS GIVEN HIM?

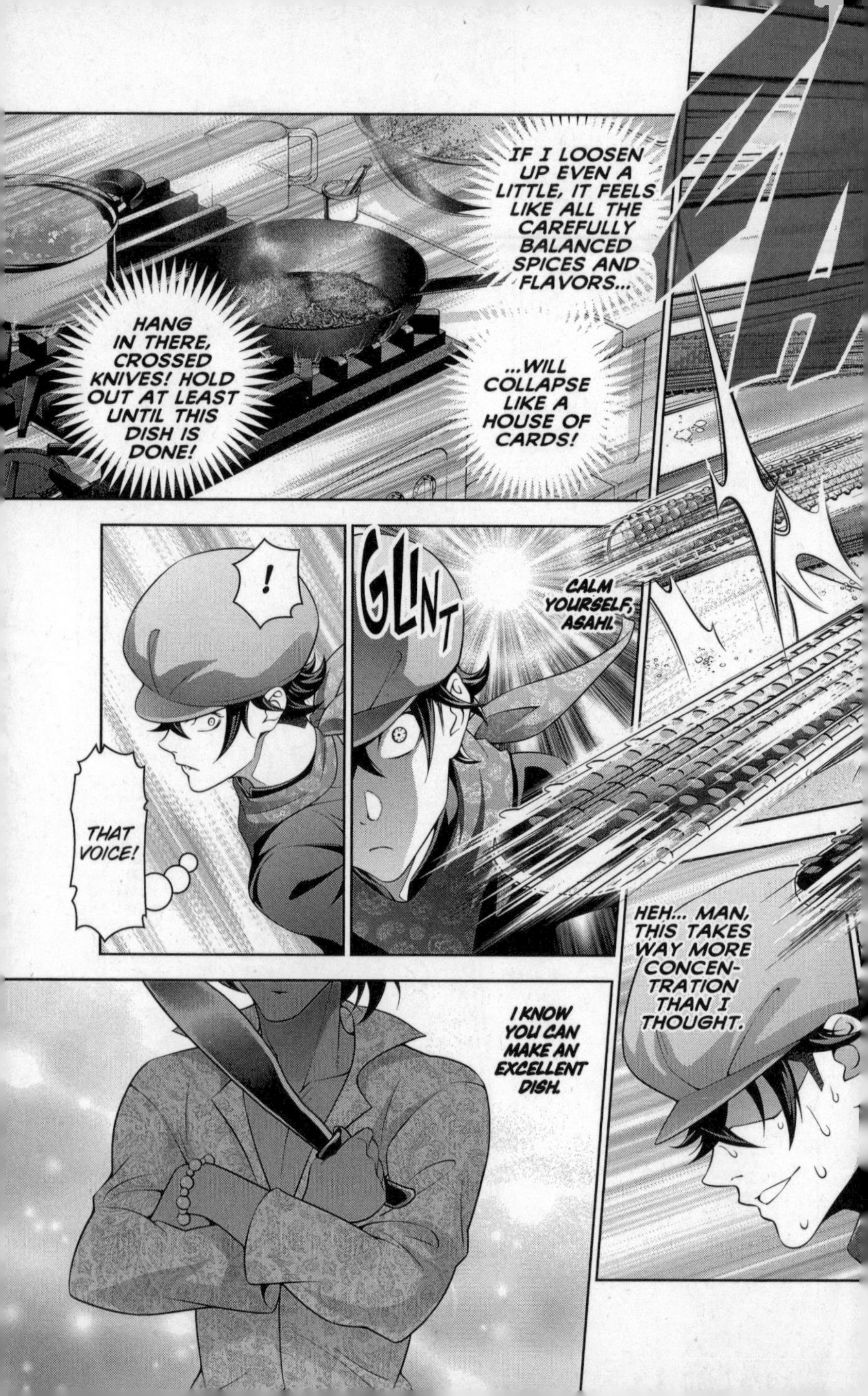
HEH... MAN, THIS TAKES WAY MORE CONCEN-TRATION THAN I THOUGHT.
IF I LOOSEN UP EVEN A LITTLE, IT FEELS LIKE ALL THE CAREFULLY BALANCED SPICES AND FLAVORS...
...WILL COLLAPSE LIKE A HOUSE OF CARDS!
HANG IN THERE, CROSSED KNIVES! HOLD OUT AT LEAST UNTIL THIS DISH IS DONE!
GLINT
CALM YOURSELF, ASAHI.
!
THAT VOICE!
I KNOW YOU CAN MAKE AN EXCELLENT DISH.

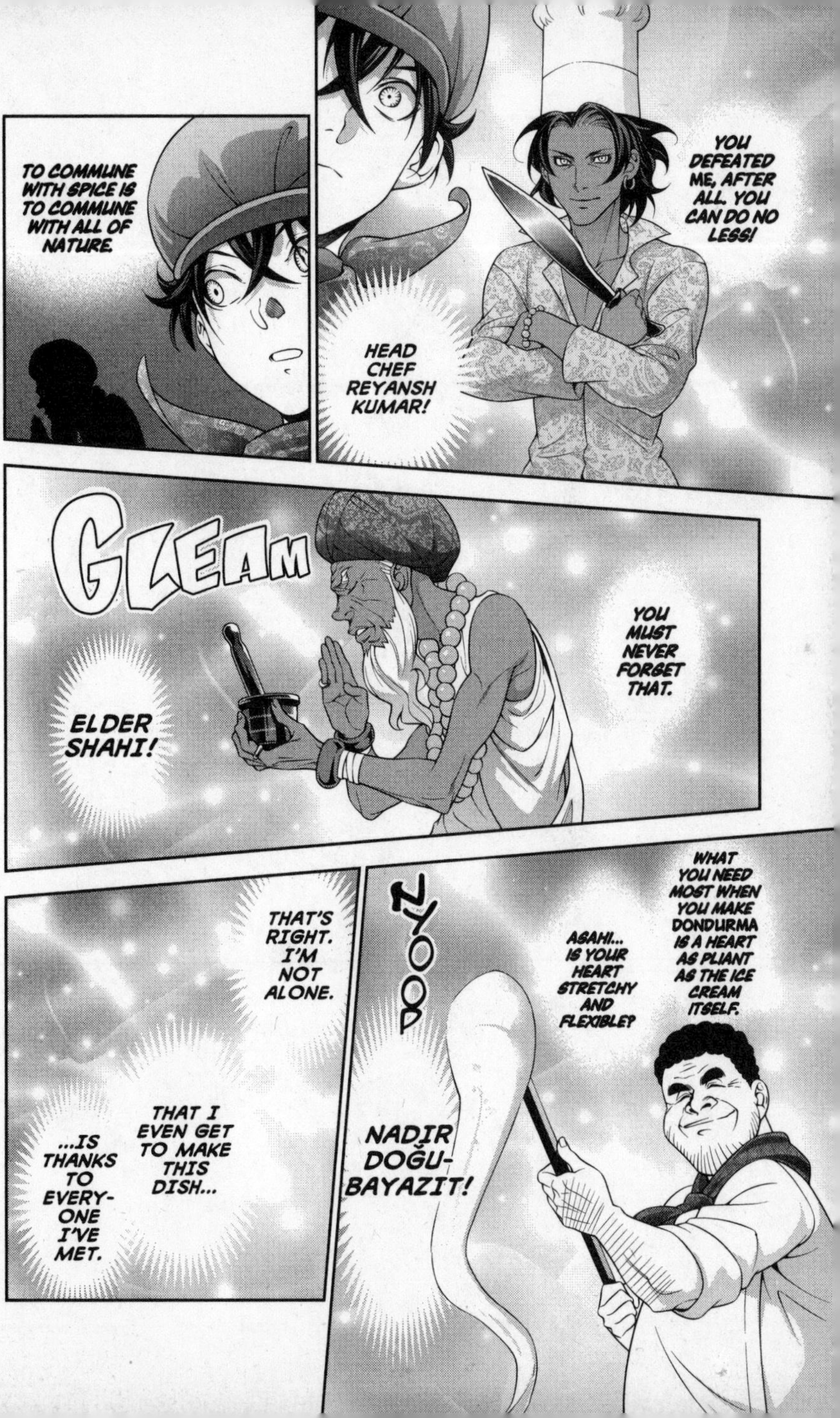
YOU DEFEATED ME, AFTER ALL. YOU CAN DO NO LESS!
HEAD CHEF REYANSH KUMAR!
TO COMMUNE WITH SPICE IS TO COMMUNE WITH ALL OF NATURE.
GLEAM
YOU MUST NEVER FORGET THAT.
ELDER SHAHI!
WHAT YOU NEED MOST WHEN YOU MAKE DONDURMA IS A HEART AS PLIANT AS THE ICE CREAM ITSELF.
ASAHI... IS YOUR HEART STRETCHY AND FLEXIBLE?
NYOOOO
NADIR DOĞU-BAYAZIT!
THAT'S RIGHT. I'M NOT ALONE.
THAT I EVEN GET TO MAKE THIS DISH...
...IS THANKS TO EVERY-ONE I'VE MET.

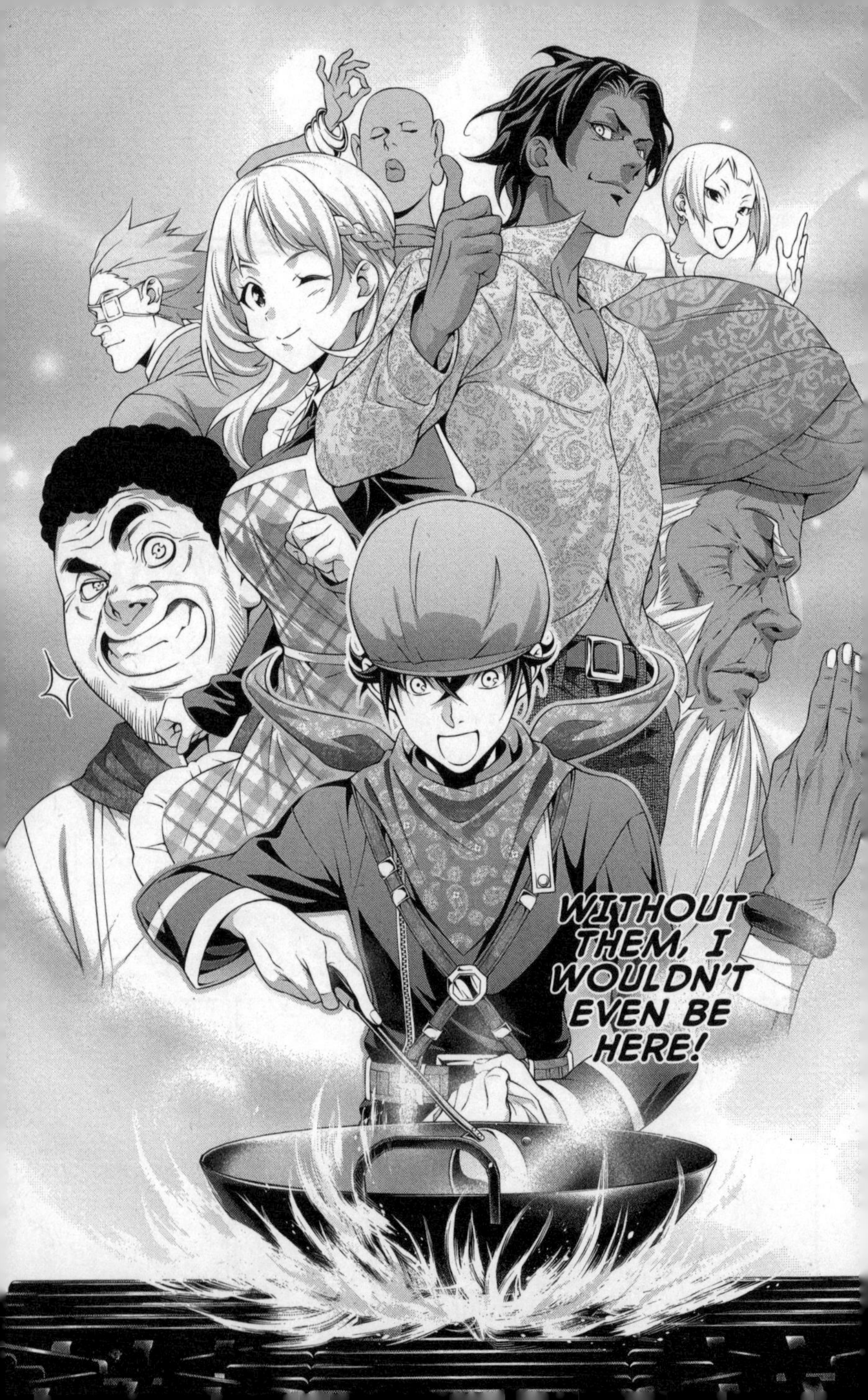
WITHOUT THEM, I WOULDN'T EVEN BE HERE!

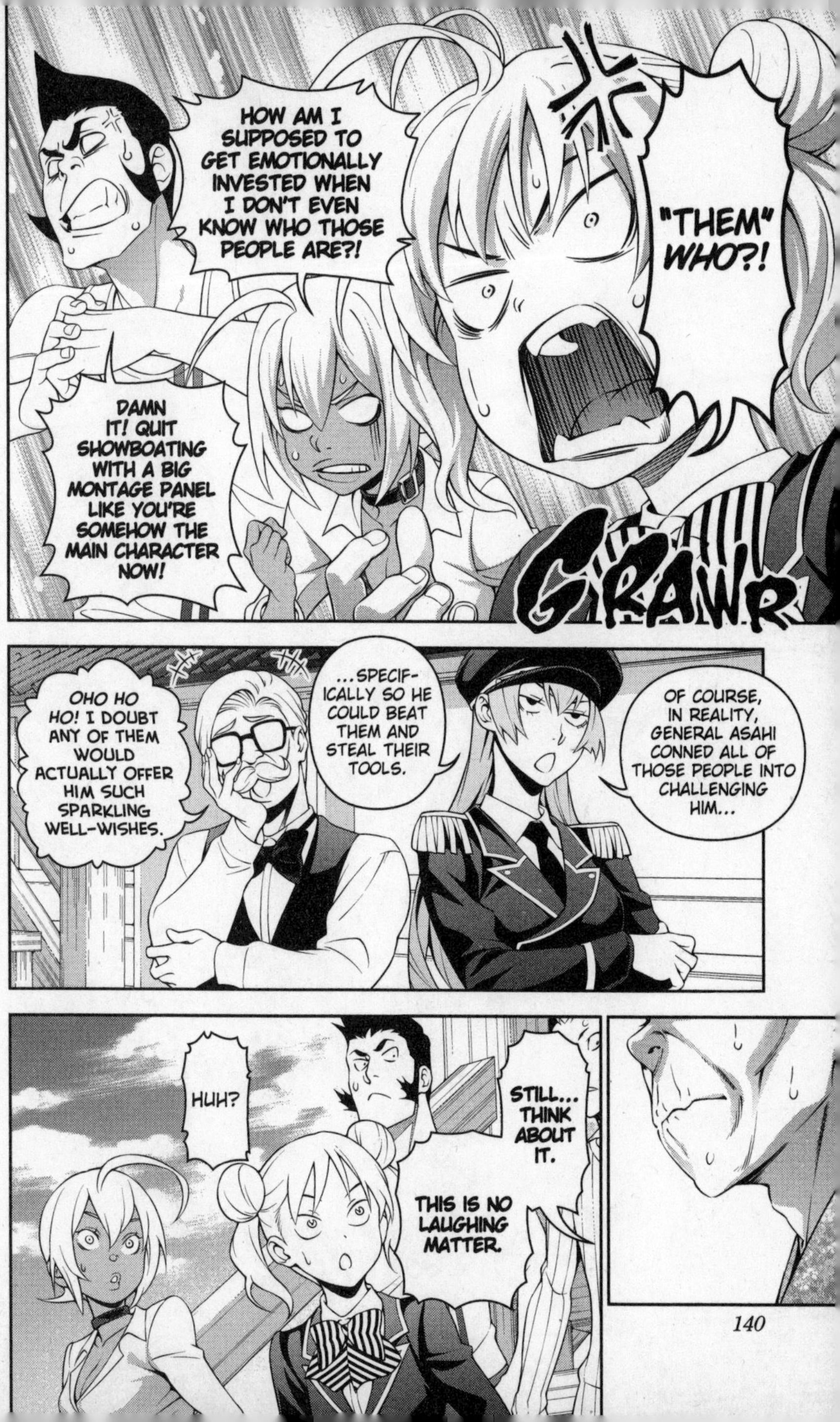
HOW AM I SUPPOSED TO GET EMOTIONALLY INVESTED WHEN I DON'T EVEN KNOW WHO THOSE PEOPLE ARE?!
"THEM" WHO?!
DAMN IT! QUIT SHOWBOATING WITH A BIG MONTAGE PANEL LIKE YOU'RE SOMEHOW THE MAIN CHARACTER NOW!
GRAWR
OF COURSE, IN REALITY, GENERAL ASAHI CONNED ALL OF THOSE PEOPLE INTO CHALLENGING HIM...
...SPECIF-ICALLY SO HE COULD BEAT THEM AND STEAL THEIR TOOLS.
OHO HO HO! I DOUBT ANY OF THEM WOULD ACTUALLY OFFER HIM SUCH SPARKLING WELL-WISHES.
STILL... THINK ABOUT IT.
THIS IS NO LAUGHING MATTER.
HUH?

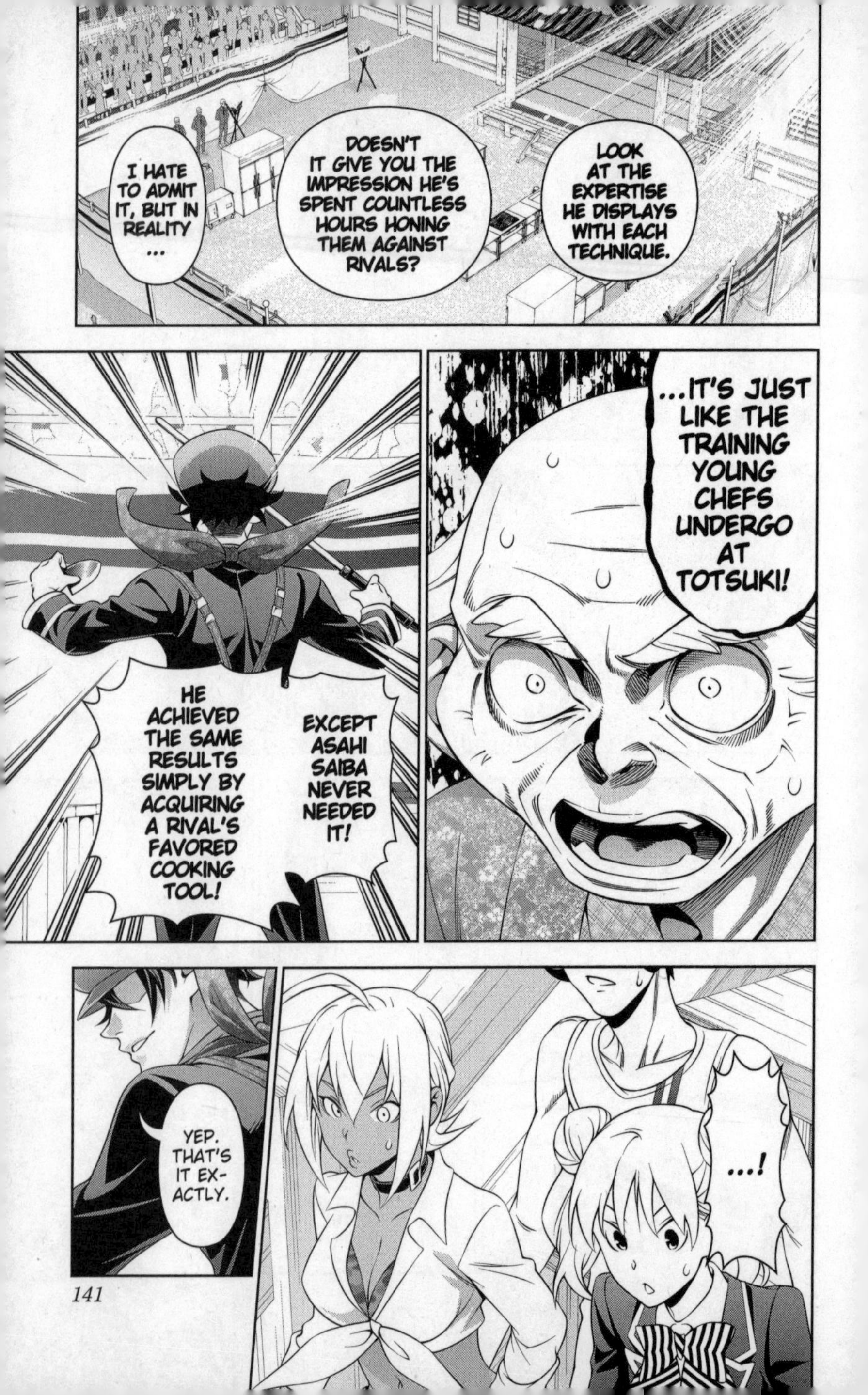
LOOK AT THE EXPERTISE HE DISPLAYS WITH EACH TECHNIQUE.
DOESN'T IT GIVE YOU THE IMPRESSION HE'S SPENT COUNTLESS HOURS HONING THEM AGAINST RIVALS?
I HATE TO ADMIT IT, BUT IN REALITY ...
...IT'S JUST LIKE THE TRAINING YOUNG CHEFS UNDERGO AT TOTSUKI!
EXCEPT ASAHI SAIBA NEVER NEEDED IT!
HE ACHIEVED THE SAME RESULTS SIMPLY BY ACQUIRING A RIVAL'S FAVORED COOKING TOOL!
...!
YEP. THAT'S IT EX-ACTLY.

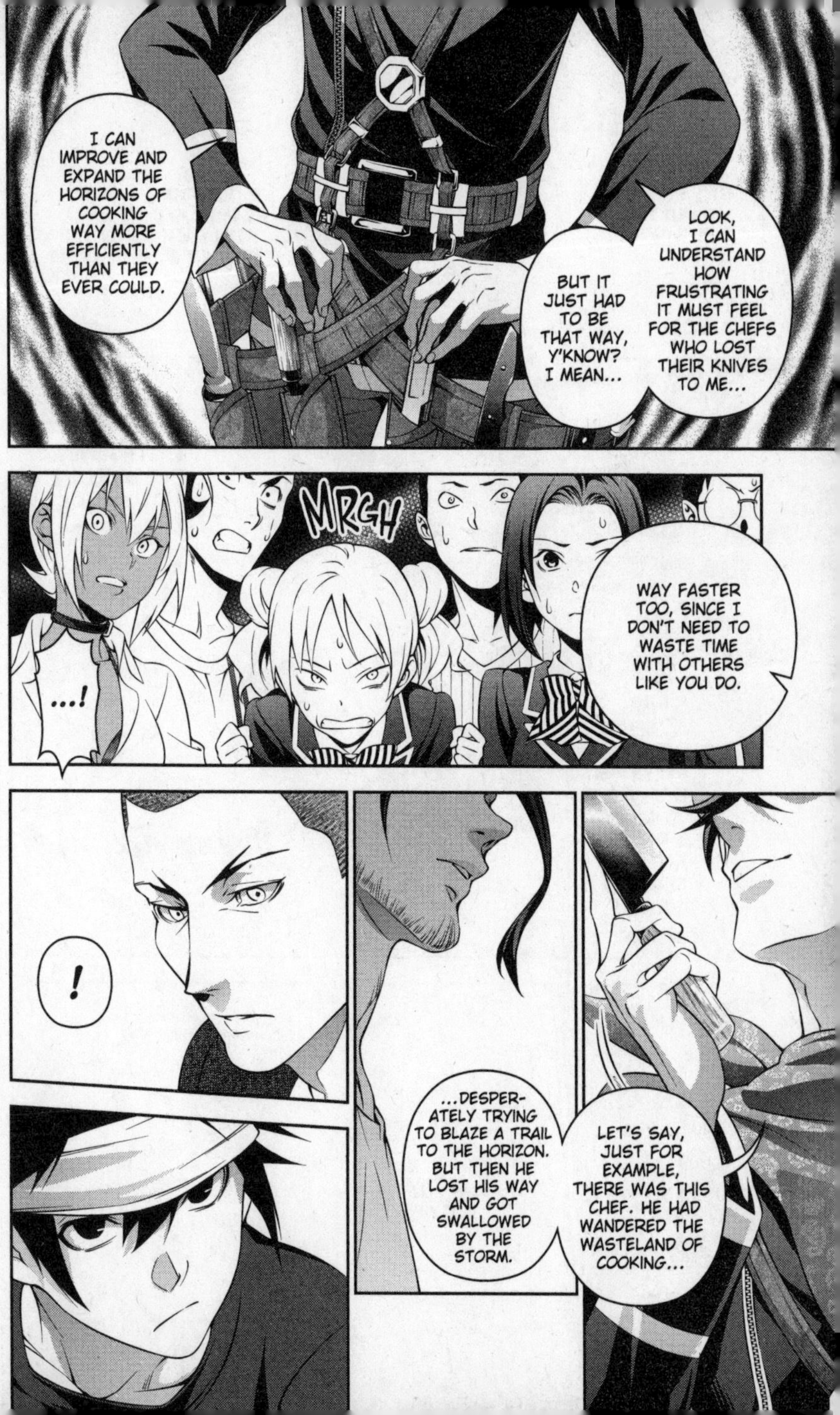
LOOK, I CAN UNDERSTAND HOW FRUSTRATING IT MUST FEEL FOR THE CHEFS WHO LOST THEIR KNIVES TO ME...
BUT IT JUST HAD TO BE THAT WAY, Y'KNOW? I MEAN...
I CAN IMPROVE AND EXPAND THE HORIZONS OF COOKING WAY MORE EFFICIENTLY THAN THEY EVER COULD.
WAY FASTER TOO, SINCE I DON'T NEED TO WASTE TIME WITH OTHERS LIKE YOU DO.
MRGH
...!
LET'S SAY, JUST FOR EXAMPLE, THERE WAS THIS CHEF. HE HAD WANDERED THE WASTELAND OF COOKING...
...DESPER-ATELY TRYING TO BLAZE A TRAIL TO THE HORIZON. BUT THEN HE LOST HIS WAY AND GOT SWALLOWED BY THE STORM.
!

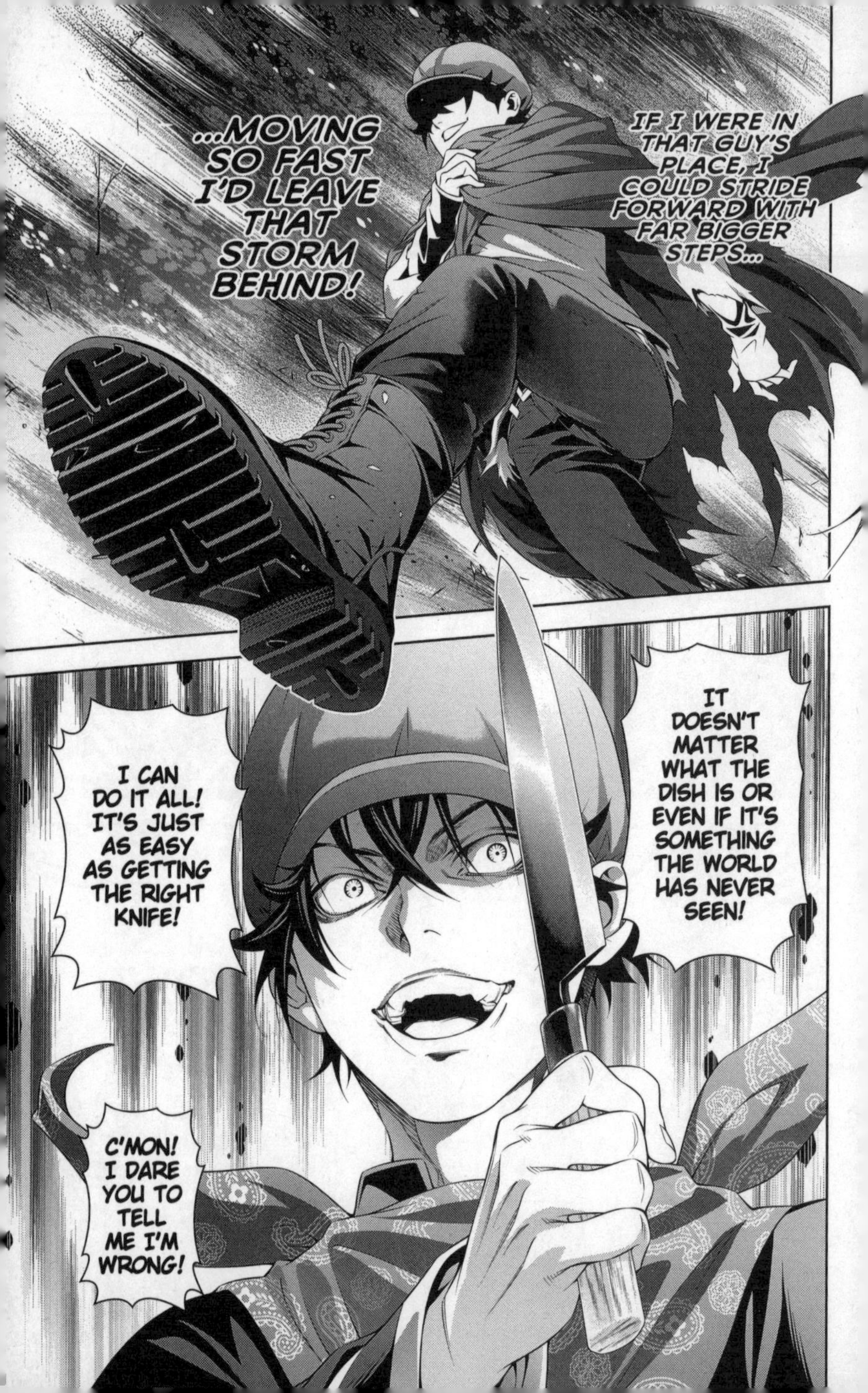
IF I WERE IN THAT GUY'S PLACE, I COULD STRIDE FORWARD WITH FAR BIGGER STEPS...
...MOVING SO FAST I'D LEAVE THAT STORM BEHIND!
IT DOESN'T MATTER WHAT THE DISH IS OR EVEN IF IT'S SOMETHING THE WORLD HAS NEVER SEEN!
I CAN DO IT ALL! IT'S JUST AS EASY AS GETTING THE RIGHT KNIFE!
C'MON! I DARE YOU TO TELL ME I'M WRONG!

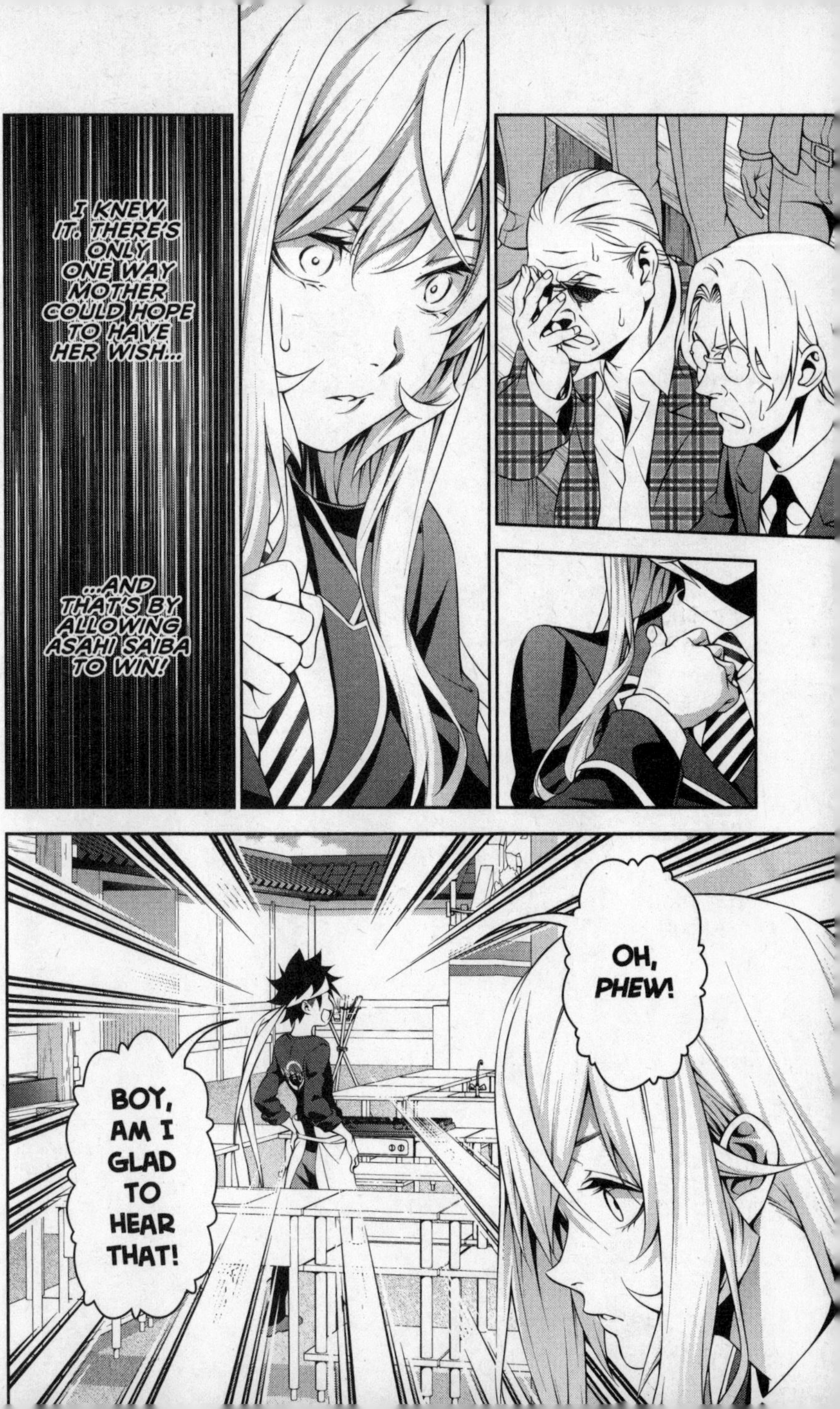
I KNEW IT. THERE'S ONLY ONE WAY MOTHER COULD HOPE TO HAVE HER WISH...
...AND THAT'S BY ALLOWING ASAHI SAIBA TO WIN!
OH, PHEW!
BOY, AM I GLAD TO HEAR THAT!

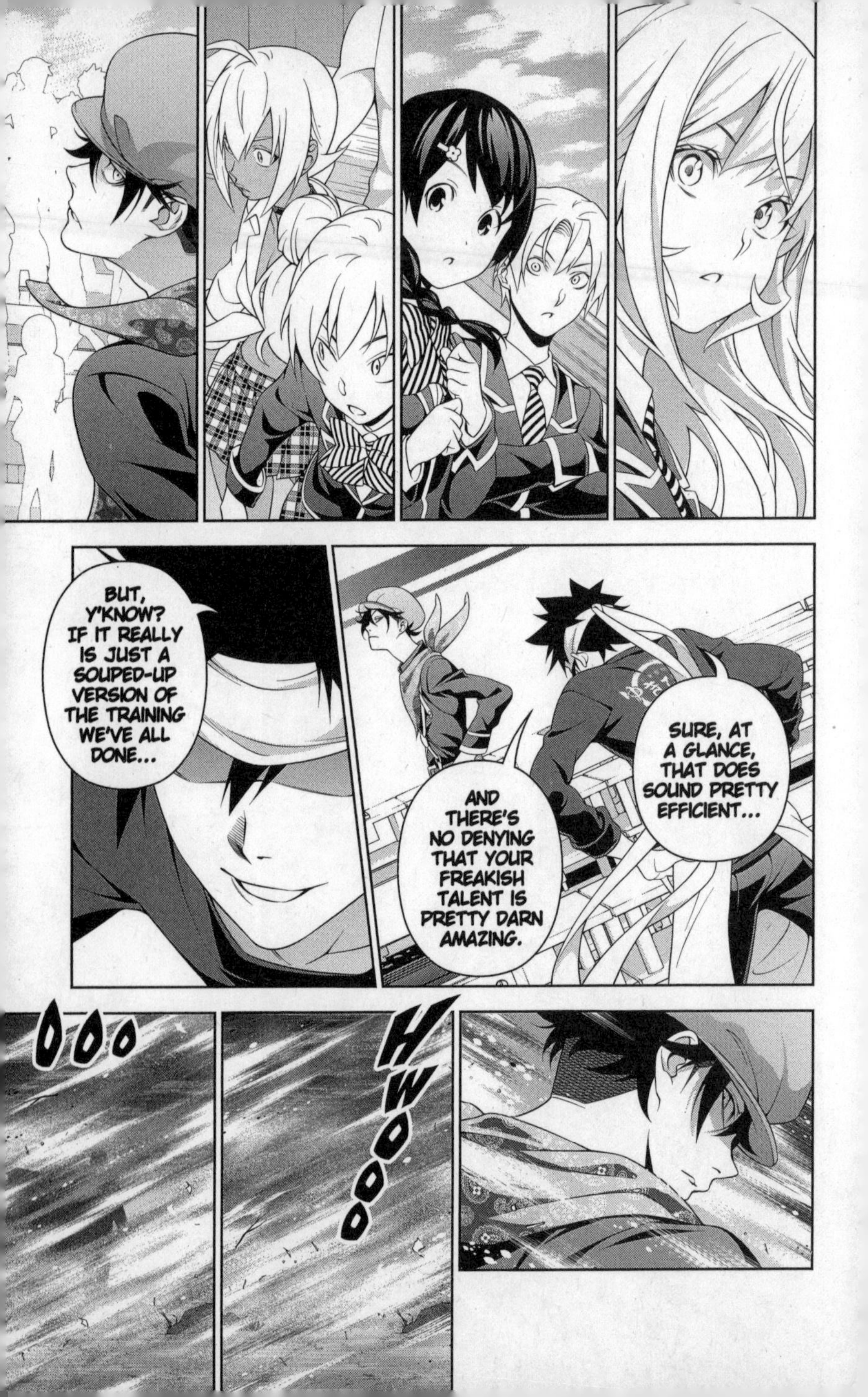
SURE, AT A GLANCE, THAT DOES SOUND PRETTY EFFICIENT...
AND THERE'S NO DENYING THAT YOUR FREAKISH TALENT IS PRETTY DARN AMAZING.
BUT, Y'KNOW? IF IT REALLY IS JUST A SOUPED-UP VERSION OF THE TRAINING WE'VE ALL DONE...
HWOOOOO
OOO

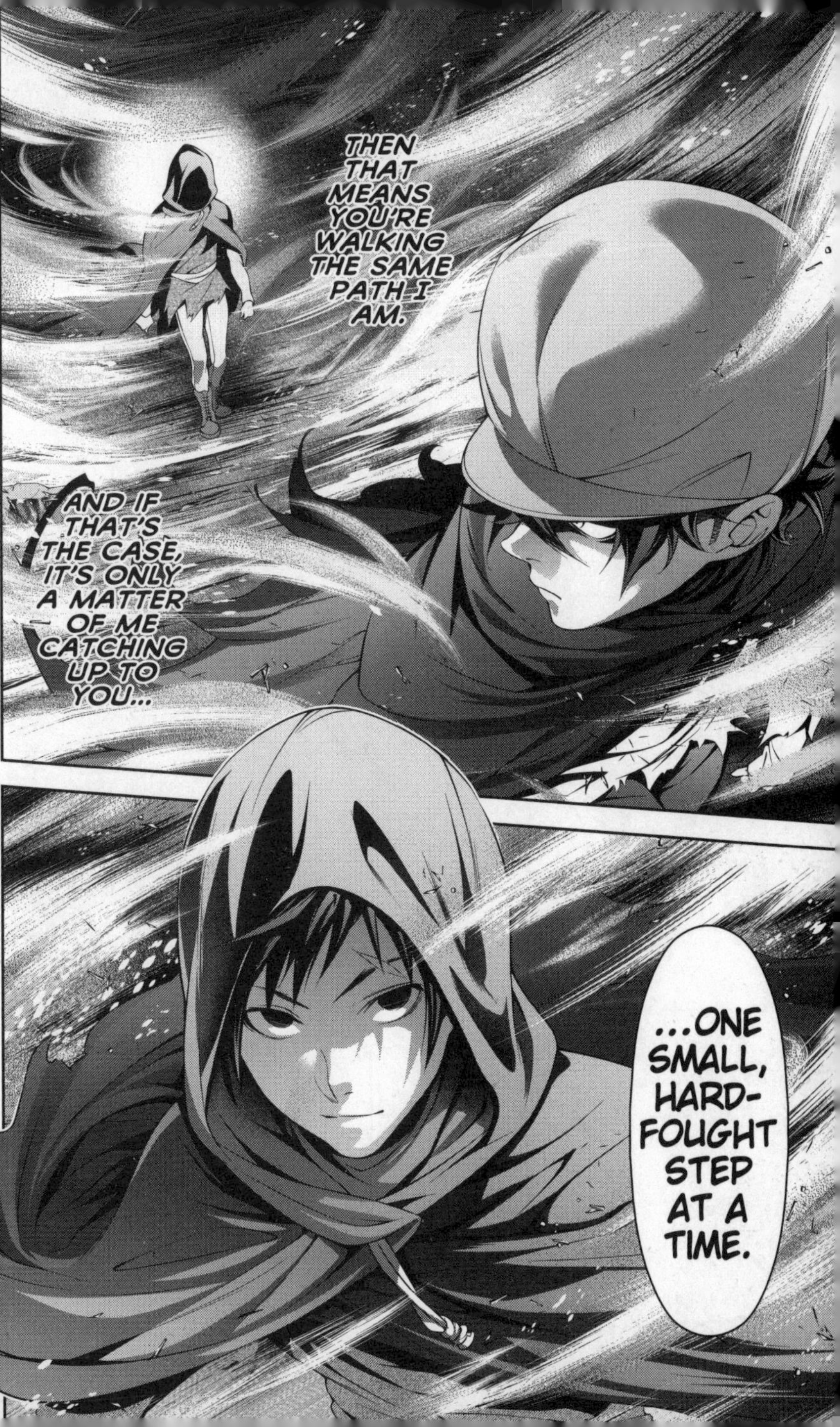
THEN THAT MEANS YOU'RE WALKING THE SAME PATH I AM.
AND IF THAT'S THE CASE, IT'S ONLY A MATTER OF ME CATCHING UP TO YOU...
...ONE SMALL, HARD-FOUGHT STEP AT A TIME.

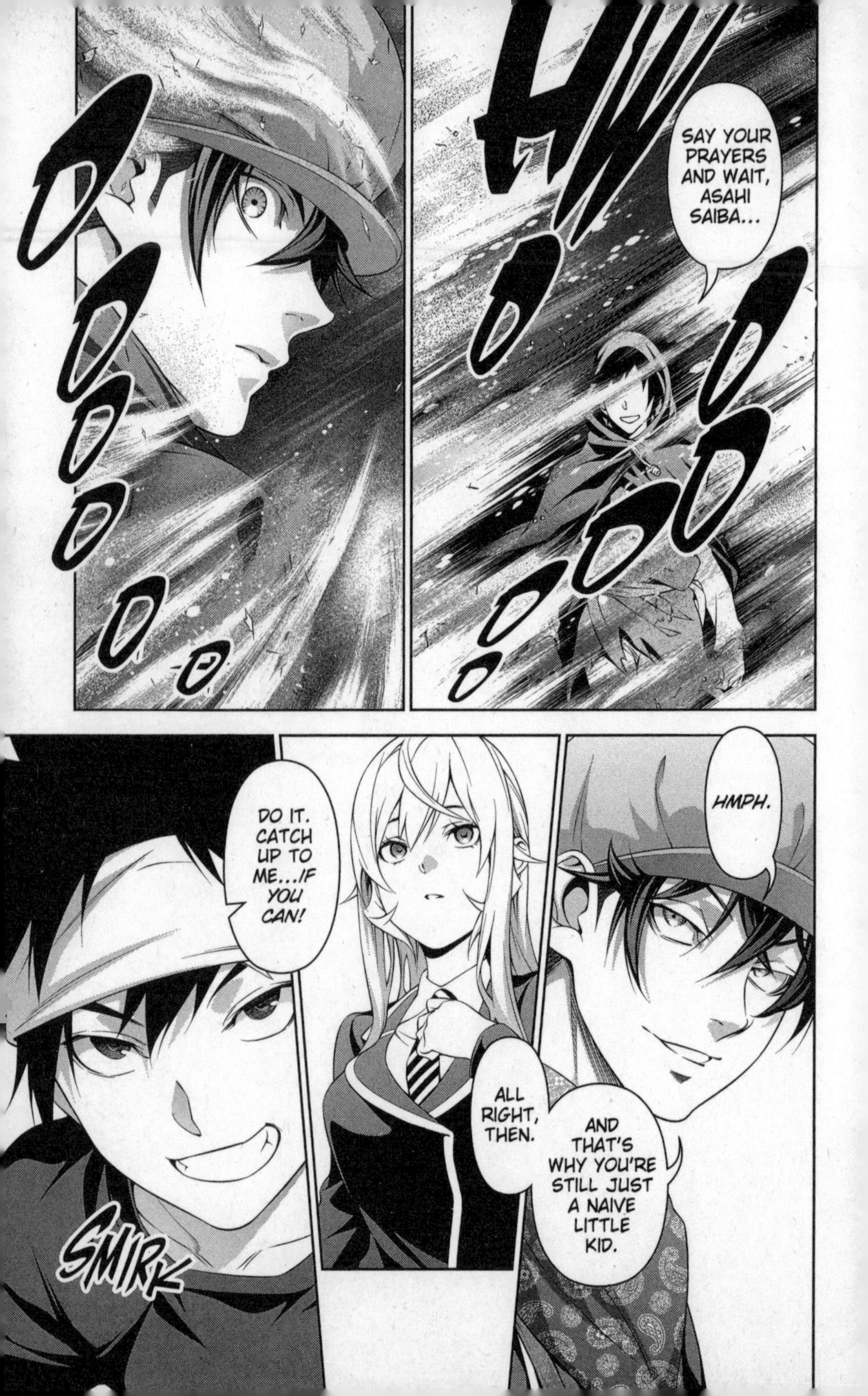
SAY YOUR PRAYERS AND WAIT, ASAHI SAIBA...
HMPH.
ALL RIGHT, THEN.
AND THAT'S WHY YOU'RE STILL JUST A NAIVE LITTLE KID.
DO IT. CATCH UP TO ME...IF YOU CAN!
SMIRK

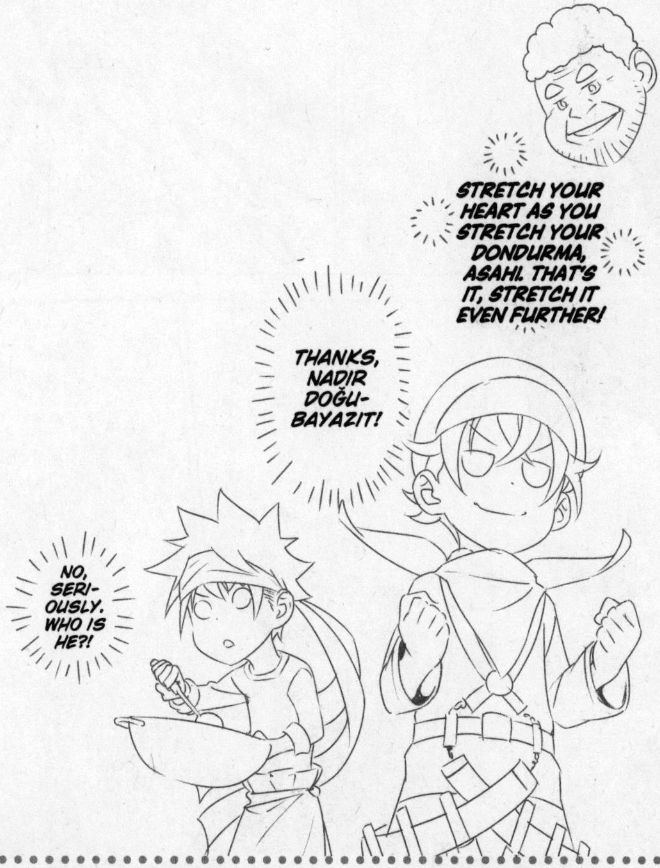
STRETCH YOUR HEART AS YOU STRETCH YOUR DONDURMA, ASAHI. THAT'S IT, STRETCH IT EVEN FURTHER!
THANKS, NADIR DOĞU-BAYAZIT!
NO, SERI-OUSLY. WHO IS HE?!

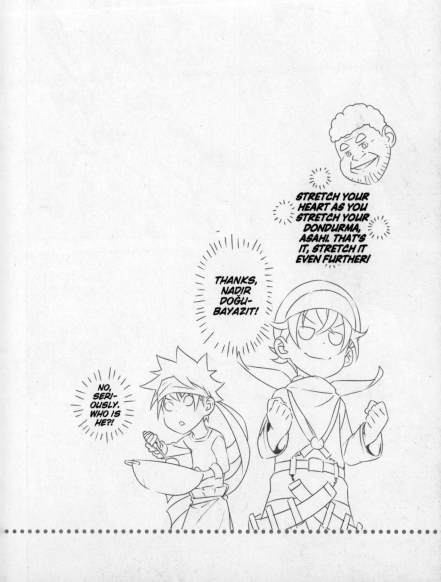

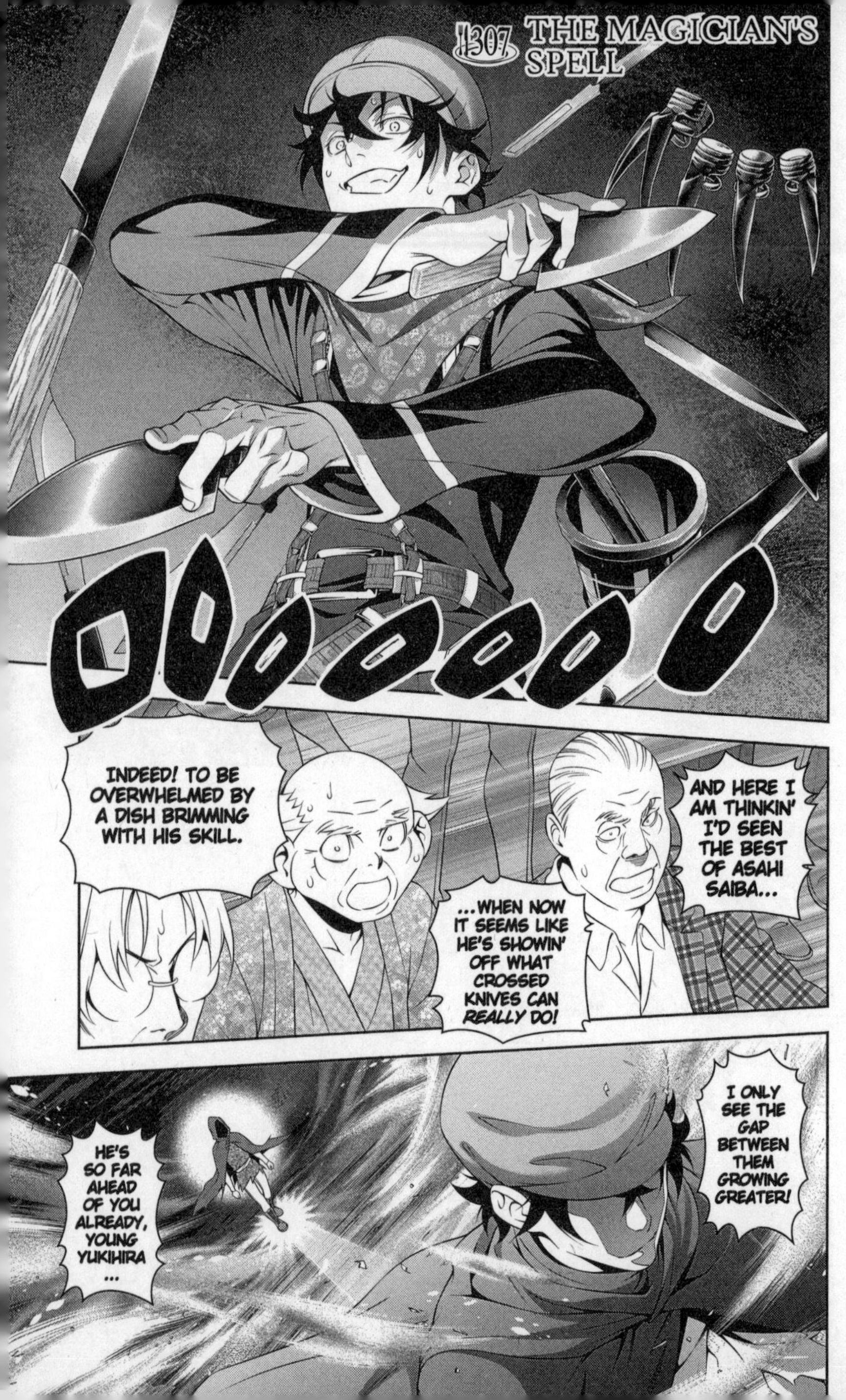
307 THE MAGICIAN'S SPELL
AND HERE I AM THINKIN' I'D SEEN THE BEST OF ASAHI SAIBA...
...WHEN NOW IT SEEMS LIKE HE'S SHOWIN' OFF WHAT CROSSED KNIVES CAN *REALLY* DO!
INDEED! TO BE OVERWHELMED BY A DISH BRIMMING WITH HIS SKILL.
I ONLY SEE THE GAP BETWEEN THEM GROWING GREATER!
HE'S SO FAR AHEAD OF YOU ALREADY, YOUNG YUKIHIRA ...

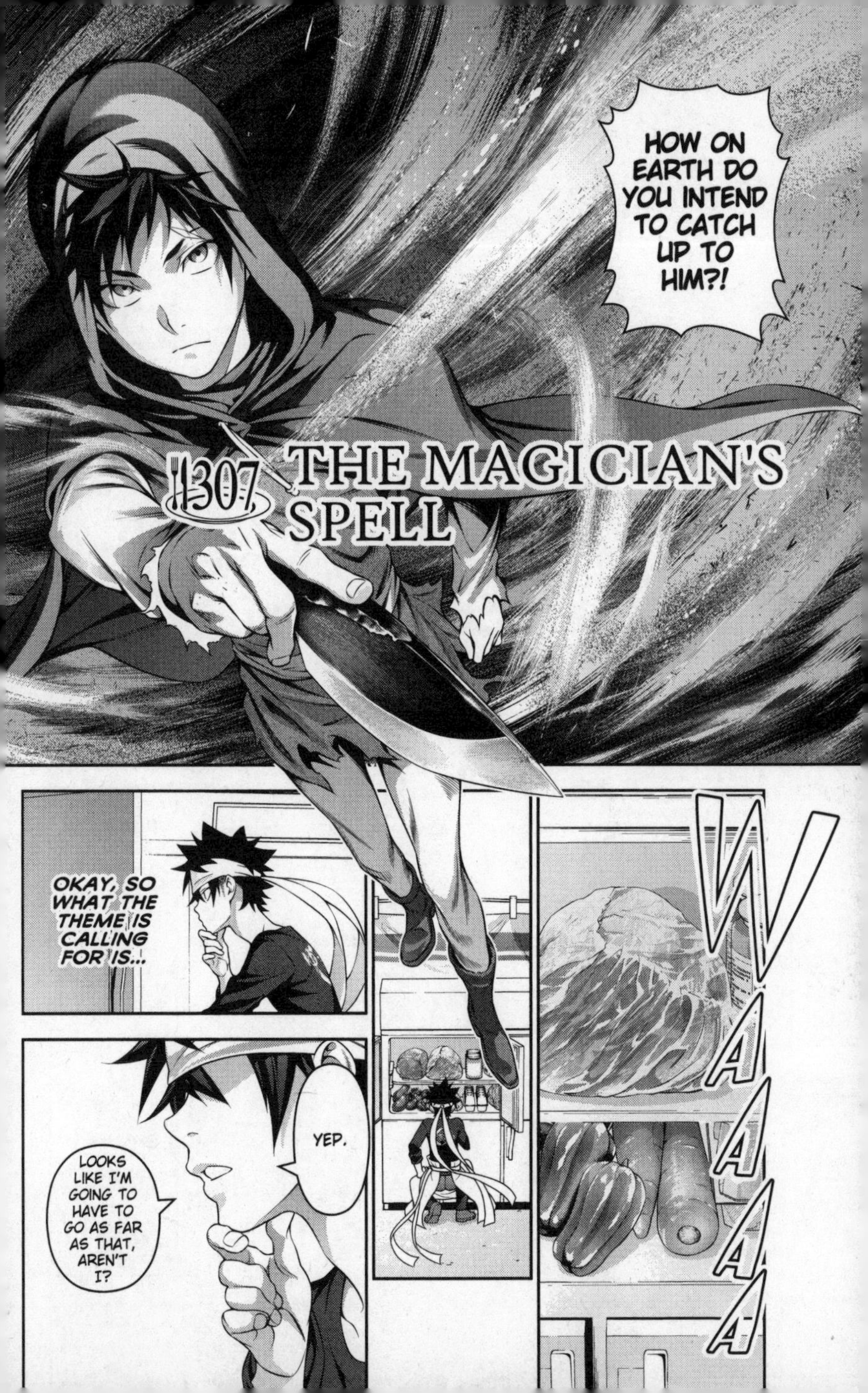

HOW ON EARTH DO YOU INTEND TO CATCH UP TO HIM?!
307 THE MAGICIAN'S SPELL
WAAAA
OKAY, SO WHAT THE THEME IS CALLING FOR IS...
YEP.
LOOKS LIKE I'M GOING TO HAVE TO GO AS FAR AS THAT, AREN'T I?

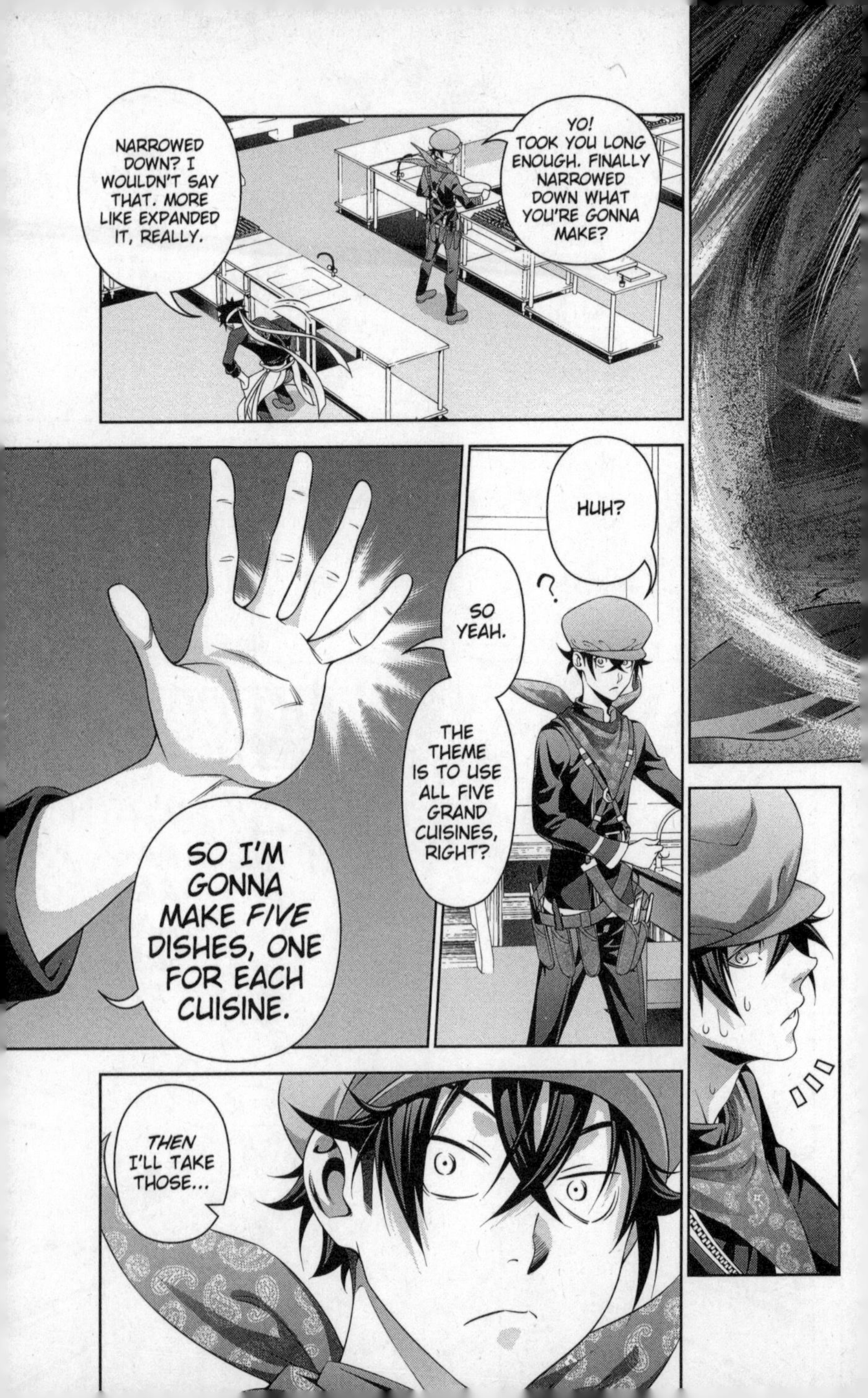
YO! TOOK YOU LONG ENOUGH. FINALLY NARROWED DOWN WHAT YOU'RE GONNA MAKE?
NARROWED DOWN? I WOULDN'T SAY THAT. MORE LIKE EXPANDED IT, REALLY.
HUH?
?
SO YEAH.
THE THEME IS TO USE ALL FIVE GRAND CUISINES, RIGHT?
SO I'M GONNA MAKE *FIVE* DISHES, ONE FOR EACH CUISINE.
THEN I'LL TAKE THOSE...

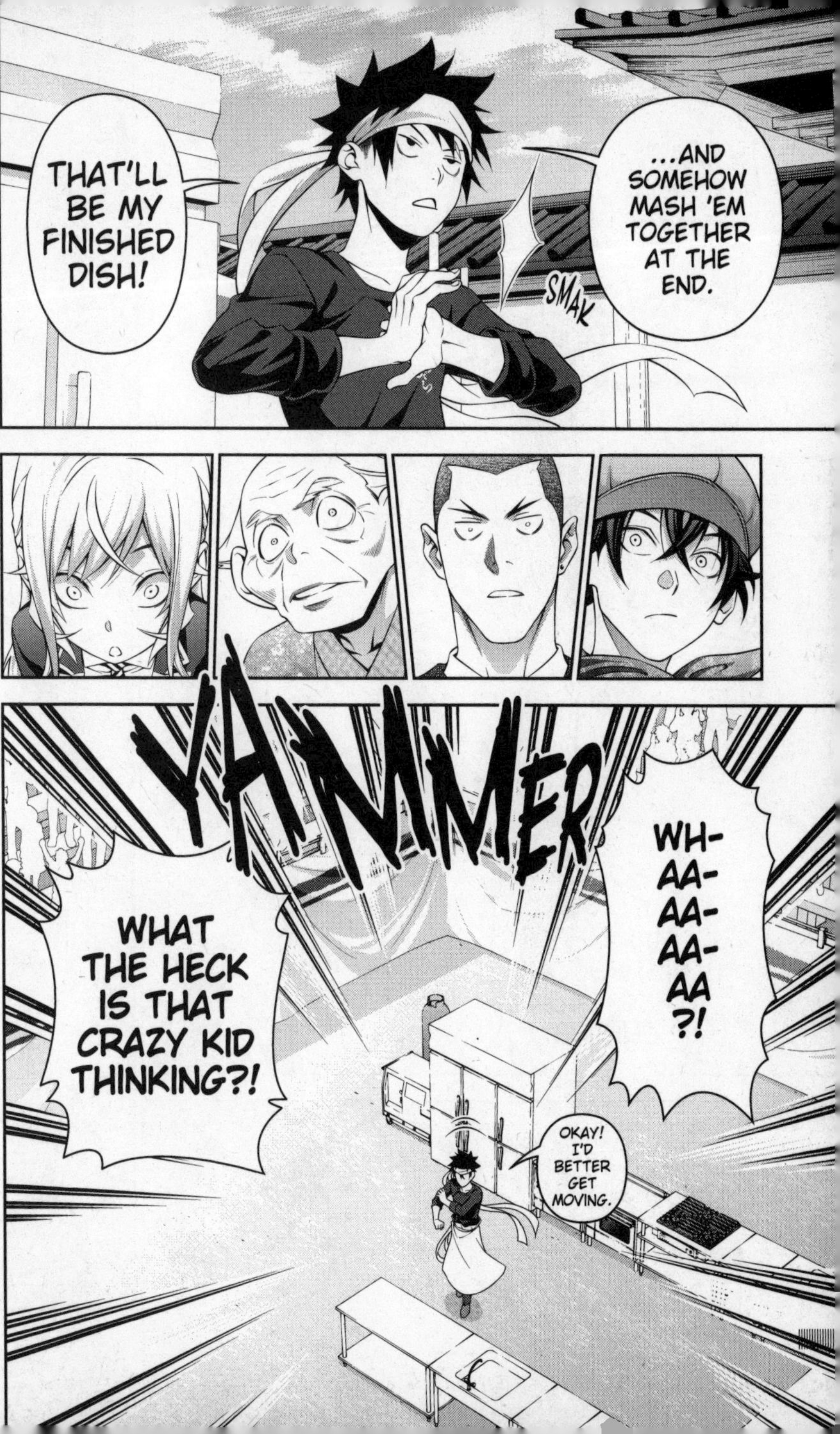
...AND SOMEHOW MASH 'EM TOGETHER AT THE END.
SMAK
THAT'LL BE MY FINISHED DISH!
YAMMER
WH-AA-AA-AA-AA?!
WHAT THE HECK IS THAT CRAZY KID THINKING?!
OKAY! I'D BETTER GET MOVING.

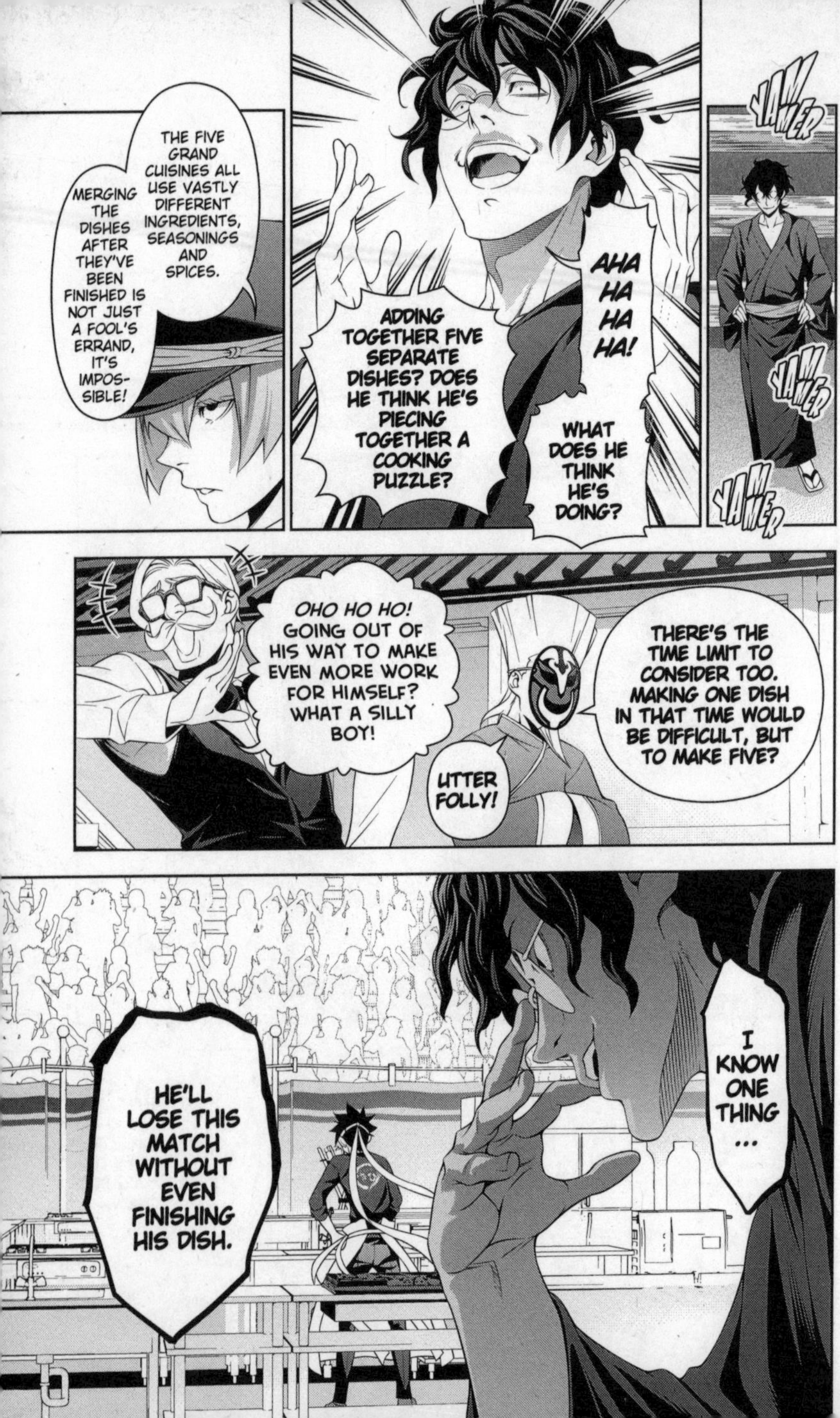
YAMM YAMM YAMM
AHA HA HA HA!
WHAT DOES HE THINK HE'S DOING?
ADDING TOGETHER FIVE SEPARATE DISHES? DOES HE THINK HE'S PIECING TOGETHER A COOKING PUZZLE?
THE FIVE GRAND CUISINES ALL USE VASTLY DIFFERENT INGREDIENTS, SEASONINGS AND SPICES.
MERGING THE DISHES AFTER THEY'VE BEEN FINISHED IS NOT JUST A FOOL'S ERRAND, IT'S IMPOSSIBLE!
THERE'S THE TIME LIMIT TO CONSIDER TOO. MAKING ONE DISH IN THAT TIME WOULD BE DIFFICULT, BUT TO MAKE FIVE?
UTTER FOLLY!
OHO HO HO! GOING OUT OF HIS WAY TO MAKE EVEN MORE WORK FOR HIMSELF? WHAT A SILLY BOY!
I KNOW ONE THING...
HE'LL LOSE THIS MATCH WITHOUT EVEN FINISHING HIS DISH.

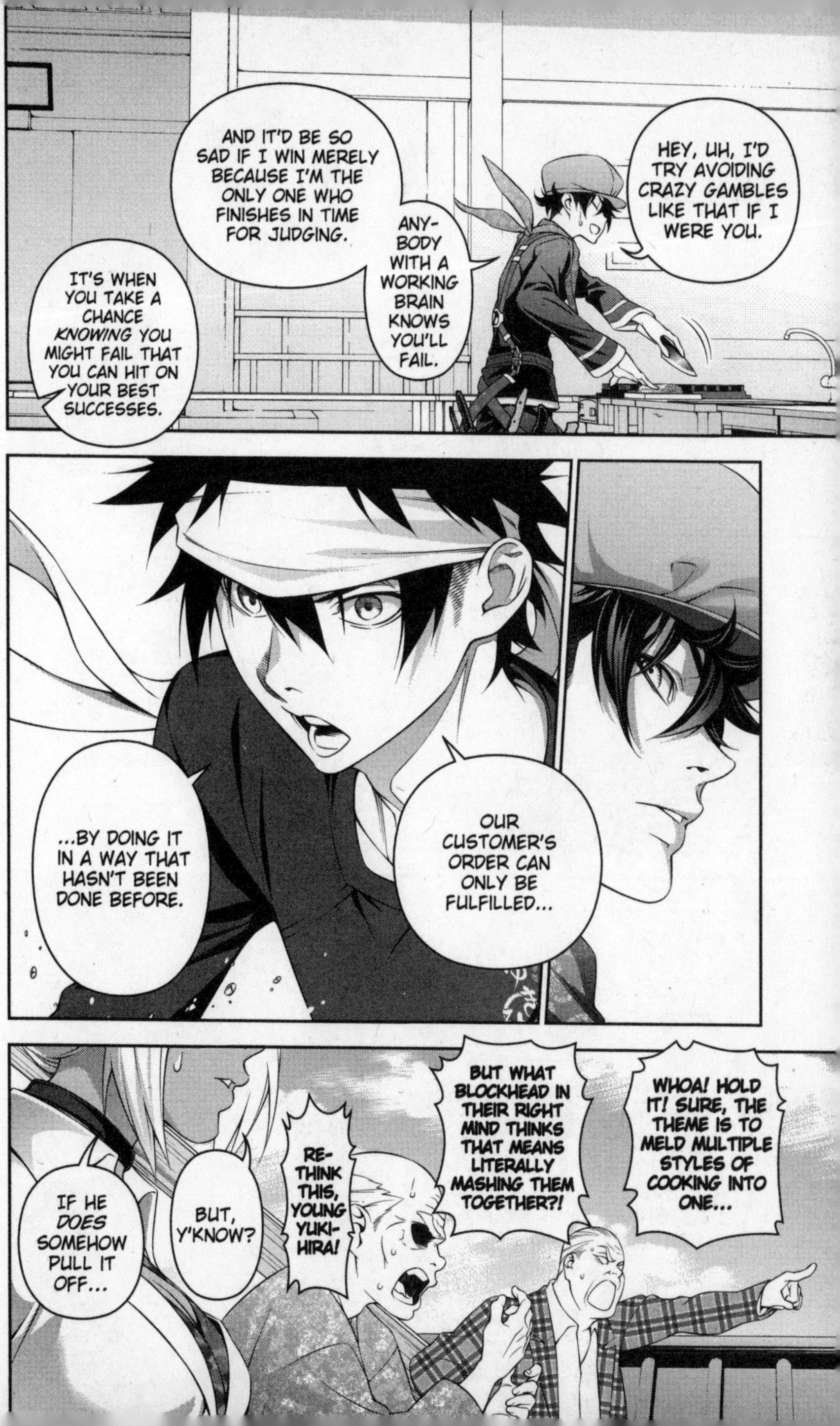

HEY, UH, I'D TRY AVOIDING CRAZY GAMBLES LIKE THAT IF I WERE YOU.
ANY-BODY WITH A WORKING BRAIN KNOWS YOU'LL FAIL.
AND IT'D BE SO SAD IF I WIN MERELY BECAUSE I'M THE ONLY ONE WHO FINISHES IN TIME FOR JUDGING.
IT'S WHEN YOU TAKE A CHANCE *KNOWING* YOU MIGHT FAIL THAT YOU CAN HIT ON YOUR BEST SUCCESSES.
OUR CUSTOMER'S ORDER CAN ONLY BE FULFILLED...
...BY DOING IT IN A WAY THAT HASN'T BEEN DONE BEFORE.
WHOA! HOLD IT! SURE, THE THEME IS TO MELD MULTIPLE STYLES OF COOKING INTO ONE...
BUT WHAT BLOCKHEAD IN THEIR RIGHT MIND THINKS THAT MEANS LITERALLY MASHING THEM TOGETHER?!
RE-THINK THIS, YOUNG YUKI-HIRA!
BUT, Y'KNOW?
IF HE *DOES* SOMEHOW PULL IT OFF...

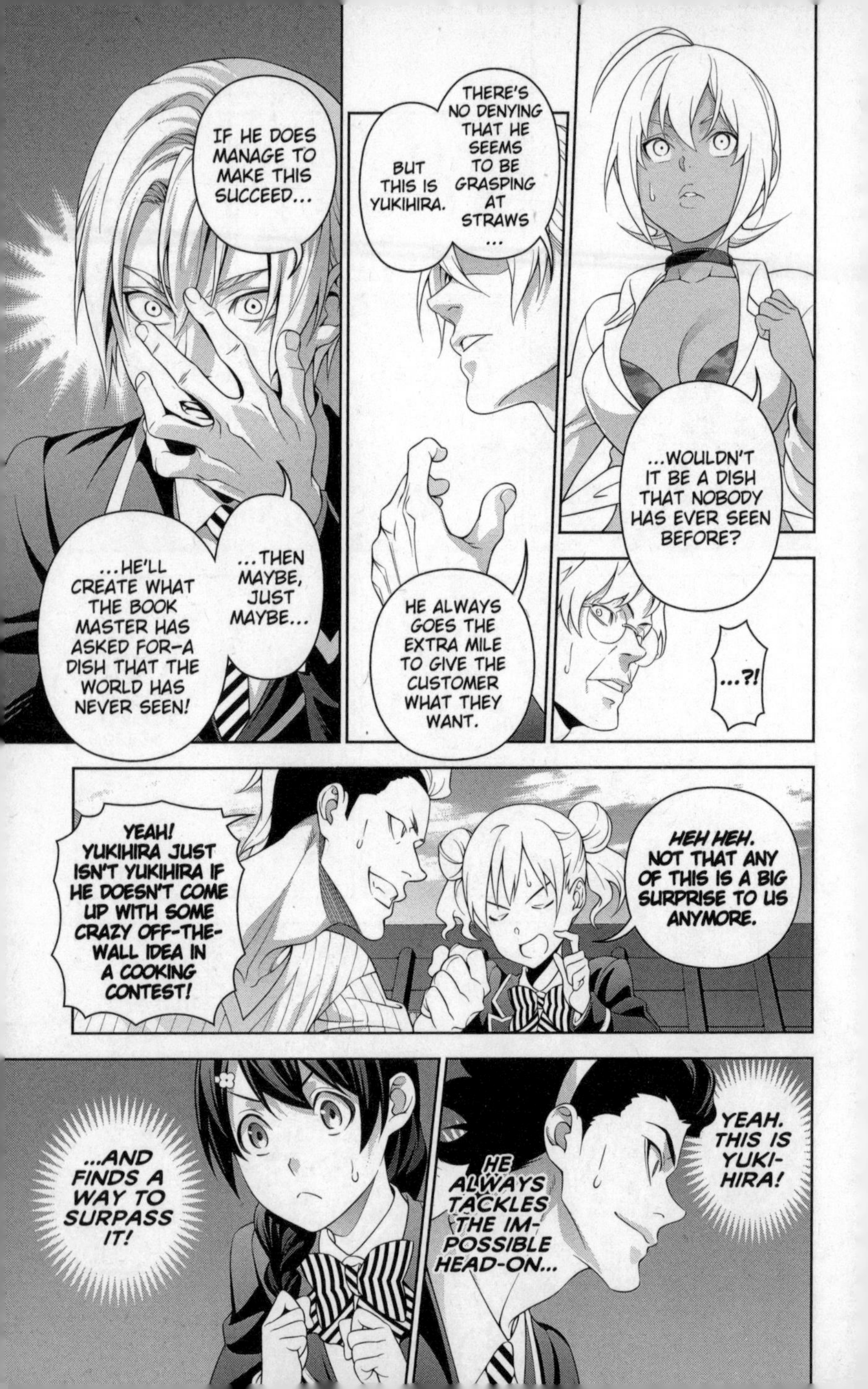
...WOULDN'T IT BE A DISH THAT NOBODY HAS EVER SEEN BEFORE?
...?!
THERE'S NO DENYING THAT HE SEEMS TO BE GRASPING AT STRAWS...
BUT THIS IS YUKIHIRA.
HE ALWAYS GOES THE EXTRA MILE TO GIVE THE CUSTOMER WHAT THEY WANT.
IF HE DOES MANAGE TO MAKE THIS SUCCEED...
...THEN MAYBE, JUST MAYBE...
...HE'LL CREATE WHAT THE BOOK MASTER HAS ASKED FOR—A DISH THAT THE WORLD HAS NEVER SEEN!
HEH HEH. NOT THAT ANY OF THIS IS A BIG SURPRISE TO US ANYMORE.
YEAH! YUKIHIRA JUST ISN'T YUKIHIRA IF HE DOESN'T COME UP WITH SOME CRAZY OFF-THE-WALL IDEA IN A COOKING CONTEST!
YEAH. THIS IS YUKI-HIRA!
HE ALWAYS TACKLES THE IM-POSSIBLE HEAD-ON...
...AND FINDS A WAY TO SURPASS IT!

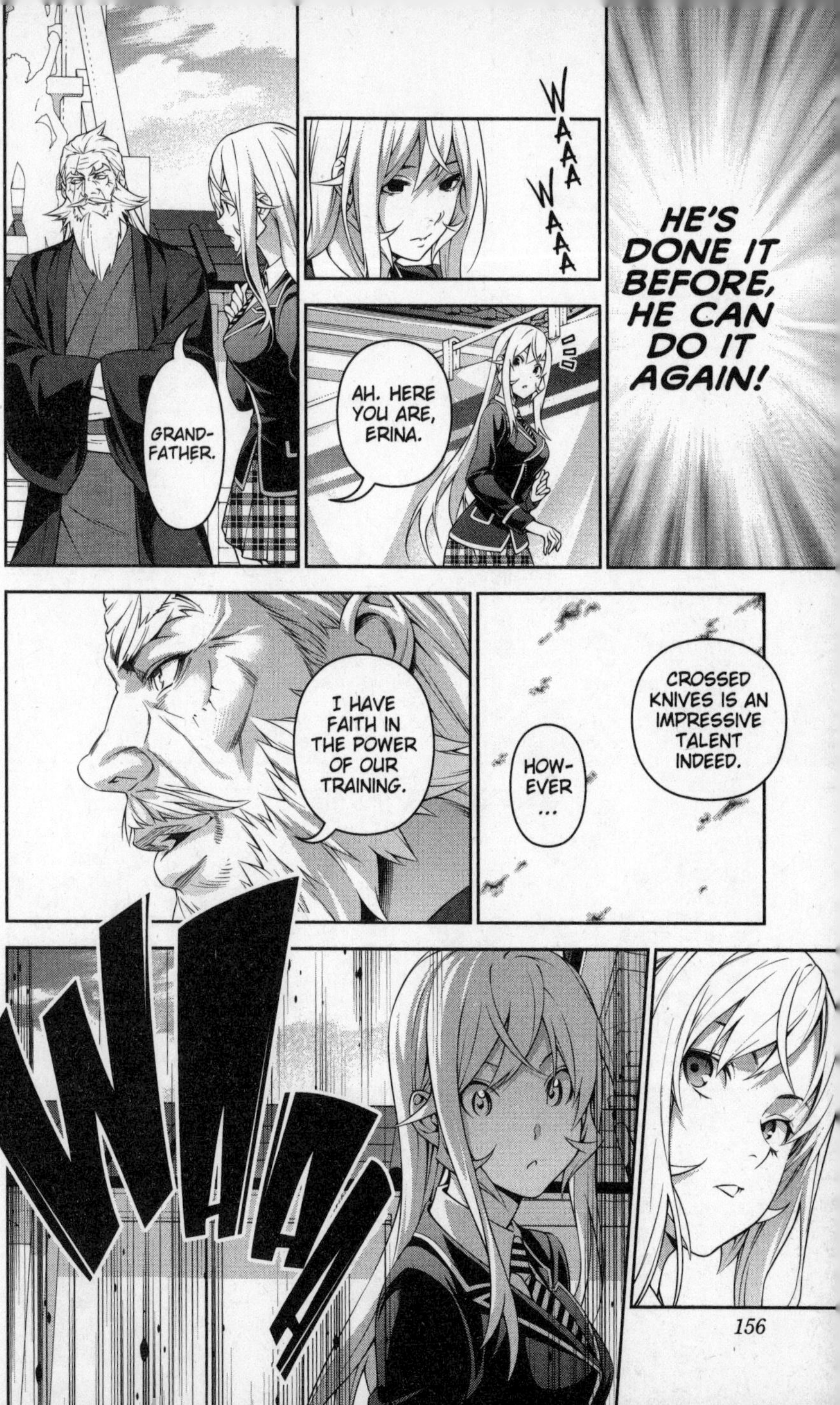
HE'S DONE IT BEFORE, HE CAN DO IT AGAIN!
WAAA WAAA
AH. HERE YOU ARE, ERINA.
GRAND-FATHER.
CROSSED KNIVES IS AN IMPRESSIVE TALENT INDEED.
HOW-EVER ...
I HAVE FAITH IN THE POWER OF OUR TRAINING.

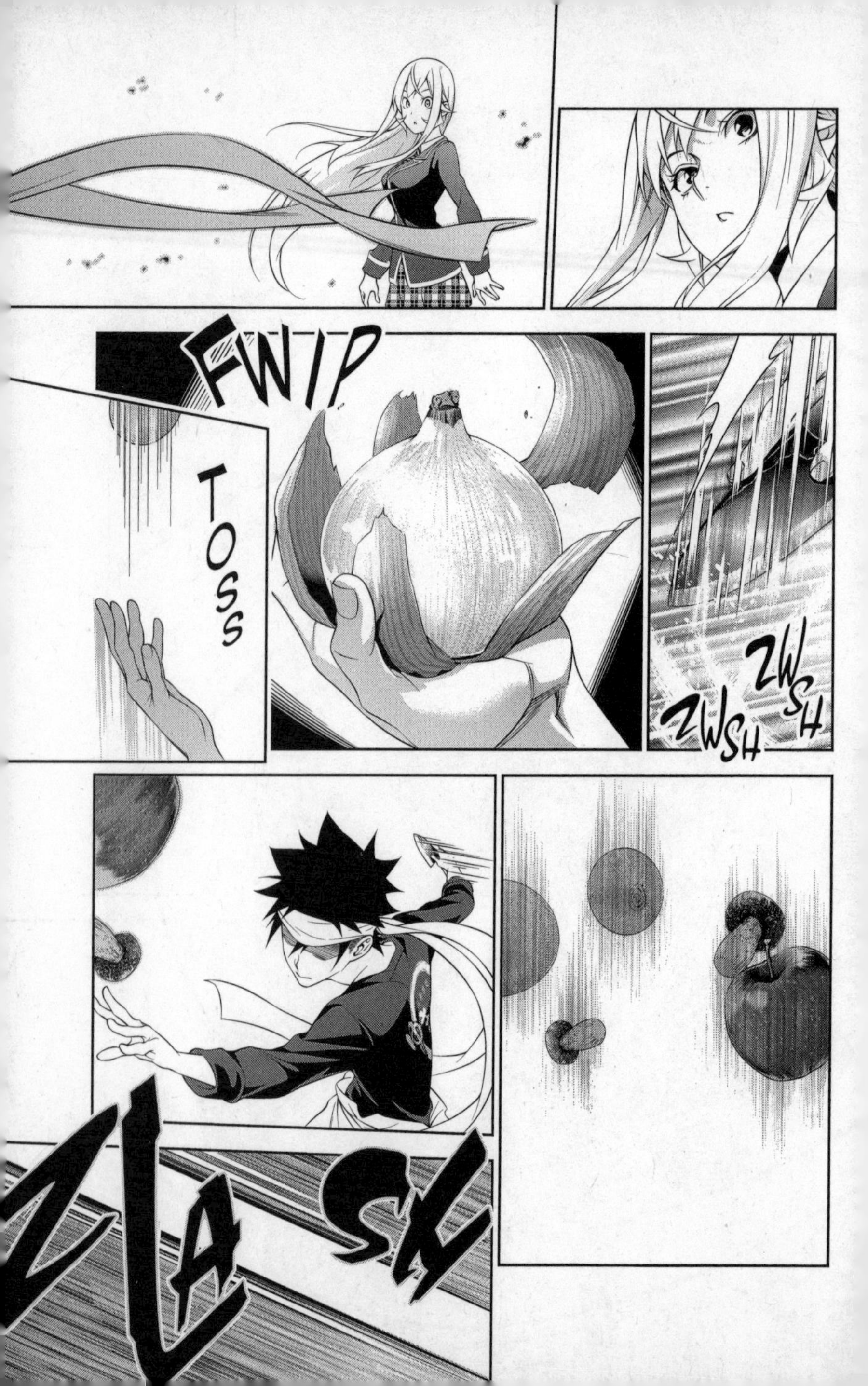
ZWSH ZWSH
FWIP
TOSS
ZLASH

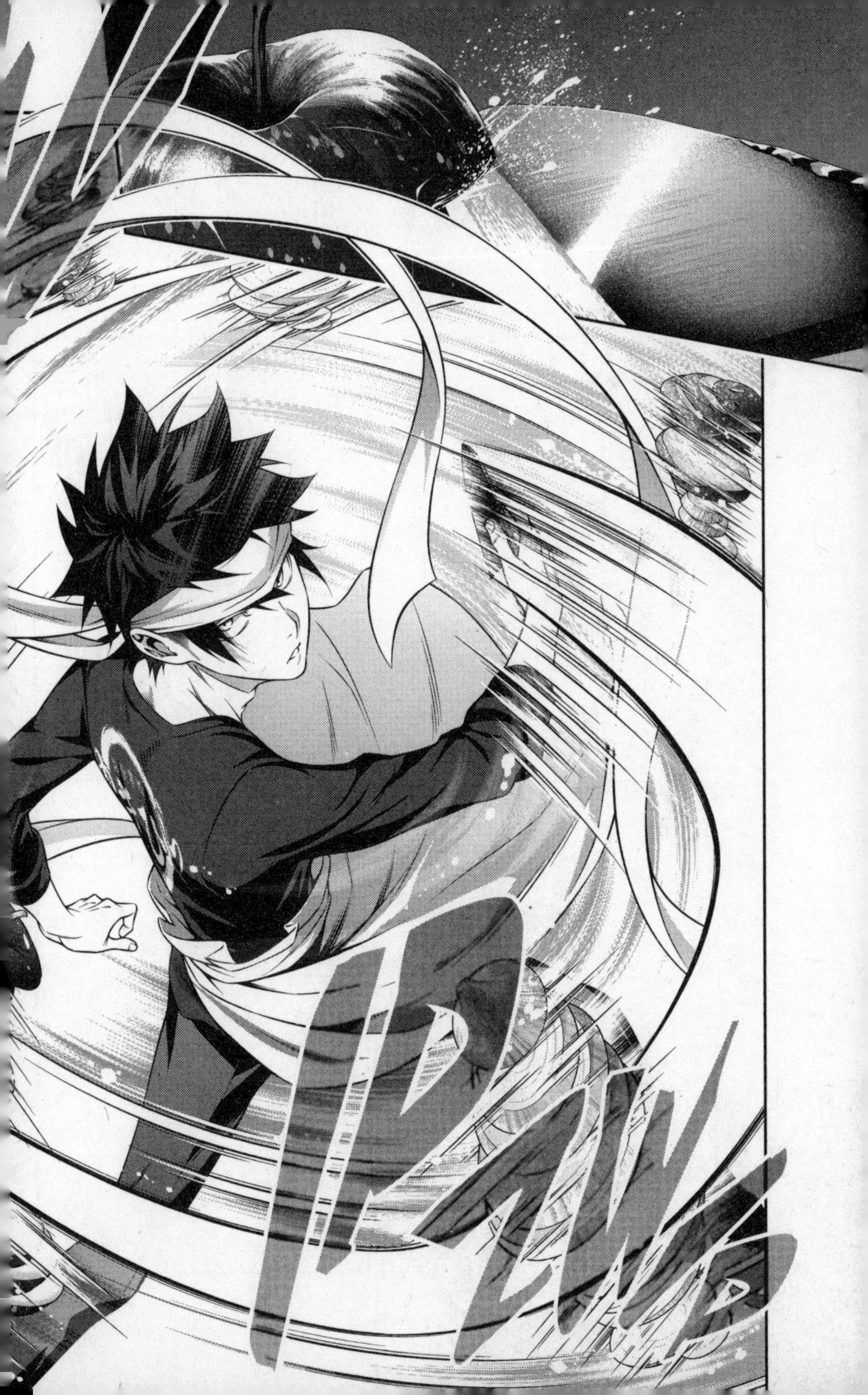

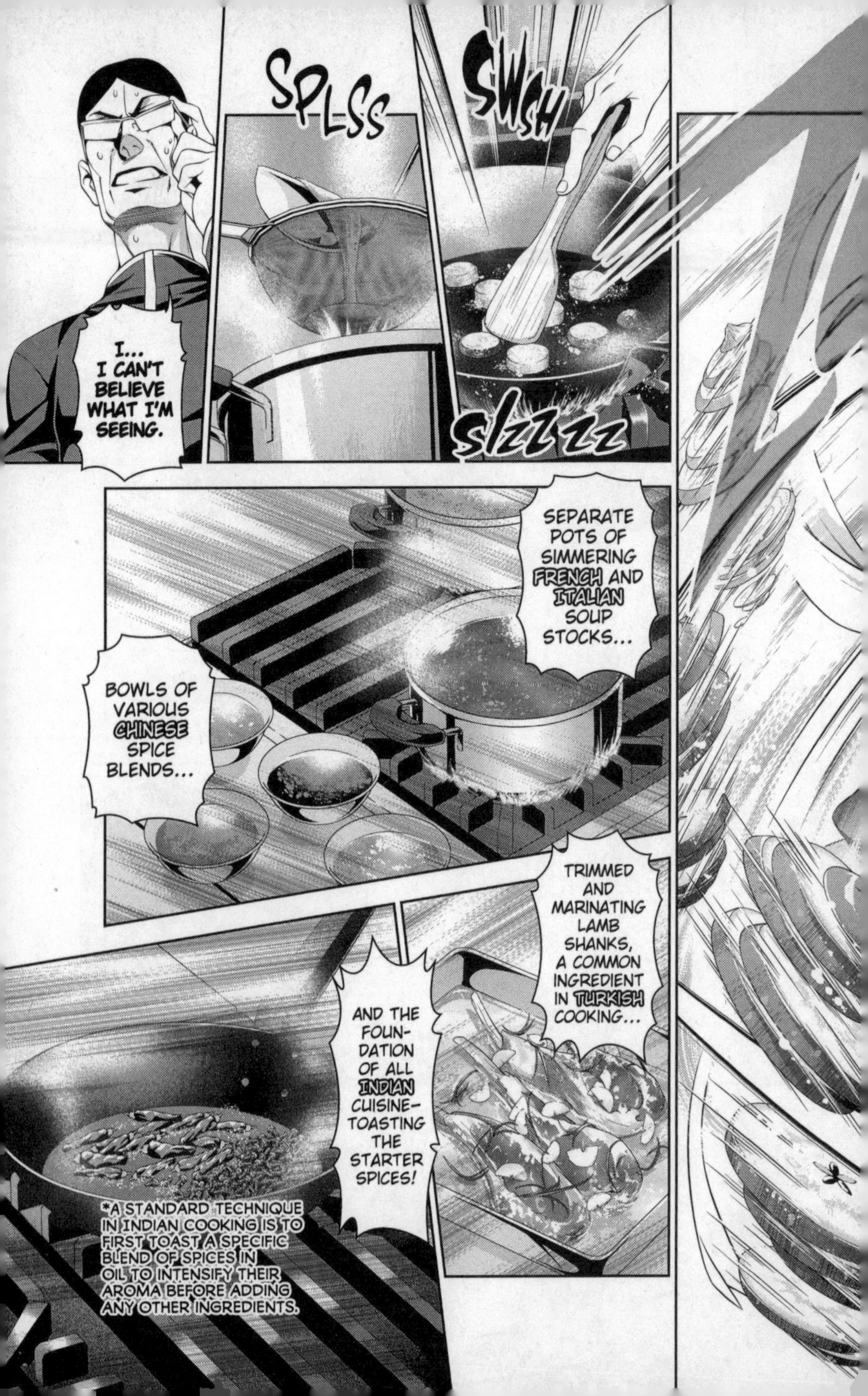
SWSH
SIZZZZZ
SPLSS
I... I CAN'T BELIEVE WHAT I'M SEEING.
SEPARATE POTS OF SIMMERING FRENCH AND ITALIAN SOUP STOCKS...
BOWLS OF VARIOUS CHINESE SPICE BLENDS...
TRIMMED AND MARINATING LAMB SHANKS, A COMMON INGREDIENT IN TURKISH COOKING...
AND THE FOUN-DATION OF ALL INDIAN CUISINE-TOASTING THE STARTER SPICES!
*A STANDARD TECHNIQUE IN INDIAN COOKING IS TO FIRST TOAST A SPECIFIC BLEND OF SPICES IN OIL TO INTENSIFY THEIR AROMA BEFORE ADDING ANY OTHER INGREDIENTS.

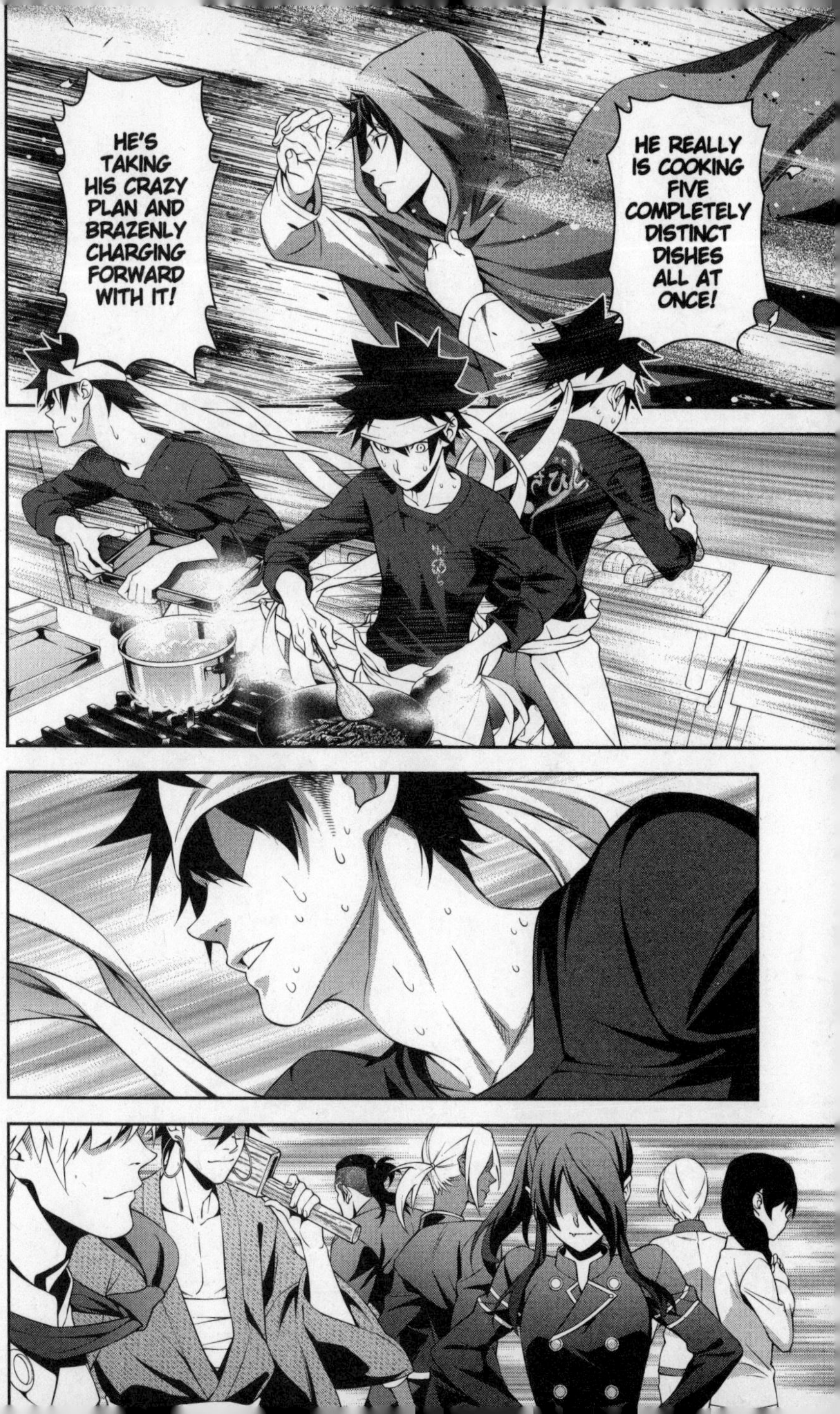
HE REALLY IS COOKING FIVE COMPLETELY DISTINCT DISHES ALL AT ONCE!
HE'S TAKING HIS CRAZY PLAN AND BRAZENLY CHARGING FORWARD WITH IT!

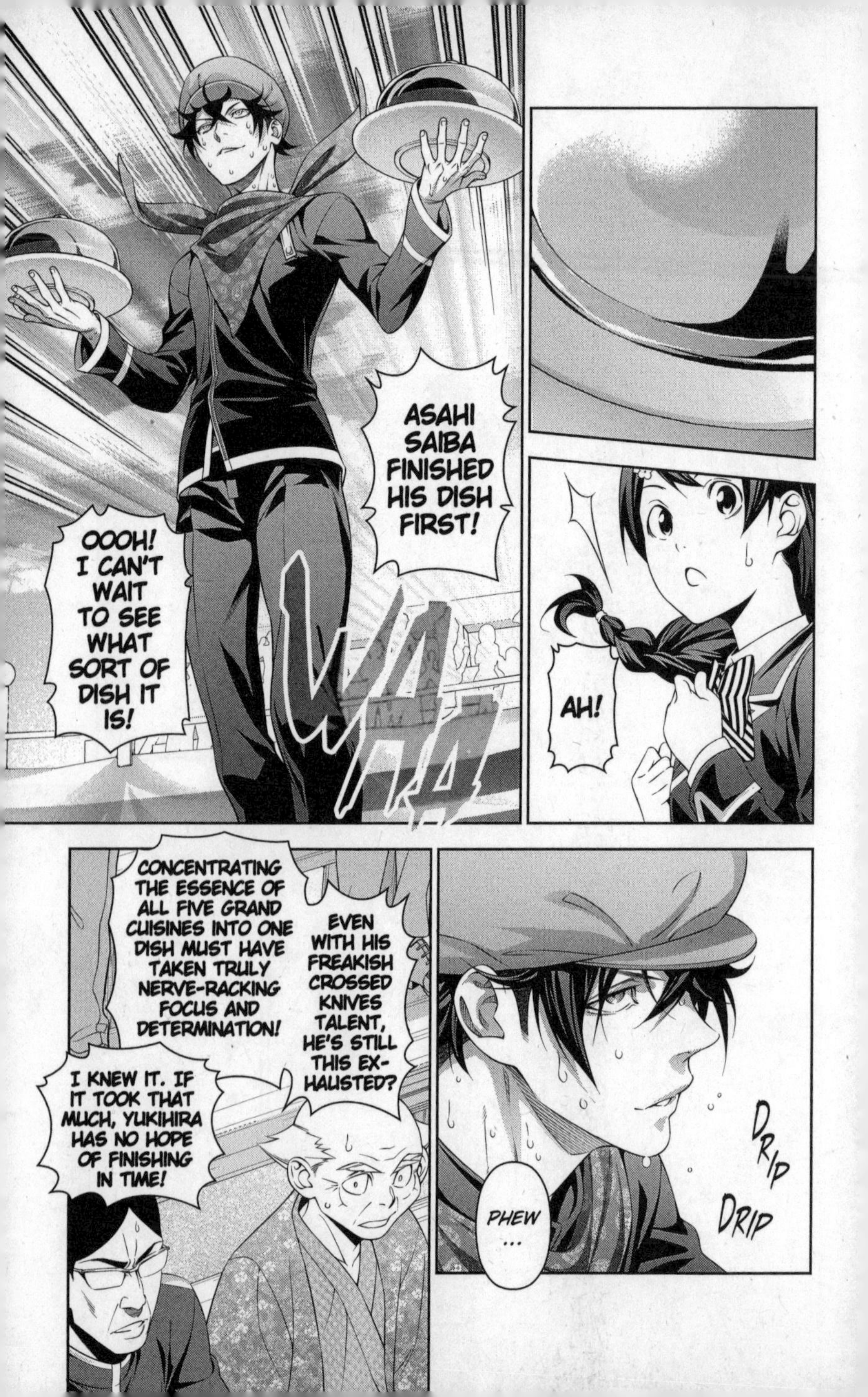
AH!
ASAHI SAIBA FINISHED HIS DISH FIRST!
OOOH! I CAN'T WAIT TO SEE WHAT SORT OF DISH IT IS!
DRIP DRIP
PHEW...
CONCENTRATING THE ESSENCE OF ALL FIVE GRAND CUISINES INTO ONE DISH MUST HAVE TAKEN TRULY NERVE-RACKING FOCUS AND DETERMINATION!
EVEN WITH HIS FREAKISH CROSSED KNIVES TALENT, HE'S STILL THIS EX-HAUSTED?
I KNEW IT. IF IT TOOK THAT MUCH, YUKIHIRA HAS NO HOPE OF FINISHING IN TIME!

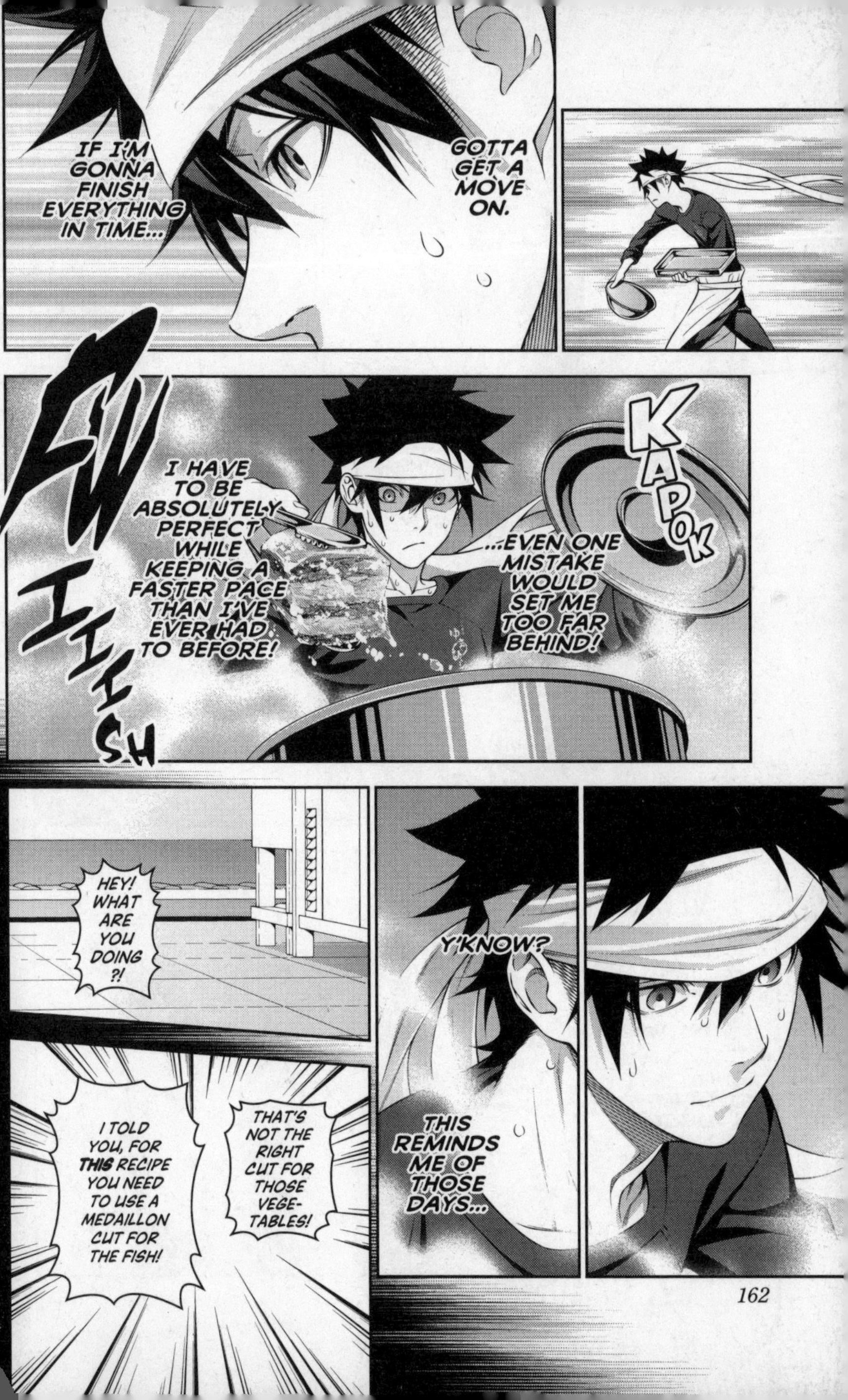
GOTTA GET A MOVE ON.
IF I'M GONNA FINISH EVERYTHING IN TIME...
KAPOK
I HAVE TO BE ABSOLUTELY PERFECT WHILE KEEPING A FASTER PACE THAN I'VE EVER HAD TO BEFORE!
...EVEN ONE MISTAKE WOULD SET ME TOO FAR BEHIND!
FWIIIISH
Y'KNOW?
THIS REMINDS ME OF THOSE DAYS...
HEY! WHAT ARE YOU DOING?!
THAT'S NOT THE RIGHT CUT FOR THOSE VEGE-TABLES!
I TOLD YOU, FOR THIS RECIPE YOU NEED TO USE A MEDAILLON CUT FOR THE FISH!

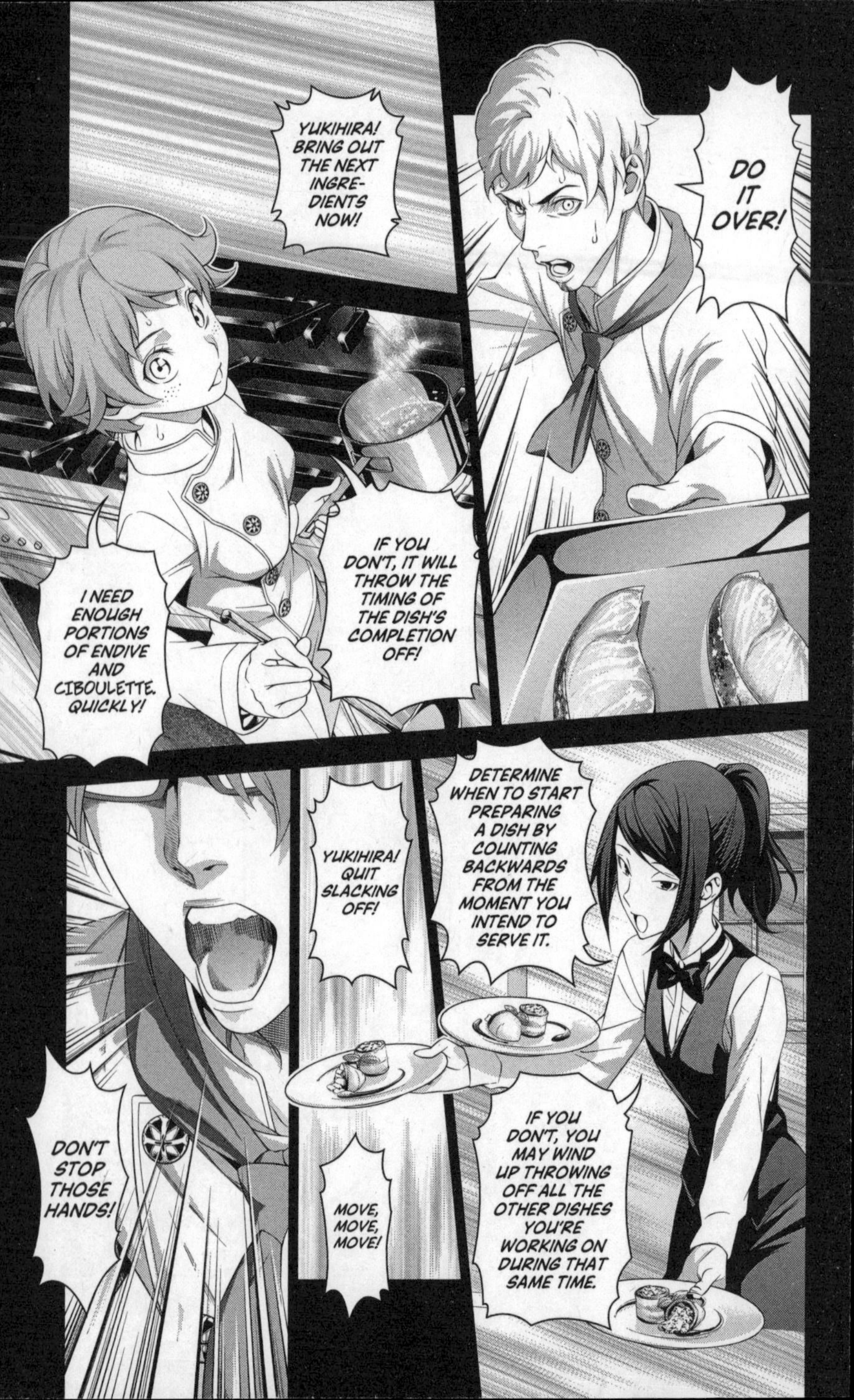
DO IT OVER!
YUKIHIRA! BRING OUT THE NEXT INGRE- DIENTS NOW!
I NEED ENOUGH PORTIONS OF ENDIVE AND CIBOULETTE. QUICKLY!
IF YOU DON'T, IT WILL THROW THE TIMING OF THE DISH'S COMPLETION OFF!
DETERMINE WHEN TO START PREPARING A DISH BY COUNTING BACKWARDS FROM THE MOMENT YOU INTEND TO SERVE IT.
IF YOU DON'T, YOU MAY WIND UP THROWING OFF ALL THE OTHER DISHES YOU'RE WORKING ON DURING THAT SAME TIME.
YUKIHIRA! QUIT SLACKING OFF!
MOVE, MOVE, MOVE!
DON'T STOP THOSE HANDS!

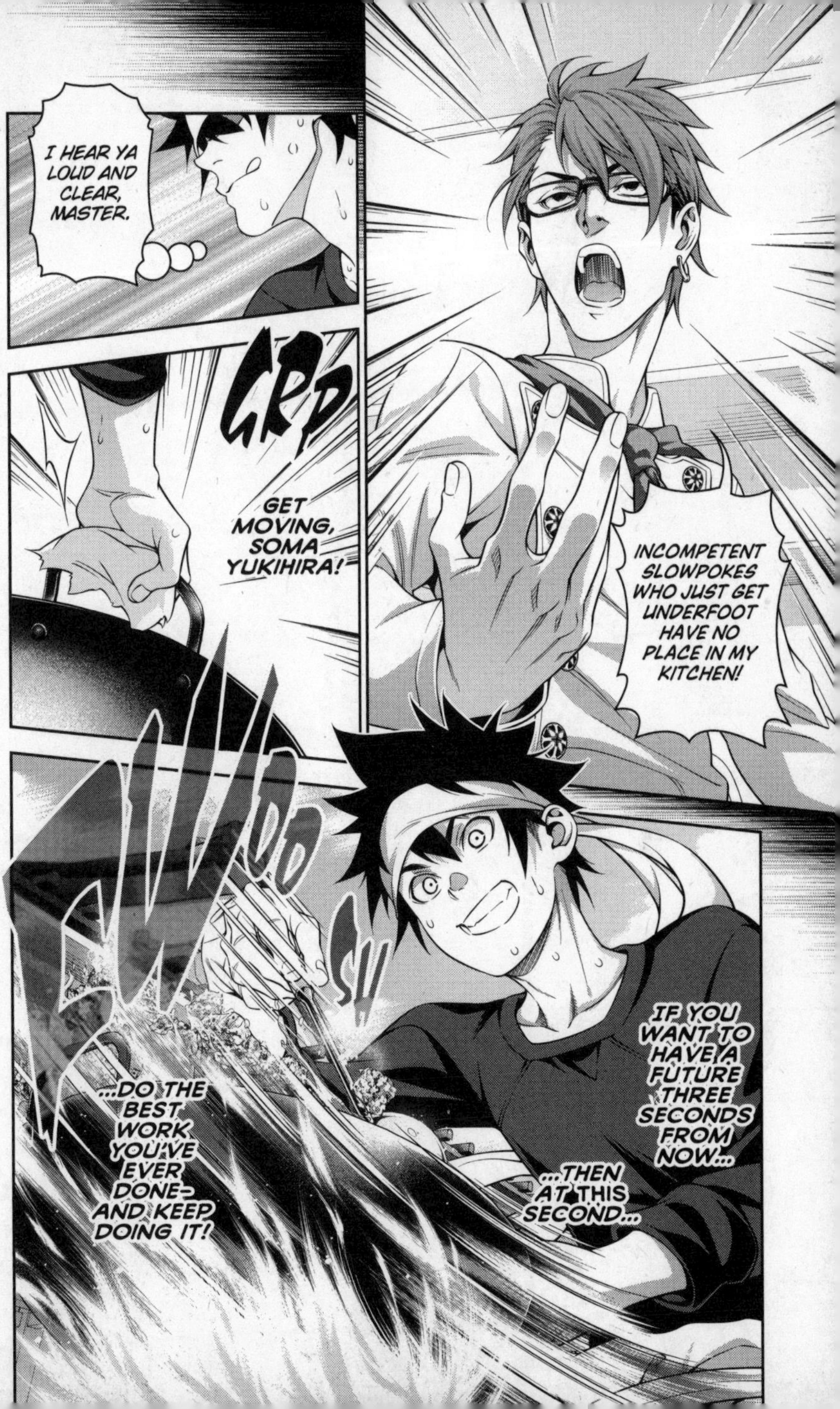
INCOMPETENT SLOWPOKES WHO JUST GET UNDERFOOT HAVE NO PLACE IN MY KITCHEN!
I HEAR YA LOUD AND CLEAR, MASTER.
GRP
GET MOVING, SOMA YUKIHIRA!
IF YOU WANT TO HAVE A FUTURE THREE SECONDS FROM NOW...
...THEN AT THIS SECOND...
...DO THE BEST WORK YOU'VE EVER DONE-AND KEEP DOING IT!

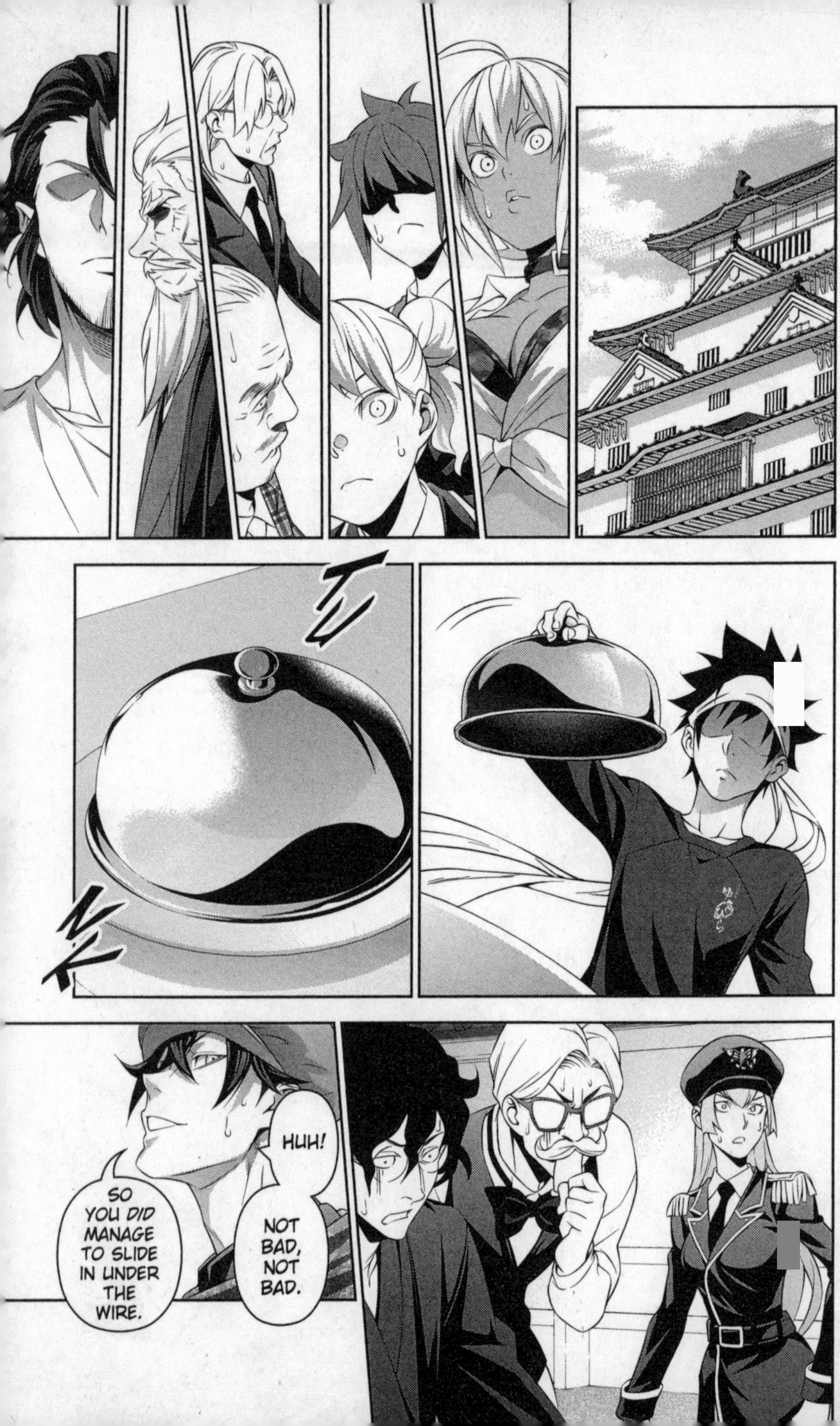
HUH!
NOT BAD, NOT BAD.
SO YOU DID MANAGE TO SLIDE IN UNDER THE WIRE.

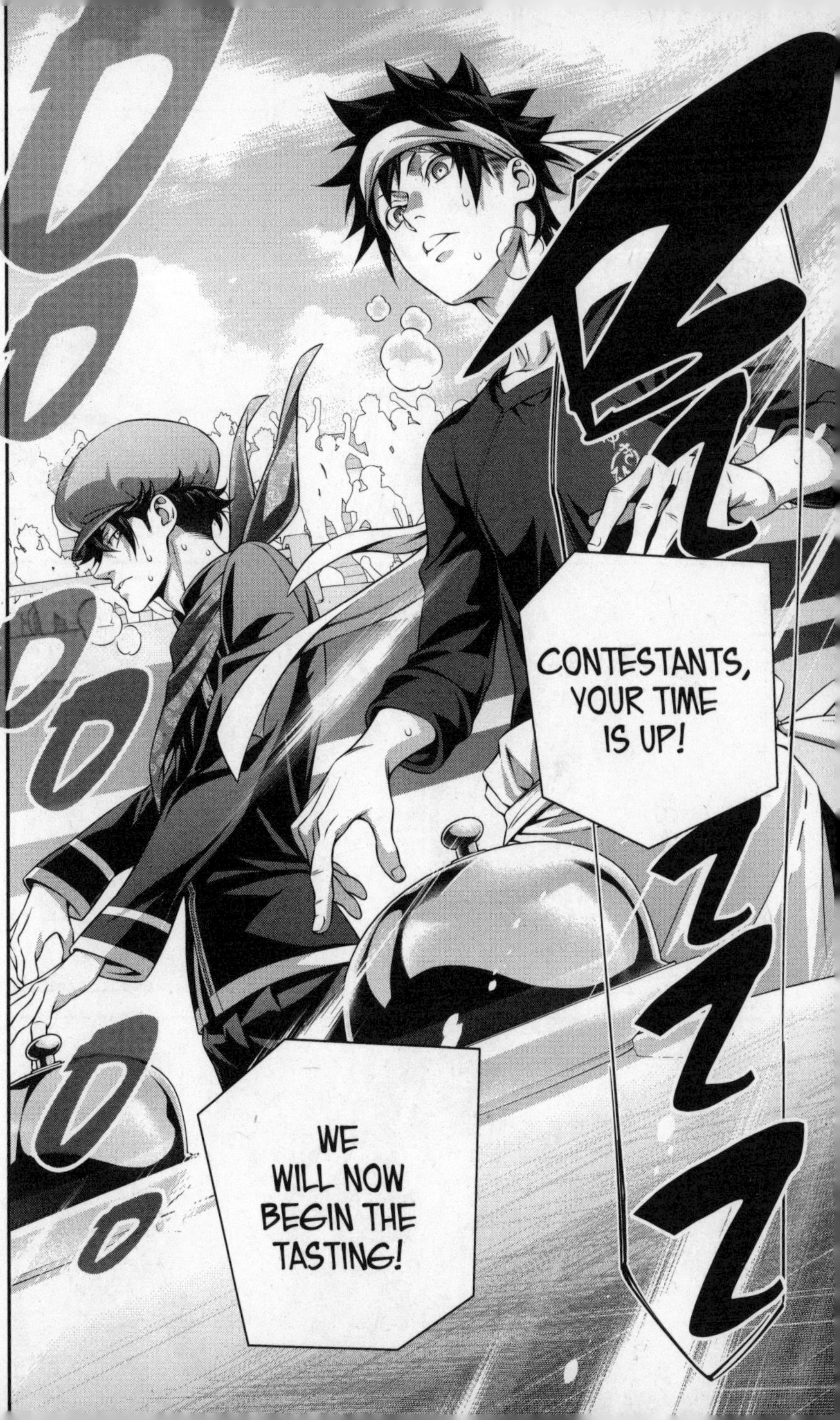
CONTESTANTS, YOUR TIME IS UP!
WE WILL NOW BEGIN THE TASTING!

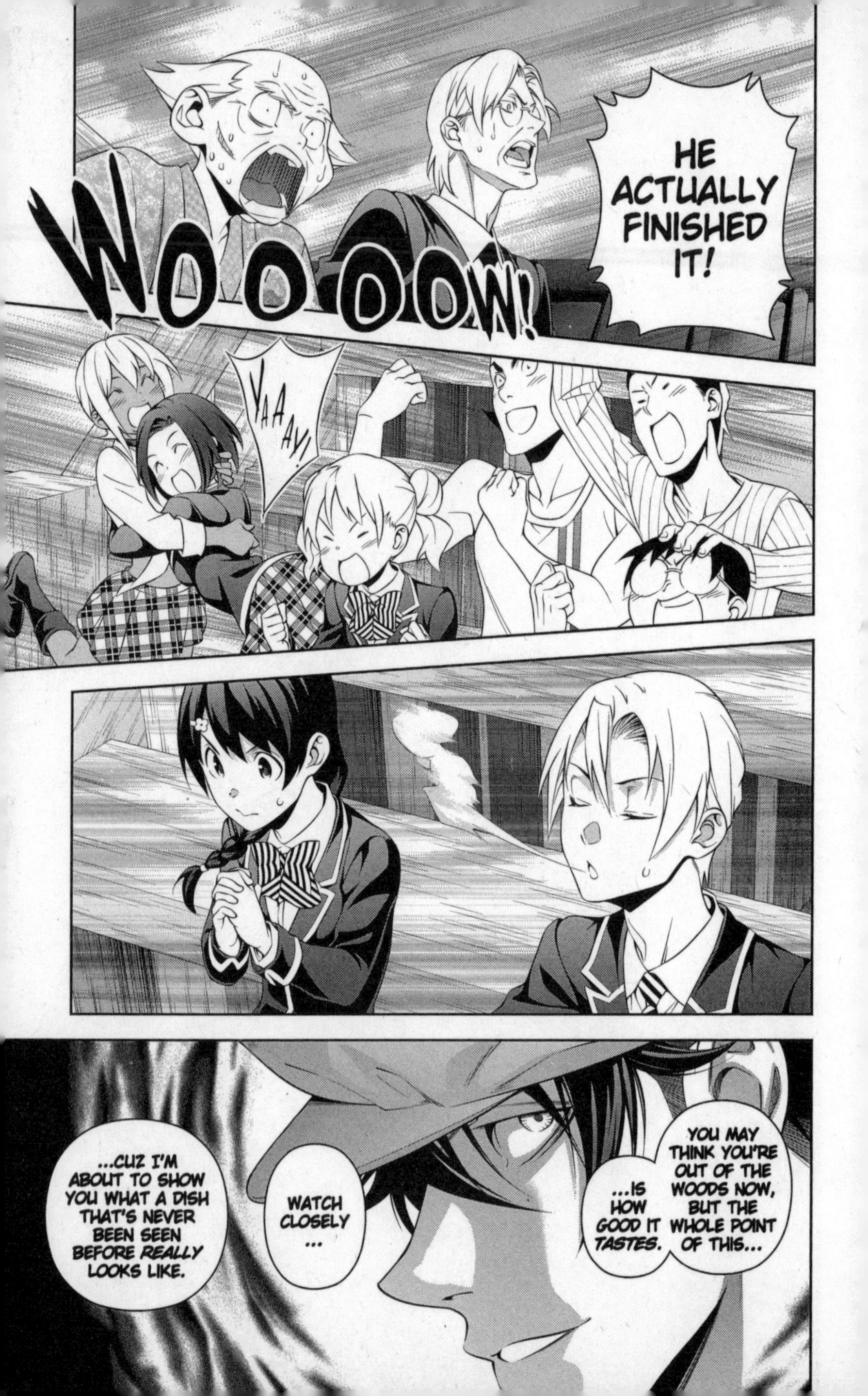

HE ACTUALLY FINISHED IT!
WOOOOW!
YAAAY!
YOU MAY THINK YOU'RE OUT OF THE WOODS NOW, BUT THE WHOLE POINT OF THIS...
...IS HOW GOOD IT *TASTES.*
WATCH CLOSELY...
...CUZ I'M ABOUT TO SHOW YOU WHAT A DISH THAT'S NEVER BEEN SEEN BEFORE *REALLY* LOOKS LIKE.

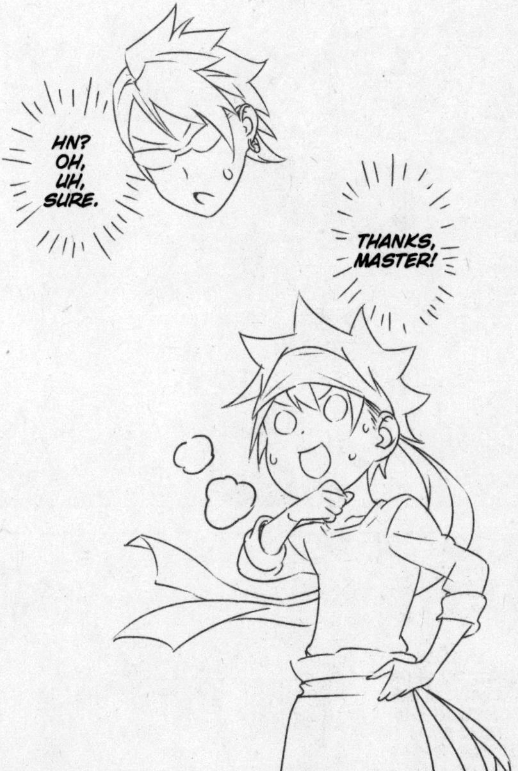
HN? OH, UH, SURE.
THANKS, MASTER!

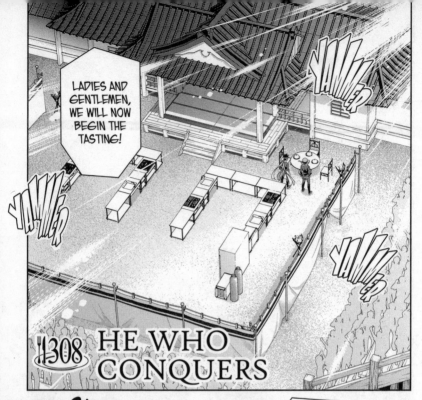

LADIES AND GENTLEMEN, WE WILL NOW BEGIN THE TASTING!

YAMMER

YAMMER

YAMMER

308 HE WHO CONQUERS

BLINK

...?!

ALLOW US TO INTRODUCE THE THREE BOOKERS WHO WILL BE OUR JUDGES!

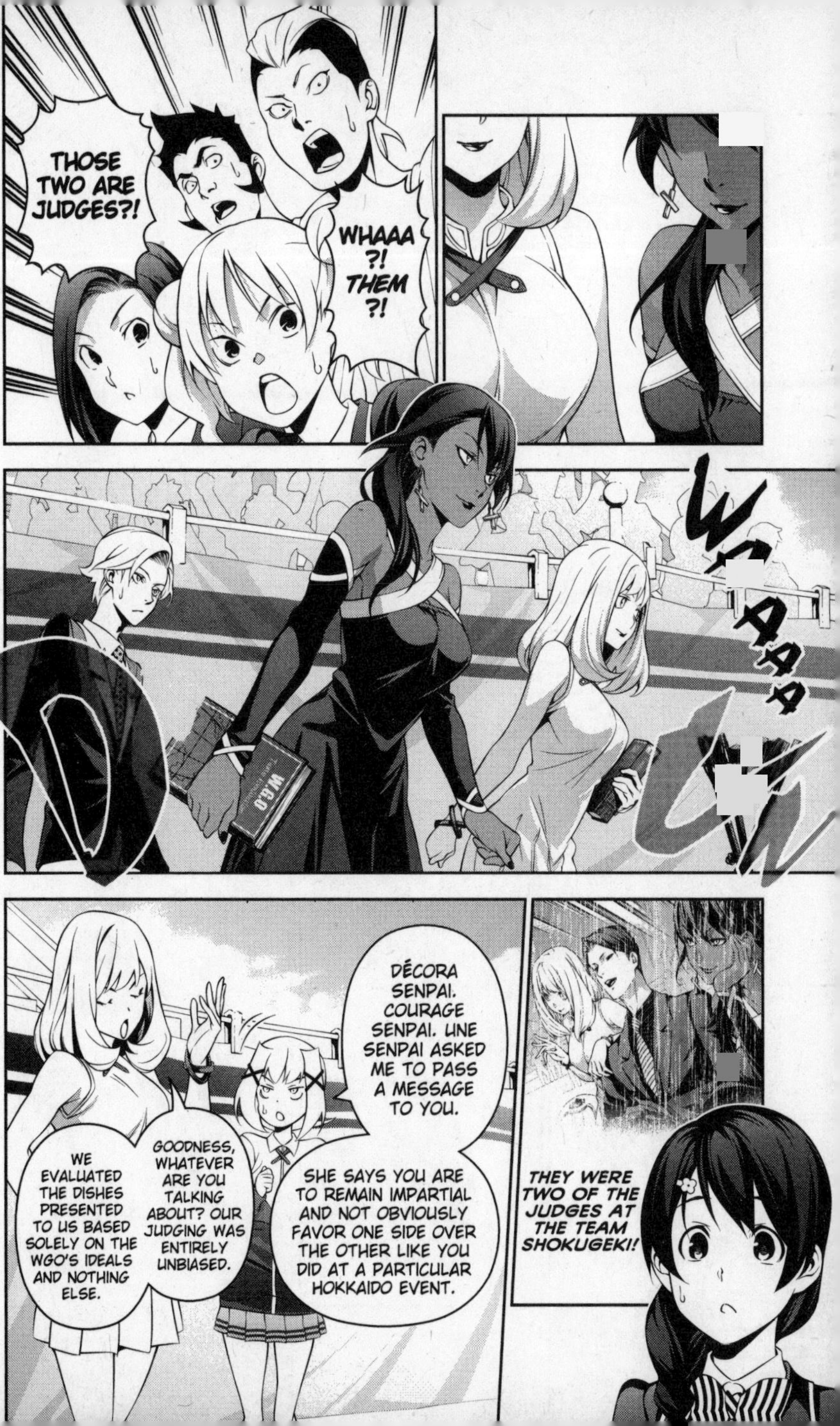
THOSE TWO ARE JUDGES?!
WHAAA?! THEM?!
THEY WERE TWO OF THE JUDGES AT THE TEAM SHOKUGEKI!
DÉCORA SENPAI. COURAGE SENPAI. UNE SENPAI ASKED ME TO PASS A MESSAGE TO YOU.
SHE SAYS YOU ARE TO REMAIN IMPARTIAL AND NOT OBVIOUSLY FAVOR ONE SIDE OVER THE OTHER LIKE YOU DID AT A PARTICULAR HOKKAIDO EVENT.
GOODNESS, WHATEVER ARE YOU TALKING ABOUT? OUR JUDGING WAS ENTIRELY UNBIASED.
WE EVALUATED THE DISHES PRESENTED TO US BASED SOLELY ON THE WGO'S IDEALS AND NOTHING ELSE.

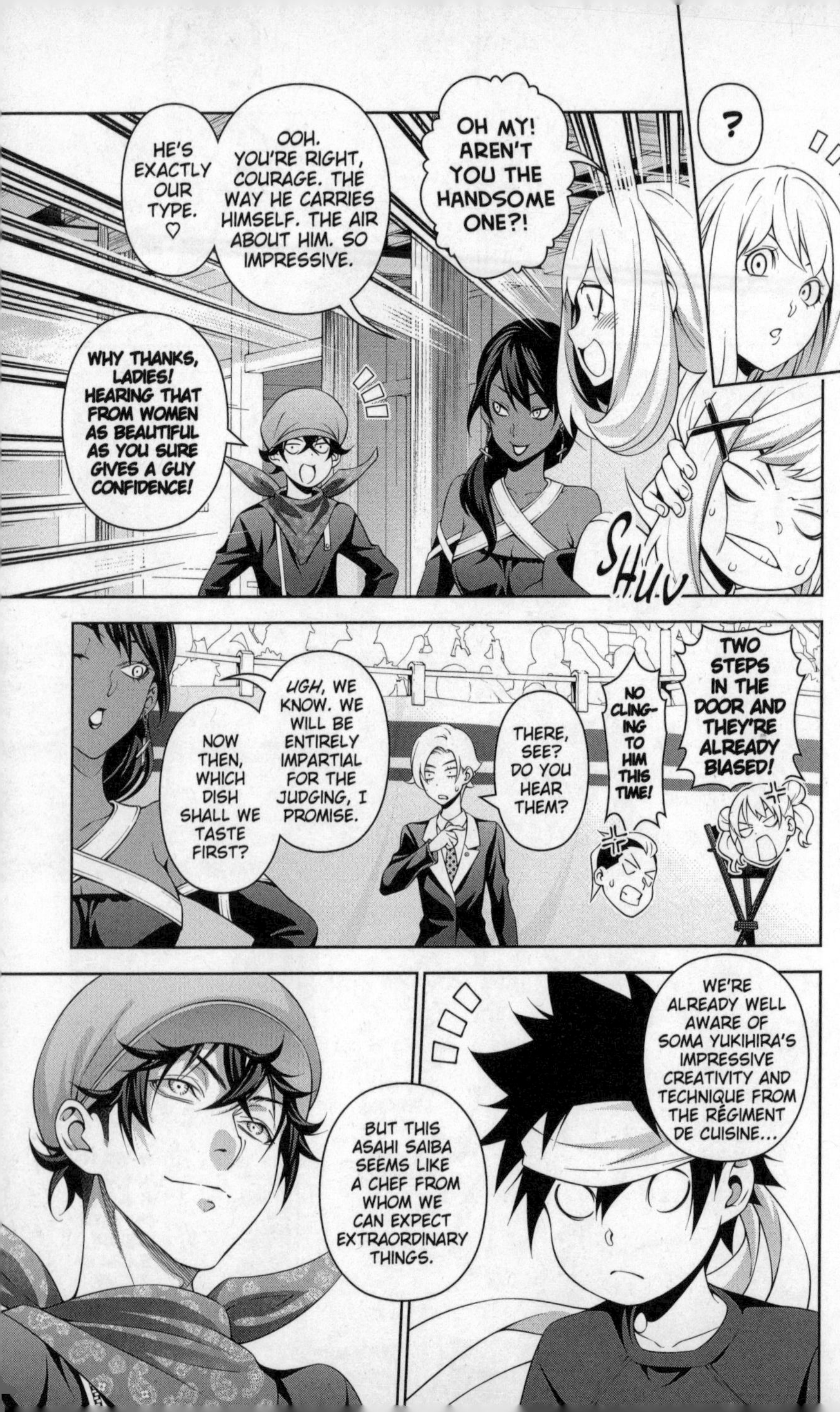
?
OH MY! AREN'T YOU THE HANDSOME ONE?!
OOH. YOU'RE RIGHT, COURAGE. THE WAY HE CARRIES HIMSELF. THE AIR ABOUT HIM. SO IMPRESSIVE.
HE'S EXACTLY OUR TYPE. ♡
WHY THANKS, LADIES! HEARING THAT FROM WOMEN AS BEAUTIFUL AS YOU SURE GIVES A GUY CONFIDENCE!
SHUV
TWO STEPS IN THE DOOR AND THEY'RE ALREADY BIASED!
NO CLINGING TO HIM THIS TIME!
THERE, SEE? DO YOU HEAR THEM?
UGH, WE KNOW. WE WILL BE ENTIRELY IMPARTIAL FOR THE JUDGING, I PROMISE.
NOW THEN, WHICH DISH SHALL WE TASTE FIRST?
WE'RE ALREADY WELL AWARE OF SOMA YUKIHIRA'S IMPRESSIVE CREATIVITY AND TECHNIQUE FROM THE RÉGIMENT DE CUISINE...
BUT THIS ASAHI SAIBA SEEMS LIKE A CHEF FROM WHOM WE CAN EXPECT EXTRAORDINARY THINGS.

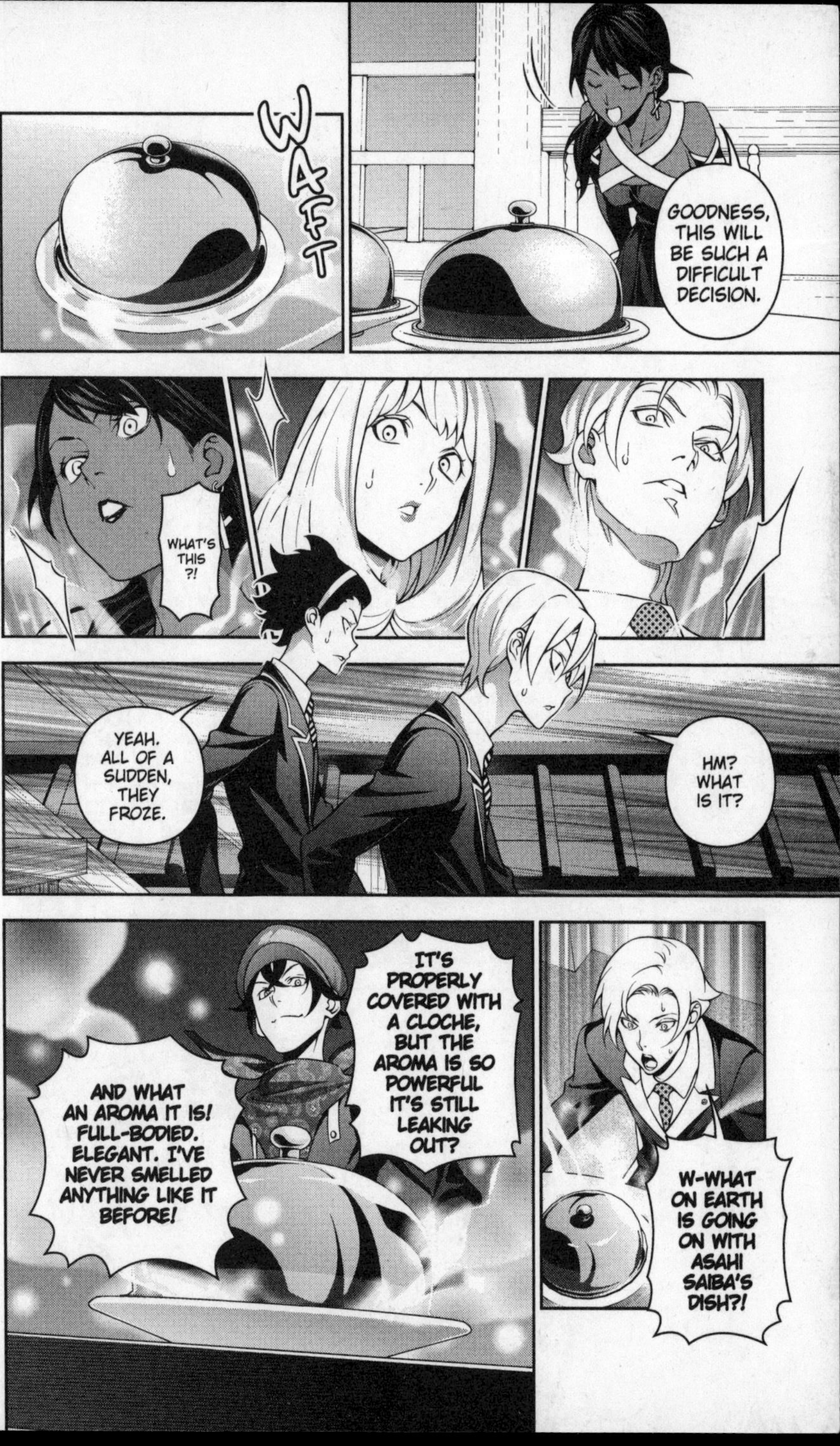
GOODNESS, THIS WILL BE SUCH A DIFFICULT DECISION.
WAFT
WHAT'S THIS ?!
HM? WHAT IS IT?
YEAH. ALL OF A SUDDEN, THEY FROZE.
W-WHAT ON EARTH IS GOING ON WITH ASAHI SAIBA'S DISH?!
IT'S PROPERLY COVERED WITH A CLOCHE, BUT THE AROMA IS SO POWERFUL IT'S STILL LEAKING OUT?
AND WHAT AN AROMA IT IS! FULL-BODIED. ELEGANT. I'VE NEVER SMELLED ANYTHING LIKE IT BEFORE!

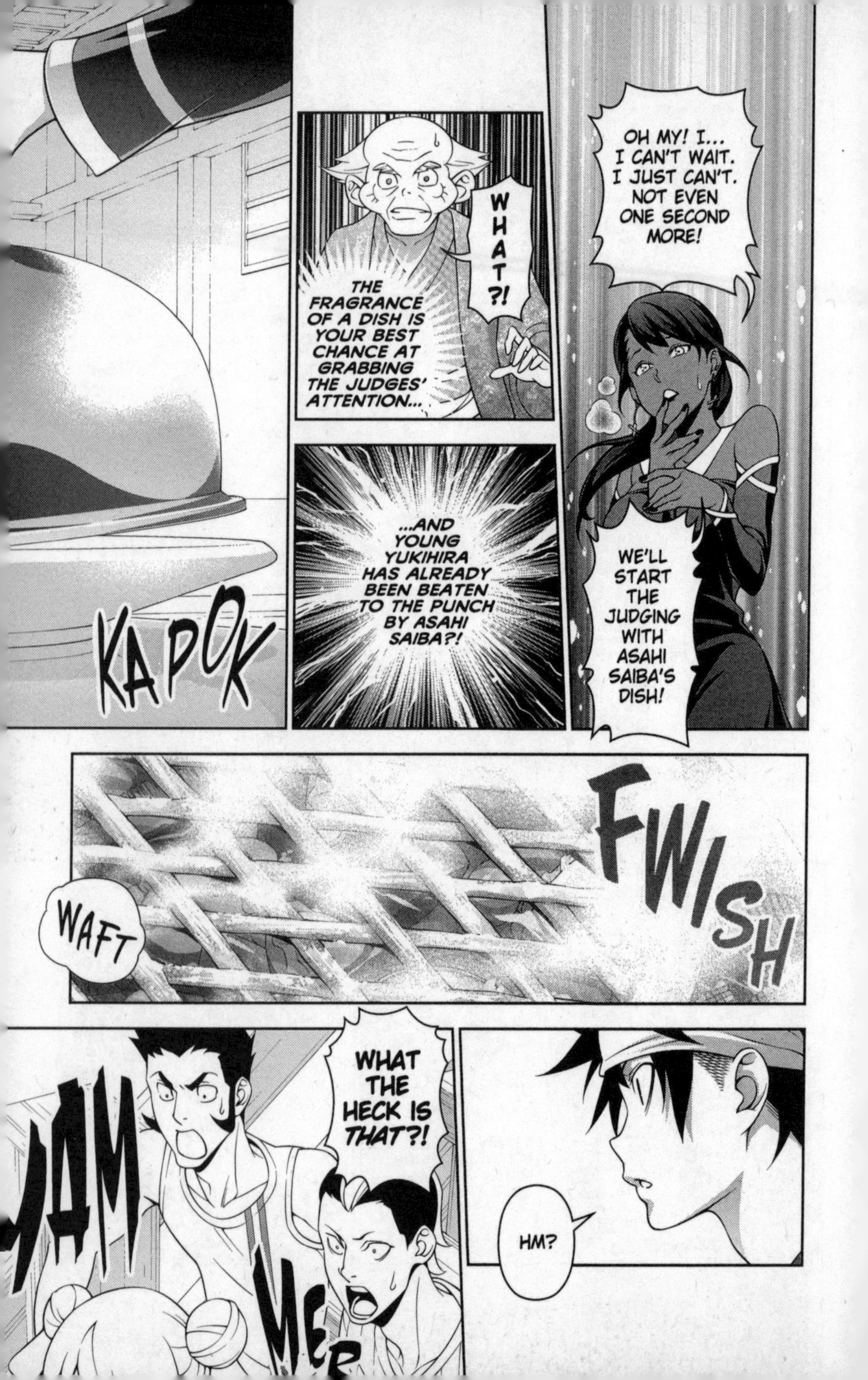
OH MY! I... I CAN'T WAIT. I JUST CAN'T. NOT EVEN ONE SECOND MORE!
WE'LL START THE JUDGING WITH ASAHI SAIBA'S DISH!
WHAT?!
THE FRAGRANCE OF A DISH IS YOUR BEST CHANCE AT GRABBING THE JUDGES' ATTENTION...
...AND YOUNG YUKIHIRA HAS ALREADY BEEN BEATEN TO THE PUNCH BY ASAHI SAIBA?!
KAPOK
FWISH
WAFT
HM?
WHAT THE HECK IS *THAT*?!

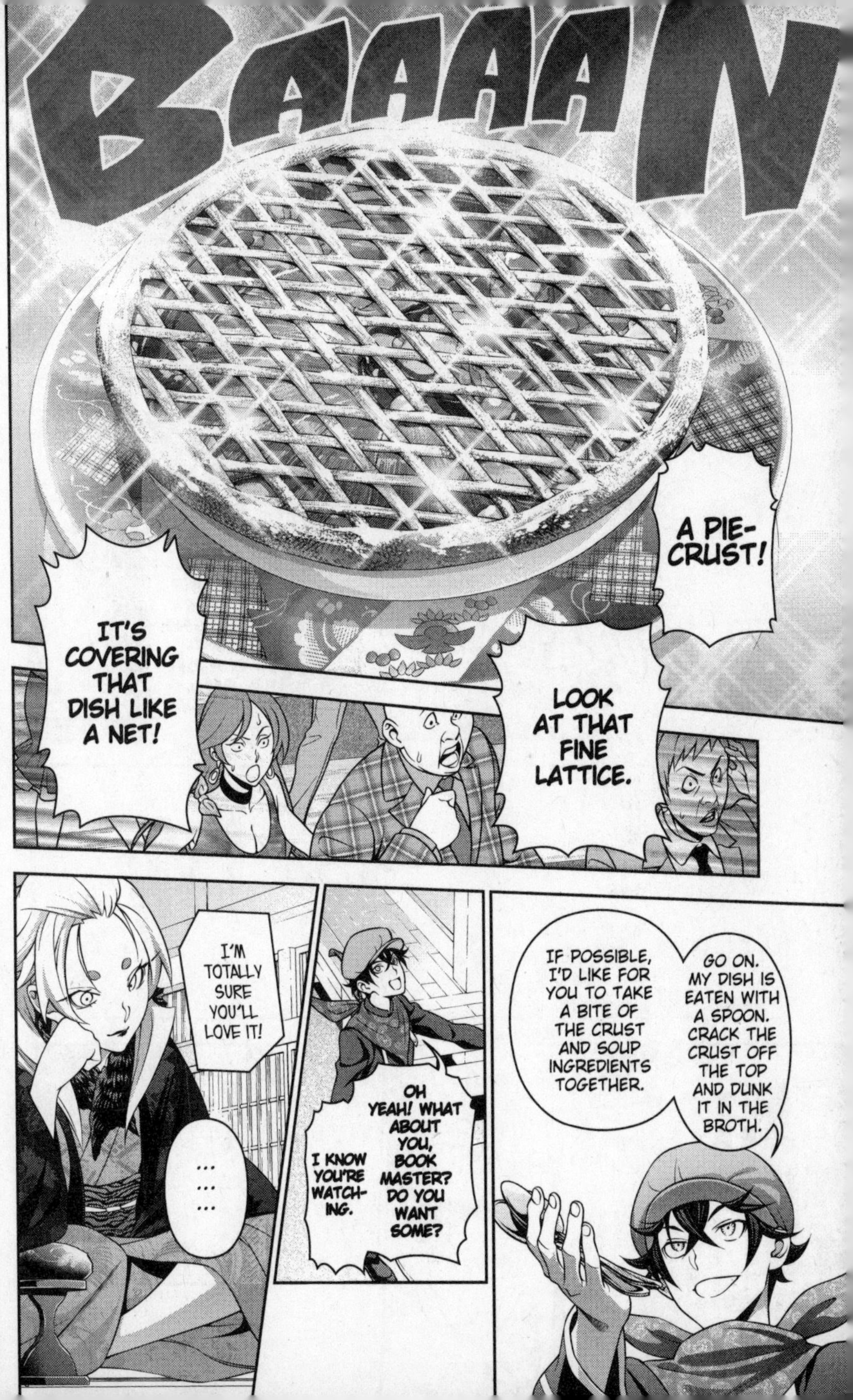
BAAAN
A PIE-CRUST!
IT'S COVERING THAT DISH LIKE A NET!
LOOK AT THAT FINE LATTICE.
GO ON. MY DISH IS EATEN WITH A SPOON. CRACK THE CRUST OFF THE TOP AND DUNK IT IN THE BROTH.
IF POSSIBLE, I'D LIKE FOR YOU TO TAKE A BITE OF THE CRUST AND SOUP INGREDIENTS TOGETHER.
OH YEAH! WHAT ABOUT YOU, BOOK MASTER? DO YOU WANT SOME?
I KNOW YOU'RE WATCH-ING.
I'M TOTALLY SURE YOU'LL LOVE IT!
... ...

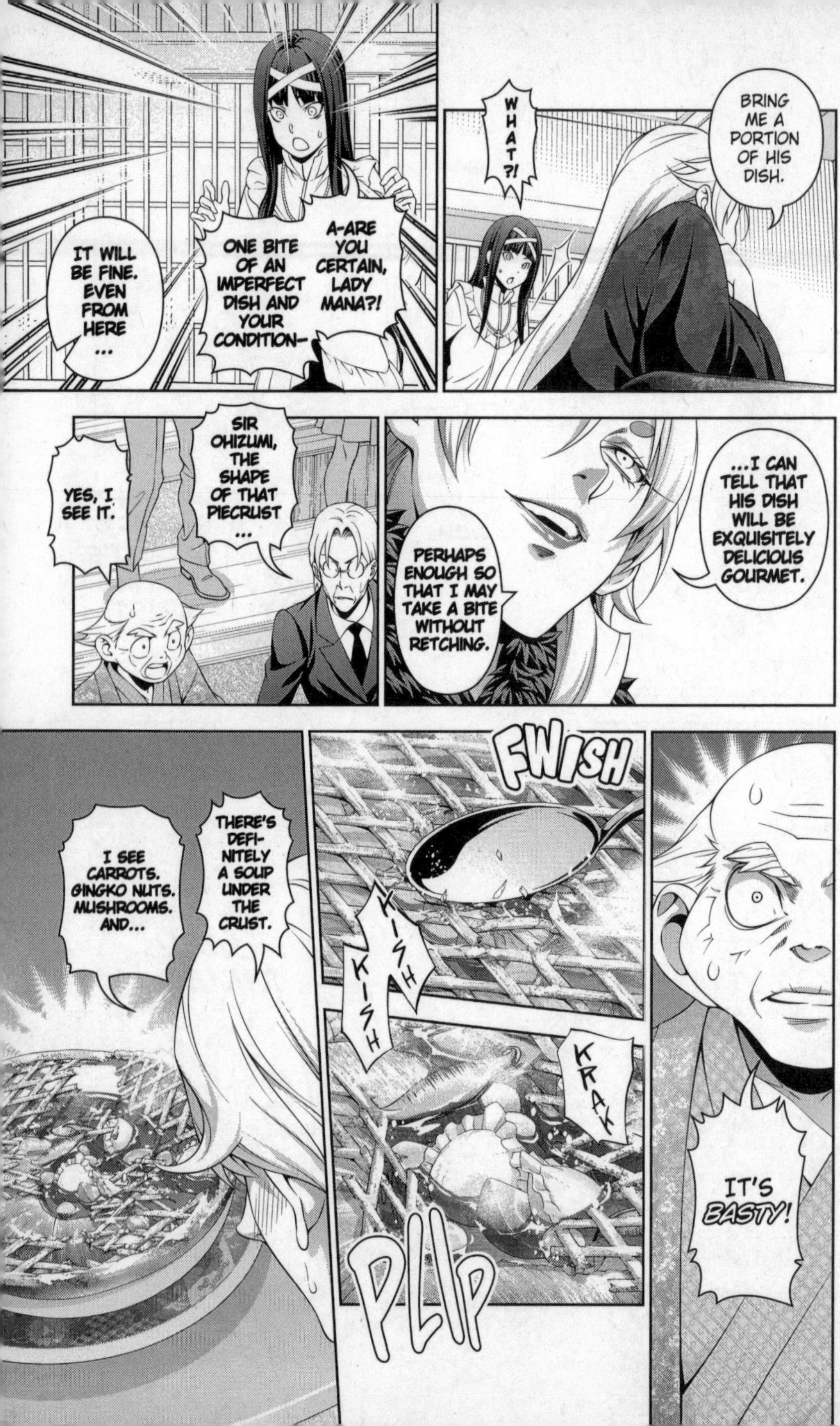
BRING ME A PORTION OF HIS DISH.
WHAT?!
A-ARE YOU CERTAIN, LADY MANA?!
ONE BITE OF AN IMPERFECT DISH AND YOUR CONDITION-
IT WILL BE FINE. EVEN FROM HERE...
...I CAN TELL THAT HIS DISH WILL BE EXQUISITELY DELICIOUS GOURMET.
PERHAPS ENOUGH SO THAT I MAY TAKE A BITE WITHOUT RETCHING.
SIR OHIZUMI, THE SHAPE OF THAT PIECRUST...
YES, I SEE IT.
IT'S *BASTY*!
FWISH
KISH KISH
KRAK
PLIP
THERE'S DEFI-NITELY A SOUP UNDER THE CRUST.
I SEE CARROTS. GINGKO NUTS. MUSHROOMS. AND...

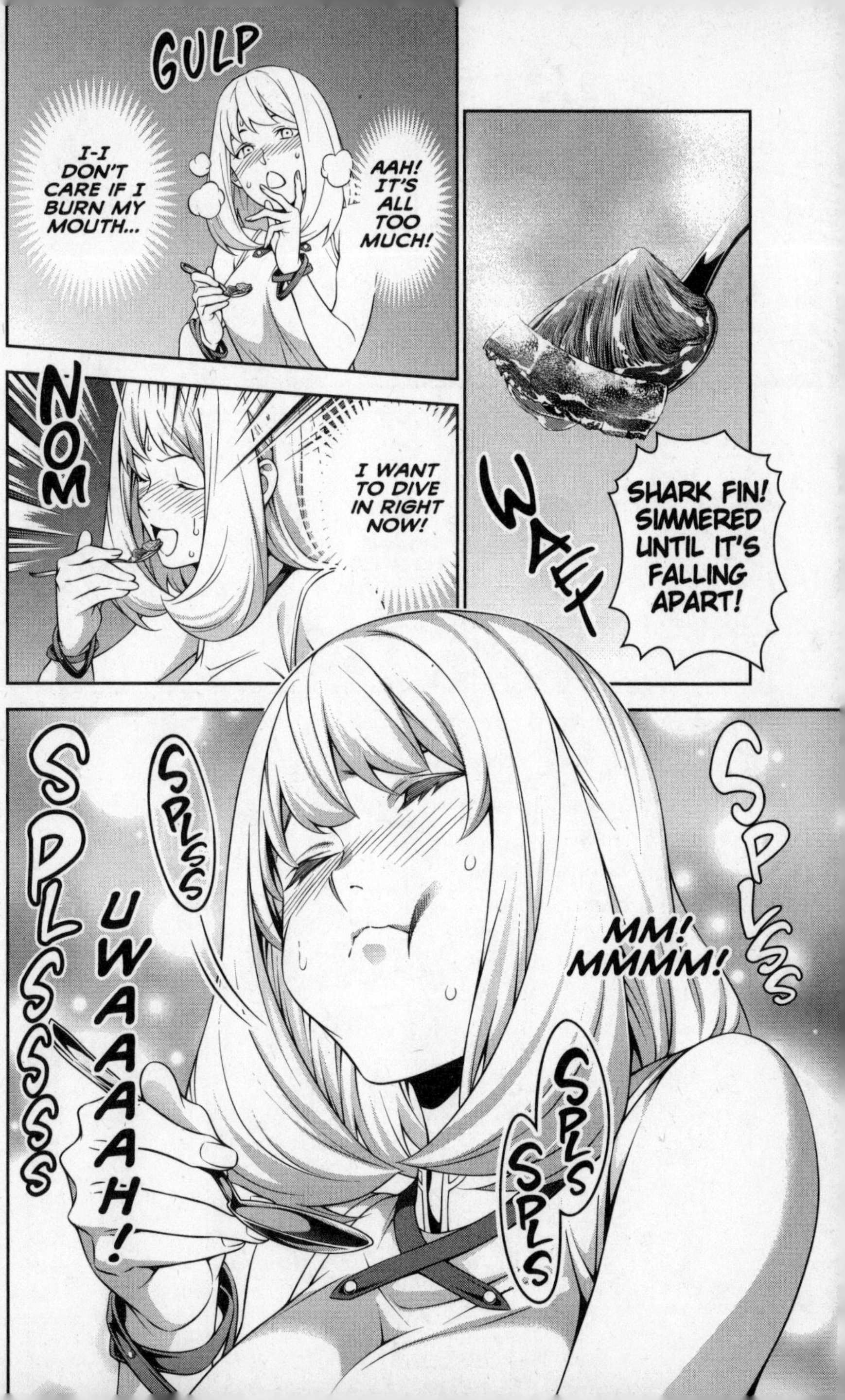
WAFT
SHARK FIN! SIMMERED UNTIL IT'S FALLING APART!
GULP
AAH! IT'S ALL TOO MUCH!
I-I DON'T CARE IF I BURN MY MOUTH...
I WANT TO DIVE IN RIGHT NOW!
NOM
SPLSS
MM! MMMM!
SPLS SPLS
SPLSS
UWAAAAAAH!
SPLLSSSSS

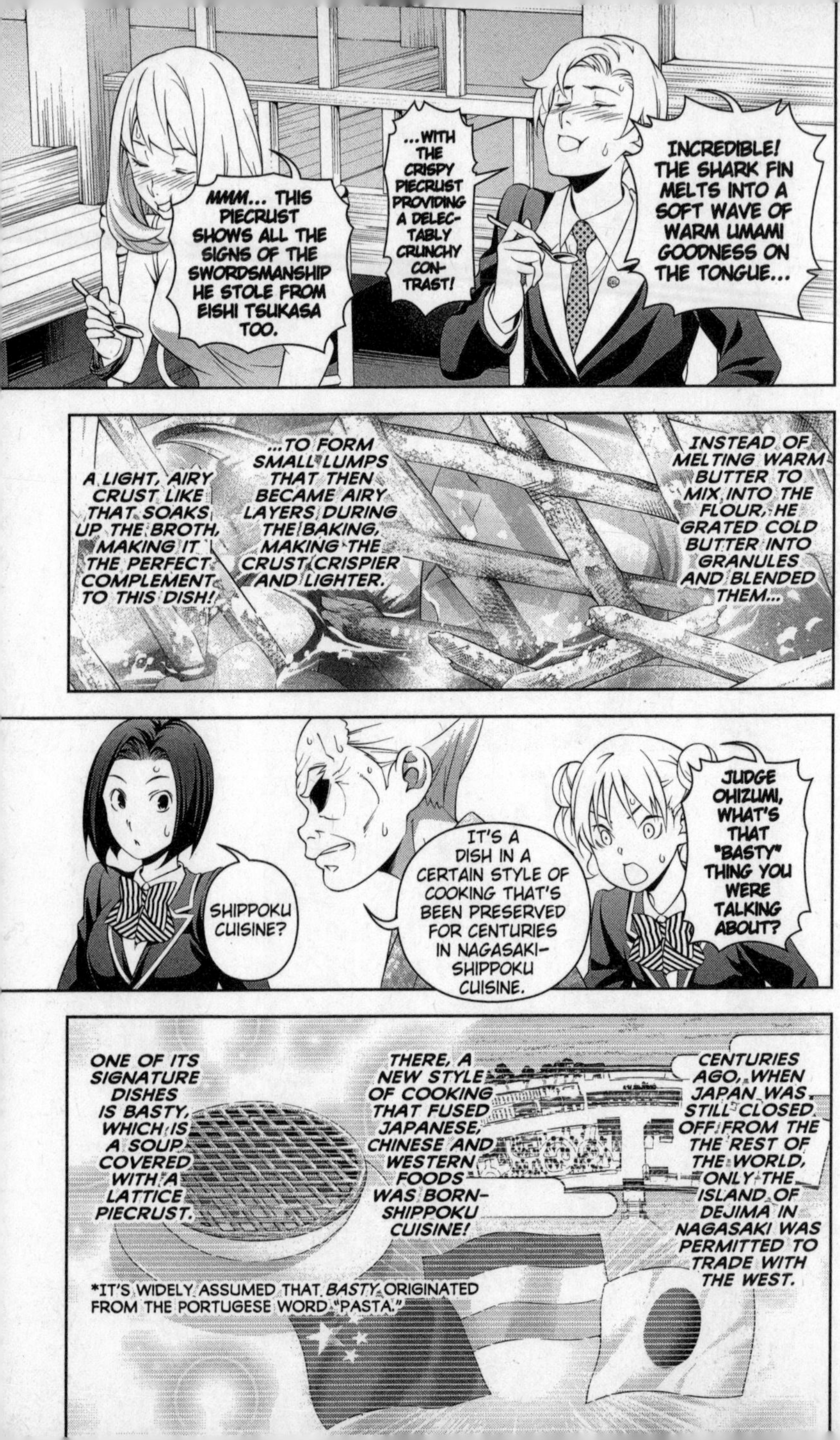
INCREDIBLE! THE SHARK FIN MELTS INTO A SOFT WAVE OF WARM UMAMI GOODNESS ON THE TONGUE...
...WITH THE CRISPY PIECRUST PROVIDING A DELEC-TABLY CRUNCHY CON-TRAST!
MMM... THIS PIECRUST SHOWS ALL THE SIGNS OF THE SWORDSMANSHIP HE STOLE FROM EISHI TSUKASA TOO.
INSTEAD OF MELTING WARM BUTTER TO MIX INTO THE FLOUR, HE GRATED COLD BUTTER INTO GRANULES AND BLENDED THEM...
...TO FORM SMALL LUMPS THAT THEN BECAME AIRY LAYERS DURING THE BAKING, MAKING THE CRUST CRISPIER AND LIGHTER.
A LIGHT, AIRY CRUST LIKE THAT SOAKS UP THE BROTH, MAKING IT THE PERFECT COMPLEMENT TO THIS DISH!
JUDGE OHIZUMI, WHAT'S THAT "BASTY" THING YOU WERE TALKING ABOUT?
IT'S A DISH IN A CERTAIN STYLE OF COOKING THAT'S BEEN PRESERVED FOR CENTURIES IN NAGASAKI-SHIPPOKU CUISINE.
SHIPPOKU CUISINE?
CENTURIES AGO, WHEN JAPAN WAS STILL CLOSED OFF FROM THE THE REST OF THE WORLD, ONLY THE ISLAND OF DEJIMA IN NAGASAKI WAS PERMITTED TO TRADE WITH THE WEST.
THERE, A NEW STYLE OF COOKING THAT FUSED JAPANESE, CHINESE AND WESTERN FOODS WAS BORN-SHIPPOKU CUISINE!
ONE OF ITS SIGNATURE DISHES IS BASTY, WHICH IS A SOUP COVERED WITH A LATTICE PIECRUST.
*IT'S WIDELY ASSUMED THAT BASTY ORIGINATED FROM THE PORTUGESE WORD "PASTA."

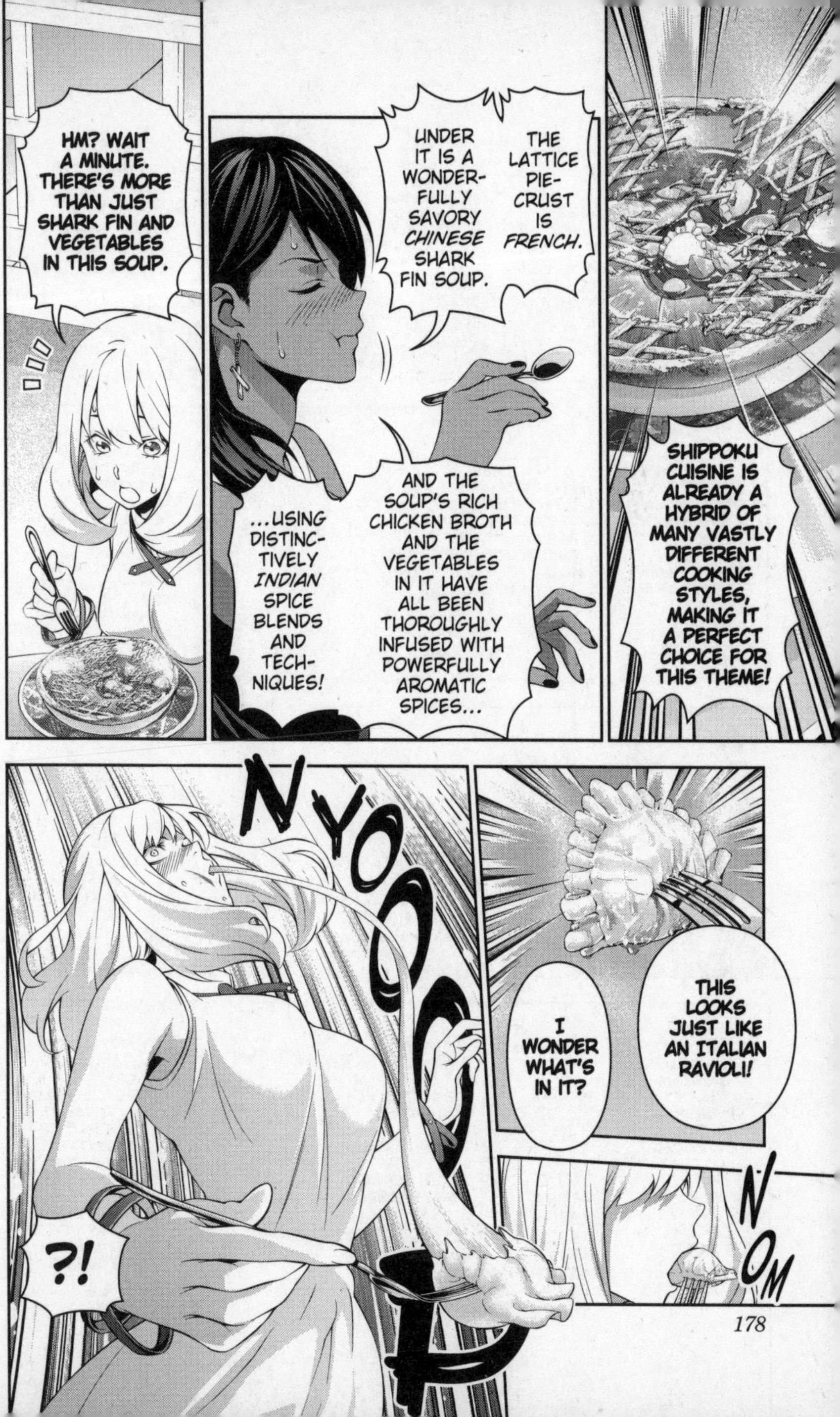
SHIPPOKU CUISINE IS ALREADY A HYBRID OF MANY VASTLY DIFFERENT COOKING STYLES, MAKING IT A PERFECT CHOICE FOR THIS THEME!
THE LATTICE PIE-CRUST IS *FRENCH.*
UNDER IT IS A WONDER-FULLY SAVORY *CHINESE* SHARK FIN SOUP.
AND THE SOUP'S RICH CHICKEN BROTH AND THE VEGETABLES IN IT HAVE ALL BEEN THOROUGHLY INFUSED WITH POWERFULLY AROMATIC SPICES...
...USING DISTINC-TIVELY *INDIAN* SPICE BLENDS AND TECH-NIQUES!
HM? WAIT A MINUTE. THERE'S MORE THAN JUST SHARK FIN AND VEGETABLES IN THIS SOUP.
THIS LOOKS JUST LIKE AN ITALIAN RAVIOLI!
I WONDER WHAT'S IN IT?
NOM
NYOOOOP
?!

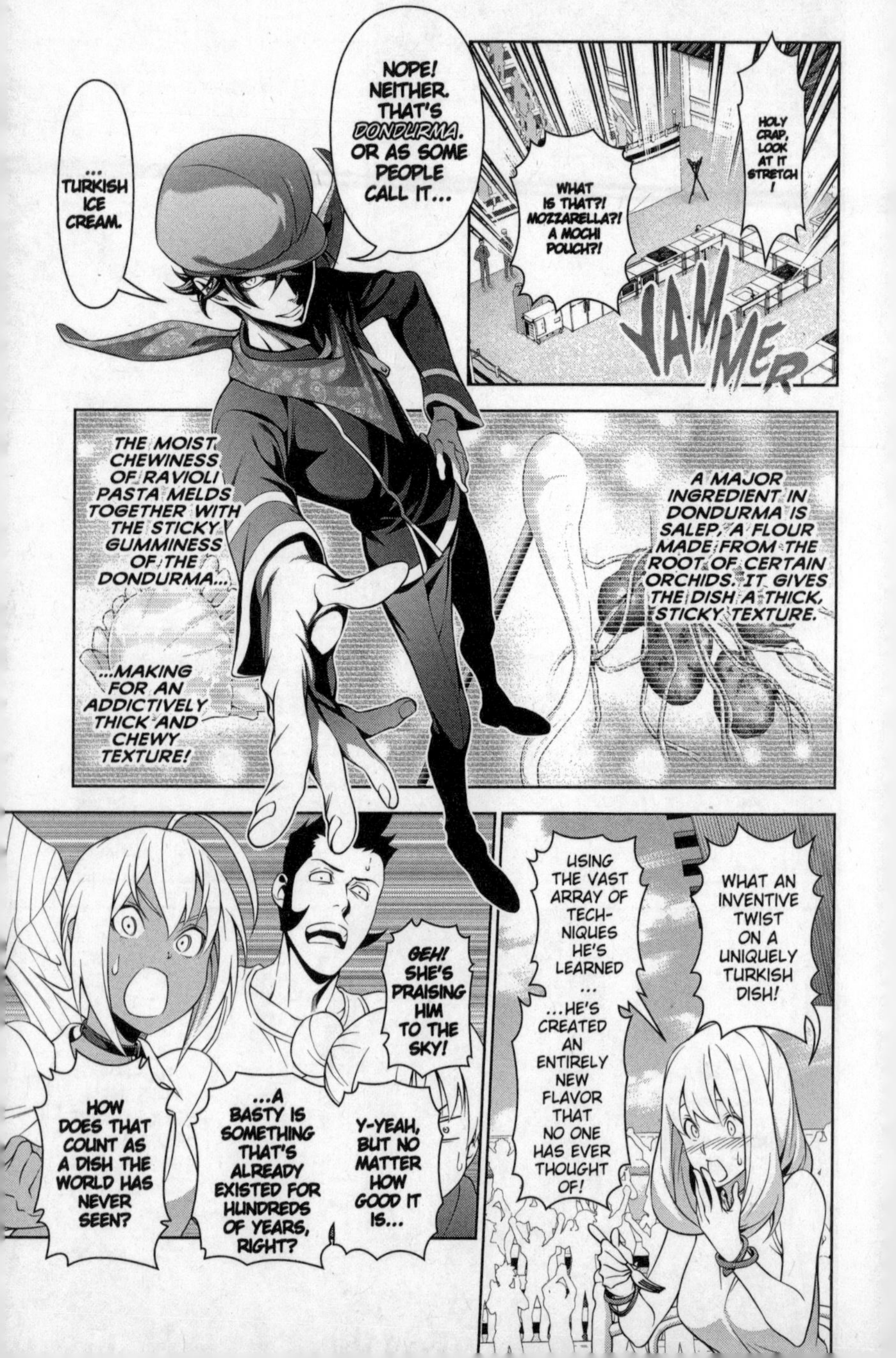
HOLY CRAP, LOOK AT IT STRETCH!
WHAT IS THAT?! MOZZARELLA?! A MOCHI POUCH?!
YAMMER
NOPE! NEITHER. THAT'S DONDURMA. OR AS SOME PEOPLE CALL IT...
...TURKISH ICE CREAM.
A MAJOR INGREDIENT IN DONDURMA IS SALEP, A FLOUR MADE FROM THE ROOT OF CERTAIN ORCHIDS. IT GIVES THE DISH A THICK, STICKY TEXTURE.
THE MOIST CHEWINESS OF RAVIOLI PASTA MELDS TOGETHER WITH THE STICKY GUMMINESS OF THE DONDURMA...
...MAKING FOR AN ADDICTIVELY THICK AND CHEWY TEXTURE!
WHAT AN INVENTIVE TWIST ON A UNIQUELY TURKISH DISH!
USING THE VAST ARRAY OF TECH-NIQUES HE'S LEARNED...
...HE'S CREATED AN ENTIRELY NEW FLAVOR THAT NO ONE HAS EVER THOUGHT OF!
GEH! SHE'S PRAISING HIM TO THE SKY!
Y-YEAH, BUT NO MATTER HOW GOOD IT IS...
...A BASTY IS SOMETHING THAT'S ALREADY EXISTED FOR HUNDREDS OF YEARS, RIGHT?
HOW DOES THAT COUNT AS A DISH THE WORLD HAS NEVER SEEN?

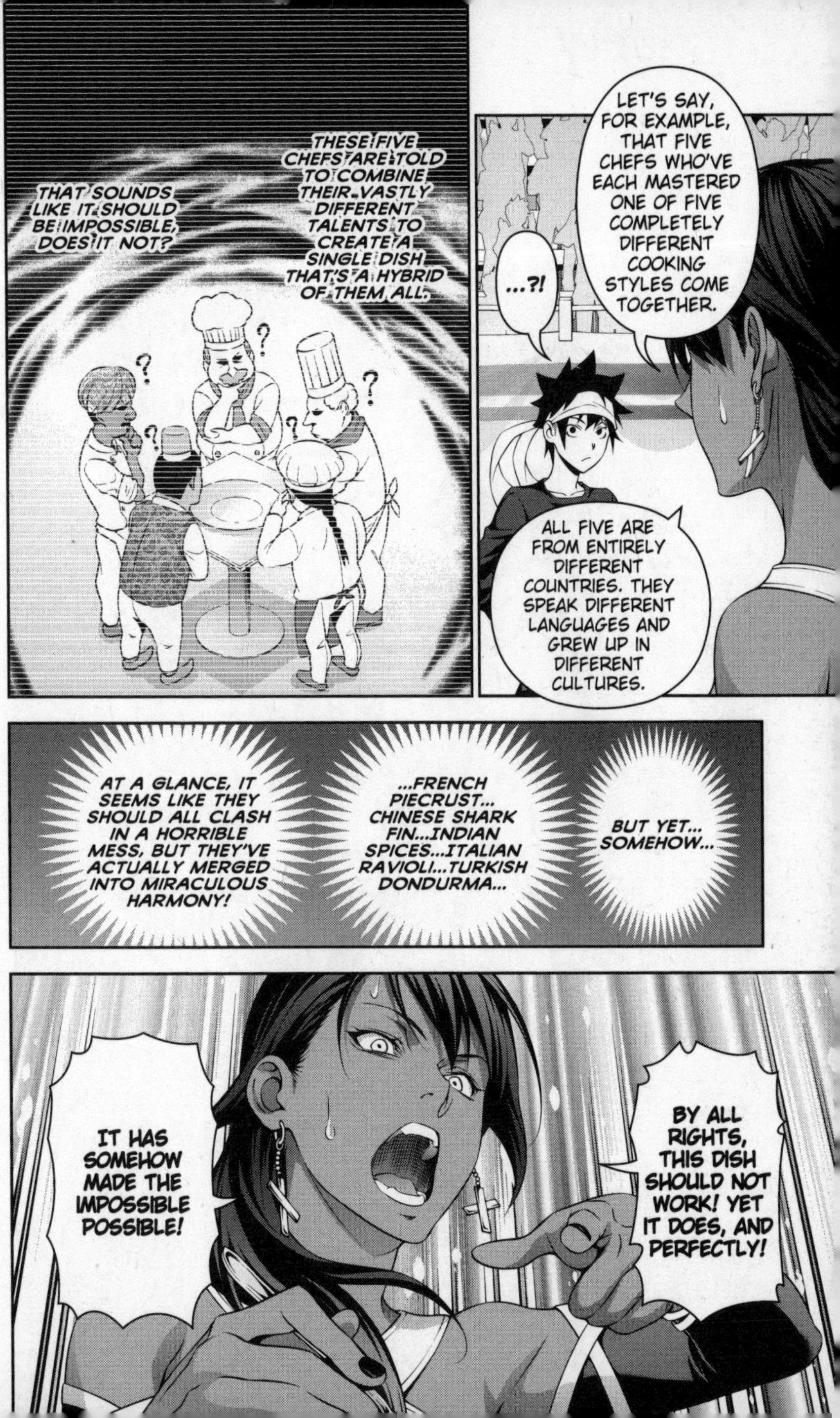
LET'S SAY, FOR EXAMPLE, THAT FIVE CHEFS WHO'VE EACH MASTERED ONE OF FIVE COMPLETELY DIFFERENT COOKING STYLES COME TOGETHER.
...?!
ALL FIVE ARE FROM ENTIRELY DIFFERENT COUNTRIES. THEY SPEAK DIFFERENT LANGUAGES AND GREW UP IN DIFFERENT CULTURES.
THESE FIVE CHEFS ARE TOLD TO COMBINE THEIR VASTLY DIFFERENT TALENTS TO CREATE A SINGLE DISH THAT'S A HYBRID OF THEM ALL.
THAT SOUNDS LIKE IT SHOULD BE IMPOSSIBLE, DOES IT NOT?
BUT YET... SOMEHOW...
...FRENCH PIECRUST... CHINESE SHARK FIN...INDIAN SPICES...ITALIAN RAVIOLI...TURKISH DONDURMA...
AT A GLANCE, IT SEEMS LIKE THEY SHOULD ALL CLASH IN A HORRIBLE MESS, BUT THEY'VE ACTUALLY MERGED INTO MIRACULOUS HARMONY!
BY ALL RIGHTS, THIS DISH SHOULD NOT WORK! YET IT DOES, AND PERFECTLY!
IT HAS SOMEHOW MADE THE IMPOSSIBLE POSSIBLE!

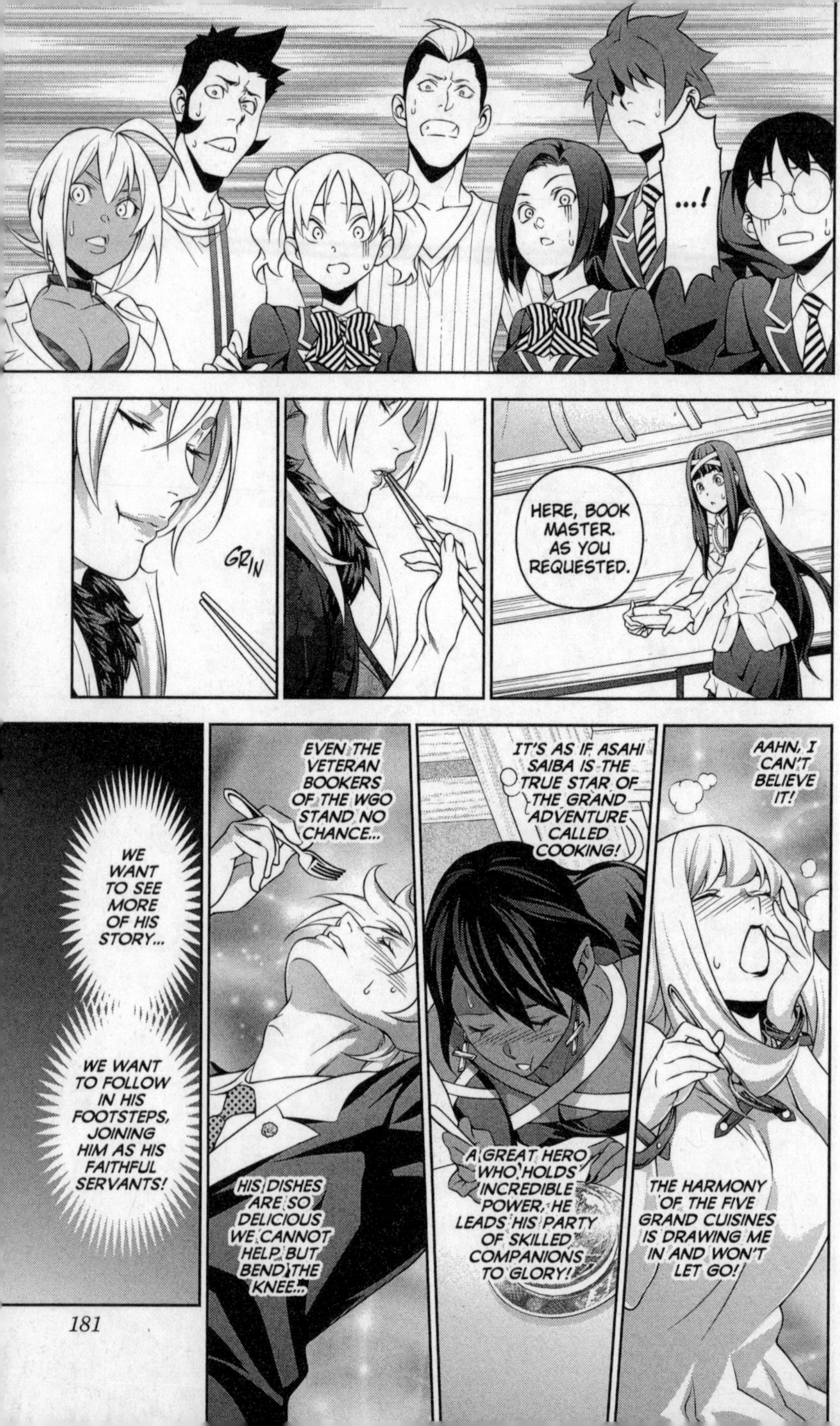
...!
HERE, BOOK MASTER. AS YOU REQUESTED.
GRIN
AAHN, I CAN'T BELIEVE IT!
THE HARMONY OF THE FIVE GRAND CUISINES IS DRAWING ME IN AND WON'T LET GO!
IT'S AS IF ASAHI SAIBA IS THE TRUE STAR OF THE GRAND ADVENTURE CALLED COOKING!
A GREAT HERO WHO HOLDS INCREDIBLE POWER, HE LEADS HIS PARTY OF SKILLED COMPANIONS TO GLORY!
EVEN THE VETERAN BOOKERS OF THE WGO STAND NO CHANCE...
HIS DISHES ARE SO DELICIOUS WE CANNOT HELP BUT BEND THE KNEE...
WE WANT TO SEE MORE OF HIS STORY...
WE WANT TO FOLLOW IN HIS FOOTSTEPS, JOINING HIM AS HIS FAITHFUL SERVANTS!

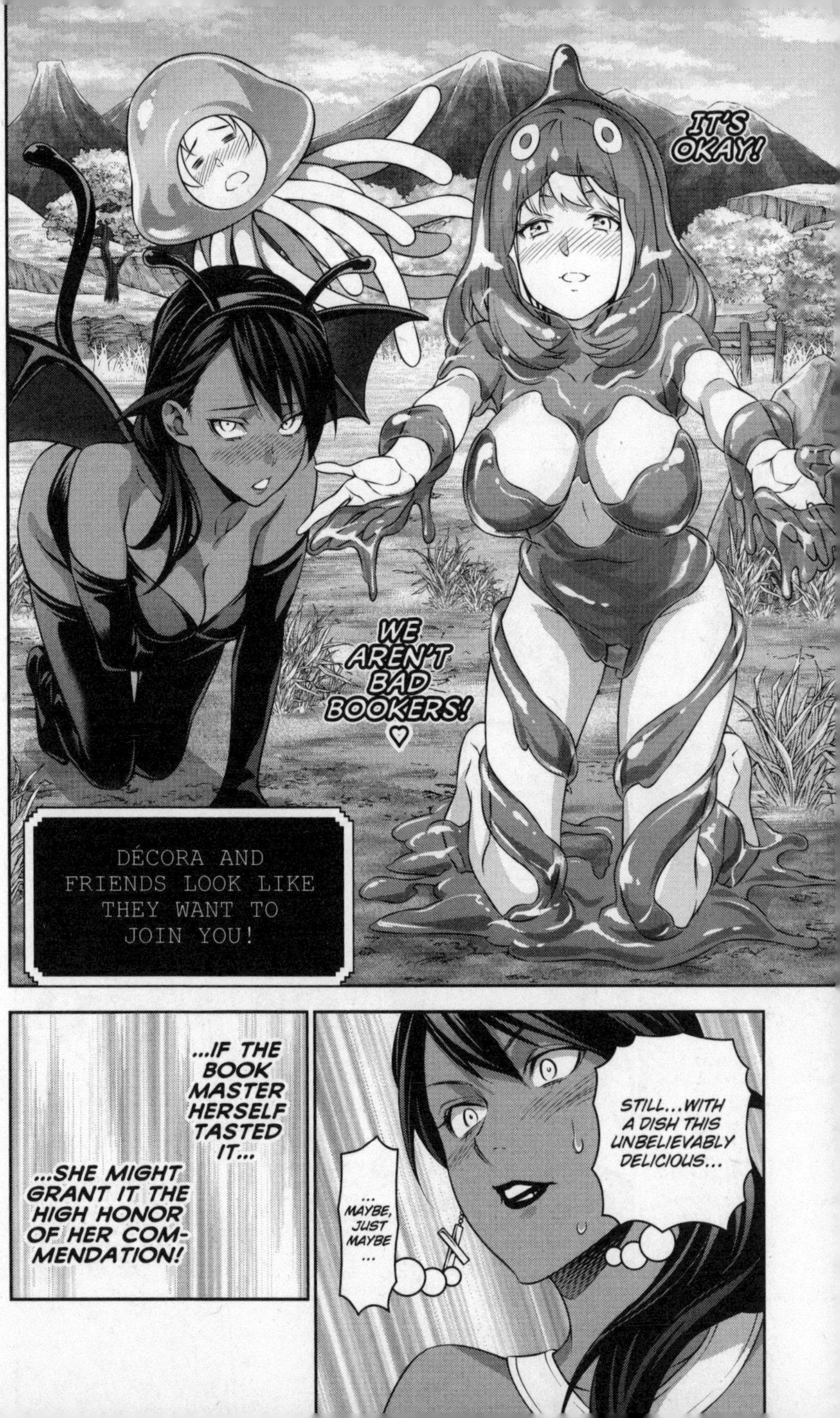
IT'S OKAY!
WE AREN'T BAD BOOKERS! ♥
DÉCORA AND FRIENDS LOOK LIKE THEY WANT TO JOIN YOU!
STILL...WITH A DISH THIS UNBELIEVABLY DELICIOUS...
...MAYBE, JUST MAYBE...
...IF THE BOOK MASTER HERSELF TASTED IT...
...SHE MIGHT GRANT IT THE HIGH HONOR OF HER COM-MENDATION!

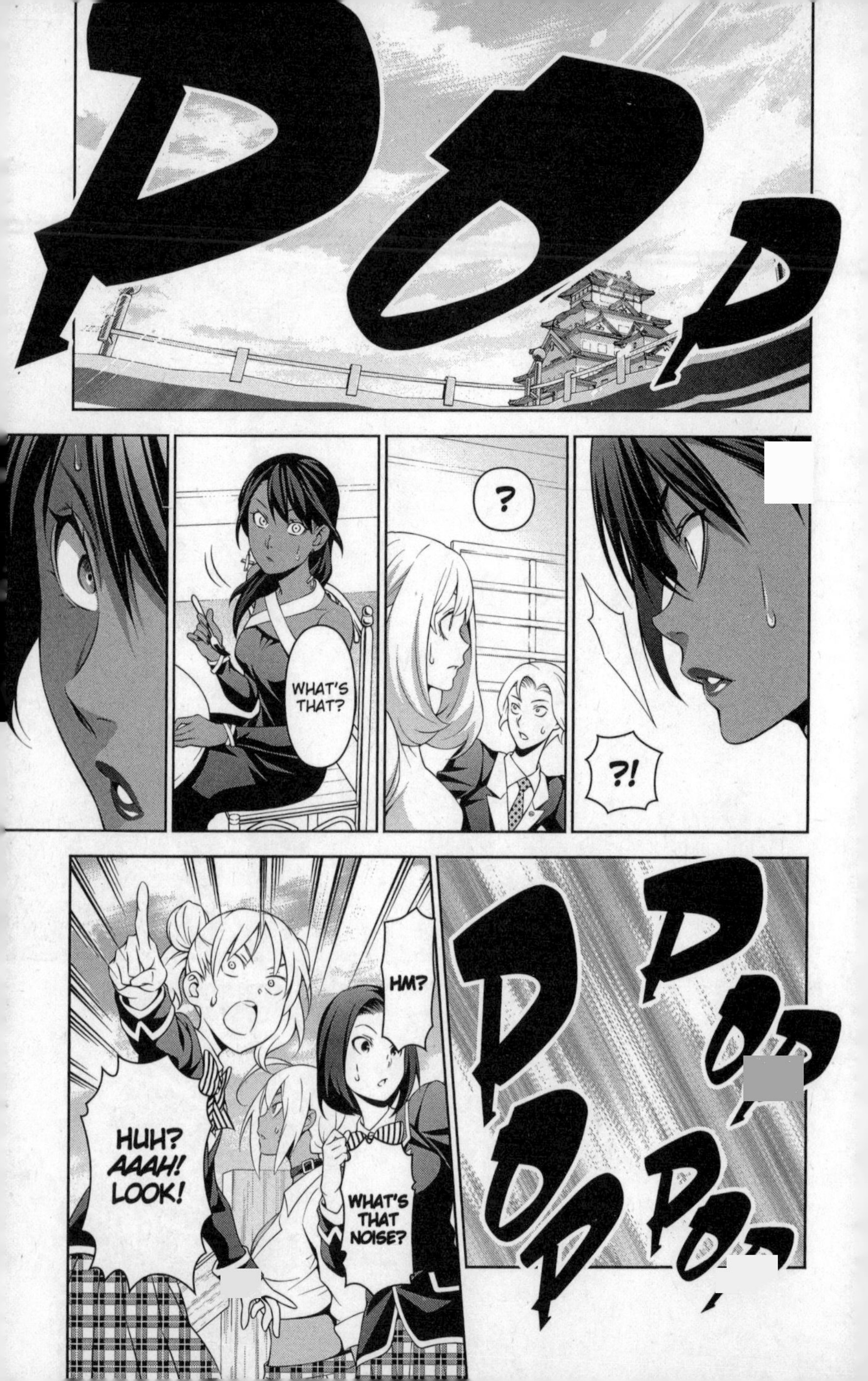

POP
?!
?
WHAT'S THAT?
POP POP
HM?
WHAT'S THAT NOISE?
HUH? AAAH! LOOK!

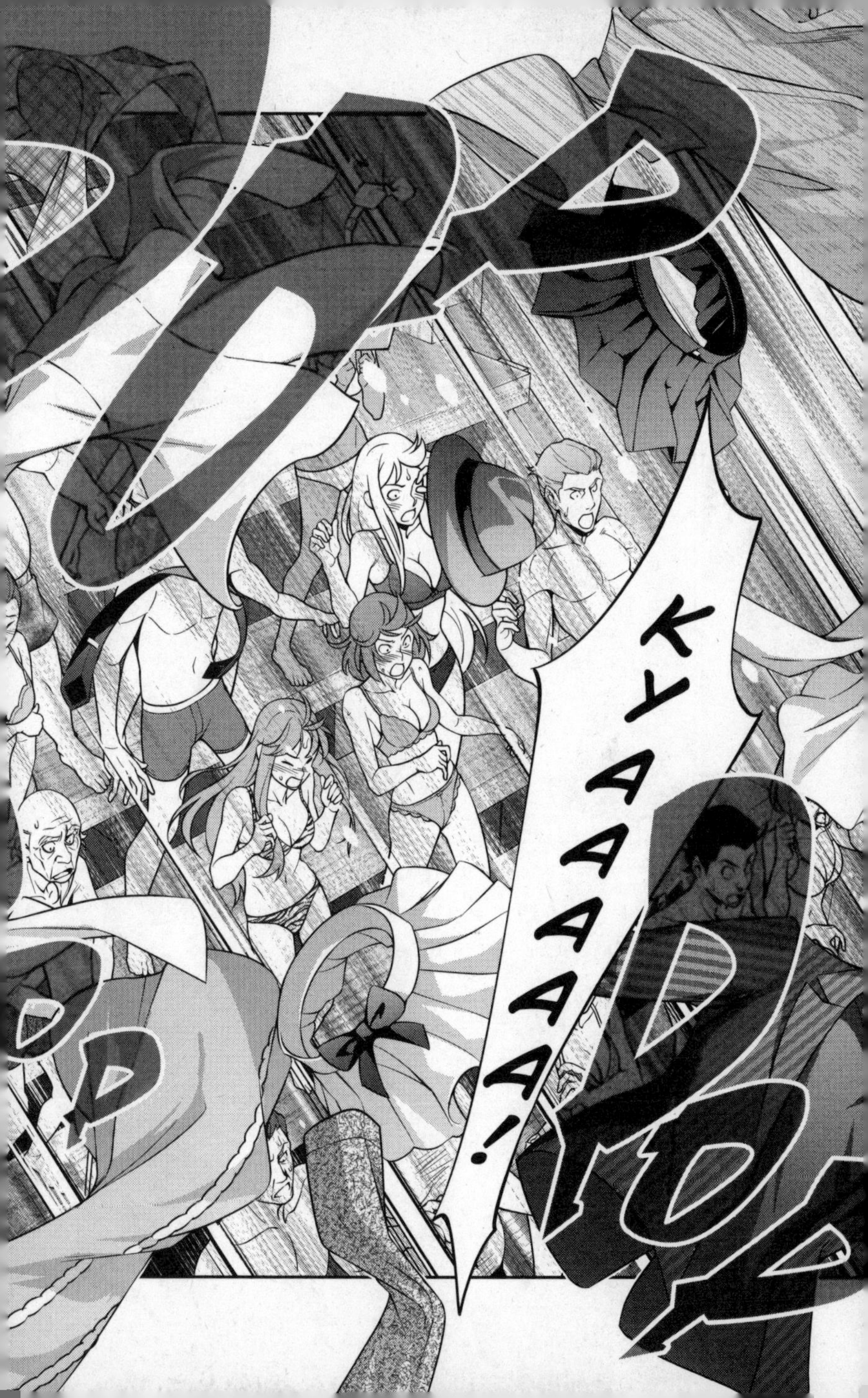
KYAAAAAA!

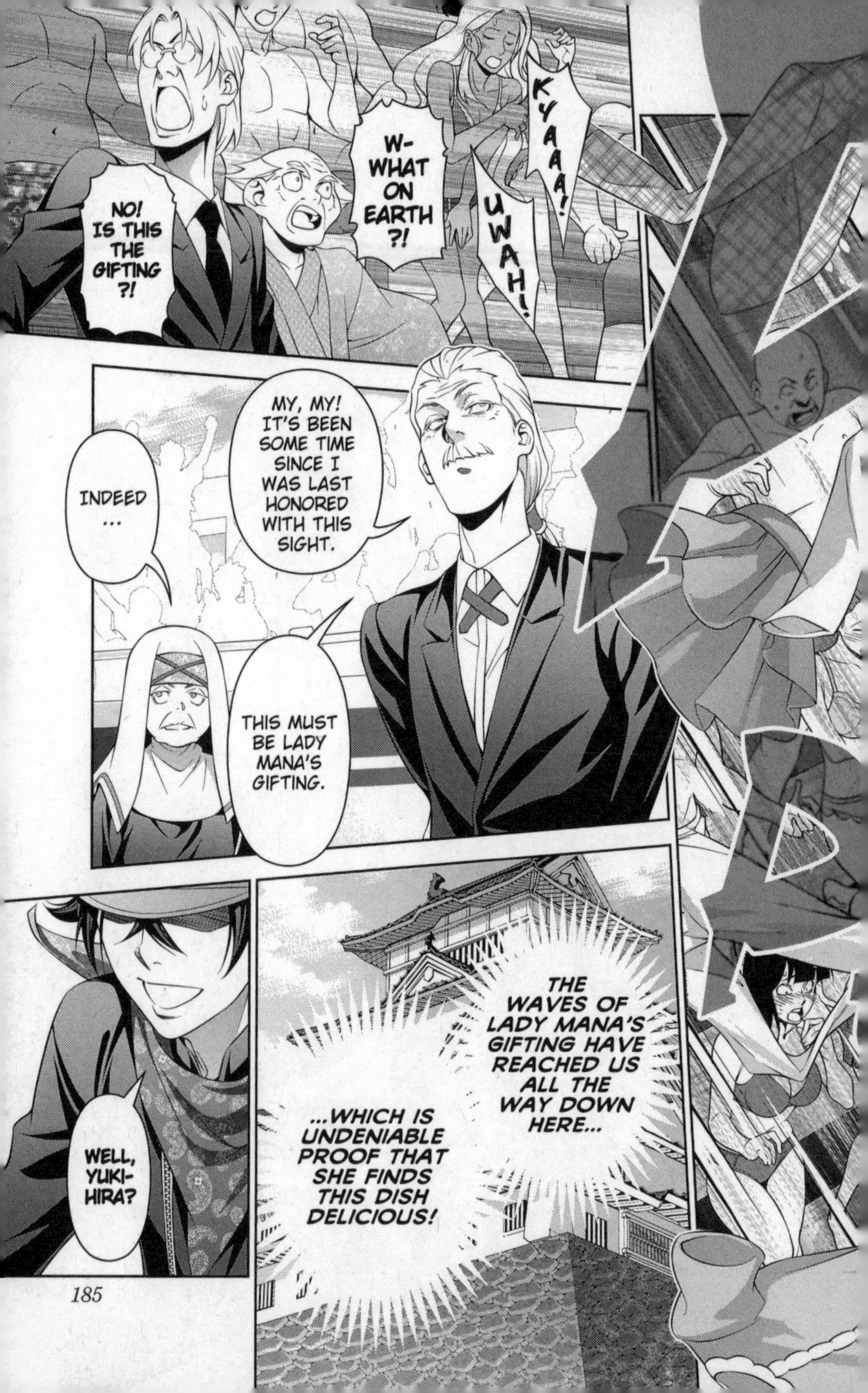
KYAAAA!
UWAH!
W-WHAT ON EARTH?!
NO! IS THIS THE GIFTING?!
MY, MY! IT'S BEEN SOME TIME SINCE I WAS LAST HONORED WITH THIS SIGHT.
INDEED...
THIS MUST BE LADY MANA'S GIFTING.
THE WAVES OF LADY MANA'S GIFTING HAVE REACHED US ALL THE WAY DOWN HERE...
...WHICH IS UNDENIABLE PROOF THAT SHE FINDS THIS DISH DELICIOUS!
WELL, YUKI-HIRA?

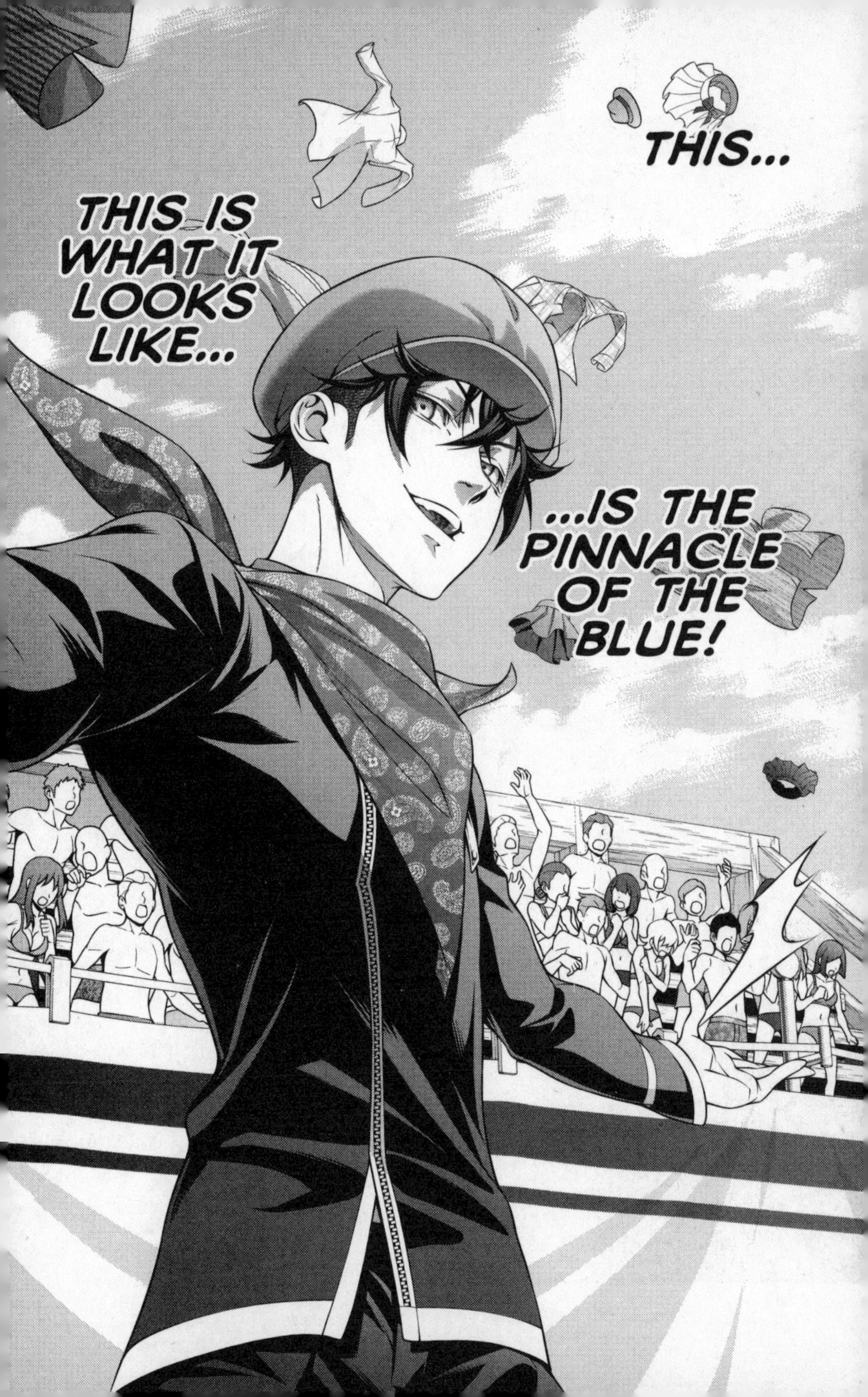
THIS...
THIS IS WHAT IT LOOKS LIKE...
...IS THE PINNACLE OF THE BLUE!

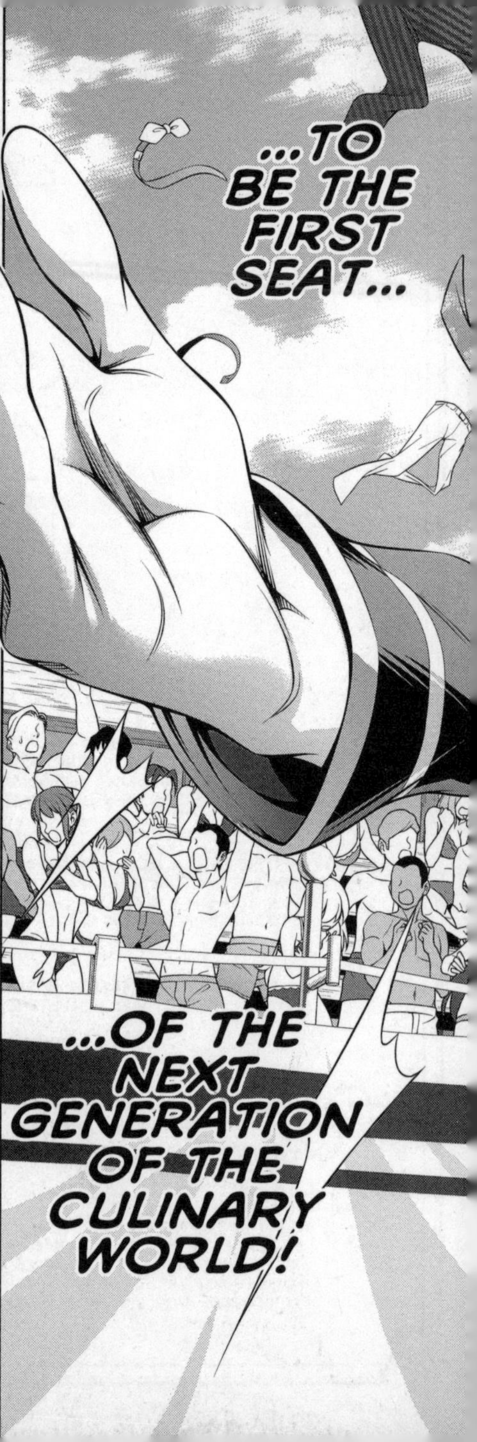
...TO BE THE FIRST SEAT...
...OF THE NEXT GENERATION OF THE CULINARY WORLD!

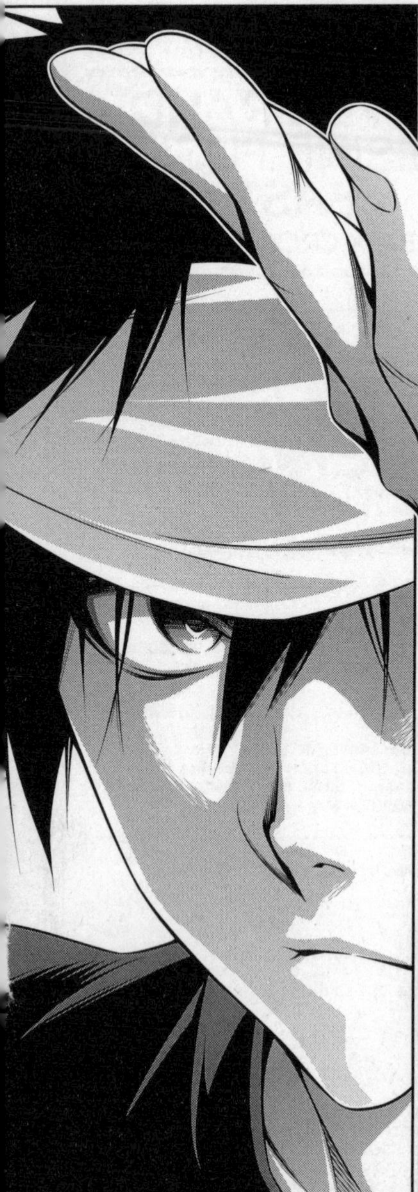

THE DIVINE TONGUE'S DESPAIR (END)

ARTIST: YUTO TSUKUDA   RECIPE BY: YUKI MORISAKI

VOLUME 35
SPECIAL SUPPLEMENT!

PRACTICAL RECIPE #1

FIVE GRAND CUISINE FUSION BASTY
EASY & NEAT

~SAIBA X CROSSED KNIVES~

STORE-BOUGHT FROZEN PIE SHEETS ARE **A PERFECT SHORTCUT!**

● INGREDIENTS ●
(SERVES 4)

1 CHICKEN THIGH

A 2 TABLESPOONS SAKE
    SALT, PEPPER

1 TABLESPOON SESAME OIL
2 THUMBS GINGER
1/2 JAPANESE LEEK
1 CARROT
200 GRAMS JAPANESE YAM

6 SHIITAKE MUSHROOMS
30 GRAMS GINKO NUTS IN WATER (DRAINED)
600 CC CHICKEN BROTH

B 1 TABLESPOON EACH
    LIGHT SOY SAUCE, MIRIN

FROZEN PIE SHEETS, SALT, PEPPER, POTATO STARCH, EGG YOLKS, SESAME OIL

1) CUT THE CHICKEN THIGH INTO BITE-SIZE PIECES. MIX (A) TOGETHER AND RUB INTO THE CHICKEN. CUT THE CARROT AND YAM INTO BITE-SIZE PIECES. MINCE THE JAPANESE LEEK AND GINGER. REMOVE THE BASE FROM THE SHIITAKE MUSHROOMS AND CUT INTO QUARTERS.

2) HEAT THE SESAME OIL IN A FRYING PAN AND SAUTE THE GINGER AND JAPANESE LEEK UNTIL FRAGRANT. POUR IN THE CHICKEN BROTH AND BRING TO A SIMMER. ADD THE CHICKEN, CARROT, GINKO NUTS, YAMS AND SHIITAKE MUSHROOMS AND SIMMER FOR ABOUT 10 MINUTES.

3) MIX IN (B). SEASON TO TASTE WITH SALT AND PEPPER. ADD POTATO STARCH AND THICKEN TO DESIRED CONSISTENCY.

4) DEFROST THE FROZEN PIE SHEET AND ROLL OUT TO DESIRED THICKNESS. SLICE INTO STRIPS ABOUT 1 CM WIDE.

5) POUR (3) INTO AN OVEN-SAFE DISH. LACE THE PIE-SHEET STRIPS OVER THE TOP OF THE BOWL IN A LATTICE, SAVING THE FINAL STRIPS TO WRAP AROUND THE RIM OF THE BOWL. MAKE AN EGG WASH WITH THE YOLK AND BRUSH IT OVER THE TOP OF THE PIE-SHEET STRIPS. BAKE IN THE OVEN AT 390° DEGREES UNTIL THE CRUST IS GOLDEN BROWN, AND DONE!

ONE MORE VOLUME TO GO!!!

LET'S DO THIS!

JoJo's

BIZARRE ADVENTURE

⬦⬦⬦⬦⬦⬦ 💎 ⬦⬦⬦⬦⬦⬦

★ PART 4 ★

DIAMOND IS UNBREAKABLE

Story & Art by
HIROHIKO ARAKI

A MULTIGENERATIONAL TALE OF THE HEROIC JOESTAR FAMILY AND THEIR NEVER-ENDING BATTLE AGAINST EVIL!

In April 1999, Jotaro Kujo travels to a town in Japan called Morioh to find a young man named Josuke Higashikata, the secret love child of his grandfather, Joseph Joestar. Upon finding him, Jotaro is surprised to learn that Josuke also possesses a Stand. After their strange meeting, the pair team up to investigate the town's proliferation of unusual Stands!

THE PROMISED NEVERLAND

STORY BY **KAIU SHIRAI**

ART BY **POSUKA DEMIZU**

Emma, Norman and Ray are the brightest kids at the Grace Field House orphanage. And under the care of the woman they refer to as "Mom," all the kids have enjoyed a comfortable life. Good food, clean clothes and the perfect environment to learn—what more could an orphan ask for? One day, though, Emma and Norman uncover the dark truth of the outside world they are forbidden from seeing.

You're Reading in the Wrong Direction!!

1
3
2
2
1
3
5
4
6

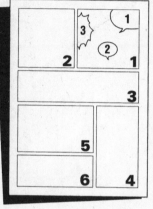

Whoops! Guess what? You're starting at the wrong end of the comic!

...It's true! In keeping with the original Japanese format, **Food Wars!** is meant to be read from right to left, starting in the upper-right corner.

Unlike English, which is read from left to right, Japanese is read from right to left, meaning that action, sound effects and word-balloon order are completely reversed... something which can make readers unfamiliar with Japanese feel pretty backwards themselves. For this reason, manga or Japanese comics published in the U.S. in English have sometimes been published "flopped"—that is, printed in exact reverse order, as though seen from the other side of a mirror.

By flopping pages, U.S. publishers can avoid confusing readers, but the compromise is not without its downside. For one thing, a character in a flopped manga series who once wore in the original Japanese version a T-shirt emblazoned with "M A Y" (as in "the merry month of") now wears one which reads "Y A M"! Additionally, many manga creators in Japan are themselves unhappy with the process, as some feel the mirror-imaging of their art skews their original intentions.

We are proud to bring you Yuto Tsukuda and Shun Saeki's **Food Wars!** in the original unflopped format.

For now, though, turn to the other side of the book and let the adventure begin...!

—Editor

MEANWHILE, ALICE NAKIRI AND HISAKO ARATO ARE OFF TO...
CHECK BACK NEXT VOLUME TO FIND OUT!

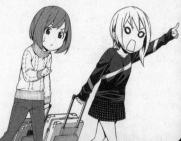